TRAWNIKI GUARDS

FOOT SOLDIERS OF THE HOLOCAUST

VOL. 2,
INVESTIGATIONS AND TRIALS

JOSH BALDWIN

SCHIFFER MILITARY
4880 Lower Valley Road   Atglen, PA 19310

Designed by Christopher Bower
Cover design by Jack Chappell
All images are in the public domain and are courtesy of the US Department of Justice via the Freedom of Information Act.
Type set in Stoneburg Condensed / Minion Pro / Univers LT Std

ISBN: 978-0-7643-6353-5
Printed in India

Published by Schiffer Publishing, Ltd.
4880 Lower Valley Road
Atglen, PA 19310
Phone: (610) 593-1777; Fax: (610) 593-2002
Email: Info@schifferbooks.com
Web: www.schifferbooks.com

For our complete selection of fine books on this and related subjects, please visit our website at www.schifferbooks.com. You may also write for a free catalog.

Schiffer Publishing's titles are available at special discounts for bulk purchases for sales promotions or premiums. Special editions, including personalized covers, corporate imprints, and excerpts, can be created in large quantities for special needs. For more information, contact the publisher.

We are always looking for people to write books on new and related subjects. If you have an idea for a book, please contact us at proposals@schifferbooks.com.

CONTENTS

Acknowledgments

I would like to thank the following people who helped make this work possible: Dr. David Rich, a historian at Catholic University in Washington, DC, recently retired, who took the time to answer a number of questions for me; Vadim Altskan, chief archivist at the US Holocaust Memorial Museum in Washington, DC, who pointed me toward the trial records that I needed to review for this volume; Lucais Sewell, who translated a number of German documents into English for me; Agata Witkowska, who translated some Polish documents into English for me; Alexander Friedman, who translated dozens of pages of Russian trial documents into English for me; Michael Melnyk and Stuart Emmett, both of whom are World War II historians and authors, for their continued moral support; and finally to my wife, Peggie, for her continued perseverance and energetic support.

I don't expect this work to be the final word on these investigations and trials, because there is still information that is missing and is still being locked away in the archives of the former Soviet Union. Whether or not someone will ever be able to complete this unfinished exploration, only time will tell.

It is my intention to revisit this subject in some form in the future.

Josh Baldwin
October 2020

CHAPTER 1

INTRODUCTION TO INTERROGATIONS AND TRIALS

Unfortunately it is not possible at this time, even seventy-five years after the war, to ascertain precisely how many Trawniki guards were identified, caught, and tried. On the basis of available evidence, the number has to be over one hundred, possibly several hundred (I have found evidence for over 120 individuals being tried). Available information indicates that there were at least thirteen "group trials" (trials with more than two defendants), starting with the Shevchenko trial with Treblinka I defendants in October 1944, and ending with the Litvinenko trial with Janowska defendants in 1968. Also noteworthy is that in the Soviet Union, the first (Shevchenko in 1944), last (Fedorenko in 1986), and largest (Schultz in 1961–1962) trials all involved defendants who had served at Treblinka, the deadliest of the Reinhard camps. Evidence of additional prosecutions may still be locked away in Russian or Ukrainian archives that have not yet surfaced or become open to public access. Fortunately, however, enough documentation does exist to state certain facts about numerous trials.

From 1945 to 1953, Soviet investigations and prosecutions of its own citizens numbered upward of 500,000. Most of these cases fell under Article 58, "Treason / Counterrevolutionary Activity," if held in Russia, or under Article 54 in Ukraine.[1] Another source stated that during the postwar years, thousands of trials against German collaborators took place, continuing up to the 1980s. Reliable figures are as yet unavailable, but according to a recent online publication of the FSB, during the 1943–1953 period, more than 320,000 Soviet citizens were arrested for collaborating with the Germans, which is nearly one-third of all arrests made by the NKVD during those years.[2] Still another source indicates that the number of trials of Nazi collaborators conducted in the Soviet Union remains unknown, but certainly hundreds of thousands of suspects were investigated. In no other country did the prosecution of Holocaust perpetrators reach this scale.[3] Most trials of collaborators under Stalin were not public. One of the reasons was that the Soviet government did not want to draw attention to the fact that so many of its own citizens had worked for the enemy during the war.[4] Judging from approximate data, there were over 140 trials of former Trawniki guards in the Soviet Union between 1944 and 1987. It is possible the actual figure is slightly higher, but due to secrecy, not all documents are available to researchers.[5]

The first Trawniki guards to be put on trial were tried even before the war ended. Six of them were captured and court-martialed by the Red Army after they had deserted from Treblinka I while it was being evacuated in late July 1944.[6] Those men were Nikita Rekalo, Valentin Roshanskij, Mikhail Poleszuk, Ivan Shevchenko, Grigorij Sirota, and Pavel Kozlov. SMERSH identified and interrogated them upon capture by the 65th Army, 1st Belorussian Front, as it swept through the Malkinia area, en route to Warsaw. The interrogations took place between August and November 1944. All were tried, convicted, and shot on the basis of Article 1 of the *Ukaz* (Order) of April 19, 1943, issued by the Presidium of the Supreme Soviet regarding Nazi collaborators.[7]

After the war, former Trawniki guards were caught by Soviet authorities through the systematic collection and cross-referencing of information—documents captured by the Red Army during the liberation of the Lublin area in July 1944—Trawniki personnel files, internal memos, and deployment rosters.[8] Soviet "investigation nets" caught former Trawniki guards from the Baltic States, Volksdeutsche from the German settlement regions of Ukraine and southern Russia, and from across Siberia.[9] Soviet security authorities in Moscow exploited the captured Trawniki documents (so-called War Trophy Documents) by extracting from them the names of Soviet citizens who had served the Germans as Trawniki guards. By early 1946, Moscow began disseminating NKVD lists of "traitors" to be investigated and arrested.[10]

Between 1946 and 1952, it is known that about a hundred or so former Trawniki guards were tried by Soviet authorities in the Stanislavov (today Ivano-Frankivsk) region of western Ukraine.[11] In 1947, Soviet military investigators in the Stanislavov/Ivano-Frankivsk region handled hundreds of young, semiliterate Ukrainian men, who had been recruited as civilians to Trawniki service in spring 1943. Twenty-five years of ITL (corrective labor camps) was the uniform sentence of punishment at the time.[12] SMERSH's interrogations of Trawniki guards in late 1944 launched cases in Stanislavov/Ivano-Frankivsk and in Lvov in 1946. By 1947, cases against former Trawniki guards began as far away as the central Asian republic of Uzbekistan and eastern Siberia.[13]

The first arrests of Nazi collaborators took place in the western border areas, especially the former Polish territories of Galicia and western Ukraine. This was facilitated by a reinforced security presence and martial law in those areas. These borderland areas remained in a state of war even after World War II had ended, as a result of nationalist insurrections by armed groups who resisted Soviet authorities. (The NKVD and NKGB eventually destroyed the Ukrainian nationalist underground movement, but it was a hard struggle. A guerrilla war with the UPA, the so-called Ukrainian Insurgent Army, continued into the early 1950s.[14])

In at least two great waves of postwar trials on Soviet territory, military and civilian prosecutors brought to account hundreds of former Trawniki guards. Between 1947 and 1952 and between 1960 and 1970, Soviet security forces identified them, investigated their activities, and placed the former guards on trial. They received sentences within the full range of criminal penalties. Secrecy was foremost among the characteristics of these proceedings, and the records of investigation remained hidden in former KGB archives until the mid-1990s.[15]

SMERSH came upon a cache of documents captured at Trawniki that listed the names of Trawniki guards and where they had served. Soviet State Security continued to search for and locate former Trawniki guards all the way into the 1980s. Those former Trawniki guards who ended up being tried twice had initially been charged with simply aiding the Germans. The second time around, however, they were specifically charged with participating in murder at the death camps. This raises the question of whether the second prosecution of some of these men violated "double jeopardy."[16]

Every Soviet citizen displaced during the war, when returning to Soviet territory, had to pass through so-called "filtration." Former Trawniki guards funneled through this screening process via various routes. In 1945, as the war drew to a close, those Trawniki guards still in German service discarded their uniforms, weapons, and identification documents and immersed themselves among the ocean of other displaced persons in Germany at the time. All of these people passed through screening or filtration camps, some of which were in the Soviet border areas, and some were labor camps in Russia's Far North or the central Asian republics such as Kazakhstan. Screenings were conducted by Soviet military or NKVD officials: they recorded the individual's name, family information, and a chronology of the person's whereabouts and activities during the war. This information was recorded on a four-page questionnaire. If the person's story was open to question, an additional interrogation took place.[17]

Probably over one hundred former Trawniki guards who had served at the Reinhard camps were interrogated after the war. The interrogations and trials were given almost no publicity, with trials in the 1940s and 1950s not even seemingly reported in the Soviet press, while the group trials of the 1960s received, at best, passing mention. It wasn't until the 1970s that there was much cooperation between Soviet authorities and war crimes investigators in either East or West Germany, and thus, not until then that former Trawniki guards' statements began to be made available in the West, first in the investigation of Franz Swidersky and then in the investigation of former Trawniki camp commandant Karl Streibel, by the state attorney's office in Hamburg under Helge Grabitz.[18]

To cite just one example of a former Trawniki guard's fate, Ivan Kozlowskij was born in 1919 into a poor peasant family in Pskov, Russia. He had worked as a grazier on a collective farm (*kolkhoz*). He was conscripted into the Red Army in 1939. At the start of the war, his unit was stationed near Lvov and began to withdraw toward Kiev. The unit was surrounded by German forces. On August 5, 1941, he was slightly injured in the neck and captured. He was taken to the POW camp in Chelm. In November 1941, he was selected for Trawniki service. In March 1942, he was assigned to Belzec. In December 1942, he transferred to Sobibor. In April 1943, he was assigned to Auschwitz-Birkenau. He was arrested by Soviet authorities in 1949. A Soviet military tribunal sentenced him to twenty-five years of imprisonment. He was sent to serve his punishment at an ore mine in the Karaganda region of Kazakhstan.[19]

During the Stalin era, Soviet procurators charged suspected collaborators under Article 58, "Counterrevolutionary Activity," of the 1926 Soviet-Russian Criminal Code. Although some of the convicted received the death penalty, evidence points to widespread sentencing to twenty-five years of ITL (punitive labor camps). Virtually all of those sentenced for collaboration and sent to the Gulag system during Stalin's time were released under the 1955 "Amnesty for Soviet Citizens Collaborating with Occupation Forces during the Great Patriotic War." The 1960s trials took place under revised statutes (1960) introduced after Stalin's death, particularly Article 181.[20]

"The fact that these trials were conducted under the Soviet legal system, many of them during Stalin's dictatorship, warrants caution in evaluating the information gleaned from the interrogations." The interrogations generally follow a specific pattern: the accused former Trawniki guard provides testimony, the MGB officer or prosecutor conducting the interrogation summarizes that testimony in a document called a "protocol," and the accused then signs the document attesting that his statements were summarized correctly. Many of the protocols of interrogation contain similar language, including rhetoric typical of the Stalin era (for example, ideological phrases used to describe the Germans during the war, "German-Fascist forces" or "German punitive organs," or the phrase commonly used to categorize collaborators—"traitors to the Motherland").[21] Interrogations were redundant except when there was a skilled interrogator who would press and ask the right questions.

However, regardless of the ideological language and slant of the summaries of these interrogations, the information they contain is generally accurate when compared against German wartime documents as well as the testimony of former Trawniki guards tried in the West.[22] The interrogations conducted in the 1940s and 1950s generally had the goal of getting the former Trawniki guard to admit that he had collaborated with the Germans during the war and was thus a traitor to the Soviet Union. If the individual denied his collaboration, he was generally confronted with his captured Trawniki personnel file, a captured Trawniki roster with his name on it, or a signed statement from other former Trawniki guards attesting to his membership in the Trawniki guard units. "Perhaps under the pressure of the real or perceived threat of physical or psychological coercion, or perhaps because he knew he had been found out, the suspect generally, though not always, confessed at this point." At the conclusion of their trials for treason, "the sentences, which were almost invariably 25 years at hard labor or death, tended to depend upon such issues as length of service and/or enthusiasm in participating in Nazi crimes." During interrogations, the Soviets also attempted to discern if any former guards had had links with the Ukrainian nationalist movement, the OUN, or UPA.[23]

Later investigations of former Trawniki guards conducted in the 1960s during the Brezhnev and Khrushchev eras, unlike the earlier investigations of the Stalin era, were more concerned with their participation in mass murder than the fact that they had been traitors of the Soviet Union. The Soviet investigators in the 1960s "did make more than just token efforts to" determine what type of activities the Trawniki guards had been involved in while working for the Germans.[24]

Few among those tried and sentenced in this second wave had avoided detection during the immediate postwar investigations and trials. For example, in July 1961, military prosecutors in Ukraine petitioned the Soviet Supreme Court to vacate the 1951 conviction of one Mikhail Gorbachev, who had received a sentence of twenty-five years in punitive labor camps and had been released following the amnesty of 1955, after they had acquired new evidence that he had personally participated in the murder of prisoners in Treblinka II.[25]

There was a suspension of the death penalty in the Soviet Union from May 1947 to 1950. As a result, former Trawniki guards sentenced during this time frame received sentences of imprisonment only.

Stalin's death in 1953 brought a legal pause to the use of Article 58 as Soviet judicial reformers had the ambitious goal of amending the Soviet criminal codes originally devised in the 1920s. The introduction of rudimentary "due process" produced a fundamental change in the way Soviet criminal investigators gathered evidence and established guilt. The redrawn codes of criminal law and procedure had a profound effect on the quality of evidence produced during investigations and the nature of accountability.[26]

After 1960, several "group trials" of former Trawniki guards took place in the Soviet Union, under the revised criminal codes using Article 54-1, and established the guilt of these men. Some examples were as follows:

(1) the "Schults" trial in Kiev, 1962: men who had served at Treblinka II and Sobibor
(2) the "Akkermann" trial in Krasnodar, 1963?: men who had served at Belzec and Lublin Detachment
(3) the "Matvienko" trial in Krasnodar, 1964: men who had served at Belzec, Sobibor, Janowska, Lublin Detachment, and Warsaw Detachent
(4) the "Zuev" trial in Dnepropetrovsk, 1965: men who had served at Belzec and Auschwitz-Birkenau
(5) the "Litvinenko" trial in Lvov, 1968: men who had served at Janowska

Each trial consisted of dozens of volumes and hundreds of defendant and witness interrogations. The case records also contain whole volumes of Trawniki-captured documents, forensic evidence, crime-scene analysis, psychological expert reports, and other diverse material.[27]

One defendant had received a sentence of twenty-five years of hard labor in 1952 from a Soviet military tribunal in the Trans-Carpathian region. The sentence was then reduced to ten years due to the individual's apparent "high-labor productivity." He was released in late 1955 under the amnesty that had just been passed by Khrushchev. As evidence emerged in the "Schults" investigation, a deputy military prosecutor had the prior conviction set aside, and the case against the man was remanded for a renewed investigation. It is probable that the origins of most cases after 1960 followed a similar course. Of the men convicted and executed, only Emanuel Schults/Vinogradov had not previously been identified, tried, and punished. After 1960, at least nine former Trawniki guards who appeared as witnesses at the trials of other former Trawniki guards had themselves never been investigated or convicted.[28]

In Ukraine alone, according to a study by Ukrainian historian V. Nikolski, on the basis of material from the SBU Archive Kiev, 1943–1953, the NKVD arrested nearly 94,000 suspected "traitors to the homeland." This number is actually an underestimate covering only the 1943–1945 period. The Communist Party archive in Kiev states that in 1946 alone, over 29,000 "traitors of the homeland" were convicted. It was not uncommon for NKVD special units to shoot collaborators without trial.[29]

In 1941, the Soviet main court enacted a decree to exile the families of collaborators to remote areas of the Soviet Union. Trials against collaborators took place at special military courts, so-called military tribunals. These tribunals were subordinate to the Military Council of the Soviet Supreme Court. Defendants had no right of appeal against sentences passed by these tribunals, although death sentences had to be reviewed by a military council and could be annulled if the council so chose (military tribunals were established back at the time of the 1917 Revolution and the Russian Civil War).[30]

Usually, military tribunals consisted of a chairman, two assessors, and a secretary. In postwar Ukraine, there were thirty-one military tribunals of the MVD. In 1948, Ukraine was divided into two legal jurisdictions: Kiev for central and eastern Ukraine, and Lvov for western Ukraine. Military tribunals in Kiev tried mostly former policemen, while most of the cases in Lvov were against members of the OUN underground. About 60 percent of Ukraine's "traitors" convicted in 1946 were from western Ukraine. Most were OUN and UPA members: 18,000 were convicted.[31]

In 1946, only eighteen of the 134 members of the leading military tribunal staff had a higher legal education. The quality of judicial investigations was therefore low. After the war, legal officials underwent an increasing number of evaluations by the political leadership. In 1948–1949, a new campaign for the perfection of legal agencies began, aiming to eliminate all symptoms of imperfection, including acquittals. This was part of the bureaucratization of Soviet justice, which continued into the post-Stalin era.[32]

Postwar Soviet military tribunals sometimes abused their responsibilities by falsifying evidence and witness testimony, extorting confessions through torture (torture was outlawed in 1953), and corruption. Military prosecutors strictly investigated cases of abuse and corruption by military tribunal staff, and if the charges could be verified, the staff member could himself be charged and tried. Corrupt staff could be expelled from the party and sent to labor camps for five to ten years. Also, judges who made several political mistakes in their punishment policies were forced to participate in judicial qualification measures.[33]

In 1946, in Ukraine, 227 members of the MVD, and forty-one members of the MGB, were convicted of offences against Soviet law: the majority of them, 216, were sentenced to five to ten years in labor camps. In 1949, 60–70 percent of defendants appealed their sentences.[34]

Two investigative bodies conducted investigations of German crimes and the crimes of collaborators: military commissions and the Soviet "Extraordinary Commission for Investigating Crimes Committed by the German Invaders."[35]

The 1934 Soviet-Ukrainian Criminal Law served as the legal basis for convicting collaborators in Ukraine until it was replaced by a new criminal code in 1960. Collaborators were tried in Ukraine under Article 54-1, which pertained to Treason / Counterrevolutionary Activity: actions carried out by Soviet citizens to the detriment of the Soviet state, its military strength, national sovereignty, or national security. Examples of this crime include engaging in espionage, passing of military or state secrets to unauthorized persons, going over to the enemy, or escaping over the Soviet border. Article 54-1 was the Ukrainian equivalent of Russia's Article 58. The sentence for civilians ranged from ten years' imprisonment up to execution by shooting. For members of the Red Army the sentence was death by shooting.[36]

In April 1943, the Supreme Soviet enacted the first regulation for war crimes, *Ukaz* (Order) 43, which dealt with "sanctions against German criminals responsible for the killing and maltreatment of the Soviet civilian population and POWs, as well as secret agents and traitors to the homeland." Spies and traitors were to be sentenced to death.[37]

The legal regulations left considerable room for flexibility, and as a result the procurator and Soviet Supreme Court passed several orders to put an end to arbitrary convictions and to curb the inflationary imposition of death sentences. In November 1943, the Soviet Supreme Court issued a definition for what type of collaboration would constitute treason: Soviet citizens serving the Germans in local administration or as policemen; providing the Germans with military or state secrets; helping the Germans persecute partisans; participating with the Germans in murdering, mistreating, and robbing the Soviet civilian population; or serving in the German armed forces. For all of these actions the sentence was death. The main Soviet prosecutor instructed regional prosecutors to review all death sentences.[38]

In May 1947, the Supreme Soviet abolished the death penalty for all crimes. However, in January 1950 the death penalty was reinstated for traitors, spies, saboteurs, and subversives. Collaborators put on trial before Soviet courts sometimes stated in their defense such things as coming from poor peasant families, having served in the Red Army, having been wounded fighting against the Germans, and working hard on collective farms (*kolkhozes*).[39]

One former Trawniki guard who had served at a death camp and was tried in Kiev in 1949 was sentenced to fifteen years of hard labor. He would have been sentenced to twenty-five years, but a mitigating factor had been that after his Trawniki service, he had recirculated back into the Red Army, where he was wounded twice and had been awarded several military decorations.[40]

During the war and its immediate aftermath, the Soviet Supreme Court complained that sentences pronounced against collaborators by Soviet military tribunals tended to be too severe. However, in the following years, 1946–1949, the Soviet Ministry of Justice several times criticized sentences that were too mild. A mild sentence meant ten years' imprisonment.[41]

During the war, between 1943 and 1945, about 5 percent of collaborators who were tried were sentenced to death. During the postwar years, 1946 to 1953, about 1 percent of collaborators who were tried received a death sentence, which was partly due to the abolition of the death penalty between 1947 and 1950. In 1946, out of 29,000 convicted collaborators, 21,000 were sentenced to ten years' imprisonment. About 650 received a death sentence. In 1950 and 1951, in the Kiev region, about 95 percent of convicted collaborators were sentenced to twenty-five years in labor camps. Only 2–3 percent of defendants were acquitted in trials of collaborators in Ukraine.[42]

In the case of the former Trawniki guards, their guilt was, in accordance with Soviet law, assumed from the very beginning, because they had broken their military oath to the Soviet Union and had served with the enemy, performing the function of policemen. However, Soviet investigators needed to prove to what extent they had participated in repressive actions, and whether they had acted under duress or had volunteered their services. A court would pass sentence on the basis of whether they had taken part in shootings or other atrocities, and also with regard to the degree of activism they displayed in carrying out their duties with the Germans. A guilty verdict was going to be delivered in any case: the only question was whether this meant a term of imprisonment or execution.[43]

To what extent can one trust the testimony given by former Trawniki guards after the war, when we know that Soviet investigators in Stalin's time used physical methods of coercion?:

My view is that they were not subjected to physical coercion, because a number of them determinedly rejected the accusation that they had participated in mass killings. They rejected the accusation both when under investigation and during trial, and Soviet investigators were not always able to prove that they had taken part in such actions. In the course of postwar investigations the majority of the former Trawniki guards denied taking any active role in mass killings, insisting that they had just stood guard or escorted prisoners, while the Germans did the actual killing.[44]

Of all the Nazi collaborators, the Trawniki guards are probably the ones that have been most thoroughly held to account by the Soviet regime:

While the Soviet Union failed to achieve a perfect record of identifying and locating all of these men, and although many served sentences far short in proportion to their crimes, nevertheless, the justice dealt out by Soviet State Security, was far-reaching and well within the bounds of justice.[45]

RG 20869 AND RG K-779

The primary source documentation on the Trawniki guards is held in various locations in the former Soviet Union, Poland, and the Czech Republic.[46] The largest single collection of captured wartime documents relating to the Trawniki guards is contained in two record groups held in the Central Archive of the Federal Security Service (FSB, a.k.a. the former KGB) in Moscow (a building that has been described as nondescript and without any identifying markings, denoting that it is an archive):

(1) Record Group 20869: consists of twenty-six volumes of Trawniki *Personalbögen* (personnel files)
(2) Record Group K-779: contains three volumes of internal reports and memos from Trawniki Training Camp, January 1943–July 1944

It is uncertain whether all of the Trawniki personnel files in RG 20869 were captured at one location or whether they were consolidated after the Soviets captured them in several locations:

If the files were consolidated only after capture, we cannot at this point say when, where, or even by whom they were captured.[47] I don't recall seeing any information that establishes a chronological pattern of where the Trawniki Identification documents moved from the time they were seized until the time they ended up in the KGB archive.[48]

The Red Army overran the Lublin area and Trawniki camp in mid- to late July 1944. At that time, they may have captured the documents in the administrative office at Trawniki before the Germans had had a chance to transport or destroy those files during their hurried evacuation of the camp. Attached to the Red Army were SMERSH (counterintelligence) units responsible for gathering intelligence and interrogating prisoners. One of their duties was document exploitation for intelligence-gathering purposes, and they may very well have secured the Trawniki documents to begin searching for war criminals.[49] It is also possible that the Germans had evacuated the Trawniki documents by train, and the Soviets had intercepted and bombed the train and confiscated the documents.

Record Group 20869 "may have originally contained as many as 2,000 Trawniki personnel files."[50] In the twenty years or so following the end of the war, the MGB/KGB transferred an undetermined number of those files from their main offices in Moscow to several of their regional offices throughout the Soviet Union in order to use those files in the criminal investigation and prosecution of individual former Trawniki guards.

The largest collection of Trawniki personnel files held outside the FSB central archive in Moscow is 240 files held by the Central State Archive in Kiev. It is unclear if this collection of files had ever formally belonged to RG 20869 in Moscow. They may have been transferred to Kiev by the KGB as early as the 1960s. Copies of a handful of these files are now held on microfilm/microfiche by the archive of the United States Holocaust Memorial Museum in Washington, DC.[51] These 240 files are primarily the files of later Trawniki recruits (those with identification numbers in the #3000 range) from Chelm, Hrubieszow, Zamosc, Zakopane, and Nowy Targ.[52] It is possible that the reason these particular Trawniki personnel files were transferred to a state archive rather than remaining in the custody of the KGB is because these former Trawniki guards were determined to have died already or were determined to live outside the Soviet Union, or the Soviet authorities had given up trying to locate them. In at least one instance, a Trawniki personnel file was destroyed by Ukrainian authorities in 1992, after they determined that there was no value in retaining it any longer.[53]

Today, Record Group 20869 contains 875 Trawniki personnel files. It also contains some postwar Soviet translations, investigation summaries, and protocols of interrogations of former Trawniki guards by Soviet investigators.[54] The MGB/KGB transferred Trawniki personnel files from Moscow to various local MGB/KGB offices in jurisdictions where the presumed former Trawniki guard being sought either was under arrest, was reported to live, was last known to have lived, or might return to live or make contact with family members still living in that area.

If the former guard was arrested, tried, and convicted, the Trawniki personnel file sent to the local office that had responsibility for the case kept it as part of the individual's criminal case file.[55] Altogether, about 1,200 of the original 5,082 Trawniki personnel files are known to exist today (about 23–24 percent of them).[56]

Record Group K-779 includes Trawniki guard rosters as well as activity, desertion, and casualty reports for the guards. The original German documents, about 450 pages, are mixed with postwar Soviet investigation notes, document translations from German to Russian, and investigative summaries of the contents of the documents, 700–800 pages.[57] Despite the valuable historical information contained in Record Group K-779, the documents contained within it cover only the years 1943–1944. Trawniki memos, correspondence, and rosters from the critical period of 1941–1942 are missing. This earlier documentation may have been destroyed by the Germans before the Red Army was able to capture it, or it may have been inadvertently destroyed in Allied or Soviet bombings.[58]

The largest single category of documentation on the former Trawniki guards is the case files of hundreds of them tried by Soviet authorities in the 1944–1968 period. Most of this documentation remains in the custody of local offices of the FSB and SBU (formerly the MGB/KGB) in the former Soviet Union.[59] Numerous Soviet trial records of former Trawniki guards have come to light in the public domain, thanks to the ongoing work of the US Department of Justice's Office of Special Investigations (now called the Human Rights and Special Prosecutions Section) in investigating some of these men who immigrated to the US, and the efforts of archival staff at the US Holocaust Memorial Museum in Washington, DC.[60] When the Department of Justice asked for judicial assistance in investigating these men, the Russian and Ukrainian governments responded by sending them copies of numerous

Trawniki personnel files, rosters, and interrogation and trial records from their FSB and SBU archives, which contain the originals of those documents.

The Trawniki rosters pertaining to the SS "Streibel" Battalion were located by OSI historians during a research trip to the Federal Ministry of Interior in Prague in 1990. They are located in the Central State Archive in Prague.[61]

Representatives of the US Holocaust Memorial Museum had been in negotiations with Russian officials in an attempt to obtain more of the Trawniki trial records and other documents from Record Groups 20869 and K-779 (those negotiations have apparently been discontinued, given the current state of relations between the US and Russia).[62]

THE RED ARMY OVERRUNS EASTERN POLAND AND CAPTURES DOCUMENTS, AND INVESTIGATIONS AND TRIALS BEGIN

THE CAPTURE OF LUBLIN

The 2nd Tank Army, as part of 1st Belorussian Front, advanced in the overall direction of Lublin.[1] 2nd Tank Army was positioned between 1st Belorussian Front and 1st Ukrainian Front and would enter the breakthrough area created by 8th Guards Army, with the task of taking Lublin.[2] 2nd Tank Army's 8th Guards Tank Corps, together with the 107th Tank Brigade of the 16th Tank Corps, and 3rd Tank Corps' 50th and 51st Tank Brigades, on July 22, 1944, began pursuing the enemy in the direction of Lublin. General Bogdanov, commander of 2nd Tank Army, decided to envelop Lublin from the north, northwest, east, and southeast.[3]

7th Guards Cavalry Corps was to advance north of the Chelm, Piaski, and Lublin highway and assist 8th Guards Tank Corps with an attack from the southeast and south.[4] The enemy, consisting of units of the German 26th Infantry Division and the 213th Security Division, fell back but attempted to check 2nd Tank Army's advance.[5] 7th Guards Cavalry Corps fought for Chelm. Meanwhile, remnants of the enemy's shattered divisions continued to retreat toward Lublin, seeking the protection of the defensive line surrounding the city. Isolated groups of the enemy feared being encircled and scattered into the woods, engaging in partisan tactics. Within two or three days, these groups were eliminated by infantry of the 8th Guards Army.[6]

By the evening of July 22, units of 3rd Tank Corps arrived on the northwest outskirts of Lublin. 7th Guards Cavalry Corps took Chelm and approached Lublin from the southeast. An attempt by the Germans to rally in the final strongpoints on the route to Lublin proved unsuccessful. 3rd Tank Corps was to take the western and northwestern outskirts of Lublin, cutting off an enemy retreat to the northwest and west.[7] 8th Guards Tank Corps was to envelop Lublin from the northeast and east and was to capture the city. 7th Guards Cavalry Corps was to attack from the southeast and south and assist 3rd Tank Corps and 8th Guards Tank Corps with taking Lublin.[8]

By the morning on July 23, 1944, the enemy had 3,000–4,000 men from remnants of the 26th Infantry Division, the 213th Security Division, the 2nd and 991st Security battalions, Police Regiment 25, and a signals company. These forces were ordered to hold on to Lublin at any cost. These forces were reinforced with twelve self-propelled guns. Defense of the city was in the hands of the commander of the Lublin garrison, Lieutenant General Hilmar Moser, who would later be captured by 2nd Tank Army. The city's defenses consisted of two rings of defensive fortifications. The first one consisted of a network of trenches, communication trenches, machine gun emplacements, mortar pits, and protected gun positions. The second ring, in Lublin itself, consisted of isolated strongpoints, for which stone buildings and cellars were turned into pillboxes for a protracted defense.[9]

Lacking adequate artillery and antitank guns, the enemy was unable to hold off 2nd Tank Army's forces in the outer ring of fortifications. By noon on July 23, the Germans abandoned the eastern part of Lublin but continued resistance along the inner ring, firing from buildings and cellars. They deployed antitank guns on the city streets and also had *Panzerfäusten* in ambush points against Soviet armored vehicles. 3rd Tank Corps, with its 50th and 51st Tank Brigades, breached the outer ring of defenses and reached the northwestern outskirts of Lublin and engaged in street fighting. 8th Guards Tank Corps, with its 59th and

60th Guards Tank Brigades, continued mopping up the northern and northeastern parts of the city. 107th Tank Brigade of 16th Tank Corps, along with 58th Guards Tank Brigade and 1817th Self-Propelled Gun Regiment, both of the 8th Guards Tank Corps, fully swept eastern Lublin along the Bystrzyca River.[10]

Attempting at first to take the city by using only tanks, 8th Guards Tank Corps encountered heavy enemy fire and had no success. Its motorized rifle brigade had not yet arrived. However, once that brigade did arrive, assault teams were formed, consisting of one to three tanks, self-propelled guns, and small groups of submachine gunners. By the end of the day on July 23, the brigades of 8th Guards Tank Corps, after stubborn street fighting, took Lublin with a concentrated assault from the north, northwest, and east. That afternoon, 2nd Tank Army's commander, Colonel-General Semen Bogdanov, suffered a gunshot wound to the shoulder. Command of the army was then taken over by his chief of staff, Major-General Alexei Radzievsky.[11] During the fighting, 8th Guards Tank Corps reportedly captured around 2,230 enemy troops and officers. The corps also reported about 120 men killed and about 340 men wounded from its own units.[12]

Author Igor Nebolsin also offered another version of the Soviet capture of Lublin, by a Polish historian, which offers some additional details of the assault on the city: On the morning of July 23, 1944, after a twenty-minute artillery barrage on German strongpoints, 2nd Tank Army launched an attack on Lublin. 50th and 51st Tank Brigades and the 1107th and 1219th Self-Propelled Gun Regiments attacked from the Slawinek, Czechow, area. Before 10 a.m., the attack broke enemy defenses in several parts of the suburbs. However, the Soviets ran into problems without their infantry units on the scene. In city combat, without infantry support, tanks become easy prey for antitank guns and *Panzerfäusten*. The Soviet attackers didn't know the city well and were surprised by the German garrison's stiff resistance. Lack of Soviet infantry made it impossible to mop up sections of buildings in the city, some of which were strongly fortified. In this situation, the attack by 3rd Tank Corps led to heavy casualties.[13]

8th Guards Tank Corps attacked toward Lublin from the northeast. 60th Guards Tank Brigade, reinforced by the 1st Battalion of the 28th Guards Motorized Rifle Brigade and the 301st Guards Self-Propelled Gun Regiment, attacked from the Rudnik area. Their attack initially faltered and the Germans counterattacked; however, this counterattack was repulsed. 60th Tank Brigade resumed its attack, now reinforced with the addition of 107th Tank Brigade, which had just arrived from Chelm. Tanks advanced toward the city center, but in the absence of covering infantry, those Soviet tanks were destroyed by the enemy.[14]

58th and 59th Tank Brigades advanced toward Lublin from the northeast and east with SU-85 self-propelled guns of the 1817th Self-Propelled Gun Regiment, supported later on by the 28th Guards Motorized Rifle Brigade. By 10 a.m., attacking units captured the eastern suburbs of the city and advanced toward the bridge over the Bystrzyca River, which divides the city. The attack was stopped by heavy German fire from the west bank of the river. Toward evening, units of the 8th Guards Army's 28th Guards Rifle Corps and the 7th Guards Cavalry Corps arrived in the vicinity of Lublin. Also, the 5th Motorcycle Regiment arrived from Chelm. These forces were more than enough to take the city. 3rd Tank Corps, 8th Guards Tank Corps, and the 107th Tank Brigade of the 16th Tank Corps maintained pressure on the enemy. That night, two battalions of 58th Guards Tank Brigade and some infantry broke through across the river to the city center.[15]

Before dawn on July 24, 1944, elements of the Lublin garrison retreated southwest toward Krasnik. That morning, both Soviet tank corps (3rd and 8th Guards) reached the city center and linked up after stubborn fighting with the enemy. The city was largely taken by noon; however, isolated pockets of defenders continued to resist until nightfall.[16] General Radzievsky ordered 8th Guards Tank Corps to continue mopping up small pockets of Germans and to hold the city until the arrival of infantry from the 8th Guards Army to replace it. Lublin was fully in Soviet hands by July 25, 1944,[17] thus bringing an end to German occupation in the city, which had once been a pinnacle of the SS empire, represented in the form of SS-Gruppenführer Odilo Globocnik, Aktion Reinhard, and the Trawniki guards.

BELZEC

The area of Belzec was liberated by Marshal Konev's 1st Ukrainian Front, specifically units of the 1st Guards Tank Army under General Katukov, sometime between July 16 and 27, 1944, and its rear areas were still in place in the Zamosc region in time to receive a report in early 1945, shortly before the Front liberated Auschwitz during the Vistula-Oder Offensive. The report included an account by Stanilslaw Kozak regarding construction of the first gas chamber, which would differ little from testimony he would give to the Polish Main War Crimes Commission in October 1945.[18] Auschwitz was liberated by the 60th Army under General Kurochkin on January 25, 1945.

In Belzec, Rudolf Reder is the only known prisoner who worked at the gas chambers and survived the camp.[19] Reder gave a lengthy testimony to Soviet investigators from the Lvov region procuracy in September 1944 regarding Belzec.[20] Reder also gave testimony before the Jewish Historical Commission in Krakow.[21] He published a book about Belzec in 1946.

In December 1945, he made a statement regarding the gassing engine used in the gas chamber in Belzec: It was "an engine with petrol fuel. It had a flywheel. This engine was always operated by two technicians, Russians from the camp staff. The engine used four cans of petrol each day. The petrol was delivered to the engine room."[22] Another witness of the gassing engine was the Polish mechanic Kazimierz Czerniak, and he stated it was a 200-horsepower engine that ran on gasoline.[23] Czerniak described the motor as a complicated installation. He later admitted to having installed a special filter on the motor, designed to separate the smoke from the pure gas that was piped into the gas chambers.[24] The SS officer, Dr. Wilhelm Pfannenstiel, who was director of the Hygiene Institute at the University of Marburg, visited Belzec in August 1942 with SS-Obersturmführer Kurt Gerstein. He stated that the engine operated with diesel fuel.[25] "I don't know if it was a diesel or gasoline engine. It was started up by a mechanic from among the auxiliaries."[26] "It was diesel exhaust."[27]

Pfannenstiel and Gerstein were given a demonstration of the gassing process by SS-Hauptsturmführer Christian Wirth. However, there were technical problems with the gassing motor, which took over two hours to fix. Furious at the delays, Wirth whipped one of the Ukrainian guards responsible for the gassing engine. Regarding that Ukrainian guard's identity, who until recently had never been named, historian Michael Tregenza said:

> I found that information quite easily: I checked the wartime patients' admission book for 1942–1943, in the local hospital. Ivan Huzija was admitted that afternoon with a "badly lacerated face." The bill was paid by SS-Sonderkommando "Belzec." He was then transferred to Treblinka. Likewise, names of Ukrainian guards admitted during a typhus epidemic in January 1943 [were also in the patient admission book]. Oddly enough, those bills were paid by the SS-Garrison Administration Lublin, SS-Sturmbannführer Georg Wippern, not Wirth in Belzec.[28]

Regarding the fate of one of the other Ukrainian guards who had worked at the gas chambers in Belzec, Edward Wlasiuk, the historian Tregenza stated:

I met "Mrs. Wlasiuk" in Belzec in the late 1990s and had afternoon tea with her in her garden one summer's afternoon. She claimed Edward was posted to Mauthausen concentration camp in late 1944. She did not go with him because she was pregnant. He returned to Poland after the war (rather silly of him!) and he found a job in a garage in Lublin. Then, he was supposedly recognized by someone in the street (as often happened in those days) who informed the *AK*. They then did a hit-and-run job on him.[29]

This story contradicts what Mrs. Wlasiuk (remarried with the last name Warzocha) told a Polish investigator in 1966 when questioned. She had at that time stated that Edward Wlasiuk had died in Austria in May 1945, having reentered the Red Army.[30]

The Polish War Crimes Investigation Commission of the Zamosc District Court (*Okregowa Komisja Badania Zbrodni Przeciwko Narodowi Polskiemo*, or OKBZ) conducted the first investigation of Belzec, starting October 10, 1945, under Judge Czeslaw Godzieszewski, and the local district court prosecutor, T. Chrosciewicz. The investigation was supervised by the head of the OKBZ in Lublin, Jan Grzybowski. Examination of witnesses took place in Zamosc, Tomaszow-Lubelski, and Lublin.[31]

The only other known survivor of Belzec to survive the war was Chaim Hirszmann. In July 1943, after Belzec was dismantled, several hundred "work Jews" from the camp, Hirszmann among them, were told that they would be transferred elsewhere for work. However, they were taken to Sobibor and executed on arrival. On the train to Sobibor, Hirszmann and another man jumped off. Hirszmann managed to reach his native area (Janow-Lubelski) and was sheltered by a friend.[32] Hirszmann did not give testimony to the OKBZ, possibly because neither he nor the investigators of that commission knew about each other's existence. However, he did testify before the Jewish Historical Commission in Lublin on March 19, 1946, regarding his time at Belzec. He stated that his job at Belzec had been removing bodies from the gas chambers.

Hirszmann was scheduled to give further testimony the following day, but he was shot and killed that same day at his apartment in Lublin by a seventeen-year-old youth who belonged to the group known as the "*TOW*" (Secret Military Organization), which was connected to the *AK-WIN* (Polish Home Army: Freedom and Independence). The testimony was completed instead by his second wife, Pola. Her testimony on Belzec is four and a half pages long.[33] The Hirszmann testimony was used for the first time by Dr. Yitzhak Arad, on the basis of a copy in the Yad Vashem Collection.[34] Hirszmann had served as an investigator in the Lublin branch of the Polish *UB* (Ministry of Public Security: essentially the Polish Communist secret police) between June 1945 and March 1, 1946, and was then voluntarily discharged for unspecified reasons. He and his wife had had a son, six days prior to his death.[35] Hirszmann's papers are located in the IPN Archive (Archive of the Polish Institute of National Memory, or AIPN). His personal file has been preserved in AIPN Lu 028/672, "Hirszmann File." However, the file is incomplete: only ten of its thirty-six documents are present; the rest were destroyed in 1975. Reducing paper in the archives was apparently a routine matter; nevertheless, why was over two-thirds of his file discarded?

Former *SS-Unterscharführer* Fritz Tauscher stated that when he was assigned to Belzec in October 1942, the camp commandant, Gottlob Hering, put him in charge of exhuming the bodies from the mass graves and burning them. The bodies were burned day and night without interruption, first with one pyre, then with two, until March 1943.[36]

The gassings, as far as I recall, stopped at the end of 1942. Then began exhumation and burning of the bodies. It should have lasted from November 1942 to March 1943. One pyre could burn about 2,000 bodies in twenty-four hours. About two weeks after the burnings began, a second pyre was built. Thus, about 300,000 bodies were burned on one pyre over a five-month period, and 240,000 bodies on the other pyre over a four-month period. Of course these are only estimates. I was assigned to the "burning kommando." The process was offensive to the senses and would probably be unimaginable to people living in a civil society under civil conditions.[37]

The estimate that cremations began in Belzec around November 1942 is corroborated by several witnesses.[38] According to a Polish investigative report, the bodies were exhumed from the ground with special cranes and burned on heaps doused with a flammable substance. Later, the procedure was improved by building structures made from railway rails, on which the bodies were placed with layers of wood drenched in a flammable substance.[39] The report refers to several witnesses, including Eustachy Ukrainski, Tadeusz Misiewicz, Stanislaw Kozak, and Kazimierz Czerniak, all of whom were local residents. The machine exhuming the bodies was mentioned by the witnesses Goch, Kirsz, Ukrainski, and Kozak.[40] The stench of burned bodies could be smelled up to 9 miles from Belzec.[41]

The burned remains were crushed with a special machine, possibly a ball mill, which resembles a cement mixer and was used for crushing bones into dust. The machine may have been borrowed from the Janowska labor camp in Lvov.[42] According to author Robin O'Neal, the machine was operated by a Janowska prisoner, a Hungarian Jew named Szpilke. Rudolf Reder mentioned this man in his report about Belzec.[43] That machine is also mentioned in statements made to the Lvov deputy district procurator by Moishe Korn on September 13, 1944, and to Heinrich Chamaides on September 21, 1944 (quoted in Ernst Klee, ed., *Gott mit uns*, p. 226).[44] Rudolf Reder stated that ashes from the cremations were scattered in fields and woods near the camp.[45]

During the liquidation of Belzec, *SS-Unterscharführer* Fritz Tauscher had at his disposal several Germans, including Werner Dubois and Robert Juhrs, and a contingent of Ukrainian guards. He also had 300–350 "work Jews." One day, Christian Wirth arrived and ordered those work Jews onto a train with eight or nine cars. He told them they were being transferred to another camp.[46] They were taken to Sobibor and shot on arrival. Afterward, Sobibor prisoners took their bodies in the narrow-gauge wagons to Camp III for cremation.[47]

On October 12, 1945, the investigative judge of the Zamosc District Court, Czeslaw Godzieszewski, presented an account of the diggings in Belzec, in which he presented the findings of a site inspection he had conducted with twelve workers. They located graves filled with ashes and sand and partly containing charred human body parts and hair:

Some remains were partly decomposed and partly mummified.[48] Some of the camp area is churned up across a width of about 100 meters. According to information from the Citizens' Militia post in Belzec, the churning-up of the camp area was done by the local population, searching for gold and jewels left behind by the murdered Jews. In the churned-up area are huge amounts of scattered bones. The camp area along the north and east border is a continuous common grave of the people murdered in the camp.[49]

Scavenging for valuables at the site of the former camp had begun even before the war had ended. When the Germans discovered that diggings were occurring there, they established a permanent guard to watch over the site.[50] However, with the approach of the Red Army, the guard fled and the locals resumed their diggings.

It was not until the second half of the 1950s, during the period of "de-Stalinization," that information concerning the condition of the former site of the Belzec camp came to public light. Voices grew, calling for the site to be made into a place of commemoration. In the meantime, a sawmill had been erected on the former site, and heavy trucks drove over the mass graves.[51]

Josef Oberhauser, the sole defendant of the Belzec trial who was convicted and sentenced to prison in West Germany in the 1960s, had his sentence reduced because he had already served a sentence in East Germany, having been convicted in Magdeburg in 1948.[52]

In 1971, as a sand quarry was being operated on the site of the former Belzec camp, nineteen carbon monoxide canisters were found. They were unearthed on the former grounds of the Trawniki guards barracks. The canisters probably originated from the time at the start of Belzec operations, when the camp was still experimenting with the killing method it would use. The Polish army took possession of the canisters, and they were later destroyed in the nearby town of Lubycza Krolowska.[53]

At least fifty-three Trawniki guards who had served at Belzec in 1942 were tried and sentenced, of which at least seventeen were executed, including three *Volksdeutsche*: Karl Deiner, Alexander Schaeffer, and Johann Tellmann. At least twelve who had served at the camp from March 27, 1943, onward were tried and sentenced, of which at least two were executed, including the *Volksdeutscher* Andrei Akkermann.[54]

In 1965, in Krasnodar, the "Matvienko" trial took place. One of the witnesses at the trial had been a participant in the Sobibor Uprising—Alexei Wajcen, and he claimed to recognize one of the former Trawniki guards on trial, Ivan Zaitsev. One of the other defendants, Vasili Podenok, was a teacher.[55]

Polish witnesses were invited to the trial, including residents of Belzec village.[56]

The documentation on the Matwijenko trial was made available to the US Department of Justice in the 1990s but focused only on a few interrogations and wartime German documents. None of the legal documents (e.g., indictments, court sessions, judgments) that identify the names of the judges and prosecutor in the case were made available.

SOBIBOR

Marshal Rokossovsky's 1st Belorussian Front liberated the areas of Sobibor, Treblinka, and Majdanek. Of these, only the investigation of Majdanek received any reinforcements from the Extraordinary Investigation Commission in Moscow. This is because it was captured largely intact and had killed both Jewish and non-Jewish victims. Most of the investigative work, as with the later 1st Ukrainian Front's investigation of Auschwitz, was the responsibility of the judge-advocate staff of the 1st Belorussian Front.[57] The crime scenes at Sobibor and Treblinka were delegated to subordinate armies: 47th Army was assigned to Sobibor.[58] General Chuikov's 8th Guards Army filed a brief report on Sobibor, Majdanek, and a number of Soviet POW camps in late July 1944 and also gathered statements from villagers in the area surrounding Sobibor.[59]

On the basis of the reports filed by the Soviet armies, it appears that they didn't have the resources or the interest in pursuing a proper systematic investigation of any of the former death camp sites. The brevity of the reports on the Reinhard camps compared to the lengthy reports filed on Majdanek and Auschwitz is obvious. However, the reports are still historically valuable. For example, the report of the 8th Guards Army summarized testimony from villagers in Sobibor who reported having heard the sound of the gas chamber motor and the cries of the victims in the camp.[60]

Descriptions of the gas chamber facility were provided in testimony and accounts from the following former Trawniki guards: Jakob Engelhardt, Emanuel Schultz, Mikhail Razgonjajew, Ignat Danilchenko, Ivan Karakach, and Vasili Pankow.[61] Testimony regarding the construction of the gas chambers was contained in a report by Kazimierz Schnierstein, district court prosecutor in Lublin, November 23, 1945 (# I. Dz. 1438/45), to the Central

Commission for the Investigation of German Crimes in Poland, Krakow, to Examining Appeal Judge Jozef Skorzynski, in Radom.[62] In 1962, Erich Bauer testified that a Ukrainian named Ivan worked at the gas chamber in Sobibor.

Former prisoner Jakub Biskupicz stated that at the end of Sobibor's existence, another camp was erected in the area for Wehrmacht soldiers. It was a large camp for reserve Ukrainian soldiers. "Those guards took an active part in chasing the escaped prisoners" during the camp uprising. Ivan Karakach, a former Trawniki guard, made mention of this camp and called it 'Camp V,' stating it had been intended for sixty western Ukrainians "brought to Sobibor to protect the new part of the camp." "Those soldiers did not have any contact with the 'main camp.'"[63] Karakach claimed Camp IV contained a bath where Jews were gassed, an area where about 150 Jewish laborers lived, a fire where Jews were burned, a German guard building, repair workshops, and a watchtower with a heavy machine gun.[64]

A sketch of Sobibor was drawn by the following persons:

(1) Michael Tregenza, with a copy in Marek Bem's private collection[65]
(2) former prisoner Arkady Weisspapier, with a copy in the MPLW Archive in Wlodawa[66]
(3) former prisoner Jakub Biskupicz, with a copy in Marek Bem's private collection[67]
(4) former *SS-Oberscharführer* Kurt Bolender, with a copy in the MPLW Archive in Wlodawa[68]
(5) former *SS-Scharführer* Franz Hodl, in 1966 or 1974, with a copy in the MPLW Archive in Wlodawa.[69]
(6) former *SS-Oberscharführer* Erich Bauer, with a copy included in the Proceedings of the District Court Hagen, December 20, 1966, 11 Ks 1/62, JuNSV XXV[70]
(7) former Trawniki guard Ignat Danilchenko, with a copy in the MPLW Archive in Wlodawa[71]

In addition,

(8) a map of the camp was prepared during judicial inquiries in the early 1960s, conducted by KGB investigators against former Trawniki guards living in the Soviet Union. That map is located in the IPN Archive Lublin.[72] It is from the records of the interrogation of Emanuel Schultz, April 27, 1961, in Vinnitsa, Ukraine.[73]
(9) A map of the camp was made by Polish geodesists in 1984, which had been commissioned by a Hagen Court in the appeal case of former *SS-Oberscharführer* Karl Frenzel, who had been sentenced to life imprisonment. In the part describing Camp III (the extermination zone) is a sketch of a crematorium pit with the caption "the place where foundation fragments and car parts with burned human bones were unearthed." This may have been a reference to grates used in the cremation pits or a frame on which a bone grinder had been installed.[74]

Historian Peter Black stated that there were 388 known Trawniki guards who had served at Sobibor during its existence. At least 29 (7.5 percent) of them deserted or attempted desertion.[75] Former Sobibor prisoner Alexei Vaitsen, who was also a Red Army veteran, testified at the Soviet trials of former Trawniki guards in the 1960s, during which he identified several Sobibor guards by name,[76] and Russian researchers produced an oral history of the Sobibor revolt from accounts of Russian survivors.[77]

The camp was surrounded by seven watchtowers, in which one guard served duty in each in the daytime. They were armed with a rifle and fifteen rounds of ammunition. At night, certain areas around the camp were patrolled by three *Volksdeutsche*.[78]

Information about Sobibor began to be gathered the moment Lublin District was liberated in July 1944. This included collecting information about the crimes committed there and estimating the number of victims. The task was undertaken by the "Historical Commission of the Central Committee of Jews in Poland," which collected survivor accounts and searched for all documents pertaining to the camp, and by the "Central Commission for the Investigation of German Crimes in Poland," which launched an official investigation into the crimes committed at the camp. The investigation, conducted in 1945–1946, began on September 28, 1945, by the prosecutor of the Lublin District Court, Kazimierz Schnierstein, and was carried out under the judges Jozef Skorzynski and Zbigniew Lukaszewicz. Investigators working under them gathered written information on the camp, compiled survivor accounts, interviewed witnesses, and conducted an inspection of the area where the camp had been.[79] An interim report by Judge Lukaszewicz was published in 1947, in the "Bulletin of the Central Commission."[80] Lukaszewicz estimated Sobibor's victims at 250,000.[81]

An initial report by M. Rozegnal, a member of the "Central Commission" in Wola Uhruska, was sent to the "District Commission for the Investigation of German Crimes" in Wlodawa, in September 1945 and put the number of Jews killed in Sobibor at around 1.5 million.[82] Information collected by the Wlodawa municipal court, prepared in 1945 by Jan Skulski, the Sobibor Commune administrator, put the number of Sobibor victims at three million.[83] The report of the regional court prosecutor in Lublin, Schnierstein, on November 23, 1945, prepared for the "Central Commission" and for Judge Skorzynski, estimated the number of victims at two million.[84] The trial of the German Sobibor staff in Hagen, in 1965–1966, put the number at at least 150,000, on the basis of research done by Dr. Wolfgang Scheffler.[85] The "Jewish Historical Institute" began a project on a historical monograph on Sobibor, to be compiled by Adam Rutkowski. In 1960, he prepared a report about Sobibor in which he stated that 350,000 victims had been killed there.[86]

Former *SS-Unterscharführer* Erich Fuchs had taken part in constructing the gas chambers at Belzec and Sobibor and stated in postwar testimony that the gas chamber engine was a heavy Russian petrol engine, presumably from an armored vehicle or tractor, with at least 200 horsepower and a V engine with eight cylinders.[87] Former *SS-Oberscharführer* Erich Bauer stated it was a petrol engine, possibly a Renault:[88]

The gas chamber gave off exhaust gasses from diesel engines. I remember hearing from other guards that there were two such diesels, supposedly from tanks. I did not personally see these engines.[89] It was a diesel engine. Near the motor worked two or three Ukrainians who serviced it. Anton Getzinger and later Franz Hodl were there to supervise. Diesel fuel was often brought to the engine. I have little knowledge about engines. I suppose it was a diesel.[90] The gassing engine was a captured Russian diesel engine, serviced by Bauer.[91] I was told it was the engine of a Russian T-34 tank. I don't know that exactly. I didn't see it. It was only what we were told to us.[92]

An excavator was brought in to exhume the bodies for burning.[93] In fall 1942, an excavator arrived in the middle of the night. SS men and Ukrainian guards unloaded it from a train and took it to Camp III (the extermination zone).[94] Probably, *SS-Oberscharführer* Herbert Floss went to Sobibor from Belzec in late April 1942.[95] Likely is that Floss supervised the preparation of the cremation pits at Sobibor. In late 1942, Floss returned to Belzec to supervise burnings there as well. *SS-Unterscharführer* Fritz Tauscher also supervised the cremations at Belzec.[96] Former Trawniki guard Ivan Karakach stated: "They take the naked bodies to the pyre and place them on the rail tracks, about 1,000–1,500 bodies at a time. Then they set them on fire."[97]

There was concern among the Sobibor camp staff that their drinking water might become polluted by leachate from the bodies, and this seemed to be the motive, or one of the motives, why Sobibor changed from burial of victims to burning victims at a relatively early stage.[98] Decomposed bodies were exhumed from the pits with an excavator and burned on huge grids in a pit. Former *SS-Oberscharführer* Erich Bauer stated that the bodies were burned in pits, on grids made of railway rails.[99] A deep pit containing burning grids was mentioned by former prisoner Chaim Engel.[100] Kurt Ticho, also a former prisoner, spoke of a "crematorium shaft" or a "burning shaft" in a letter to the World Jewish Congress dated December 3, 1961. In a letter to the Dutch Red Cross, of September 3, 1946, Ticho had mentioned what he called a *Kremationgrube*: a cremation grave/pit.[101] The Polish witness, Jan Piwonski, lived in the village of Zlobek, 1.5 miles from the camp, and was told by some of the Ukrainian guards that one day as many as 5,000–6,000 bodies were exhumed at Sobibor to be burned.[102] Piwonski, who had worked at the Sobibor train station, stated that he had learned of the burning of bodies in a pit from a non-German camp guard named Waska.[103]

Few details about body burning at Sobibor are known because no prisoners from that area of the camp, Camp III, survived. Witnesses spoke of a pyre being doused with gasoline or other flammable liquid, and huge fires flaring up that could be seen quite a distance away.[104] Former *SS-Oberscharführer* Hubert Gomerski stated that there had been three huge pits, of which the third was no longer used to bury bodies because the camp's disposal method had changed to cremation.[105] Ukrainian guards in their watchtowers found it hard to breathe when the wind blew in their direction from the burning grids.[106]

At Sobibor, ashes were used as fertilizer for vegetable plots, were mixed with sand and spread out across the soil, or were removed from the camp altogether.[107] According to Kurt Ticho, ash was loaded into barrels and sent to Germany as fertilizer or mixed with coal and dirt and scattered on the camp's roads.[108] The witness Bronislaw Lobejko stated that he was told by Ukrainian guards that the human ashes were mixed with gravel from locomotives (?) and scattered on the camp's roads and paths, whereas unburned bones were crushed by Jewish prisoners with hammers and then mixed with grit.[109] According to the witness Jan Piwonski, the ashes were removed from the camp and loaded onto a train or trains.[110]

After the Sobibor Uprising, the camp's remaining prisoners were shot in Camp III, on orders from the HSSPF (senior SS and police commander) of Lublin District, Jakob Sporrenberg.[111] In another statement regarding the Jews who were killed during or after the camp uprising, Felix Gorny, a member of German Army Security Battalion 689, based in Chelm from March 1942 to July 1944, shed light on this issue. He stated that he had been told by SS men at Sobibor that all the Jews who had failed to escape had been shot and then burned with gasoline in a pyre near the ramp by the railway line. Gorny claimed to have seen the burning site himself.[112]

The work in Camp III included filling in the ash pits, leveling the ground, and planting trees for camouflage. Two hundred Jews were brought from Treblinka to obliterate all traces of Sobibor. On October 20, 1943, five freight cars left Treblinka for Sobibor.[113] On November 4, 1943, about seventy-five Jews were brought to Sobibor from Treblinka. On orders from *SS-Oberscharführer* Gustav Wagner and Karl Frenzel, the prisoners were divided into groups and assigned particular tasks. Most of the prisoners were engaged in demolishing the camp, especially Camp III.[114] In late October–early November 1943, several men of the Treblinka staff were assigned to Sobibor to help liquidate the camp: Kurt Franz, Heinrich Matthes, Gustav Munzberger, Karl Potzinger, and Franz Suchomel. Also assigned there were Karl Schluch, Ernst Zierke, and Robert Juhrs, all three of whom had formerly served at Belzec.[115]

Former *SS-Unterscharführer* Robert Juhrs stated that in early December 1943, the last prisoners were shot in Camp III or somewhere near the wooded area of the camp. Wagner and Frenzel supervised the executions. Juhrs claims the Ukrainian guards carried out the shooting, the most active being the *Volksdeutscher* Alexander Kaiser. Erich Bauer, Franz Hodl, Erwin Lambert, Heinrich Unverhau, and the *Volksdeutscher* Franz Podessa also took part. Additionally, the rest of the camp staff were present, and some of them cordoned off the execution site. The prisoners were shot in the back of their heads, and they didn't put up any resistance.[116]

About two weeks after Sobibor closed down, and up until April 1944, a group of *Baudienst* (Construction Service) laborers from Chelm lived at the site of the former death camp. On a daily basis, escorted by German and Ukrainian guards, they departed the camp to go dig defensive embankments by the Bug River. The laborers lived in barracks previously occupied by the Ukrainian guards. Many of the laborers found valuables left behind by Jews murdered in Sobibor. In March 1944, some were caught digging in the camp, and their work supervisor authorized the Ukrainian guards to shoot anyone who continued doing these digs. However, digging continued, this time by the Ukrainian guards themselves.[117] "People from the local area suspected that the Jews might have buried valuables in the ground where the camp once stood. Shortly after the Germans left, they came around to dig. The train stationmaster saw a local road builder who staked out an area of about 15 meters square and dug up several gold rings, including wedding rings, and gold coins."[118]

On September 28, 1945, the Main Commission for the Investigation of German Crimes in Poland sent a request to the prosecutor of the Lublin District Court to conduct an inquiry of Sobibor. The commission informed the prosecutor that it knew the names and locations of four witnesses who had been prisoners in the camp: Zelda Metz, Shlomo Podchlebnik, Salomea Hanel, and Hersz Cukiermann.[119] The case was handled by the prosecutor of the Lublin District Court, Kazimierz Schnierstein, and the investigating district judge, Sergiusz Urban.[120]

An official investigation of Sobibor began on October 4, 1945, conducted by Judge Urban. On October 11–12, the whole area of the camp was examined. Former prisoner Eda Lichtman took part in this site inspection. A site plan and photographic documentation were prepared. Locals in Wlodawa who might have information on the camp were interviewed. From October 13 to 18, nine witnesses, including two former prisoners, were questioned. They were residents of Wlodawa, Sobibor, and the immediate area. Between October 29 and November 7, further investigation was done in Chelm. Witnesses were questioned, including one former prisoner. A sample of ashes and bones were taken from the camp area to establish if they were human remains. In October 1946, the investigation was closed.[121]

After escaping the camp during the uprising, Alexander Pechersky joined a Soviet partisan unit. When that unit joined the Red Army in April 1944, Pechersky was arrested and assigned to a penal battalion. That was his penalty for having been taken prisoner by the Germans as a Red Army officer. He served in the battalion from June to August 1944. After telling the battalion commander, Andrejew, about Sobibor, Andrejew authorized Pechersky to go to Moscow and relate his information to the "State Special Commission for the Investigation of Nazi Crimes." Pechersky met with two members of the commission: Wieniamin Kawierin and Pawel Antokolski. They were also on the editorial board of *The Black Book*, a collection of documents regarding the extermination of the Jews on Soviet territory. Pechersky's account became known as "Pechersky's Notes."[122] Pechersky would later testify in the trial of former Trawniki guards held in Kiev, the "Schultz" trial.[123]

In July 1944, soon after the Red Army crossed into Poland, war correspondents of *Komsomolskaja Pravda* (the *Komsomol Truth*, a Soviet newspaper), including Major Rutman and Guards Lieutenant Krasilszczyk, in Chelm, came upon three Sobibor escapees—Selma Engel, Chaim Powroznik, and Dov Freiburg—and wrote down their accounts of the camp. Those accounts were published in the above newspaper on September 2, 1944, in an article titled "*Fabryka smierci w Sobiborze*" ("The Sobibor Death Factory"). It was the first published account of Sobibor, except for information on the camp uprising that was published earlier by the Polish underground press.[124]

TREBLINKA

General Pavel Batov's 65th Army, of the 1st Belorussian Front, investigated the area of Treblinka I and II.[125] However, the Red Army seemed to have no guidance from higher authority when conducting the investigation. The investigators in Treblinka included Lieutenant of Justice Jurowski, Lieutenant Rodionov, Lieutenant Kadalo, Major Konoyuk, Major Apresian, and Major Golovan.[126]

The most thorough investigation of Treblinka was conducted in November 1945 by Judge Zdzislaw Lukaszkiewicz. In a report dated December 29, 1945, he wrote the following:

> With assistance of an expert land surveyor and witnesses, I conducted an inspection of the terrain. The area of the camp is approximately 13.5 hectares and is shaped like an irregular quadrilateral. In the northwest part, the surface is covered for about 2 hectares by a mix of ashes and sand. Also, bones and tissue remain, decomposing. With assistance from an expert in forensic medicine, it was determined that the ashes are of human origin. Skulls were also examined. There is an unpleasant odor of decay.[127]

Judge Lukaszkiewicz went to the former site of the camp in late 1945 to investigate the area, with help from several camp survivors. Excavations were conducted from November 9 to 13, 1945, focusing on locating the mass graves. A search was also undertaken to locate the site of the former gas chambers. Pits 10–15 meters long and 1.5 meters deep were dug.[128] The search for the site of the gas chambers was not successful, since the witnesses who assisted had not themselves worked in that part of the camp when they had been prisoners there.[129]

The prisoner Abraham Goldfarb worked at the Treblinka gas chamber building for a few days, dragging bodies to the pits, and he described the chambers during a September 1944 statement given to Soviet military investigators.[130] A plan of the old gas chambers was drawn by a Soviet investigator, Lieutenant of Justice Yurovsky, in September 1944, on the basis of the statement from Goldfarb.[131]

As for the type of gassing engine used in the gas chambers, "It was a four-cylinder engine that used gasoline and, according to the German machine operator, was of Russian make."[132] "The gas chamber engine worked on petrol or ligroin."[133] Several other former Trawniki guards spoke of a diesel engine.[134]

The identity of the two Trawniki guards who operated the gas chamber, Ivan Marchenko and Nikolai Shalayev, was given in the testimony of numerous former guards during the Schultz trial in Kiev in 1961. Those statements were also later included in the case file of the Fedorenko trial in Simferopol, in 1986, and were used by the defense team in the Demjanjuk appeal in Israel in 1990 to save Demjanjuk from a death sentence.[135]

In Simferopol, the Fedorenko case file was kept. The Demjanjuk defense team went to see Oleg Tatunik, the judge in the Fedorenko case. He stated that in preparation for the Fedorenko trial, the court had collected all statements that former Trawniki guards from Treblinka had given to the KGB prior to their war crimes trials. In many of the statements there is mention of the two who operated the gas chambers, Marchenko and Shalayev.[136]

A description of what occurred was given:

An incinerator for burning bodies was situated 10 meters beyond the gas chamber. It had the shape of a cement pit about 1 meter deep and 20 meters long. A series of furnaces covered the top, with four rows of rails along the length of the pit. The bodies were laid on the rails, set on fire, and burned. About 1,000 bodies were burned at a time.[137] After the bodies had been burned, the prisoner "work crew" passed the ashes and remains through a sieve. Body parts that were left over were put into a special mortar and were pounded into flour. This was done to hide the traces of the crimes committed. Then the ashes were buried in deep pits.[138]

Some of the ashes were removed from the camp, according to a Soviet investigation report on Treblinka I and II dated August 24, 1944.[139]

In late 1942–early 1943, following instructions from higher up, the bodies began being burned. At first, a burning grid was made of trolley rails. However, these could not bear the weight of the mountains of bodies. Then, a bigger grid was built next to the gas chamber and was made of railway rails placed on concrete foundations. At first, there were also difficulties with this. A specialist for burnings was brought in, an NCO named Floss. After some trial and error, he got the grids working successfully. In a pit underneath the grid, a wood fire burned. The bodies were placed on the grid in layers and burned.[140]

One witness stated that there were five or six pyres, each of which could burn 2,500 bodies at a time.[141] A similar description of the cremations was given earlier by former *SS-Untersturmführer* Kurt Franz.[142] An August 24, 1944, report by the Soviet investigation commission found that there were statements from hundreds of village residents from within a 6-to-8-mile radius of the camp who saw giant columns of black smoke coming from the camp.[143]

"For many years, no preservation efforts were taken at Treblinka other than the erection of a fence around the former camp perimeter in 1947. Appeals made in subsequent years for the safeguarding of the area went unheeded. Commemoration of the victims at the three Reinhard death camps finally took place in the 1960s." Trials of many of the former camp staff members and guards in the same decade (the 1960s) may have prompted Polish authorities to finally preserve the former camp sites for fear that the neglect of those sites might become known.[144]

Historian Jozef Kermisz went to the former site of Treblinka several times after the war. He saw crowds of locals digging all over the terrain. Additionally, he witnessed Soviet soldiers using explosives to blow holes in the ground, looking for valuables. There were skulls, bones, and body parts unearthed.[145] "Clean-up and inventory at the site of the former camp began in 1958," wrote Treblinka historian Martyna Rusiniak. "During this period, it wasn't uncommon for clean-up workers and the police to also occasionally join in with the diggers."[146] A man named Dominik Kucharek was indicted for attempting to sell a diamond in Warsaw that he had found while digging at the former site of Treblinka. According to historian Martyna Rusiniak, this was the only instance of a person being legally charged for attempting to sell loot from the former camp site. Regardless, the indictment was dropped.[147] An AK unit from Vilnius moved into the area of Treblinka in February 1946. When the partisans were told of diggings taking place at the former camp site by local peasants, the unit sent patrols there over a three-night period. In the nearby town of Wolka-Okraglik, they arrested several diggers and punished them with whippings.[148]

The US Holocaust Memorial Museum (USHMM) Archive has files of the "Soviet Extraordinary State Commission" investigations of several of the Reinhard camps, and copies of Red Army investigative reports from the Russian Military Archive in Podolsk.[149]

The Central Judicial Office (*Zentrale Stelle*, or ZStL) for the Investigation of Nazi Crimes, in Ludwigsburg, was organized into a number of *Referat* (desks), each assigned to a particular region or category of crimes. The Reinhard camps fell under *Referat 8*, later *Referat 208*, which also investigated other German SS and police units that had been assigned to the Lublin District.[150] There were about 130 trials held in West Germany for crimes committed in Poland during the war, of which ten focused on the Reinhard death camps and Treblinka I. In contrast, East Germany prosecuted only eight such cases, of which one concerned Treblinka I.[151]

CHAPTER 3

POLISH INVESTIGATIONS AND LEGAL PROCEEDINGS

In 1965, the Polish Ministry of Internal Affairs informed the Citizens' Militia (Police) HQ in Lublin that the National Security Committee of the Soviet Council of Ministers had delegated to the Bureau of Investigation of the Ministry of Internal Affairs two of its officials to collect evidence concerning Nazi crimes committed in Poland. They were interested in, among other things, Belzec, Sobibor, and the SS training camp Trawniki.[1] As the investigation was underway, Polish citizens who had been in Trawniki service were scrutinized. For example, a former employee of the Provincial National Security Office in Lublin, Wladyslaw Sliwinski, was sentenced by a district court in Lublin for his Trawniki service.

In 1965, the Investigation Department completed its legal investigation and reported to the Soviet security authorities regarding crimes committed by Soviet citizens at Belzec, Sobibor, and Trawniki. Witness interrogations, site inspection reports, and other documentation was handed over to Soviet officials. Copies of interrogation records and lists of suspected war criminals were deposited in the archive of the Citizens' Militia (Police) HQ, Lublin.[2] Some of the individuals investigated for Trawniki service included:

Viktor Vorobyev, #1004: served in the SS-"Streibel" Battalion
Alexei Rozenko: served in Belzec
Profirij Szpak: served in Belzec
Semyon Dovgalyuk, #352: served in Auschwitz-Birkenau
Timofej Gura, #903: served in Belzec and Auschwitz-Birkenau
Yakov Kierezor, #1929: served in Auschwitz-Birkenau
Nikolaj Sewieryn
Alexander Bylena
Alexander Frolov
Andrej Kirilov
Vladimir Pavluchenko
Dimitri Staroshchenko
Andrej Timakov
Sergej Vinachodov
Viktor Enoch

The Bureau of Investigation of the Ministry of Internal Affairs conducted an investigation commissioned by the Prosecutor's Office. Dozens of witnesses were questioned, evidence was collected, and preliminary archival research was carried out.[3] Most likely, proceedings were ended in 1968.

Polish authorities had conducted a secret investigation of Polish citizens who had been in Trawniki service. The investigation was given the code name "*Raki*" (Crawfish).[4] The Citizens' Militia (Police) HQ, Lublin, checked Trawniki guard lists for men with Polish names. Some of the initial names they came across were Lucjan Flisinski, Bronislaw Zajac, Jan Szpringer, and Dymitri Bartnik, from Okuninka, Wlodawa District (near Sobibor); Jan Martyniuk, from Korolowka, Wlodawa District; Alexander Nawoznik, from Korolowka, Wlodawa District; and Jan Pawluczuk, from Korolowka, Wlodawa District.[5]

An investigation was also conducted in Chelm District. In the village of Okopy in the Dorohusk commune, information was collected on Ignacy Gardzinski, suspected of having been in Trawniki service. He is believed to have served at Treblinka II. Wladyslaw Lichotop, an employee of the Chelm Cement Plant who lived in Wolka Okopska, knew Gardzinski. They both had gone to school together in Okopy. Lichotop had also been in Trawniki service and had served with another man, Czeslaw Krzykocki, from Dobrylow, Chelm District. After liberation of the Lublin area, Krzykocki was arrested by a member of the Citizens' Militia (Police) at the railway station in Chelm. He was tried and sentenced for his Trawniki service. After being released, he moved to western Poland. Gardzinski, on the other hand, had avoided arrest because he had fled westward together with the retreating German forces.

Investigators also established that Franciszek Hajczuk, from Okopy, had been in Trawniki service with Gardzinski. He, like Gardzinski, was suspected of having served at Treblinka II. After liberation of the Lublin area, Hajczuk fled to western Poland and probably settled somewhere in Szczecin Province. Investigation showed that Wlodzimierz Zinkiewicz, from Beredryszcze in Dorohusk commune, had been in Trawniki service. After liberation of the area, he was arrested and sentenced. Upon release, he returned to his home in Beredryszcze.[6]

In 1949, lists of former Trawniki guards born between 1923 and 1925, with identification #s in the 3800–4100 range, were investigated by the *UB* (Polish Security Service). They were from the following localities: Lublin area, Chelm, Wlodawa, Stulno, Sobibor, Adampol, Kosow, Zamosc, Hrubieszow, and Drogobych. A few examples included Michael Kalisz, #3897, from Zbereze, Sobibor area; Stefan Tesulko, #3928, from Stulno; Pavel Alebik, #3974, from Sobibor; and Ignacy Woloszyn, from Chelm.

From 1965 to 1968, the criminal activities of the former Trawniki guards who served at Belzec were investigated by Polish authorities. A list of some of their names was compiled by the "Main Commission for the Investigation of Nazi Crimes in Poland" and given to the Majdanek State Museum and the Lublin Militia (Police). In 1965 and 1966, the *SB* (Polish Security Service) in Lublin questioned several local civilians in the Belzec area regarding their recollections of the Trawniki guards who served at the camp, and the crimes that they had committed there. The main interrogator appears to have been Captain Eugeniusz Katiuszyn.[7]

In 1967–1968, at the request of the Soviet KGB, the Polish secret police (SB) began an investigation of the Trawniki guards who had been assigned to Belzec during the war. Documentation of this investigation wasn't declassified until thirty years later.[8] By the time the KGB had made this request, Soviet authorities had already tried and convicted a number of former Trawniki guards who had served at Belzec, including two groups of men tried in the 1960s, in the Matwijenko trial in Krasnodar in 1964, and in the Zuev trial in Dnepropetrovsk in 1965. Also, by the time this request was made, Polish authorities had already had an investigation underway into former Trawniki guards who served at Belzec. It was titled (translated into English) *FILE INVESTIGATION, Case: Criminal Activities of the Wachmänner at Belzec*, AIPN Lu-08/298, 1965–1968. The file includes documents from the Majdanek State Museum, documents from the Main Commission of the Investigation of Nazi Crimes in Poland, copies of other documents regarding Belzec, protocols of interrogations of witnesses, and photos from Belzec. In 1965, a list of Ukrainian guards who had served at Belzec, compiled by the Main Commission, was given to the Majdanek State Museum and the Lublin MO (militia/police) office. In charge of this investigation was Captain Jozef Floroczak, from the Department of Investigations of the Lublin SB (Office of Public Security).[9]

Interrogations were conducted by the following officials, in the following locations, in connection with this investigation: Captain Jan Solis in Belzec in 1965; Captain Eugeniusz Katiuszyn in Belzec in 1966; and Sergeant Franciszek Skawinski in Belzec, Tomaszow-Lubelski, and Lublin in 1966. These investigators were either from the SB or MO office in

Lublin. They interviewed the following persons who were local residents of the Belzec area and had in one way or another come into contact with the camp or the Trawniki guards who had served there: Krystyna Natyna, Edward Luczynski, Michael Kusmierczak, Maria Warzocha (formerly married to the Trawniki guard Edward Wlasiuk), Josef Lewko, Mieczyslaw Kudyba, Jozefa Stefaniec, Jan Glab, Andrzej Panasowiec, Eugeniusz Goch, Kazimierz Czerniak, and Maria Misiewicz.[10]

The local witnesses were asked to look at photo spreads of some of the former Trawniki guards to see if they could recognize any of them. Some did and some did not recognize them. The photos reportedly showed the men in civilian clothing and at their current ages (as of the years 1965–1966), whereas these witnesses had known them in uniform and when they were over twenty years younger (in 1942–1943). Witnesses who did make positive identifications had reportedly recognized a number of those who were currently defendants or witnesses in current (1964–1966) trials in the Soviet Union, including[11]

(1) Ivan Zuev (defendant in Zuev trial, Dnepropetrovsk, 1965)
(2) Nikita Mamchur (defendant in Zuev trial, Dnepropetrovsk, 1965)
(3) Alexei Lazarenko (defendant in Zuev trial, Dnepropetrovsk, 1965; mentioned by six witnesses)
(4) Ivan Woloszyn/Voloshin (witness in Zuev trial, Dnepropetrovsk, 1965; mentioned by nine witnesses, most of whom correctly recalled that he had been the ringleader of a mass desertion of guards from the camp in March 1943)
(5) Samuel Trautwein, a *Volksdeutscher* whose fate after the war is unknown (mentioned by four witnesses)
(6) Alexej Pietka, fate unknown (mentioned by three witnesses)
(7) Saszka or Szaszka Komar, fate unknown (mentioned by five witnesses)
(8) A man known only as Grisza (possibly a nickname), whom the witness Maria Warzocha stated had been responsible for running the gassing engine in the camp, along with the guard Stefan (Jadziol). She had reportedly been told this by her husband at the time, Edward Wlasiuk, who also ran the gassing engine.

Several of the witnesses referred to the Trawniki guards from Belzec as "*Vlasovites*" (a term referring to members of a German collaborator force consisting of Russians and known as the "Vlasov army," led by the former Red Army general Andrei Vlasov).[12]

A recurring theme in the testimony of witnesses in the Belzec investigation was that the Trawniki guards had spent a significant amount of their off-duty time buying vodka in Belzec village.

For the investigation, the following additional documents were included in the file:[13]

(1) a list of Trawniki *Wachmänner*, born 1923–1925, with Trawniki ID #s in the 3800–4100 range, from the following localities: Lublin area, Chelm, Wlodawa area, Sobibor area, Zamosc, Adampol, Kosow, Hrubieszow, Sniatyn, and Drogobycz
(2) Personnel rosters with the names of hundreds of Trawniki *Wachmänner* in the 3000–4000 ID # range. The largest proportion of these men appear to have been recruited from the Chelm area and Hrubieszow. They were assigned to places such as Sobibor, the Rejowiec Detachment, the Krasnystaw Detachment, the Zamosc Detachment, and the Gendarmerie Post in Lublin.
(3) several protocols of interrogation or court appearances of former Trawniki guards recorded in the files of the Procurator's Office in Lublin, 1968

(4) A list of names of men who had served as Trawniki guards and who were from the Chelm area. They were sought for investigation. Some of them were known to have served in the Red Army after their Trawniki service, and some of them also moved to the Soviet Union after the war. (Many, possibly hundreds of Trawniki guards were from the Chelm area and had been assigned Trawniki ID #s in the 4000 range.) This list had originally been filed with the UB Office in Chelm in 1949.

(5) A list of names of men who had served as Trawniki guards and were sought for investigation. The list had originally been filed with the UB Office in Wlodawa in 1949.

EUGENIUSZ MAYTCHENKO[14]

Eugeniusz Maytchenko lived in Chelm. His mother and sisters identified themselves as Ukrainian, but his father considered himself Polish. Maytchenko himself claimed that he identified himself as Polish, and that this was the nationality listed on his Trawniki identification (*Dienstausweis*). He listed his occupation as student at a technical school.

In 1943, he was recruited for Trawniki service and claims that he deserted in July 1944 and then joined the AK. At some point thereafter, he was apparently arrested by the UB (Polish Security Service). Released several weeks later, he then enlisted in the Polish army. Promoted to sergeant, he served at the front and was decorated for bravery. After the war, he served as a political officer. He was arrested in 1947 and imprisoned for almost a year. He then lived in Krasnik. Rearrested in 1952, along with other former Trawniki guards living in Poland, he was put on trial. He claimed that he had volunteered for Trawniki service because he had been instructed to do so by the AK in order to gather intelligence on the Trawniki camp.

Another former Trawniki guard testified that Maytchenko had denounced a fellow guard who had deserted while he was on home leave in Chelm. Maytchenko reported him to the German gendarmerie. The same former comrade also stated that Maytchenko had given his family goods stolen from Jews at Trawniki.

Maytchenko admitted to being present at Trawniki when the "*Erntefest*" massacre occurred, but said that he had not participated in it. The judge sentenced Maytchenko to ten years' imprisonment.

In 1967, when the "Polish Main Commission for the Investigation of Nazi Crimes" opened an investigation on the Trawniki camp, Maytchenko was interrogated as a witness (see Archive of the Majdanek State Museum; Commission for the Investigation of Nazi Crimes in Lublin District; Main Commission for the Investigation of Nazi Crimes in Poland, Investigation of the Trawniki Camp, 1966–1967).

CHAPTER 4

INTERROGATIONS OF FORMER TRAWNIKI PERSONNEL

Protocol of Interrogation of Pavel Kozlov, August 1944[1]
On August 24, 1944, I, deputy chief of Section 4 of SMERSH Counterintelligence of the
65th Army, Guards Captain Postovalov, interrogated the arrestee Pavel Mikhailovich Kozlov.

Q: How long did you work in the German camp of Treblinka, and what were your duties?
A: After being captured by the enemy on May 25, 1942, and after spending two and a half
months in several POW camps, I was assigned to a guard school located in Trawniki (Poland).
After undergoing training there for four months, I along with 100 other trainees was sent
to the Lipowa camp in Lublin as a camp guard. In January 1943, I returned to Trawniki. In
April 1943, with fifty-five other men, I was assigned to serve at the Treblinka labor camp
in Warsaw region. I was a guard there until July 25, 1944.
Q: Describe the criminal acts committed by the Germans against prisoners at the camp.
A: I was an eyewitness and participant in the criminal acts instigated by the Germans
imprisoned in the camp. All of the criminal acts were committed under the supervision of
the camp commandant, SS-Hauptsturmführer von Eupen; his assistant, SS-Untersturmführer
Prefe; SS-Unterscharführer Schwarz; and SS-Unterscharführer Stumpe.

In April 1943, when I arrived, the camp held approximately 750 Jewish and Polish
prisoners. The prisoners were used to repair the railroad line, in various agricultural projects,
and in other kinds of work in the camp. During the first six months of 1943, approximately
300 people died in the camp, mainly Jews, from exhaustion from heavy labor, shortage of
food, and also various diseases. No medical assistance was offered.

Jews who became incapable of work because of exhaustion were taken away from the
camp and shot on the order of the camp commandant, SS-Hauptsturmführer von Eupen.
The bodies were dumped into pits in the forest, 500 meters from the camp, toward the
village of Malshevo.

In addition to the people who were shot and died from hunger and diseases, which
included 750 people, in late 1943 approximately 250–300 Jewish prisoners, who were
exhausted and no longer fit for work, were sent to a camp located about half a mile from
our camp, on the order of von Eupen, and they were killed there. I myself was never in this
camp, even in cases where the guard detail escorted prisoners to the camp. We heard reports
that the prisoners in that camp were killed by being gassed, and that people were herded
into a building resembling a bathhouse.

During my time as a guard at the camp, according to my not very accurate count, about
1,200 people died from exhausting work, hunger, and disease, and by being shot. In spring
1944, a typhus epidemic broke out in the camp, and within two months, up to 150 Polish
prisoners died in the camp.

In summer 1943, I was at my guard post in a tower. This was about 3 p.m., and I fell
asleep at my post. Taking advantage of this, about twenty-two prisoners made a hole in the
barbed wire and escaped the camp one by one. The escape was noticed by Oberwachmann
Ljajtsh, and he sounded the alarm. When I awoke, Germans from the camp pursued the
escapees on horseback. Wachmann Reznichenko and I opened fire on the escapees with
our rifles and killed one Jew.

In November 1943, one morning, SS-Unterscharführer Stumpe ordered me and Wachmann
Gubar to bring out and bury the bodies of nine men who had died the previous night. Two Jews
who were physically exhausted were placed on a cart. We were given orders to shoot them. We

went to the forest to a previously prepared pit and then threw the bodies into the pit, and those two Jews were made to stand up near the pit. I shot one, and Wachmann Gubar shot the other. On July 24, 1944, on the order of the camp commandant, von Eupen, an operation was conducted to kill the 570 remaining Jewish prisoners in the camp. The executions were carried out south of the camp in Malashevsky forest. This was done from 6 to 10 p.m. The prisoners were brought to the forest in groups of ten to fifteen. I was part of the cordon, and I accompanied the next-to-last group of approximately twenty people to the forest. Here, all of the prisoners were placed with their faces to the ground, and the Germans shot all of them with their pistols. The following persons carried out the executions on that day: SS-Unterscharführer Schwarz and SS-Unterscharführer Rege. I don't know exactly, but I heard that the Polish prisoners were released from the camp. I don't know the reason behind the large-scale operation to kill the prisoners.

The protocol was written down from my words correctly and read to me. [Signature] Kozlov
Interrogated by deputy chief, 4th Section, SMERSH, Counterintelligence Department, 65th Army, Guards Captain Postovalov
True Copy: Operations Deputy, 2nd Section, 4th Directorate, MGB, Shepobolik

September 26, 1947
Reference: Original copy of the Kozlov interrogation protocol is located in archival investigation file #0408181
True copy from a copy: Senior investigator, MGB, Counterintelligence Section, 14th Air Army, Guards Captain Isayev
I attest to the authenticity and accuracy of the copy of the interrogation protocol of Pavel Kozlov, and that the original is located in the archive of criminal case #11991, against Alexander Moskalenko, pp. 107–108, of the folder.
Security Service of the Ukraine
Directorate of the Lvov region
Certified
Chief of the Archive, Dobrytsnev
October 27, 1995
Chief, State Archive of the Security Service of the Ukraine. [Signature] A. Pshennikov

Protocol of Interrogation of Nikolaj Olejnikov[2]
January 10, 1947

Q: Under what circumstances did you enlist to serve in the SS guard forces?
A: After being captured, I was sent by the Germans with a large group of POWs to the Chelm POW camp. In June 1942, German SS officers arrived at the camp. They selected POWs for service in the SS. Healthier men were chosen. I was among them. About 250 were selected. We were brought to the camp headquarters. There was a storehouse there, and we were issued green tunics and pants. We were taken in vehicles to the town of Trawniki. We were issued military uniforms and equipment.

SS-Hauptsturmführer Streibel appeared before us and, through an interpreter, told us that we had been enlisted in the SS guard forces and we would undergo military training. We were to serve as guards around the Trawniki SS camp and at other German military facilities. We were assigned to companies. My company commander was SS-Oberscharführer Mayevskij. We began training, and we were given black shoulder boards for our SS uniforms.

Q: How was your enlistment to serve in the SS guard force formalized?

A: In July 1942, I swore an oath to serve the German-Fascist government faithfully.

Q: You are being shown a copy of a signature on a form bearing information and your photograph. Is this your signature?

A: Yes, the signed document bearing a photograph of me with #2263 was issued to me by the Germans when I swore the oath in July 1942.

Q: How long did you serve in the SS guard force, and what did you do in that service?

A: I served from July 1942 until May 1945. I served at Trawniki transit camp, where Jews were held before being sent on by train to Lublin and Krakow. The number of Jews held in Trawniki fluctuated between 700 and 3,000.

Q: What crimes were inflicted on the Jews by members of the SS guard force?

A: I know that there were separate detachments from Trawniki SS training camp operating in Trieste, Treblinka, Krakow, Lublin, Austria, and other places. There, roundups were carried out to force Jews into ghettos. They were guarded there and were later sent away to be exterminated.

Q: Describe the circumstances in which you participated in crimes against Jews.

A: Besides guarding the Jews in the camp, on three occasions I also directly took part in shooting Jews. In September 1942, one morning SS-Hauptscharführer Bartechko brought three male Jews into the guard facility and ordered the German on duty to have them shot. I do not know why. The duty man ordered me and two other *Wachmänner* to shoot them. We did. We escorted them about 200 meters out of the camp, dug pits, and shot them in the back of their heads.

On another occasion about a month later, again while I was on guard duty, Bartechko brought five Jews to the guard facility. The German duty officer woke me, the Pole Bronislaw Zhimanskij, and another Pole and ordered us take the Jews out of the camp and shoot them. We carried this out in the same manner as the previous shootings a month earlier.

I was also frequently sent to round up Poles. On one occasion, around November 1943 in Kielce, the Poles raided German storehouses containing uniforms and equipment. We were sent along with sixty to seventy other *Wachmänner*, under the supervision of SS officer Shrumpf, to Kielce, where we carried out a sweep of the houses near the storehouse. We detained several Poles who were caught with uniforms and equipment in their homes. We confiscated these items, then returned to Trawniki. In April 1944, some Poles blew up the Krasnik railroad station, about 50 miles southwest of Lublin. We surrounded the station and swept through the nearby homes. We did not find any suspects, so we returned to Trawniki. Besides this, in summer 1943 I participated in a search for Jews who had escaped from the camp. This operation yielded no results.

In mid-June 1944, along with Wachmänner Fedor Perig and Fedor Fedechko, I was sent, under the supervision of SS-Unterscharführer Shubert, to the town of Milets to pick up ammunition for the guard detachment. We were supposed to pick up a truckful of it. Due to Soviet forces breaking through the German defenses, however, all transportation heading east was halted. We returned to the detachment, where we learned that all the Jews who had been held in Trawniki had been shot, and that the detachment was preparing for a rapid evacuation.

The same day we departed Trawniki, as members of the guard detachment, after being loaded onto trains in the direction of Lublin. Along the way, at Swidnik station, our train was bombed by Soviet aircraft, and we were forced to head on foot for Krasnik station. There, we were again loaded onto a train and we traveled through Krakow, Czestochowa, and Breslau, and we arrived in Regensburg in July 1944. There, I was left to guard military factories. We were quartered in barracks next to an armaments factory. There were sixty of us under the command of Shrumpf. I served in this detachment as a *Gruppenwachmann* and assigned guards to their posts.

I guarded this factory until January 1945. Then, we were attacked by British or American aircraft, which began bombing military factories. I was wounded by shrapnel in my shoulder blade. I was sent to Regensburg and put in a German military hospital. I was captured by American forces.

Q: What was the last rank you held in the SS guard force?

A: *SS-Gruppenwachmann*

Q: For what reason were you promoted by the Germans to the rank of *SS-Gruppenwachmann*?

A: I was promoted for having a good attitude about service in the guard force. I also followed all the orders of the Germans, and I earned their trust.

Q: Name the traitors to the Motherland you know who served with you in the SS.

A: 1) Vasili Salnikov. From Tula. *Gruppenwachmann*.

2) Alexander Vlasov. From Moscow. *Gruppenwachmann*. Served in Trieste.

3) Nikolai Vozhkin. From Moscow. Served in Krakow.

4) Alexander Nosov. Russian. *Zugwachmann*.

5) Vasili Madamov. *Oberwachmann*. Served in Krakow.

6) Vasilij Gusev. From Saratov. Served in Krakow.

7) Grigorij Stoilov. Escaped from Trawniki, June 1943.

8) Nikolaj Timin. Escaped, summer 1943.

9) Nikita Bondar. From Kiev. *Gruppenwachmann*.

Q: It is known that at Trawniki SS training camp there was a school for *Oberwachmänner*. Did you undergo training there?

A: Yes. I underwent training there.

Q: Describe the circumstances under which you enlisted in the school for *Oberwachmänner*.

A: In August 1942, I was summoned by company commander Mayevskij. He offered me enrollment in training to become a *Gruppenwachmann*. I agreed to do so. The school was in Trawniki. Training lasted about four months.

Q: Who was trained at this school?

A: Squad commanders for the SS forces.

Q: What did you do at this school?

A: We studied the German language, weapons: rifles and machine guns, military drill, political training, and guard duty regulations.

Q: When did you complete the school?

A: December 1942. I was promoted to *Oberwachmann*. Six months later I was promoted to *Gruppenwachmann* and served as a squad commander.

Q: Who was in charge of the school for *Gruppenwachmänner*?

A: SS-Oberscharführer Rolixmann.

Q: How many men underwent training at this school?

A: During my time, 120. During my service in the SS forces, starting in 1942, the school graduated three groups of trainees. The last two groups were selected by the Germans exclusively from among western Polish Ukrainians, so-called Galicians.

Q: Name the trainees who trained with you at the school for *Gruppenwachmänner*.

A: Arkhipenko, Stepanov, Stoilov, Ovchinnikov, Vlasov, Balchys, and Zajankauskas. Those are the names I remember.

Q: Why had you concealed your training at the school for *Gruppenwachmänner* from this investigation until now?

A: I had forgotten about this.

The interrogation was recorded from my words correctly and read to me. [Signature] Olejnikov
Interrogated by chief of 2nd Section, Investigations Department, MGB, Major M. Stoyakin

Excerpt of Protocol of Interrogation, Vasili Smetanyuk[3]
July 11, 1947
City of Stanislavov (Ivano-Frankivsk)
I, chief of 2nd Section, 4th Department, of the MGB in Stanislavov region, Guards Major Stromyatnikov, interrogated the following detainee: Vasilij Smetanyuk, born 1921 in Stanislavov region, Ukraine. No party affiliation. Did not serve in the Red Army.

I have been warned in accordance with Article 89 of the Criminal Code of the Ukrainian Soviet Socialist Republic.

Q: Tell me a little about yourself?
A: My father was a poor peasant. He died in 1933. I worked on my family farm until 1939. In 1939, I attended the Kolomya Pedagogical School. I finished courses in 1941. I, however, did not become a teacher. Instead, I worked as an apprentice at the office of forest administration.
Q: What did you do during the German occupation?
A: In February 1943, I volunteered for German service and was enrolled in the SS police training camp in the town of Trawniki. I was deemed fit for service by a medical commission, and I boarded a train in Kolomya bound for Trawniki. Training there included drill, field tactics, physical exercise, weapons, search and arrest, guard duty regulations, and antipartisan combat. I was assigned personal ID #3617 and was promoted to *Oberwachmann* after additional training.
Q: Did you receive leave time while service at the SS camp in Trawniki?
A: Yes. I used it to go home to my village in Stanislavov region. I soon learned that partisan detachments of the "Kovpak" Brigade were passing through my home area. I feared being detained by the partisans, so I left my village for the city of Kolomya and spent my leave there instead.
Q: How long did you serve at the SS camp in Trawniki?
A: For six months. Then, in August 1943, I was sent to Italy with eight to ten others from Trawniki. My detachment was escorted there by SS-Obersturmführer Schwarzenbacher. We were issued new uniforms and were also accompanied there by SS-Sturmbannführer Lerch.

We left for the city of Trieste. In Trieste, Lerch organized an SS Police headquarters in the Adriatic Coast Operational Zone. We were tasked with guarding the headquarters. This headquarters was subordinate to SS-General Globocnik. Also present was SS-Hauptsturmführer Michalsen.
Q: What was the objective of Lerch's headquarters?
A: To fight the partisans in Yugoslavia and Italy on the Adriatic coast, in Trieste. In addition to us *Wachmänner* (guards), Schwarzenbacher also trained detachments of Slovenian and Italian youths. Operationally, a Cossack Corps was also subordinate to Lerch's headquarters. They also fought the Yugoslav partisans.
Q: How do you know that Cossack units were subordinate to Lerch's headquarters?
A: On two occasions, I saw senior Cossack commanders visit the headquarters. I also handled documents at headquarters, and correspondence.

Recorded from my words accurately which I affirm with my signature. Smetanyuk.

Protocol of Interrogation, Josef Masyuk[4]
August 20, 1947
City of Stanislavov (Ivano-Frankivsk)
I, chief of the 4th Department of the MGB, Stanislavov region, Guard Major Stromyatnikov, interrogated the following detainee: Josef Masyuk, born 1923 in Stanislavov region, Ukraine. He has no party affiliation and no prior convictions.

I have been warned of my liabilities for giving false statements in accordance with Article 89 of the Criminal Code of the Ukrainian Soviet Socialist Republic.

Q: Briefly describe your background.
A: My father died when I was very young. I worked on a farm. I also worked as a tailor. Starting in 1937, I worked as both a tailor and a farmer at the same time. In February 1943, I enlisted to serve at the SS police training camp in the town of Trawniki.
Q: Clarify how you enlisted for service at the training camp.
A: In February 1943, I was called before a medical commission in the city of Kolomiya. I was determined to be suitable for military service with the Germans. A week later, I went to an assembly point in Kolomiya with 100–150 other recruits. A German officer loaded us onto a train. We arrived at the SS police training camp in Trawniki.

I was issued an SS uniform and was photographed. I signed a commitment attesting to voluntary service in the SS police. I swore an oath to serve the German government faithfully. I signed a commitment not to reveal secrets. Each of us was assigned a personal number. Mine was #3183. Each of us was armed with a rifle. I trained at Trawniki camp for two months. Training included drill, weapons, and guard duty. Then I was sent with others to the city of Warsaw. I was there for two months, then sent back to Trawniki. I was then sent to Austria and served there until April 13, 1945.
Q: What did you do in Warsaw?
A: I participated with other *SS Wachmänner*, under the command of a Gestapo member, SS-Obersturmführer Franz, in the liquidation of the Jewish ghetto.
Q: Who did the Germans choose for service in the SS police at Trawniki?
A: They accepted only volunteers. Basically, Russian traitors to the Motherland who had chosen to go over to the German side. Others were taken from the western regions of Ukraine.
Q: Did you participate in the extermination of prisoners?
A: I did not directly participate in this activity.
Q: Describe how the liquidation of the Jewish ghetto in Warsaw was carried out.
A: In May 1943, the command at Trawniki camp sent a group of about 300 *SS Wachmänner*, under the command of Gestapo officer Franz, to participate in the liquidation of the ghetto. We provided reinforced guard around prisoners held in a building. These prisoners were escorted to a site where they were loaded onto trains. They were then sent to death camps for extermination. About 25,000 people were escorted out of the ghetto in this manner. *SS Wachmänner* also escorted the trains that took the people to these camps. In this way, prisoners were sent to Poniatowa, Trawniki, Auschwitz, and so on. Later on, I deployed with other *SS Wachmänner* to Gusen, Austria. It was about 12 miles from the city of Linz.
Q: What were your duties there?
A: A detachment of eighty to ninety of us guarded prisoners in the Gusen camp. About 8,000–9,000 POWs from the Red Army and Allied forces were held there. The Germans had intended to exterminate these prisoners, but the advance of Soviet forces prevented this. On April 13, 1945, the Germans disarmed all of us in Gusen. We were taken to a camp in Steyr, where I remained until the arrival of American forces.

I was handed over to Red Army authorities on May 17, 1945. I underwent screening with the 210th Army Reserve Regiment and enlisted in an Air Defense Artillery Battery. I served in this unit until I was demobilized from the Red Army.

Q: During your screening, did you explain why you were in German territory?

A: No, I feared being held responsible for the crimes I committed before the Motherland, so I told the counterintelligence organs that the Germans had sent me to a concentration camp. They believed me. I never disclosed my German service to anyone.

This statement was recorded from my words accurately and read aloud to me. I affirm this with my signature. [Signature] Masyuk

Interrogated by chief of 4th Department, MGB, Stanislavov region, Guards Major Stromyatnikov

Excerpt of Protocol of Interrogation, Dimitrij Korzhinskij[5]

August 1947

City of Stanislavov (Ivano-Frankivsk)

I, chief of 2nd Section, 4th Department, of the MGB in Stanislavov region, Guards Major Stromyatnikov, interrogated the following detainee: Dimitrij Korzhinskij, born 1922 in Stanislavov region, Ukraine. No party affiliation. Did not serve in the Red Army. I was sent to the SS police training camp in Trawniki.

Q: Describe what happened at the Trawniki camp, and who was sent there?

A: The *SS Wachmänner* (guards) at the camp consisted of traitors to the Motherland who had gone over to the German side. The prisoners who were brought to Trawniki were all eventually exterminated. The bodies were placed in large pits and then burned.

Q: Did the *Wachmänner* participate in shooting the prisoners?

A: I was on leave when the mass shootings occurred. From the statements of other *Wachmänner*, no, they did not. They only stood guard. The Germans did the shooting.

Q: Where were the *SS Wachmänner* trained at Trawniki assigned, and for what purpose?

A: In May 1943, a 300-man detachment was sent to Warsaw to liquidate the Jewish ghetto. SS officer Franz was in charge of this detachment. In August 1943, a 400-man detachment was sent to Italy to engage Italian and Yugoslav partisans. SS officer Lerch was in charge of this detachment. Also, small units of *Wachmänner* periodically deployed against Polish partisans, and to gather supplies from the Polish population to supply the needs of the German army.

Q: Did you participate in all of the operations that you just described?

A: Yes. In May 1943, I deployed to Warsaw and participated in liquidating the Jewish ghetto.

Q: Describe this operation in detail.

A: We guarded captured Jews held in the ghetto. The Germans liquidated the ghetto. About 2,500 Jews were shot on the spot. The remaining 2,300 Jews were transported to Trawniki, Poniatowa, and Treblinka.

Q: Did you participate in shooting Jews in the ghetto?

A: I did not. Members of the Gestapo and SD did the shooting. We *Wachmänner* either stood at guard posts or in cordons. We also escorted the trains that carried the prisoners away to the camps. In July 1943, I escorted a train to Treblinka. The train carried about 1,500 people.

Q: Where were you sent after the liquidation of the Warsaw ghetto?

A: To the Poniatowa camp.

Q: What happened at this camp?

A: In November 1943, all of the prisoners in the camp were exterminated.

Q: Did you participate in the shootings?
A: No. The Germans did the shooting. We *Wachmänner* only stood at our guard posts.

The statement has been recorded from my words accurately. It has been read to me. My signature affirms its accuracy. [Signature] Korzhinskij
Interrogated by chief of 2nd Section, 4th Department, MGB, Stanislavov region, Guards Major Stromyatnikov

Note: Korzhinskij was convicted by a military tribunal of the MVD forces of Stanislavov region on November 3, 1947. As of November 10, 1947, he was held in the jail of the MVD in Stanislavov region.
True copy: deputy case officer, 4th Department, 4th Directorate, MGB, Major Shelobolin

**Protocol of Interrogation
of the Arrestee Vladimir Emelyanov**[6]
September 23, 1947
V. Emelyanov. Born 1919 in Lukhovitsi District, Moscow region, Russia. He had six years of education. He is a barber by occupation. He resides in the city of Moscow.

Q: Where were you during the Patriotic War?
A: From 1939 to May 1942, I served in the Red Army as a squad commander in the 10th Replacement Company, 302nd Replacement Division. I was captured by the Germans on May 15, 1942, at the front in Crimea. I was later held in a POW camp in Rovno.
Q: How long were you held in the Rovno POW camp?
A: For about two weeks. In June 1942, I was transferred to Trawniki camp.
Q: What caused this to occur?
A: I was transferred along with 250 other men from the Rovno camp to Trawniki by the Germans. I do not know what caused this to occur.
Q: An original German document indicates that you were transferred to the Trawniki camp in order to serve in the SS forces. Do you intend to admit to this?
A: Yes.
Q: State when you began to serve the Germans.
A: In June 1942.
Q: Did you swear an oath to serve the Germans faithfully?
A: Yes, I provided the Germans with my signature on a commitment form stating that my service in the SS forces was voluntary.
Q: In which SS unit did you serve?
A: The SS training detachment in the Trawniki camp. I was trained there for about one month until July 20, 1942.
Q: Describe the SS detachment.
A: It was a training detachment. Trawniki camp was a school in which the Germans trained cadres for service in SS military units, punitive detachments, and camps for mass extermination. The detachment consisted of physically healthy former servicemen of the Red Army, POWs who had crossed over to the German side and declared their desire to serve for the Germans in the police forces and special punitive detachments. The squad and platoon commanders were persons of German nationality who had lived in the USSR. The SS training detachment was structured like a military unit. It consisted of five or six companies and a headquarters. The commander of the unit was a German SS officer with the rank of *SS-Sturmbannführer*

(major). I do not remember his name. When we joined this detachment, we all became *SS Wachmänner* (guards). Our squad commanders attained the rank of *SS Gruppenwachmann* (guard sergeant). At my time in Trawniki, about 700 men were being trained at the camp.

Q: What were you taught in the SS detachment at Trawniki camp?

A: We were taught how to carry out roundups of the population, how to undertake arrests and searches, and the rules for escorting and guarding prisoners. We also trained in drill, weapons practice, physical training, and German regulations for guard duty.

Q: Were you taught how to shoot people in the SS detachment at Trawniki?

A: I know nothing about this.

Q: You are being read an excerpt from the statement of the arrestee Ivan Voloshin dated March 13, 1947 (the statement was read). Do you confirm Voloshin's statement.

A: I have known Ivan Voloshin since July 1942, from our mutual service in the SS detachment that was assigned to Belzec camp. I confirm his statement regarding the shootings of people carried out by the SS training detachment of Trawniki camp. I know that on German orders, the men trained in Trawniki, in the course of their preparation and training, shot and escorted Jews to be shot.

Q: Where did you serve after training at the Trawniki SS training camp?

A: On July 20, 1942, I was sent to serve at a camp in the town of Belzec. It was located about 12 miles from the town of Rava-Russkaya. I served there until March 4, 1943.

Q: What functions were carried out by the SS detachment at Belzec camp?

A: It carried out the mass extermination of Jews by asphyxiating them in special gas chambers. By my estimate, from July 1942 until February 1943, a minimum of 50,000 people were exterminated in Belzec. During the period from July to October 1942, railroad trains arrived in the camp almost every day carrying Jews from the western parts of the Soviet Union and Poland.

Q: Describe in detail how the Belzec camp was equipped to carry out mass extermination.

A: The camp was located in the woods about 700 meters from the Belzec railroad station. A railroad spur extended from this station into the camp. The people were brought to the camp in trains along this track. The people were unloaded within the camp. The camp was surrounded by many rows of barbed wire that stood 2 meters high. The outer part of the camp was camouflaged by a thick belt of small pine trees. There were wooden barracks for us, a kitchen, a dining hall, and a medical station. Another part of the camp contained barracks for haircutting and storing the valuables of the victims. There were six gas chambers inside a brick building. Each had a capacity to hold about 300 people. People were asphyxiated in these chambers. As many as 500 Jewish prisoners were assigned to work in the camp. They pulled the bodies out of the gas chambers and buried or burned them. They also sorted the confiscated possessions. We later exterminated them as well.

Q: Who primarily was exterminated in the Belzec camp?

A: Only Jews. This included men, women, and children of various ages. They were brought to the camp from the western regions of the Soviet Union and Poland. I personally participated in suffocating people in the gas chambers.

Q: What was done with the bodies of the people suffocated in the gas chambers?

A: The bodies were thrown out of the chambers and carried to pits in the camp. At the end of 1942, the bodies were burned in specially dug trenches within the camp. Before being buried or burned, gold teeth were removed from the mouths of the victims.

Q: What type of gas was used in the chambers?

A: I do not know. A powerful engine operated during the asphyxiation process. It stood in a shed at the back wall of the gassing facility. Two *SS Wachmänner* worked with this engine, but I do not remember their names.

Q: Who was the commander of the Belzec camp?

A: A German officer. He was about fifty years old. I do not remember his name. His deputy was a German lieutenant named Schwarz. He was about thirty-five years old. Schwarz directly supervised the activities of the SS detachment in the camp. He personally gave the orders to carry out the exterminations in the gas chambers.

Q: Name the persons you remember as having served with in the SS detachment at Belzec camp.

A: Magilov: of Russian nationality. Born in Chernigov region.

Dimitrij Timoshkin: of Russian nationality. Told me that he lived in Siberia in the Buryat-Mongol region, about 25 miles from the Soviet-Mongol border. After Belzec, he also served with me at a camp in Krakau. I escaped from this camp in September 1943, so I don't know about his subsequent fate.

Naumenko: I was sent back to Trawniki from Belzec on March 4, 1943; however, he remained on duty at Belzec.

I have read the interrogation protocol. My statements have been recorded correctly from my words. [Signature] Emelyanov

Interrogated by investigator, 2nd Section, 4th Department, MGB, Senior Lieutenant Zaschlev

True copy:

Deputy department chief, Investigations Department, MGB, Sverdlovsk region, Guards Captain Klejmenov

Protocol of Interrogation, Ivan Knysh[7]

January 29, 1948

City of Stalino (Donetsk)

I, deputy department chief of the Investigations Department, MGB, Stalino region, Guards Captain Klejmenov, interrogated the following accused: Ivan Kirillovich Knysh, born 1922 in Stalino region, Ukraine. From an average peasant background. Worked as a director on a collective farm. He is married. Has no party affiliation. Has seven years of education. Was convicted in 1946 for illegally storing combat weapons. He was sentenced to one year ITL (corrective labor camp) under Article 192 of the Criminal Code of the Ukrainian Soviet Socialist Republic. He resides in Stalino region.

Q: Describe your traitorous activities.

A: While serving in the Red Army, I was assigned as a soldier to the 83rd Marine Rifle Brigade. I participated in combat in the area of Kerch. I ended up in encirclement by German forces on May 16, 1942. We surrendered. By doing so, I violated my military oath and betrayed the Motherland.

I was evacuated in formation to the Dzhankoj station and loaded onto a train and sent to the city of Rovno. I was put in a POW camp there for about ten days. On June 27, 1942, German officers ordered all POWs born in 1920–1921 to form a line. The German officer and his interpreter then selected seventy to eighty prisoners. I was among those. We were asked if we wanted to serve in the German military. They promised that we would be better fed and would receive a salary and a uniform. We all volunteered. We were then loaded into two cargo vehicles and taken to the Trawniki camp. We were housed in one of the camp barracks.

We were issued green German uniforms and a black service cap. We received military drill training and learned the rules for guard duty, the parts of a rifle, and how to carry out arrests and searches. We were also given lectures on political subjects, in which the German military and Germany were praised and the Red Army and Soviet authorities were denigrated.

Our trainer was an *SS-Zugwachmann*. He spoke Polish and also broken Russian. The training lasted about 2.5 months. All of us were photographed. A Volksdeutscher completed a form on each of us in the barracks where we resided. Each of us signed a commitment to serve the Germans faithfully. We also gave a thumbprint on the form. I was fully processed for service in the SS. I was assigned ID #1892 and was designated as an *SS Wachmann* (guard).

In August 1942, I was sent along with a 120-man detachment to Lublin to serve under the authority of *Hauptwachtmeister* (Police Master-Sergeant) Basener. I do not remember his first name. He was in charge of the Lublin ghetto / concentration camp. It was located next to a Polish cemetery. Basener was also in charge of the city jail.

Q: Describe what you know about the crimes committed in the Trawniki camp and the ghetto.

A: Mass shootings of Jews had been carried out in this camp before I arrived. The bodies were buried in pits in the vicinity of the camp. The Lublin concentration camp imprisoned Jews, Russians, Ukrainians, Poles, and other peoples. They numbered up to 800 or 1,000. They were exterminated either by shooting or in gas chambers.

While serving in the SS detachment in Lublin, I guarded the local camp. There was a so-called bathhouse there. The prisoners were killed in this facility by use of some sort of gas. I do not know the process by which people were put to death. I stood guard in the ghetto to ensure that none of the prisoners escaped. Every morning the *SS Wachmänner* escorted fifty to sixty prisoners to the "bathhouse" barracks. I also participated in this. This was carried out under the supervision of an *SS-Sturmführer*, whose name I do not know. I do not know what was done with the bodies. Perhaps they were burned. The bodies were cleared by a work detail of Jews. I escorted prisoners to the "bathhouse" gas chamber on four occasions.

Q: What other punitive activities were carried out by the SS detachment of Hauptwachtmeister Basener in Lublin?

A: Our detachment also guarded the central Lublin jail. I also guarded the jail. We also guarded the commander of Majdanek concentration camp, an *SS-Sturmbannführer*, whose name I do not know. In June 1943, I participated as a member of an SS detachment in an operation during which we carried out the mass arrest of Jews in a town, whose name I do not remember, that was about 40 miles from Lublin. This was carried out under the supervision of a Schutzpolizei officer from Lublin. Hauptwachtmeiser Basener told us through a Volksdeutscher *SS-Zugwachmann* interpreter, whose name I cannot remember, that we were going to a town to carry out the mass arrest of Jews. We were instructed to establish a cordon around the town. With the help of the local Polish and German police, we were then to arrest all of the Jews. We had to go through homes in the town to force out all the Jews to go to the town square. Those who resisted were to be beaten and shot. We escorted a total of about 200 Jews. They had to surrender all of their valuables, including money, watches, rings, etc. They were then all escorted to the railroad station and loaded onto trains sent to I do not know where.

In September 1942, I was sent along with a sixteen-man detachment to the city of Rostock in Germany. We were to serve at a slave labor concentration camp at the "Heinkel" aviation factory. As many as 600 Soviet citizens were held in this camp. Our detachment guarded the camp and escorted the workers to and from the worksite. I served in this camp until April 1944. I then returned to Trawniki.

In May 1944, SS-Wachmann Ivan Solovskij and I were granted a one-month leave. We spent this time with Solovskij's relatives in Poland. Our leave ended in June 1944, and we returned to Trawniki. By that time, Soviet forces had nearly reached Poland. Lublin was being bombed by air. Other *SS Wachmänner* told us of the declining morale among the SS detachment. Some of the *Wachmänner* began to escape. I conspired with Wachmann

Solovskij, and on June 11, 1944, we escaped from the camp and joined the partisans. We remained with the partisans until 1945.

Q: Name the persons who served with you at the Trawniki camp and at other locations.

A: The following persons served with me:

(1) *SS-Sturmbannführer* Streibel, German. The commander of Trawniki camp.

(2) *Hauptwachtmeister* Basener, German. Commander in Lublin.

(3) *SS-Zugwachmann* Nikolai Shapovalov, Russian. Deputy commander of 4th Company. Worked as a teacher before the war.

(4) *SS-Oberzugwachmann* Rudolf Becker, a Volksdeutscher. From Zhitomir region. A platoon commander.

(5) Vasilij Kirillyuk. From Kiev. Ukrainian. A driver by occupation. Had served as a driver in the Red Army. Captured near Kerch. Held in Rovno POW camp. He was assigned either to Sobibor or Treblinka.

(6) Alexei Nagornyj. From Kiev. Ukrainian. Worked as a plumber or fitter. Captured by the Germans near Brody. Served at Treblinka and Rostock. He told me he had participated in the shooting of 3,000 prisoners.

(7) Ivan Stepanov, Russian. From Tula. Served in Rostock.

(8) Ivan Solovskij, Polish. From Lublin.

(9) Nikolaj Chernyshev, from Stalino region. Ukrainian. Worked as a blacksmith.

(10) Andrej Sergienko, from Stalino region. Ukrainian.

(11) Petr Babin, Russian. From Tula. Served in Rostock and Treblinka. He has the name "Petya" tattooed on the palm of his hand.

(12) Vasilij Kharchenko, from Poltava. Ukrainian. Had served in the Danubian flotilla. Served in Rostock.

(13) Konstantin Gureyev, Russian. From Stalingrad. Had served as a senior sergeant in the Red Army. Apparently worked as a teacher before the war. Served in Lublin, at the ghetto. Has "1920" tattooed on his hand or arm.

The interrogation protocol was read to me. My answers have been correctly recorded from my words. I affirm this with my signature. [Signature] Knysh

Interrogated by deputy department chief of the Investigations Department, MGB, Stalino region, Guards Captain Klejmenov

Protocol of Interrogation, Nikolaj Potyatynik[8]

February 9, 1948

City of Stanislavov (Ivano-Frankivsk)

I, chief of 2nd Section, 4th Department, of the MGB in Stanislavov region, Guards Major Stromyatnikov, interrogated the arrestee: Nikolaj Potyatynik, born 1923 in Stanislavov region, Ukraine.

Q: Where did you live, and what did you do during the Patriotic War?

A: Up until 1943, I lived with my father and worked on his farm with him. In 1943, I betrayed the Motherland by entering into German service and was enlisted into the security police at the SS police training camp in the town of Trawniki.

My village elder had told me to report to the city of Kolomya, where I went before a medical commission to determine my fitness for service with the German military. A week later, I was summoned to an assembly point in Kolomya with other young men from my region. A German officer put us all on a train to the Trawniki camp. At Trawniki, special forms were filled out on us. We were each photographed and assigned a personal ID #. Mine was #3251. We took an oath of loyalty to the German-Fascist government. We gave a signed statement subordinating ourselves to the orders of the German punitive organs. We also gave a signed statement not to divulge any secrets known to us. We also each received a weapon: a rifle.

Q: What was the purpose of the Trawniki camp?

A: It was a school where the German punitive organs trained a cadre of police and executioners who were sent to various camps to exterminate people held by the Germans. Also, special units of *SS Wachmänner* (guards) were to combat the partisan movement in Poland and other countries.

Q: What training did you receive at the SS police training camp?

A: Drill, weapons, special police service, and SS punitive service training: how to guard and escort prisoners and how to combat partisans, and political training; anti-Soviet lectures and praising of the German-Fascist system and the Aryan race. All the training was conducted by Gestapo and SD personnel through an interpreter.

Q: Where were you assigned after training, and for what purpose?

A: In May 1943, I was sent with 300 other *SS Wachmänner* to Warsaw to liquidate the Jewish ghetto. This unit was led by Franz. The Jews were loaded onto trains and sent for extermination to the death camps of Poniatowa and Treblinka. Some prisoners, including the elderly and children, were shot on the spot, and the bodies were burned. The ghetto itself was also burned.

Q: Did you take part in shooting Jews in the Warsaw ghetto?

A: I did not. The shootings were done by Gestapo and SD personnel. All of us *SS Wachmänner* stood at posts and provided security to prevent escapes. I stood at my post too.

Q: Where were you sent after Warsaw, and what did you do?

A: I was sent on three occasions to liquidate partisan units active near Zamosc. The punitive unit I belonged to was designated for combat against partisans. The unit had about 100 men and was led by SS-Oberscharführer Rolixmann.

Q: Do you know the fate of the prisoners held at the Trawniki camp?

A: I know from what other *SS Wachmänner* said that all of the prisoners held in the camp were shot. I did not take part in that. At the time, I was in a unit training in Lublin.

Q: What unit were you in in Lublin?

A: It was a unit of about 150 men that was to be trained in Lublin for combat against partisans. We trained in weapons, military reconnaissance, and tactics against partisan units. The training lasted about three months. We then transferred to the city of Dresden in Germany. I remained there until the Red Army arrived. I then reported to an assembly transfer point. There, I concealed my service in the German punitive organs and was sent to the Drogobycz region. From there, I was called up for Red Army service. However, I instead enlisted in the fire brigade in the city of Lvov, where I served until July 1947.

The statement was accurately recorded from my words and has been read to me. I affirm this with my signature. [Signature] Potyatynik

Interrogated by chief of 2nd Section, 4th Department, MGB, Stanislavov region, Guards Major Stromyatnikov

Excerpt of Protocol of Interrogation, Alexander Yeger[9]

April 2, 1948

I, investigator of the Investigations Department of the MGB of the Ukrainian Soviet Socialist Republic, Molotov region, Lieutenant Popov, interrogated the defendant: Alexander Ivanovich Yeger, born 1918 in Saratov region. He is a German citizen of the USSR.

In September 1942, I served as a platoon commander in the guard company at the Treblinka death camp.

Q: What was the purpose of Treblinka?
A: The Germans established it for the mass extermination of Jews, brought there from all the European countries occupied by German troops. Trains arrived every day in the camp.
Q: How many people were exterminated daily at Treblinka?
A: Two or three trains arrived daily with a total of 2,000–5,000 people. Some two million people were exterminated at Treblinka during my service there, but I cannot name the exact figure.

Interrogation continued, April 7, 1948
Q: How was the guard company organized, and what functions did it carry out at Treblinka?
A: The company consisted of 100–120 men. It was divided into three platoons. The first platoon did external guard duty outside the camp for twenty-four hours. The second platoon was subdivided into two squads. One squad worked inside the camp; it unloaded the incoming trains and escorted the new arrivals to the undressing barracks and then to the gas chambers. The other squad was given leave for about eight hours to go to the nearby villages. The third platoon performed domestic tasks in the camp. The platoons each rotated through these duties every twenty-four hours. So in three to six days' time, all the guards of the company took direct part in the extermination process.
Q: What was the purpose of the "Lazarette"?
A: Jews were shot there. Those who resisted during the unloading of the trains and those unable to walk on their own to the gas chambers were shot there. All the guards and the Germans took part in shooting prisoners there. They were brought there, undressed, and laid near a pit; the guards shot them; and the bodies were shoved into the pit. A fire burned at the bottom of the pit, and the bodies were burned right there.
Q: Who made up the "labor crew" in the camp?
A: The "labor crew" was made up of healthier Jews from the incoming trains. It consisted of about 300 men divided into two companies. The 1st company, which had 200 men, unloaded the trains, helped the prisoners undress, and took away their belongings. The 2nd company, which had 100 men, unloaded the bodies from the gas chambers and hauled them away to the pits. Roughly every fifteen to twenty days, all the men of the labor crew were shot at the "Lazarette," and new companies formed from among the incoming trains.
Q: What role did you play in the atrocities and shooting of Jews?
A: Like all the guards in Treblinka, I took part in beating and shooting Jews during the unloading of the trains, in the undressing area, on the way to the gas chambers, and at the "Lazarette." I personally shot about 200 people.

Written down from my words correctly, read by me, and signed. [Signature] Yeger
Interrogated by investigator, Investigations Department, MGB, Ukrainian Soviet Socialist Republic, Molotov region, Lieutenant Popov
True copy: 1st deputy procurator of the Crimea region, Senior Counselor of Justice Kuptsov

Protocol of Interrogation, Fedor Tartynskij[10]
June 7, 1948
City of Konstantinovka
I, deputy chief of the 4th Department of the MGB in Stalino region, Colonel Blednykh,

interrogated the person: Fedor Dimitrivich Tartynskij, born 1911 in Voronezh region, Russia. From an average peasant background. Has four years of education. No prior convictions. Worked as a fire stoker at a zinc factory. Resides in Stalino region.

Having been warned of his liabilities for providing false statements in accordance with Article 89 of the Criminal Code of the Ukrainian Soviet Socialist Republic, he provided the following answers to the questions posed:

Q: Describe your Red Army service.
A: I was called up for service by the Konstantinovka City Military Commissariat on May 20, 1941, in Stalino region. I served with the 227th Rifle Division. On June 29, 1941, the division was sent by train to the area near Belaya Tserkov, Kiev region. We engaged the Germans in the battle around Baranovichi. I served as a telephone technician in the division's communications unit. In late July 1941 our division was encircled. I was captured along with other men from the division. We were sent to a POW camp in Chelm. In October or November 1941, we were in formation, and three Germans selected about forty-five of us POWs, including me. We were selected on the basis of our physical appearance. We were told that we would be taken elsewhere. We did not ask where. We were just grateful to leave the POW camp, where we were poorly fed.

A bus took us to the town of Trawniki. We remained in a quarantine barracks for about two weeks. We were then assigned to companies. We were trained to become part of the SS Wachmannschaften (Guard Force). We were issued SS uniforms. We were told that we would guard Jews. After training for several months, I was assigned to Lublin in April 1942. We escorted groups of Jews from the Lublin ghetto to Majdanek camp. In fall 1942, after the liquidation of the Lublin ghetto, our company was sent to guard Majdanek. When we arrived there, over 100,000 Jews were being held there. They were being systematically exterminated. The camp had been guarded by a Lithuanian SS unit before we arrived. I learned later that there had been discontent among them, and they were relieved of duty. In their place, German SS men stood guard in towers with machine guns. We Russian SS men patrolled between the guard towers. We guarded Majdanek until the end of 1942. Majdanek had two crematoria. There was also a gas chamber. During the period of my service there, no fewer than one million Jews were exterminated there.

On December 31, 1942, our company was sent back to Trawniki. There were rumors at the time that Russian POWs were to be exterminated at Majdanek, and that the Germans sent us away out of fear that we would mutiny. Only German SS remained in the camp.

Next I was assigned to the Warsaw ghetto. A member of our company, Alexei Mikhin, was shot by the Germans for taking money from the Jews to release them. Along with my company commander, a Volksdeutscher named Josef Blank, I also took money, 1,000 zloty, from a Jew. We released him from the ghetto. We were caught and sent back to Trawniki, where we spent ten days under arrest.

My next assignment was again in Lublin, as a guard for the German police. In summer 1943, eighteen of us guards were sent to a camp in Krasnik, about 20 miles from Lublin. We guarded the staff of the German police there. In spring 1944, the Red Army began to approach. We were evacuated to Krakow. We remained there for about two days. My German commander was SS-Untersturmführer Tits. We then departed for Slovakia. There, we carried out arrests along with the German SS. More accurately, they were members of the SD. We guarded their staff. We arrested no fewer than 100 people in Slovakia. They were suspected partisans or people who were pro-Soviet. The Germans later shot them. I did not participate in the shootings.

I became ill with pneumonia and was sent to a German hospital in Slovakia. With Red Army units approaching, we evacuated in a train to Germany. My fever dropped and I recovered. I was then sent to serve with the staff of the ROA (Russian Liberation Army). A Cossack cavalry unit of the ROA was stationed there where I was (I can't remember the name of the city). We dug trenches to maintain a defense against the advancing Red Army. My ROA commander was a former Red Army officer named Medvedev. We were sent to the front against the Americans. Our ROA commander was named Trukhin. We did not see combat. American units captured Medvedev, and we scattered to a city near Vienna. We changed into civilian clothes and presented ourselves to American forces as Red Army POWs.

On May 24, 1945, the Americans brought us to a camp and handed us over to the Soviet authorities. We went on a train to Budapest. There, we were sent to a screening camp. I gave false information about myself to the screener. I was then sent to a camp in Neukirchen, Austria. From there, I was taken to work as a cook for a Red Army unit in the city of Baden. I worked there about two months. I returned to the Soviet Union via Zighet, Romania. I arrived back in my home in Stalino region on May 24, 1946.

The protocol is recorded from my words accurately and has been read to me. I affirm this with my signature. [Signature] Tartynskij
Interrogated by deputy chief of 4th Department, MGB, Stalino region, Colonel Blednykh
True copy: Deputy chief of Investigations Department, MGB, Stalino region, Guards Captain Klejmenov

Excerpt of Protocol of Interrogation, Nikolaj Tkachuk[11]
September 2, 1948
City of Stanislavov (Ivano-Frankivsk)
I, investigator of the Investigations Department of the MGB in Stanislavov region, Lieutenant Tortsov, interrogated the following person: Nikolaj Tkachuk

Q: We have evidence that you served in the German punitive organs during the war: specifically in the SS Security Police. Do you acknowledge your guilt?
A: Yes. In February 1943, I was enlisted in the SS Security Police and was sent to the SS Police training camp in the town of Trawniki. Following training, I was part of a unit they deployed to guard the Warsaw ghetto in May 1943. I did guard duty on Pawia Street. While I was assigned there, the Germans transported the Jews from the ghetto to death camps. In September 1943, I deployed for guard duty at the Poniatowa camp. I then went on leave for a few weeks and returned to Trawniki.

My unit then deployed to the area around Hrubieszow, where a savage battle was being fought between Poles and Ukrainians. Our mission included putting a stop to this battle. By the time we arrived in the area, twenty villages had been burned. After this operation, we returned to Trawniki.

In 1944, we retreated, ending up in Dresden, where we regrouped. I escaped to Czechoslovakia in April 1945. In May 1945, I was drafted into the Red Army, where I served until being demobilized in August 1946. I then returned home.
Q: Did you participate in the shooting of prisoners while serving at Trawniki and Poniatowa?
A: No, I did not participate.

Interrogated by investigator, Investigations Department, MGB, Stanislavov region, Lieutenant Tortsov

Assistant military prosecutor of MVD forces, Ukrainian Soviet Socialist Republic
Lieutenant Colonel Smyshlyayev

Protocol of Interrogation, Nikolaj Belous[12]
March 15, 1949
City of Lvov
I, chief of 2nd Section, 1st Department, Security Directorate, MGB, Lvov region, Major Vasilev, interrogated the detainee: Nikolaj Petrovich Belous, born 1918 in Krasnopol District, Sumy region, Ukraine. No party affiliation. Completed five years of education. Works as a stevedore at the Lvov Locomotive and Rail Car Plant (LPVRZ). Resides in Lvov.

I have been warned about my liability for giving false statements according to Article 89 of the Criminal Code of the Ukrainian Soviet Socialist Republic.
[Signature] Belous

Q: State your whereabouts and activities for the period 1941–1945.
A: Before the Soviet-German war, I lived in the city of Kharkov and worked at the tractor plant as the duty metalworker. A month after the start of the war, I was drafted into the Red Army, and after completing a three-week military-training course, I was sent to the front as part of a rifle regiment. In the first battle with the Germans in the area of Mironovka Railroad Station, near the city of Kiev, our unit was defeated and surrounded. We were forced to surrender. After being taken prisoner I remained in a POW camp near the city of Dresden.
Q: This is not true. You were sent to Trawniki and then Treblinka, and not as a POW. Give truthful statements.
A: After I was taken prisoner by the Germans, I was sent to a POW camp in the town of Chelm, where I stayed until the end of 1941. In January 1942, German officers arrived and began selecting some of us prisoners. They selected about fifty, and I was one of them. At the time, I did not yet know the purpose of the selection. We were loaded into vehicles and brought to the town of Trawniki. There we were informed that we were assigned to the SS training camp and must undergo training in how to guard camps, escort prisoners, and conduct roundups. I spent more than a year in this training camp, until about March 1943. During that time, we completed military training, studied German weapons, learned how to guard prisoners, [learned] proper conduct on duty, and so on. I was then sent the Treblinka punishment camp as part of a group of guards. This camp held Jews and Poles who had gotten in trouble with the German authorities.

At the camp, the other *Wachmänner* and I had to escort prisoners to forced labor and guard the camp. For this work, the camp administration paid me a salary, provided three meals per day, and provided a uniform. I was armed with a German rifle. I spent six to seven months at this punishment camp.

When the Red Army began approaching the camp, by order of the camp commandant, almost all of the prisoners were shot. There were over 500 people in the camp, and very few managed to escape.

I, together with the camp staff and the other *Wachmänner*, went to the other side of the Vistula River to a small town called Zloty, where we had to force local residents to dig ditches and antitank trenches and build military fortifications to deter the approaching Red Army. I retreated with the Germans until we got to the city of Dresden. After Germany's defeat, I wound up in the Soviet zone of occupation and was sent to a processing and screening (filtration) camp in Gorlitz. While going through the screening process, I hid my service with the Germans. I was then sent as a repatriate to Lvov and got myself a job at LPVRZ.

Q: Describe your participation in shooting the prisoners at Treblinka.

A: I did not personally participate in shooting prisoners at the camp. When the Red Army approached, the prisoners were shot to death by the Germans and the *Wachmänner* who were not on guard duty. At that time, I was on guard duty in the camp.

Q: Did you participate in raids the Germans conducted?

A: Yes I did. In spring 1943 the citizens of Warsaw rebelled against the Germans. After suppression of the rebellion, I took part in several roundups of Jews and guarded the Jewish ghetto. I did not participate in shootings. However, while escorting prisoners, I had to beat them, and of this I am guilty.

Properly recorded from my words. My statements were read to me. [Signature] Belous
Interrogated by chief, 2nd Section, 1st Department, Security Directorate, MGB, Major Vasilev
    I attest to the authenticity and accuracy of the copy of the Interrogation Protocol for Nikolaj Belous, and that the original is located in the archive of criminal case #27090 against Nikolaj Belous, pp. 15–19 of the folder.

Security Service of the Ukraine
Directorate of the Lvov region
Chief of the Archive, Dobrydnev
October 27, 1995
Chief, State Archive of the Security Service of the Ukraine, A. Pshennikov

Protocol of Interrogation, Nikolaj Pavli[13]
November 17, 1949
City of Stalino (Donetsk)
I, deputy chief of the Investigations Department of the MGB for Stalino region, Lieutenant Klajmenov, interrogated the accused: Nikolaj Antonevich Pavli, born 1921 in Stalino region, Ukraine. He is of peasant background. Works as a replacement civil engineer in the agricultural department of the General Council in the Dnepropetrovsk region. Not a party member. Married. Has no state decorations. No prior convictions.

Q: Specify the circumstances under which you were captured by German forces in July 1941.

A: While I was a soldier in a 120 mm artillery battery in the 75th Division, my unit was moving toward the city of Kovel, and we were surrounded by the enemy. Everyone split up in different directions, with the objective of reaching the rest of our forces. I and another soldier, Rafalnikov, advanced on our own. We found an abandoned Soviet vehicle and tried to get it started. But we were suddenly overtaken by German soldiers. We were taken to the town of Lutsk and put in a POW camp. I then transferred to a POW camp in the town of Chelm in Poland. I was held here until September 1941. I was conscripted by the Germans, along with other POWs, to serve in the SS force at the Trawniki camp in Lublin District, as an *SS Wachmann* (guard).

Q: Under what circumstances were you conscripted by the Germans to serve in the SS force at Trawniki camp?

A: Around late September 1941, a German, SS-Oberscharführer Mayevski, came to Chelm POW camp and ordered that we be put in parade formation. He selected about sixty POWs from among us, including myself. No one told us for what purpose we had been selected. We were put on two trucks and taken to Trawniki. We were divided into groups and were given basic training in weapons and guard duty. We had to submit information about ourselves so forms could be filled out on us, and we had to submit a fingerprint. We also provided our signature.

In November 1941, I was sent with a forty-man detachment of *Wachmänner* to the Belzec death camp, where I served until August 1942. I guarded civilians who were brought to the camp for extermination in gas chambers. The prisoners arrived by train. We and the Germans took these people off the trains and escorted them to the gas chambers. Adjacent to the gas chamber was an internal-combustion engine from which exhaust gas would be piped into the chambers, killing the prisoners inside. After fifteen to twenty minutes, the doors to the chambers would be opened, and a Jewish work detail removed the bodies and took them to pits. There, they were buried. I participated in guarding the trains when they arrived with people, and I also escorted the people to an area where they would undress. Other *Wachmänner* and Germans took the prisoners to the gas chambers. I also guarded the work detail when it unloaded bodies by the pits. I also guarded a pit in which sick and weak people were to be shot. From every train load that arrived, about twenty to thirty people would be shot here. During my service at Belzec, 40,000 people were killed, most of them by suffocation with gas.

In August 1942, I was sent as part of a thirty-man *Wachmänner* detachment to the Sobibor death camp. There, I performed the same service as at Belzec. I took part in surrounding the pits in which the sick would be shot. I personally did not shoot any prisoners. A German SS officer did the shooting. I and the other *Wachmänner* only had to stand around the pit. Apart from that, I guarded the prisoners within the camp and also on the watchtowers around the camp. The bodies of the dead were arranged in pits on a special surface by work details on rail lines and burned. I also guarded the work details.

In November 1942, I was sent with a thirty-man *Wachmänner* detachment to the city of Lublin. There, we guarded prisoners who worked. They did various jobs: at a wood-processing plant, on a farm, and demolishing houses. I served here until October 1943. I was then sent as part of a sixty-man *Wachmänner* detachment to the Flossenburg concentration camp in Germany. Here, we guarded prisoners who did construction work at the "Messerschmidt" Aviation Plant, and other work.

At this time, I and the other *Wachmänner* were given an SS tattoo for medical reasons. I removed it in 1945 with a burning cigarette because I was afraid of punishment for my crimes if I were caught with it. I served at Flossenburg until March 1944. Then, I served at a camp where I guarded prisoners who worked in German military warehouses, at a brick works, and within the camp. As the front drew near, I and the other *Wachmänner* evacuated the prisoners to the rear, but with the approach of American forces, all the *Wachmänner* and prisoners fled in various directions. I and Wachmann Rafalovski changed out of our uniforms and put on civilian clothes.

When the American forces arrived, I was sent to a transit camp, with the aim of being returned to my country, among many other Soviet citizens who were now in Germany. I was transferred by the American forces in a truck to the area of Czechoslovakia that was under the control of Soviet forces. Then, with many others, I was sent to a camp for Soviet citizens designated for repatriation back to the homeland. From this camp, in June 1945, I was reconscripted into the Red Army, in which I served until May 31, 1946.

The protocol of interrogation was recorded according to my words in correct form and was read to me. I affirm this with my signature. [Signature] Pavli

Interrogated by deputy chief of the Investigations Department, MGB, Stalino region, Major Klejmenov

Confirmation: Nikolaj Pavli was found guilty by a military tribunal of the Cherkov Command, under Article 54-1b of the Criminal Code of the Ukrainian Soviet Socialist Republic, and sentenced to twenty-five years of ITL (corrective labor camps), December 23, 1949.
Attorney-general of the USSR
Director of the Office of the Attorney-General of the USSR. [Signature] A. P. Vladimirov
True copy: The original document is located in archival criminal file #56434, volume 2, pp. 118–121, charging Petro Goncharov, Nikolaj Sherbak, et al.

Protocol of Interrogation, Andrej Kuchma[14]
February 8, 1950
City of Kiev
I, case officer with the 4th Department of the MGB for Kiev region, Lieutenant Krivonos, interrogated the following detainee: Andrej Vasilevich Kuchma, born 1907 in Kiev region, Ukraine. No party affiliations, two years of education, married, has no prior convictions. He has no government decorations or wounds. He served in the Red Army from June to August 1941. He lives in Kiev region and works as a collective farmer.

He has been warned of the liabilities for providing false statements in accordance with Article 89 of the Criminal Code of the Ukrainian Soviet Socialist Republic.

Q: Where and under what circumstances were you captured by the Germans?
A: In August 1941, in the area of the village of Mironovka, my battalion was left behind to delay advancing German units. German units surrounded us, and after a long battle, those of us who were still alive were captured.
Q: In which POW camps were you held?
A: I was held in Belaya Tserkov and Chelm.
Q: How long were you held in Chelm POW camp?
A: Until about January 1942. At that time, a German officer arrived in the camp and selected fifty of us to transfer to the Trawniki camp.
Q: What was the Trawniki camp like?
A: It was a training camp in which the Germans trained cadres of *Wachmänner* (guards) for service in the SS forces.
Q: When did you swear an oath to serve the Germans?
A: I do not remember whether or not I swore an oath.
Q: What were you taught in the Trawniki SS training camp?
A: We underwent drill training, tactics to battle partisans, how to perform roundups of Jews, rifle training, and German commands and songs, and we also listened to anti-Soviet lectures.
Q: How long did you undergo training at the Trawniki SS training camp?
A: Five or six months. Until May or June 1942. I was then assigned to Lublin for two months. In August or September 1942, I was sent to the town of Belzec.
Q: What did you do in Belzec?
A: I served in the special detachment of the Belzec death camp. I drove a tractor in the camp. I moved bricks for the construction of a garage.
Q: Why was Belzec called a death camp?
A: Because in the camp, the Jewish population was exterminated in gas chambers and by shooting.
Q: What did you do while serving in the Belzec death camp?
A: As I already stated, I drove a tractor to undertake construction work. I also stood guard over the camp in a tower to ensure that no one escaped from the camp. On several occasions, I also buried the bodies of Jews who had been killed in the gas chambers or shot.

Q: How many times did you participate in shooting Jews in the camp?

A: I never participated in shooting Jews in the camp because there were special units designated for this purpose in the camp.

Q: How long did you serve at the camp?

A: For two months. After that, we were sent back to Trawniki because we had wanted to release the Jews in the camp. Next, we were sent to the Auschwitz concentration camp.

Q: What did you do in Auschwitz?

A: I guarded people imprisoned in the camp.

Q: How long did you serve at Auschwitz?

A: Two or three months. After which, we were put on a train bound for Germany. On the way, I escaped and resided in the city of Kassel until 1945. I remained there until the city was occupied by American forces.

The interrogation protocol was recorded from my words accurately and was read aloud to me, which I affirm with my signature. [Signature] Kuchma

Interrogated by case officer with the 4th Department, MGB, Kiev region, Lieutenant Krivonos

Protocol of Interrogation, Nikolai Shalayev[15]

November 27, 1950

After being captured in June 1941 by the Germans in the vicinity of the village of Ternovka, which is near the city of Belaya Tserkov in Kiev region, the Germans sent me as a POW to the town of Chelm and put me together with other POWs in the camp. I was kept as a POW in this camp from early August 1941, and sometimes I was sent to work at a lumber mill to stack boards. In November 1941, together with selected POWs totaling twenty-five men, I was taken by the Germans to the town of Trawniki by bus. At first, 400 of us were placed in huts, where the Germans made everyone weave straw boots for the German army. Being at the training camp in Trawniki, I was trained for two months at the school for *Wachmänner* (guards). After this, I was sent as a member of the Trawniki 3rd Company to the city of Lublin to guard the Jewish ghetto. Every day we were lined up and inspected three times a day, then dismissed. In June 1942, thirty of us were sent to the Treblinka camp. In Lublin, our detachment was put on a train, accompanied by a German, and taken to Malkinia station, to Treblinka, via Warsaw. I stayed in this camp for about a year and was an armed guard at the camp. Being a guard, I, like the others, wore an SS uniform: a khaki cap, service tunic, black pants, and boots. I, together with the guard Ivan Marchenko, stood at the motor that supplied exhaust gas to the gas chambers. There were three gas chambers, or as they called them, "baths." About 150 people were put through the "baths" at a time, and in eight to ten minutes they were dead. Aside from men and women, children as young as nursing age were among the victims. It is difficult for me to say how many Jews were exterminated at the Treblinka death camp during my stay there, but in any case 50,000–70,000 and maybe even more.

Q: Where did you go after leaving the Treblinka camp?

A: From Treblinka I was sent to Italy, to the town of Trieste.

Q: For what purpose?

A: It took them five days to take us in vehicles along a route from Treblinka to Warsaw–Krakow–Klagenfurt–Villach–Udine–Trieste; in other words, from Poland through Austria to Italy. About twenty-five German policemen went with us. They were armed; we were not.

Q: How many guards from Treblinka camp left with you for Trieste?

A: They sent five of us: two Russian Volksdeutsche from the Povolzhiye (Volga region), two Ukrainians, and me.

Q: What did you do in Trieste?

A: They put the five of us in the port to guard stores of food and goods, and we were armed with Italian pistols. We arrived in Trieste in summer 1943 and guarded the port warehouses until April 1944. After stealing two rolls of leather from the warehouse, I was caught trying to sell them by the Italian police. I tried to get away from them. The police handed me over to the Germans. A German police officer detained me for three days and then sent me to a garage to work as a mechanic. The garage belonged to the German police, with whom we retreated in April 1945 from Italy to Austria, where I was captured on May 6 or 7, 1945, by the British. The British tried to persuade all the Russians, including me, to stay with them in Austria and not to go back to the Soviet Union. But I did not want to stay, and therefore I was transferred to the Soviet authorities in Laibach (Ljubljana) together with other Soviet POWs and civilians forced out of the Soviet Union by the Germans during the war. During processing in the town of Getzendorf (12 miles from Vienna), I concealed from the Soviet authorities my service with the Germans and my criminal activity.

The interrogation was conducted by investigator of the Investigations Section, MGB, Captain Gorokhov

Head of the Office of the Procuracy of the USSR

Procuracy of the USSR, E. F. Vladimirov

The original of this document in located in criminal file #17214 of the Archives, on the accusation against Nikolai Egorovich Shalayev, pp. 30–34.

Protocol of Interrogation, Nikolai Shalayev[16]
December 8, 1950

Q: You have been accused, according to Article 58-1b of the Criminal Code of the Russian State, of having voluntarily entered the guard school at the SS training camp in Trawniki in October 1941, and taking a military oath to Fascist Germany, after having been taken prisoner by the Germans. After training at the camp, in February 1942 you guarded the Jewish ghetto in Lublin as part of an SS detachment and escorted people of Jewish nationality from the ghetto to the Sobibor death camp. From June 1942 until November 1943, you were at the Treblinka death camp, and as an engine operator of the gas chambers you took a direct part in the mass extermination of the peaceful population by means of gas suffocation and shooting. Then, in Italy in 1944, you took part in arresting civilians and punitive operations against Italian partisans and guarded the prison of political prisoners in Trieste. Do you admit that the accusations against you are accurate?

A: I completely admit the accusations against me are correct. I understand what I am accused of. Serving in the Red Army, I was captured on July 3, 1941, by the Germans during a battle near the village of Ternovka in Kiev region. I served in the Red Army as a trainee at the regimental school of the 126th Battalion of the 58th Rifle Division, 13th Corps, 12th Army, with the rank of private. The war started before I could finish the regiment school, and all trainees, including me, were sent to fight. We retreated from the Soviet-Hungarian border toward Kiev. After I was captured, I was sent to the POW camp in Belaya Tserkov, in Kiev region, and then to the town of Chelm (Poland), where I was put in another POW camp. I remained in Chelm camp for more than four months, and in November 1941 I happened to be with a group of twenty-five men selected by a German officer together with the commander of the camp. All those selected, including me, were put on a bus, escorted by a Polish policeman and the German officer who selected us, and we were taken to the town of Trawniki, to an SS training camp. None of us knew where we had been taken or for what reason. On arrival, we were used by the Germans for different kinds of jobs in the camp. Then we were divided into detachments that weaved straw boots for the German army. Then all of us, and others in the camp, were divided into companies. I was in the third company. We were trained as *Wachmänner* (guards). The commander of the company was a German with the rank of *Oberwachtmeister* (police sergeant-major). The training was conducted by *Volksdeutsche* from the Volga region. The training included drill, German commands, learning German songs, and studying German military ranks. It took about a month to cover these subjects, and we were then sent to Lublin to guard the Jewish ghetto there. When we were at Trawniki guard school, we filled out some questionnaires when we were called into the German clerk at the headquarters.

During our stay in Lublin, we also performed drill, and in June 1942 our group of twenty-five to thirty guards was sent to the Treblinka death camp for guard duties. During my time at that camp, I guarded the exterior of the camp, and later I was appointed an engine operator of the gas chamber. Ivan Marchenko worked together with me as an engine operator. During my time at the camp, more than 70,000 people of Jewish nationality went through the gas chambers, called "baths." All of them were killed by exhaust gas supplied to the chambers after the engine was turned on. There were three chambers, in each of which seventy-five people could fit, among whom were men, women, and children. After five to eight minutes in the chamber, all the people died of gas poisoning from the engine.

Q: Did you have a dog when you worked as an engine operator at the gas chamber?

A: Yes, I did. The dog belonged to Oberwachmann Alexander Yeger, who after getting sick gave it to me to take care of.

Q: Did you beat Jews in the camp with a stick?

A: There were instances when I beat Jews in the camp; I do not deny this.

Q: Did you take part in pushing the Jews into the gas chambers?

A: Yes, sometimes I had to force those Jews that refused to go into the chambers. They obviously guessed that something was wrong, and they began to shout.

Q: Tell us about your participation in the shooting of Jews during your time at the Treblinka camp.

A: I also shot Jews at the camp.

Q: How long did you serve at the camp, and where did you go from there?

A: I served at Treblinka camp from June 1942 to June 1943. After that, I left for Trieste in Italy with a group of nine people and German officers. On the way to Italy, we stopped in Warsaw, where we joined a German police detachment of about eighty men. We were taken to Trieste by motor vehicle.

Q: Why were you sent to Italy?

A: I cannot say, since none of us knew where we were going and why. Only upon arrival in Italy did we figure out that we were brought there to guard military installations in Trieste and to participate in punitive operations against Yugoslav partisans and the population.

Q: Who among the *Wachmänner* left for Italy with you?

A: Ivan Marchenko, Voloshenko, Lebedenko, and the two Volksdeutsche from the Volga region, Pilman and Schultz. Three German officers also came with us.

Q: What did you do in Italy?

A: I was an armed guard, guarding German storage areas in the port of Trieste and the local prison. I also took part in punitive operations against Italian partisans, and roundups of local citizens whom the Germans forcibly sent to work in Germany. Being a policeman, I also escorted German officers back and forth on trips by car from Trieste to Fiume.

Q: What uniform did you wear, and how were you armed?

A: Being a *Wachmann*, I wore a German uniform and was armed with a rifle and an ammunition belt.

Q: How much money did you get from the Germans for your service with them?

A: During my service in Italy, as a policeman, I was paid 125 liras in cash, plus free meals and the uniform. In Trieste we ate at a dining room at the town prison where our detachment was quartered.

Q: On your arrival at the SS training camp in Trawniki, you had voluntarily agreed to be trained as a *Wachmann*?

A: I must admit, I accepted the offer of the Germans and was trained as a guard, worked in Treblinka, served as a policeman in Italy, and did everything the Germans ordered me to do.

The interrogation was conducted by investigator of the Investigations Section, MGB, Captain Gorokhov
Assistant military procurator of the MVD, Major of Law, Vdovin
Head of the Office of the Procuracy of the USSR
Procuracy of the USSR, E. F. Vladimirov
The original of this document is located in criminal archive file #17214, on the accusations against Nikolai Egorovich Shalayev, pp. 30–34.

Protocol of Interrogation, Nikolai Shalayev[17]
December 18, 1950

Q: What were your duties when you guarded the Jewish ghetto in Lublin?

A: My duties as a *Wachmann* included not allowing anyone living in the ghetto to leave, to guard the property of arrested Jews who remained in their homes following their evacuation, and not allowing local Poles into the area of the ghetto.

Q: Where did the Germans send the Jewish population from the ghetto?

A: I did not know where they were being sent. It was only later that I learned from other *Wachmänner* that the Jews were being sent by the Germans to the Sobibor death camp.

Q: Did you escort Jews who were arrested in the ghetto to the Sobibor death camp?

A: No, I only guarded the ghetto.

Q: What was the Jewish ghetto in Lublin?

A: Several blocks in Lublin where the Jewish population lived, and it was fenced in by barbed wire.

Q: What kind of weapon did you have when you guarded the ghetto?

A: I was armed with a rifle of French manufacture, I believe.

Q: Did you escort arrested Jews from the ghetto to the Sobibor death camp?

A: No.

Q: You are trying to hide the fact that you did this. Tell us about this.

A: I am not hiding anything, and I was not involved in escorting arrested people during my time in Lublin.

Q: Did you participate in the mass executions of the Jewish population that was held in the Lublin ghetto?

A: No, I did not.

Q: What did you do when you were not on guard duty?

A: Sometimes we took part in rifle training at the place where our company was deployed. More frequently the *Wachmänner* went into Lublin on leave passes or even without permission. I also went into town without permission, where we would often sell items we had stolen from the Jewish houses that we were guarding, and, having money, drank vodka and visited prostitution houses.

Q: In Lublin, were there any cases of desertion by the *Wachmänner* from your company?

A: Yes, I knew of two cases, when two *Wachmänner* deserted, but I don't remember their last names.

Q: Where were you sent after Lublin?

A: I was part of a detachment of approximately fifteen men in June 1942 sent to serve at the Treblinka death camp.

Q: Why were you assigned to serve at the Treblinka death camp, and out of the entire company, why were those particular fifteen men chosen?

A: The entire company of *Wachmänner* was lined up near a hut, where we were quartered, and a German officer of the company selected fifteen men, who were ordered to leave the formation. I was among the men selected. I don't know what guided the officer in selecting the *Wachmänner*, but after this the officer stated through an interpreter that we were going on guard duty, but where it was not said, and the next day, accompanied by a German police NCO, we left by train for Treblinka.

Q: Please give the last names of the *Wachmänner* who were sent with you as part of this detachment from Lublin to the Treblinka camp.

A: I no longer remember the last names of all the guards, but I do remember some: Petr Shilov, Prokofij Ryabtsev, Semen Pashkov, and Ivan Tsitsurin. Of the guards whose names I just gave, all four before the war were residents of Voronezh region and my compatriots.

Q: What did the death camp of Treblinka consist of?

A: The camp was located in a forest on an area of about 5 hectares, approximately 5 miles from the railroad station of Malkinia and 1 mile from the villages of Vulka and Kutaska. The camp was surrounded by a high wire fence, and several tens of meters from the fence there was a line of antitank iron obstacles, which later were interwoven with barbed wire. Inside the camp was a narrow passage 2.5 meters wide, fenced in on both sides with barbed wire, camouflaged with tree branches. This passageway went from the huts where the people undressed, to the gas chambers in a single-story stone building, which in the camp was called the "bath." There were also nine huts, where the Germans, guards, and Jewish work detail stayed; a dining room; a shoemaker and tailor shop; and huts for storing the personal items taken from the killed people. Outside the camp, at the corners, were four sentry towers, in which there were guards on duty at all times. In the camp were sixty Germans and seventy-five *Wachmänner*. The camp itself was divided in half by barbed wire, as if to divide it into two camps. Camp I included the huts that housed soldiers of the Waffen-SS and German police, [as well as] the *Wachmänner* detachment, the dining room, and warehouse. Camp II included the hut for the Jewish work detail and the stone building with the gas chambers, and behind this building was a pit where the bodies were buried. Later, these bodies were dug up from the pit and burned. Evidently the Germans wanted to hide the traces of their crimes, and from then on, the bodies were burned immediately. At first there was one gas chamber with three compartments with a capacity for 225 people to be exterminated at one time, and later, in early 1943, the Germans began to construct a new chamber with five compartments alongside the old one.

Q: How did the process of killing people in the camp take place?

A: Trainloads of Jews, among them men, women, and children, arrived at Malkinia station.

The train then entered the death camp. The area of the camp could hold ten railroad cars at a time. The arriving people were then taken off and sent to the undressing room and then lined up, to turn in for storage their personal belongings and money. Five Jewish men, sitting down, explained to the people that they would later receive their belongings back. Men and women undressed separately in different dressing rooms. The naked people were then grouped into batches of seventy-five and in turn sent in groups along the narrow passageway to the "bath." All three compartments were filled in turn. Once the outer door was closed, I crawled into the attic of the chamber, where I opened the pipe valve along which the gas went into the chambers, and I went to the machine room, where I started the engine. After five to eight minutes, the people died. The chamber was then opened and the work detail went in to remove the bodies, which were loaded onto narrow-gauge railroad cars and taken to a large pit where the bodies were buried. After the bodies were removed, the chambers were washed by the workers with water and damp rags because they accumulated a small amount of soot. Before the arrival of a train in the death camp, all guards were assigned to their designated places: meeting the train in the camp, unloading, directing people to the undressing room, and guarding the narrow passageway from the undressing room to the gas chambers. Together with the *Wachmänner*, German Waffen-SS soldiers were also assigned to designated duties. I, together with Ivan Marchenko, two Germans, and two Jews, was stationed at the engine that generated exhaust gas into the gas chambers.

Q: What did the gas chambers consist of?

A: Each chamber was 4 by 4 meters and 2 meters high. The walls and floor were inlaid with parquet slabs. A gas pipe passed from the attic to the ceiling of the chamber. In order to camouflage it and deceive the people who had entered the chamber, three water spouts hung from the ceiling like in a real bathhouse with shower stalls. In the ceiling there was a small window made of thick glass, through which a murky light entered. The gas pipe passed along the ceiling, and there was a ladder that I climbed to open the valves.

Q: What was the engine like that supplied the exhaust gas to the chambers?

A: It was an ordinary, four-cylinder engine, which used gasoline and, according to the German machine operator, was of Russian make. The engine was installed on a wooden frame and started as soon as the people were herded into the gas chamber, whereupon the exhaust pipe was covered and the valve of the pipe opened, through which the exhaust gas entered the room. This engine was located in the machine room through a wall from the first chamber.

Q: What did your duties include?

A: My duties as the *Wachmann* working in the machine room included opening and closing the valves, through which the exhaust gas entered the chambers, starting the engine, and sometimes helping the other *Wachmänner* to herd the people into the chambers.

Q: What else did you have to do when stationed at Treblinka?

A: In addition to working as an engine operator, earlier I also had to be a perimeter guard outside the barbed-wire fence surrounding the camp. Our posts were located between the sentry huts and were a reinforcement for camp security to prevent members of the Jewish work detail from escaping. These posts were also active at night, and in addition to them, patrols walked around the camp, usually two German soldiers and two Russian *Wachmänner*. I also was assigned to meet the arriving trains and to direct the people to the undressing rooms.

Q: Tell us about the "Lazarette" at Treblinka and what its purpose was.

A: It had an area of about 80 square meters, enclosed within a fence made of evergreen trees, 2.5 meters high. All sick Jews unable to walk from the arriving trains to the gas chambers on their own were brought here. This place was intended for their execution in a pit.

Q: Who shot the Jews in this "Lazarette"?

A: The Germans and *Wachmänner*.

Q: How many people from each arriving train were sent to the "Lazarette"?

A: It is difficult to answer this question exactly, but in any case there were several tens of people in almost every train sent there. There, all of them were indiscriminately executed.

Q: In what manner did these executions occur?

A: All sick Jews were led in by hand or carried on stretchers. The Jews from the work detail accompanied them and undressed them, and then *Wachmänner* and Germans shot them.

Q: Give us the last names of the *Wachmänner* who served at the "Lazarette."

A: I no longer remember the names of these *Wachmänner*, because they were assigned there in turns, and this duty was assigned to many of them.

Q: What did the Germans do with the clothing and valuables taken from the executed Jews?

A: The clothing, money, and valuables were taken somewhere by the Germans. These items were taken away by motor vehicle, protected by German soldiers, or loaded onto railroad cars and sent to some unknown place from the camp.

Q: Were the *Wachmänner* able to steal money and valuables at the camp?

A: Yes, almost all of the *Wachmänner* without exception managed to steal items.

Q: How much money did you personally acquire and take away from the Jews who arrived in the camp?

A: I was able to take about 100,000 Polish zlotys and several watches, which I sold in the village of Vulka, where I visited a Polish woman by the name of Zosya, or I bought vodka and food from Poles who came to trade in the forest near the camp. I also stole a warm blanket from the warehouse, which I also sold to a Pole.

Interrogated by investigator of the Investigations Department, MGB, Voronezh region, Captain Gorokhov

Certified copy: Senior investigator of the Investigations Department, KGB, Crimea region, Captain Linnik, 18th [illegible], 1985

Note: The original of this document is located in archival criminal file #17214

Deputy chief of the Administration,

Procuracy of the USSR, E. F. Vladimirov

Xerox copy made from a copy in the criminal file on the accusations against Fedorenko, vol. 15, pp. 158–166

Protocol of Interrogation, Ivan Shvidkij[18]

July 10, 1951

City of Dzerzhinsk

I, assistant case officer of the Dzerzhinsk District Office of the MGB, Senior Lieutenant Evseyev, interrogated the detainee, Ivan Danilovich Shvidkij, born 1909 in Dzerzhinsk District, Stalino/Donetsk region, Ukraine; no party membership, works as a loader at the Kryga station. Resides in Dzerzhinsk District.

Subject was warned of his liabilities for providing false statements in accordance with Article 89 of the Criminal Code of the Ukrainian Soviet Socialist Republic.

Q: Recite your autobiography.

A: I was born into an average peasant family. In 1919 I completed two years of school, then from 1919 to 1930 I worked on a farm. In 1930 I began work on a collective farm and remained there until 1932. From 1932 to 1941, I worked as a face cutter in the Dzerzhinsk District mines. On June 28, 1941, I was summoned to serve in the Red Army.

Q: Which district military commissariat called you up to serve in the Red Army, and to what unit were you assigned?

A: I was called up by the Dzerzhinsk District Military Commissariat. I was sent to the front with the 15th Replacement Company as a soldier until August 2, 1941, when I was captured by the Germans.

Q: Where and under what circumstances were you captured by the Germans?

A: I was captured in the area around the village of Mironovka. I do not recall what region we were in. I had been sent to the front, with my unit, to join Timoshenko's army. Those captured with me included Mikhail Lysak, Danil Shivlyak, Nikolaj Pogrebnyak, and fifty to sixty other men whom I do not know.

We were taken to the town of Belaya Tserkov, and we remained there about two days. Then we were loaded onto a train and sent to a POW camp in the town of Chelm (Poland). I remained there until November 1941, after which the Germans sent 100 of us to a village to gather the harvest, including carrots, cabbage, and corn. Then, in late December 1941, Germans selected thirty of us from this group, including me, and we were sent to the Trawniki SS training camp.

Q: What did you do in the SS training camp in Trawniki?

A: We were trained to become *Wachmänner* to guard concentration camps. The training consisted of drill, weapons, and how to perform guard duty. I provided my signature to the Germans to commit to serve as an *SS Wachmann*. In May 1942, I completed training at the camp and was sent to Lublin. There, I was assigned to guard residential blocks in which Jews had once resided but have now been evicted.

In July 1942, I was sent to the Treblinka camp, in which Jews, Russians, Ukrainians, and people of other nationalities were held. Prisoners were brought to this camp from Lublin and were pushed into gas chambers and killed. I served as a guard at this camp. I was ordered to shoot people if they tried to escape. I served at this camp from July 1942 until September 1943. During that period, about 30,000 Soviet citizens were exterminated there.

Q: Describe how Soviet citizens were exterminated in the camp. What was done with the bodies, and what was your personal participation in the process?

A: The camp was divided into two sections. The camp staff, including the Germans and we *Wachmänner*, were housed in the first section. Soviet citizens brought for extermination were held in the second section.

Every day, on two or three trains, people were brought to the camp. After undressing and surrendering their valuables, they were pushed into the "bathhouse," which was a bathhouse only in name. In fact, it was a gas chamber. When the gassing was finished, the doors were opened and the bodies were removed and taken to pits on carts. The pits were located 40–50 meters from the gas chambers, and the bodies were burned in them. I personally participated in forcing Soviet citizens into the gas chambers. After they had been killed, I also carried them to the pits and burned them.

In September 1943, I and other members of the camp guard were transferred to Stutthof, about 20 miles from Danzig (Gdansk). In Stutthof, I guarded a concentration camp until February 1945.

In February 1945, the Germans divided us into groups of fifteen to twenty men, and each group guarded up to 100 prisoners. The groups were sent in different directions. In the town of Putsiki (Poland) in March 1945, I was taken into custody by Soviet forces and sent to Stolp (Germany). I arrived in a screening camp. I was redrafted into the Red Army that same month and served as a soldier in the 10th Rifle Division. I was demobilized in November 1945. I went to Dzerzhinsk District, Stalino region, where I have resided ever since.

Q: Other than the signature you provided to serve the German authorities as an *SS Wachmann*, did the Germans have you sign anything else?

A: I also allowed them to give me a tattoo on my left arm. I still have this tattoo. It was put on at the same time that I signed the service commitment in Trawniki.

Q: While being screened by Soviet authorities, were you asked where you were held in POW camps by the Germans, and if they asked, what was your reply?

A: At the time, the representative of the Soviet command asked me what I had done during the period of my detention in German POW camps from 1941 to 1945. I responded that I was held in a concentration camp and worked just like all other Red Army POWs.

Q: Why did you not acknowledge, while undergoing screening, that you had served the Germans as an SS *Wachmann* and guarded concentration camps and Jewish ghettos? Why did you also not acknowledge the fact that you personally participated in executing Soviet citizens at the Treblinka camp?

A: I did not confess to them that I had betrayed the Motherland because I was afraid of being held responsible before the Motherland for the crimes I had committed.

Q: Provide the names of other traitors to the Motherland who served with you at the SS training camp in Trawniki and at the Treblinka death camp.

A: These are the men whom I know at Trawniki:

(1) Mikhail Lysak
(2) Nikolaj Pogrebnyak
(3) Nikolaj Grebenyuk

All three of these men were from the Dzerzhinsk District, Stalino region, like me. I do not remember any others. From service in Treblinka death camp, I remember

(1) Ivan Makarenko: from Kiev region
(2) Pritsch: from Kiev region
(3) Brik: from Ternopil region
(4) Tsukhin
(5) Vasilij Shilov: from western Ukraine
(6) *Zugwachmann* Schultz: from the Volga region, a Volksdeutscher
(7) *Zugwachmann* Rogoza: from Kiev region
(8) Nedozrelov
(9) Sergej Bilan: from Kiev region
(10) Unrau: from Volga region, a Volksdeutscher

The interrogation protocol was read to me. It was recorded from my words accurately, which I affirm with my signature. Shvidkij
Interrogated by assistant case officer of the Dzerzhinsk District Office, MGB, Senior Lieutenant Evseyev

Protocol of Interrogation, Fedor Tikhonovskij[19]
January 21, 1955
I, senior case officer of the KGB, in the Karaganda region, Lieutenant Moldashev, interrogated the following person: Fedor Petrovich Tikhonovskij, born 1907 in Dnepropetrovsk region, Ukraine. He has no party affiliation. He has three years of education and worked as a planer in a mechanical repair factory. He is married. He has no prior convictions.

He was warned regarding his liabilities for providing false statements according to Article 95 of the Criminal Code of the Russian Soviet Federated Socialist Republic.

Q: Give your autobiography in detail.

A: I was born in 1907 in Dnepropetrovsk region, in an average peasant family. Until 1934, I worked on my own farm along with my father. In 1934, I took work at a bread factory as a counter of bread in the city of Dneprodzerzhinsk. In 1937, I went to work at a metallurgical factory as a planer until I was called up to serve in the Red Army. I was called up to serve on June 23, 1941, by the Dneprodzerzhinsk City Military Commissariat.

Q: Describe your service in the Red Army.

A: After the call-up, we recruits were taken to the city of Dnepropetrovsk. There I was assigned to a communications battalion. I do not remember the unit number. Around June 25, 1941, I was sent to the front with this battalion. In a village about 30 miles from the city of Shepetovka, I was captured by German forces after having been encircled on July 6, 1941.

Q: Describe your captivity in detail.

A: After being captured, I was taken by the Germans to a camp in the town of Chelm in Poland, along with a group of other POWs. In this camp, the Germans sometimes took us out to work unloading cargo at a railroad station. But we spent most of our time there without work. While working at the railroad station one day, I took the advice of a Pole who worked at the station, and escaped from the camp. I got into a railcar going eastward. I got off the train in western Ukraine. I was detained by the Germans and sent to Rovno, then to Germany, where I did farmwork for a landowner. I remained on this farm until being liberated by American forces on April 12, 1945.

Q: This investigation has information that you did not, in fact, escape from the Chelm camp, but from November 1941 onward, you underwent training at a German training camp in the town of Trawniki, in Lublin District, Poland. Why are you concealing this?

A: Yes, I in fact did not give the truth up until now. I acknowledge that I did not escape from the Chelm camp. In November 1941, the Germans took a group of prisoners from this camp, including myself, in two vehicles, to Trawniki. In Trawniki, I was enrolled in a German school where I underwent training until March 1942. We were brought one at a time to the German camp headquarters, where we completed forms with our biographical information, which we had to sign, and then submit a fingerprint of our right thumb. We then underwent drill training, learned some German, and learned the workings of a rifle. Upon completion of training in Trawniki in March 1942, I was sent to the city of Lublin with my unit. About 100 us were assigned to Lublin.

Q: State the names and other information of men who received training with you at Trawniki.

A: I remember the following persons:

Taras Olejnik: from Dnepropetrovsk region
Nikifor Bulykishko: from Dnepropetrovsk region
Grigorij Bulat: he served with me at Auschwitz and Buchenwald.
Grigorij Kniga
Grigorij Nesmejan

Q: Why did you not admit up front that you had undergone training at the Trawniki school?

A: Because I felt responsible before the Soviet government for having undergone this training and for serving as a *Wachmann* at the death camps of Belzec, Auschwitz, and Buchenwald.

Q: Where were you sent after completing the Trawniki school?

A: In March 1942, my Trawniki unit was sent to guard the Jewish ghetto in Lublin. In May 1942, we were transferred to the Belzec extermination camp. Jews were brought there for extermination, and I performed guard duty there. Jews were brought here in groups, and the Germans suffocated them in a death chamber. I was assigned to the camp from May 1942 until spring 1943. From among the *Wachmänner* who served with me at this camp, thirteen escaped. After this incident, some of the *Wachmänner*, including myself, were recalled to Trawniki. In spring 1943, we were sent to the Auschwitz death camp. Soviet citizens were held in this camp, some of whom went to work at road repair. I remained at this camp until July 1943. From there, we were sent to the Buchenwald concentration camp in Germany.

Q: Describe your participation in the mass shooting and extermination of people in the abovenamed camps.

A: I performed guard and escort duty, armed with a weapon at these camps. I guarded people and maintained order. In Belzec, I guarded Jews who were gathered by the Germans for mass extermination. In Auschwitz and Buchenwald, there were Soviet citizens and POWs among the Jews. My duties included guarding prisoners and escorting people to work. I did not participate in any shootings or extermination of people held in these camps.

Q: Why did you conceal the fact that you trained at the German school in Trawniki and your service in the concentration camps, when you underwent screening?

A: Because I feared taking responsibility before the Soviet government.

B: How do you now view your training in the SS school and your service as a guard over defenseless people held in death camps?

A: I acknowledge that while in difficult circumstances during time of war, I was forced to serve the Germans. I ask the investigative organs to give me an opportunity, with honest effort, to atone for my guilt before the Motherland.

The interrogation protocol was recorded from my words correctly and was read to me. [Signature] Tikhonovskij
Interrogated by senior case officer, 2nd Section, 4th Department, KGB, Lieutenant Moldashev
True copy: Senior investigator, Investigations Department, KGB, Dnepropetrovsk region, Captain N. Shkonda
Note: The original document is located in the archival criminal file charging V. Podenok, F. Tikhonovskij, and others, which is stored with the KGB in Krasnodar District.
December 24, 1965

Protocol of Interrogation, Prokofij Ryabtsev[20]
April 18, 1961
City of Vinnitsa
I, senior investigator of the Investigations Department of the KGB for the Kaliningrad region, Captain Shabanov, interrogated the following person as a witness: Prokofij Nikolayevich Ryabtsev, born 1915. Other identifying information on him is contained in the file.

The witness was warned of his responsibilities for refusing to give a statement and for giving false statements under Articles 178 and 179 of the Criminal Code of the Ukrainian Soviet Socialist Republic.

Q: Describe in detail the specifics of performing guard duty at the Treblinka death camp.
A: The basic task of the guards and Germans at the camp was the extermination of people brought to the camp. Practically every *Wachmann* in the camp performed the following: stood

guard in one of the towers located at the corners of the camp; stood guard in a cordon around the railcars when trains arrived with the people, to prevent escapes; participated in unloading the trains, guarded the people in the undressing area, guarded the outer side of the path along which the people were forced from the undressing area to the gassing facility, and served at the "Lazarett," where they shot people. I do not remember exactly, but it is possible that *Wachmänner* also escorted the people to the gas chambers. I personally did not do this.

I remember well that at the gas chambers, duties were performed by the Germans and the *Zugwachmänner* Shalayev and Marchenko. I remember well that on the platform where the Jews from the work detail unloaded the bodies from the gas chambers and carried them to the pits, there was always a German who watched their work. Whether or not there was also a *Wachmann* posted there, I cannot exactly say; I have forgotten.

There was no permanent division of responsibilities among the *Wachmänner*, which is why all of them served at each of the posts that I described above. They participated directly in the mass extermination of people by forcing them toward the gassing facility and by shooting them in the "Lazarett." All of the Germans who served in the camp also participated in all of these functions. Besides the platoon commanders, one of the Germans was always present during the unloading of the trains, in the undressing area, at the gas chambers, and at the "Lazarett."

Discipline in the camp was very tough. For this reason, there were no attempts to avoid following orders. Regardless of the fact that they could be punished with whips, *Wachmänner* frequently went on unauthorized absences, took gold and money left behind by the exterminated people, and used these valuables to buy alcohol in local villages. Practically all the *Wachmänner* had an unlimited amount of money and a great deal of gold. The *Wachmänner* constantly drank with Polish women from the local villages and were frequently sick with venereal diseases. The conditions of life and character of service caused the Germans and *Wachmänner* to lose their humanity, and they treated the Jews very cruelly.

Q: Describe how the Germans and *Wachmänner* in Treblinka treated the people who were brought to the camp.

A: Because the people who were brought to the camp were designated for extermination, they were treated accordingly. Human life was worthless. Franz, who was very cruel, and the other Germans could shoot Jews for any reason, and they frequently did. I saw this myself. All of the Germans walked around the camp carrying whips, which they used frequently. Franz regularly set his dog on people. The *Zugwachmänner* beat people as well. Binnemann, for example, was also very cruel. The *Wachmänner* were cruel also.

Q: How many dogs were owned by Germans and *Wachmänner* in the camp?

A: A very large dog named Barry was owned by Franz, the deputy camp commander. Also, as I remember, *Zugwachmann* Schultz, who worked in the camp headquarters, and the motor operator Nikolai Shalayev owned dogs.

Q: What did you do during your service in the SS special detachment in the city of Lublin?

A: From February or March 1942 until July 1942, our service there consisted of guarding the Jewish ghetto and also rounding up Jews from the ghetto for deportation to various death camps. The Jewish ghetto occupied a section of the city on the outskirts of Lublin and consisted of a group of houses surrounded by barbed wire. Our job was not to allow anyone out of or into the ghetto. The Jews who were held in the ghetto were periodically deported by railcars to death camps. We escorted them in groups of 600–700 at a time, to the Lublin station, and loaded them onto trains, which were sent away. By July 1942, all the Jews in the Lublin ghetto had been sent away in this manner. I knew they had been sent away to death camps, because I once escorted one of these trains as a guard. This was in May or

June 1942. This train, carrying 600 Jews, was taken to . . . I believe it was Sobibor. It was located in the woods about 100 miles from Lublin. Other than guarding and deporting the Jews from the ghetto, we escorted [those] Jews to work who were held as a work detail in a large camp for Soviet POWs located on the outskirts of Lublin. We brought them to the opposite side of the city from there to work laying cable. This was in June 1942.

There were incidents of Jews being shot in Lublin, even mass shootings. I did not personally participate in these shootings, but other *Wachmänner* from our group were taken along by the Germans. They drove the Jews into the woods and shot them there. Other *Wachmänner* who participated in these operations told me of this, including Semen Pashkov.

Q: Name your fellow service members in the SS forces.

A: I remember the following:

> Semen Pashkov: born in Voronezh region
>
> Vasilenko: Served with me in Treblinka. He participated in the shooting of 150 Jews outside the camp zone.
>
> Alexander Yeger: A platoon commander in Treblinka. I was in his platoon.
>
> Yakov Vazin: a German from the Saratov region
>
> Skydan: served in Treblinka
>
> Alexander Rittich: Served at Treblinka. From the Caucasus region.
>
> Biennemann: A Volksdeutscher from the USSR. Served as a *Zugwachmann* in Treblinka. Then served in Italy. Very cruel.
>
> Robertus: From the Saratov region. Served as a *Zugwachmann* in Treblinka. Then served in Italy.
>
> Nikolai Shalayev: served as a motor operator in Treblinka
>
> Ivan Tsitsurin: Born in Voronezh. Served in Treblinka.
>
> Ivan Terekhov: Born in Voronezh region. Served in Treblinka with me in Yeger's platoon.
>
> Vasili Shishayev: Born in Voronezh region. Served in Treblinka.
>
> Skakodub: served in Treblinka
>
> Petr Shilov: Born in Voronezh region. Served in Treblinka.
>
> Tadich: Born in Voronezh region. Served in Treblinka, from where he escaped in July 1943.
>
> Grigorij Rubez: Born in Voronezh region. Served in Treblinka.
>
> Kulak: Served in Treblinka. His statement was read to me during the investigation into my case.
>
> Dimitri Borodin: I do not remember if he served at Treblinka with me.
>
> Schultz: A Volksdeutscher from the USSR. Served in Treblinka in the camp headquarters. He was a clerk and held the rank of *Zugwachmann*.

Q: Do you know Levchishin, Kuzminskij, Karplyuk, Tkachuk, Parfinyuk, Ryabeka, Pritsch, Govorov, or Gorbachev from service in the SS forces?

A: I do not remember any of those named. It is possible that they might have served with me, but I do not remember those names.

Q: Did you know Wachmann Ivan Kurinnij from service at Treblinka?

A: I am not familiar with that name.

The interrogation protocol was read to me. It was recorded from my words correctly. [Signature] Ryabtsev

Interrogated by senior investigator, Investigations Department, KGB, Kaliningrad region, Captain V. Shabanov

The original interrogation protocol is located in the investigation file #14, charging Schultz, a.k.a. Vertogradov, and others, which is held with the KGB in Vinnitsa region.

True copy:

Office director

Procurator's Office of the USSR, E. F. Vladimirov

Copy made from a copy located in the archival criminal file #66437 (volume 17, pp. 32–37), charging Schultz (a.k.a. Vertogradov) and others. [Signature] Vladimirov

Archive of the Federal Counterintelligence Service of the Russian Federation, Krasnodar District, Protocol of Interrogation, Nikolai Leontev[21]

June 30, 1964

City of Krasnodar

Nikolai Semenovich Leontev, born 1917 in Penza region, Russia; not a party member, convicted in 1948 by a military tribunal in accordance with Article 58-1b of the Criminal Code of the Russian Soviet Federated Socialist Republic to fifteen years of imprisonment in corrective labor camps, and released in June 1956. Lives in the city of Penza and works as a mechanic at a clock factory.

Concerning the activities of the SS forces and the traitors of the Motherland serving in its ranks, I state the following: While serving in the Red Army, I was taken prisoner by the enemy in around November 1941. The Germans selected about thirty to forty men from the POW camp in Chelm and transported us in vehicles to the town of Trawniki (Poland). This group included myself, Korzhikov, Ivan Khabarov, and some others I don't remember. Nothing was explained to us in Chelm, but after arriving in Trawniki, we were quartered in a training camp that trained cadres for the SS forces. In the camp were Germans and Russians in SS uniforms and undergoing military training. We were informed that we were being enlisted to serve in the SS, a questionnaire was filled out for each of us, we were photographed, and we each signed a vow of service to Nazi Germany, after which we were issued SS military uniforms and bedding.

There were more than six companies of us Russian POWs in the camp. The company commanders were German officers, and the platoon commanders were Volksdeutsche such as Traut, Akkermann, Reimer, and others. For two to three months we were trained in marching, weapons, how to perform guard duty, and commands in the German language.

In March 1942, Mikhail Korzhikov, Ivan Khabarov, and I were in a detachment of about ninety men deployed to Lublin. We were escorted there by Oberwachmänner and Gruppenwachmänner Reimer, Akkermann, Traut, and others. In Lublin we guarded some houses of the Jewish ghetto that contained property. We also took large groups of prisoners from the Majdanek concentration camp and escorted them to work. They dug a ditch where cable was going to be laid. On one occasion, we guards were driven out of Lublin and guarded a site in the forest where 250–300 people were shot in a single day. After that, we returned to Lublin.

In July 1942, our detachment deployed to Warsaw. We were there for two weeks guarding the Jewish ghetto. We then returned to Trawniki for two weeks. Then fifteen of us were assigned to the Belzec death camp. The camp was separated into three zones, which were divided from each other by barbed wire. One of these zones, which faced the town of Belzec, had three barracks, a kitchen, and a cafeteria. The *Wachmänner* and other staff lived in this zone. The Jewish labor detachment lived in the only barracks in the next zone. They unloaded the bodies of people killed in the gas chambers, and buried them. The third zone of the camp was where the people were killed.

When trains arrived, people had to turn in their valuables and get undressed. The women had all their hair cut off. When all the chambers were filled with people, exhaust gas was conducted through a pipe system into the chambers and poisoned the people inside. Death occurred in fifteen to twenty minutes.

The zone where people were suffocated had some large trenches where the bodies were buried. Later, some rails were erected on a scaffolding, and large stacks of the bodies were laid on top and burned. The bonfires of the bodies burned around the clock.

When we arrived in Belzec, an SS detachment was already there. The members I remember were *Wachmänner* Ivan Voloshin, Alexander Dukhno, Vasilij Podenok, Litus, Kozlovskij, Petr Brovtsev, Sirota, Krivonos, Kiryanov, and some others whom I do not remember. The *Zugwachmänner* were Schmidt and Schneider, and *Gruppenwachmann* Alexeyev. I arrived in the camp with Korzhikov, Khabarov, Baskakov, and Treshin.

Almost every day, trains arrived in the camp from Poland, Germany, Czechoslovakia, Romania, France, and the western areas of the Soviet Union, bringing Jewish citizens who were exterminated by suffocation in gas chambers or by shooting. The victims included men, women, and children of all ages. When the trains arrived, all SS men not on specific guard duty detail participated in the extermination process, including unloading the people from the railroad cars, escorting them to the undressing rooms, and pushing them into the gas chambers. Each week, we participated in three or four actions involving the extermination process.

While serving in these duties, I often saw the German officers, Zugwachmänner Schmidt and Schneider, and *Wachmänner* Podenok, Kozlovskij, and others armed with whips and clubs beat the victims to force them to undress. Then the victims were chased into the gas chambers by these same men. In other instances, I myself helped those men I have named push the victims into the gas chambers, but I did not use such brutality against the people as they did.

Statement was accepted and recorded by senior investigator of the KGB, Krasnodar District, Major [illegible signature]
Archive of the Federal Counterintelligence Service of the Russian Federation, Krasnodar District[22]

Protocol of Interrogation, Mikhail Korzhikov
September 9, 1964
City of Krasnodar
Senior investigator of the Investigations Department of the KGB, Krasnodar District, interrogated the witness: Mikhail Egorovich Korzhikov, born 1921 in Orenburg region, Russia, not a party member, convicted by a military tribunal in 1947 in accordance with Article 58-1b of the Criminal Code of the Russian Soviet Federated Socialist Republic, to twenty-five years of imprisonment in corrective labor camps, but released in 1956 in an "amnesty." He lives in the town of Kuvandyk, Orenburg region, and works as an assistant excavator mechanic.

The witness responsibilities stipulated by Article 73 of the Russian-Soviet Code of Criminal Procedure were explained to Korzhikov, and he was warned about the criminal liability for providing false testimony or refusing to give testimony, in accordance with Articles 181 and 182 of the Russian-Soviet Criminal Code.

In response to questions asked about the activities of traitors to the Motherland serving in the SS forces, he testified as follows: In November 1941, while I was serving in the Red Army, I was taken prisoner by the enemy, and I found myself in a group of thirty men who were supposedly selected to be used on a work project, but instead the Germans transported us in a vehicle from the POW camp in the town of Chelm (Poland) to the town of Trawniki.

After arriving there, we were quartered in some kind of estate surrounded by a stone wall, and without any request for our agreement, we were enlisted into the service of the SS. The SS officers were quartered in stone buildings, and we, dressed in SS uniforms and undergoing military training, lived in barracks.

After being enlisted to serve, a questionnaire on each of us was filled out in the staff office, we were photographed, and we signed an "obligation of service" form, after which we were issued SS uniforms and bed linens.

At Trawniki, the place where we had been brought, we learned that this was a training school where we would be trained as SS guard troops. Marching drill was taught to us by Volksdeutsche who had the ranks of *Oberwachmann, Gruppenwachmann*, and *Zugwachmann*. The individual Volksdeutscher I remember were Reimer, Traut, and Akkermann, and the other trainees in my unit were Nikolai Leontev, Alexander Melnikov, Alexander Surayev, Stepan Vershinin, Vasilij Kiryanov, Ivan Khabarov, and Semen Morin, and I don't remember any other names.

During the course of two to three months in Trawniki, we underwent instruction in marching drill, procedures for carrying out guard duty, weapons training, and learning commands in the German language. There were about twelve companies formed from us POWs who went through this military training.

After training was complete, we were all given the rank of *Wachmann*. In March 1942, our company deployed to Lublin. Three German officers went with us. One of them was the company commander, and the other two were platoon commanders. In Lublin we were quartered in the city center and remained until June 1942 guarding the Jewish ghetto, which occupied a large number of residential blocks. At various times, prisoners in the ghetto were taken away in columns of 1,000 or more, including men, women, and children, with the participation of Volksdeutsche such as Reimer and Akkermann, and us SS *Wachmänner*. We escorted them to the railroad station and loaded them into freight cars. While putting them in, the Germans beat them with whips, and the SS *Wachmänner* shoved them with rifle butts to make them get in faster. I personally helped load people into the cars but did not use force. I do not know the destination of where these trains were taken.

Also in Lublin, the other *Wachmänner* and I occasionally escorted groups of 100–200 prisoners from Majdanek concentration camp. We would escort them into town and guard them while they worked constructing a building or laying some kind of cable n trenches. After the work was done, we took the prisoners back to Majdanek.

One day, a group of about twenty of us SS guards were driven about 10 miles out of Lublin in a vehicle and were unloaded onto a highway. Our commander and his deputy arrived by car. *Gruppenwachmann* Akkermann and Reimer were with us. The *Wachmänner* with me included Vershinin, Khabarov, Leontev, and others whom I do not remember. Twenty-five to thirty people—men, women, and children—were delivered in a covered truck to the same spot that we were at. On orders from the Germans, these people climbed out of the truck. We surrounded them and led them down a country road into the forest. Some of the people started to cry when they realized that they were being led to their deaths. In the forest was a large pit that had been dug. Standing at this pit were four SD officers. They were armed with submachine guns. The people we escorted were ordered to sit down on the ground about 15–20 meters from the pit. We *Wachmänner* were positioned around the execution site. On orders from the Germans, Akkermann, Reimer, and another *Gruppenwachmann* used their rifle butts to hit the terrified people, to make them stand up, and they were pushed to the pit in groups of five to seven people at a time, and then they were shot by the German officers and Volksdeutsche. After the people were finished off, we repeated this process with several other groups of people brought to the forest, until about 250–300 people were shot in total. After this we returned to Lublin.

In June 1942, I left Lublin with my company and we traveled to Warsaw. For two weeks there, we guarded the Jewish ghetto. Then, about twelve of us were returned to Trawniki, where we spent two weeks doing basically nothing. In July 1942, twelve to fifteen of us SS guards were sent to serve in a mass extermination camp located in the town of Belzhets (Belzec), on the Soviet-Polish border.

Belzec camp measured 400 meters long by 250–300 meters wide. It was surrounded by two rows of barbed wire. Two sides of the camp were camouflaged with trees. A railroad spur from the train station entered the camp. The camp was surrounded by guard towers. One of these towers was equipped with a machine gun inside the camp. A separate half of the camp was equipped to exterminate people. There were five barracks along the platform of the railroad tracks at the camp entrance. Two were for storing the victims' belongings when they arrived, and the other three were undressing rooms for the victims. Money and valuables were handed over at the so-called cashier's office, and then the women's hair was cut off. A corridor with wire fencing on both sides then led to the gas chambers. There were six gas chambers altogether, separated into two sets of three chambers by an internal corridor within the building. The chambers were equipped with a pipe system that was connected to a motor outside. Near the gas chambers were some large, excavated trenches where the bodies of those murdered were buried. Later, the bodies were burned on some rails that were set up on scaffolding.

The camp commandant's headquarters was located outside the camp. The commandant was a German officer with the rank of *Stabsscharführer* (staff sergeant). I do not remember his name. There were eight other officers besides him, but I remember only the names Schwarz and Franz. When I arrived in Belzec camp, I was accompanied by Nikolai Leontev, Ivan Khabarov, Alexander Melnikov, and some others whom I do not remember. An SS detachment was already posted in the camp when we arrived. I later became acquainted with and still remember the following SS men: *Zugwachmänner* Siebert, Schmidt, and Schneider; *Oberwachmann* Alexeyev; and *Wachmänner* Ivan Voloshin, Ivan Zakota, Alexander Dukhno, Mikhail Gavrilyuk, Alexander Bogdanov, Olejnik, Vasilij Podenok, Timoshkin, Nikolaj Dotsenko, Petr Brovtsev, Tikhonovskij, Zakharov, Kirillov, Ivan Baskakov, Emelyanov, and Lysak.

During my service at Belzec camp, each of us SS men was assigned at various times to details guarding the camp and helped unload the people from the train cars, forced the people to undress, then beat them with clubs or whips and chased them into the gas chambers. The gas chambers could simultaneously hold more than 800 people, who were killed by the exhaust gas that was blown into the chambers by the motor.

The trains that arrived in the camp came from Poland, Czechoslovakia, the western areas of Ukraine, and other countries. I can say that Soviet citizens were brought to be exterminated in the camp, because I heard many of these people talking among themselves in Russian or Ukrainian.

During a typical extermination operation, this is what occurred: A train would arrive and perhaps eight cars would enter the camp along the unloading platform. Present to receive the people were the commandant; the officers Schwarz, Franz, and others; *Zugwachmänner* Siebert, Schmidt, and Schneider; *Oberwachmann* Alexeyev; and *Wachmänner* Zakharov, Podenok, Tikhonovskij, and Semenov (whom I came to know well during our service together), and some others. The Germans and SS men I named were carrying whips and clubs.

I was assigned with some other *Wachmänner* to guard the train cars and undressing rooms. The train cars were opened and the people inside were ordered out. Anyone who didn't get out quickly enough was pushed out. Then a German and a Jewish *kapo* told the people that they were to wash themselves in the "bathhouse" and would then travel on to some labor project. On instructions, the people left their baggage and outer clothing in two barracks. Then everyone undressed in barracks, men and women separately. While I was with the other *Wachmänner* in the detail guarding the undressing rooms, we saw some people getting undressed, but other people hesitated and looked upset because they sensed that something was wrong. Women then had their hair cut off. We then joined the other *Wachmänner* whose names I have mentioned above, and formed a semicircle around the victims and chased them into the corridor that led to the gassing facility.

The victims in a single transport numbered in the hundreds. The victims cried; women and children in particular screamed in despair. The SS and guards paid no attention. The Germans and Schmidt, Schneider, Alexeyev, Podenok, and Tikhonovskij beat the victims with whips and clubs up to the very doors of the gas chambers, pushing them inside. Once everyone was inside, the doors were closed and the motor started to blow the exhaust gas into the chambers. Horrible screams were heard, and the people inside died within twenty to twenty-five minutes. Then the doors were opened and the Jewish labor detachment pulled the bodies out.

Trains full of people arrived every day in the camp. During my service at Belzec camp from summer 1942 until March 1943, except for those days when I did routine camp guard duty, the other SS men and I constantly assisted in the actions involving mass murder.

I named Vasilij Podenok as a guard who often helped undress and shove the victims into the gas chambers. Podenok tried to appear disciplined whenever he was in view of the German officers and *Zugwachmänner*. When trains arrived, he tried to put himself into a position where he could show the Germans his capabilities or where he could take as much money and as many valuables from the people as possible. When assigning the details to carry out this or that duty involved in the killing process, Zugwachmann Schmidt or Schneider often took Podenok and similar *Wachmänner* into their group that was to force the people to undress and to push them into the gas chambers. They distinguished themselves with their extreme brutality, so the *Zugwachmänner* knew them. Tikhonovskij, Alexeyev, and Zakharov also made strong impressions on me. They too often helped push people into the gas chambers, beating them as they undressed beforehand.

Interrogated by senior investigator of the Investigations Department, KGB, Krasnodar District
Senior investigator of the KGB, Major [illegible]

Excerpt of Protocol of Interrogation, Grigorij Kniga[23]
December 9, 1964
City of Krasnodar
I, senior investigator of the KGB in the Krasnodar region, 1st Lieutenant Metelkin, complying with the requirements of Article 158 and 160 of the Criminal Code of the Russian Soviet Federated Socialist Republic, interrogated the following person as a witness: Grigorij Efimovich Kniga, born 1910 in Dnepropetrovsk region, Ukraine. No party affiliation, barely literate. Works as a member of the Ingulyatsk Geological Exploration crew. He resides in Dnepropetrovsk region and is married. He was tried in 1949 under Article 54-1b of the Criminal Code of the Ukrainian Soviet Socialist Republic and sentenced to twenty-five years of ITL (corrective labor camps).

The witness received an explanation of his responsibilities under Article 73 of the Criminal Code and was warned about his criminal liability for refusing or evading from providing testimony under Article 182 of the Criminal Code, and for knowingly giving false testimony under Article 181 of the Criminal Code.

On the subject matter, the witness testified: On May 28, 1941, I was drafted into the Red Army and was assigned as a private in a communications battalion.

December 10, 1964

Q: Continue your testimony about the practices of the *Wachmänner* unit at the Belzec death camp in regard to executing the civilian population.

A: Yesterday, during my interrogation, I talked about the location of the Belzec death camp and described the crimes against the prisoners. The camp was truly a death camp in every sense of the word. Prisoners were executed immediately upon arrival in gas chambers. I was in the camp from spring or summer 1942 until fall 1943. During that time, civilians were executed almost every day on a massive scale. Upon arrival of the crowded trains into Belzec station, all *Wachmänner* not on specific guard duty were called in and had to be involved in the operation. We were placed in a surrounding position around the train, or part of it. Our goal was to prevent escapes of the newly arriving people.

December 11, 1964

Q: On your case in 1949, you did not disclose your service at the Belzec death camp. Why didn't you?

A: Because after my arrest, the investigation authorities pressed charges against me on serving in the SS forces in Trawniki, Auschwitz, and Buchenwald. I was never charged with serving at Belzec; that's why I thought that since the authorities knew nothing about that, then I shall keep secret about my service there, and that is the reason why I did not tell about Belzec. If the investigators had charged me with serving there, I would not have hidden this information.

Q: Then why now, during this interrogation, don't you want to truthfully tell about the involvement of *Wachmänner* in executions at Belzec?

A: During the previous interrogation process, I testified and told everything that I knew about this matter. During yesterday's interrogation I testified that the most-active contributors to the mass executions in Belzec were Schmidt, Schwartz, Siebert, Schneider, Kunz, and the camp commandant, whose name I don't recall, as well as other German officers and *Zugwachmänner*.

Protocol of Interrogation, Alexander Zakharov[24]

January 8, 1965

City of Krasnodar

I, senior investigator of the KGB in the Krasnodar region, 1st Lieutenant Metelkin, complying with the requirements of Article 158-160 of the Criminal Code of the Russian Soviet Federated Socialist Republic, interrogated the following person as a witness: Alexander Sergeyevich Zakharov, born 1915 in the city of Irkutsk, Russia. No party affiliation, married, has seven years of education, and resides in the city of Novgorod. He was tried in 1947 by the military tribunal of the MVD forces in Moscow region under Article 58-1b of the Criminal Code of the Russian Soviet Federated Socialist Republic and sentenced to twenty-five years of ITL (corrective labor camps).

The witness responsibilities, in accordance with Article 73 of the Criminal Code, were explained to the witness. He was also warned about criminal liability for refusing to provide testimony or knowingly giving false testimony under Article 181-182 of the Criminal Code.

Q: Did you serve at the Belzec death camp during the years of the Great Patriotic War, and what do you know about the crimes that were committed there?
A: Yes, I did serve at the Belzec death camp, from spring 1942 until fall 1943, up until it was closed down. However, there was a break during my service, because in November 1942 I got sick with relapsing typhoid fever and was placed in a hospital in the town of Tomashev. The illness caused complications, so I was sick until almost the spring of 1943.

January 9, 1965
Q: Continue your testimony in regard to the crimes committed at the Belzec death camp.
A: Yesterday, during the interrogation, I told the court about the general location of the camp and that railroad trains, filled with people of Jewish nationality, arrived in the camp. As soon as the convoys with people started arriving, we *Wachmänner* had to deal with their extermination. We received the trains daily, sometimes two sets per day. As soon as they arrived, the extermination process would commence immediately. The killing was normally done by the method of gas chamber, but some people were also executed by firing squad.
In response to another question, the witness gave the following answer: In Belzec, I served under the last name Pruss. I got this name even before joining the SS, while I was in a POW camp. I took this name because I wanted to appear as a Volksdeutscher, hoping that I would be removed from the POW camp to work somewhere.
Q: Why didn't you, either during the investigation of your own case or during the trial, identify Vasili Podenok, who was among those whom you knew during service in the SS, but now you are giving testimony about him?
A: During the investigation I wasn't asked about him, and I did not name him because it simply did not occur to me. If interest would have been expressed about Podenok during the investigation, then I would have named him, since I remember him very well.

The protocol of interrogation has been read to me and documented from my words accurately.
[Signature] Zakharov
Interrogated by senior investigator of the Investigations Department of the KGB of Krasnodar region, Senior Lieutenant Metelkin
Note: The original document is located in criminal case #4, charging Tikhonovskij, Podenok, et al., and is stored in the archive of the KGB Criminal Codes section. [Signature] Senior Lieutenant Metelkin

Protocol of Interrogation, Zaki Tuktarov[25]
February 1, 1965
City of Krasnodar
I, senior investigator of the KGB for the Krasnodar District, Captain Pavlyukov, interrogated the following person as a witness in compliance with the requirements of Articles 158 and 160 of the Criminal Code of the Russian Soviet Federated Socialist Republic: Zaki Idrisovich Tuktarov, born 1918 in Saratov region. He is of Tatar nationality. He has no party affiliation and a four-year education. He worked as an order placer for a village consumer office. Was convicted in 1948 under Article 58-1b of the Russian Soviet Criminal Code and was sentenced to twenty-five years of ITL (corrective labor camps). He was released in 1955. He resides

in the city of Kadievka, Lugansk region, Ukraine. He possesses a military ID booklet issued in 1964 by the Kadievka city military commissariat. He is married with two children.

The witness was explained his responsibilities under Article 73 of the Criminal Code and was warned of his criminal liabilities under Article 182 of the Criminal Code for refusing to give or avoiding giving a statement, and under Article 181 of the Criminal Code for knowingly giving false statements.

In response to the questions posed, the witness stated the following: While serving in the Red Army as a soldier, I was captured by the Germans in July 1941. Having gone through several camps for POWs, in spring 1942 I ended up in a camp for POWs in the town of Majdan [Majdanek] (Poland). One day in spring 1942, all of us POWs were put in formation, and the Germans selected about thirty of us who were of Tatar nationality. I was among those selected. We were allegedly being selected for work. We were put on a train and sent to the town of Trawniki. There was an SS training camp located there. Upon arrival in this camp, a form was completed on each of us. We were photographed, and each of us signed a commitment to serve the Germans. We were issued SS military uniforms and linens. We had been enlisted in the SS forces. We underwent military training for about two months. We were called *Wachmänner* (guards).

In summer 1942, I was part of a 150-man *Wachmänner* company sent to the city of Lublin. We were escorted there by a German and *Gruppenwachmann* Akkermann. In Lublin, we were housed in three or four barracks. We guarded a Jewish camp where prisoners worked in various types of shops. Soon afterward, I was sent along with a *Wachmänner* detachment to serve at the Majdanek concentration camp.

Majdanek was large. It was surrounded by two rows of barbed wire. There were guard towers with machine guns located every 150–200 meters around the camp. The prisoners were held in barracks. There was a gassing facility located near our barracks. Each chamber could hold over 200 people. A large pipe opening was built into the roof. This facility was used to kill prisoners with some type of poisonous substance. I do not know what type of poison it was. The camp also had a crematorium. The prisoners' bodies were burned there.

Several tens of thousands of prisoners were held in this camp. They included Jews, Poles, Soviet POWs, and others. Prisoners were not fed enough and had to do heavy physical labor. Once prisoners were too emaciated to work, they were taken to the gassing facility and exterminated. The tasks of the *Wachmänner* at Majdanek were to guard the prisoners, escort them to work, participate in unloading newly arrived prisoners from the trains, and push the prisoners no longer suitable for work into the gas chambers.

I served in Majdanek from summer 1942 to January or February 1943. During that time, I participated along with the other SS men in guarding and exterminating camp prisoners. The following persons also served with me in this camp: *Gruppenwachmann* Akkermann, Oberwachmann Denisenko, and *Wachmänner* Tusin, Gilmiyarov, Shvejko, Sabirov, and Vasili Oljunin. I do not remember any other names. Just like me, they all participated in guarding and escorting prisoners to work and pushing prisoners no longer suitable for work into the gas chambers. These were our normal daily duties. I personally had to participate in pushing people into the gassing facility on about three occasions.

On one particular occasion in fall 1942, a *Gruppenwachmann* whose name I do not remember, but who was Latvian, selected a group of about twelve of us *Wachmänner*. Oberwachmänner Denisenko and Tusin, and I were among those selected. I do not remember the names of the others. He brought us to the camp gates, where a group of Germans were waiting. Some of these Germans, as well as the Latvian *Gruppenwachmann* and *Oberwachmann* Denisenko, each with a whip or stick in his hand, entered a barracks, and then two or three other barracks, and they forced out the prisoners who were emaciated and no longer suitable for work. While being driven out, the prisoners were pushed and hit with the whips and sticks. There was yelling. We surrounded them and forced them into the gassing facility. On this occasion, about 350–400 male prisoners were forced into the gassing facility. I participated on two other occasions in putting people in the gassing facility along with Akkermann, Sabirov, Oljunin and other *Wachmänner*. Each time we put about 300–400 people to death. I do not remember any incidents of shootings of prisoners at Majdanek. Usually they were all killed in the gassing facility.

From Majdanek, I was sent back to Trawniki and then assigned to serve in the SS detachment in Radom.

The interrogation protocol was read to me by the investigator at my request. The statement was recorded from my words accurately. [Signature] Tuktarov
Interrogated by senior investigator of the KGB for Krasnodar District, Captain N. Pavlyukov
Note: The original of this document is located in criminal file #4, which charges Nikiforov and others. The file is stored with the KGB in the Krasnodar District.

Protocol of Interrogation, Prokofij Ryabtsev[26]
February 3, 1965
City of Krasnodar
I, senior investigator of the KGB for Krasnodar District, Captain Pavlyukov, in compliance with the requirements of Articles 158 and 160 of the Criminal Code of the Russian Soviet Federated Socialist Republic, interrogated the following person as a witness: Prokofij Niolayevich Ryabtsev, born 1915 in Voronezh region, Russia. No party affiliation, four years of education, works as a mason for the collective farm construction administration. He was tried in 1948 under Article 58-1b of the Criminal Code and sentenced to twenty-five years of ITL (corrective labor camp imprisonment). He was released on January 9, 1962, and has since lived in Kavkaz District, Krasnodar region.

His obligations, as listed under Article 73 of the Criminal Code of the Russian Soviet Federated Socialist Republic, were explained to him as a witness. He was also warned about his criminal liability under Article 182 of the Criminal Code for refusing to provide a statement, and under Article 181 of the Criminal Code for knowingly providing false statements.

On the substance of the questions posed to me, I can state the following: While serving at the front during the Patriotic War, as a soldier in a reconnaissance unit, I was captured by the Germans in late August 1941 in the area around Rovno. After this, having gone through a number of transit camps, I ended up in the Chelm POW camp in Poland in September 1941. I remained there until the end of November 1941. Then, among a group of twenty to twenty-five other POWs, I was taken by the Germans to the town of Trawniki, where there was a training camp for the SS forces. There, I signed an obligation to serve Nazi Germany, and until about February 1942 I underwent military training.

I remember that our squad commander at Trawniki was Alexander Yeger, who at the time held the rank of *Oberwachmann*. In February or March 1942, I was sent to the city of Lublin as a member of a thirty-five-to-forty-man unit of *Wachmänner*, under the command of the abovenamed *Oberwachmann* Yeger and some Germans. There, I guarded the Jewish ghetto from which the Jewish population was sent to German death camps. On one occasion, I myself had to escort a train with Jews to the Sobibor death camp.

In July 1942, I was sent as a member of a twenty-to-twenty-five-man unit of *Wachmänner* to Treblinka. In the camp I served in the platoon commanded by Zugwachmann Yeger. This was a death camp located in the woods near the village of Vulki and the Malkinia railroad station. The entire camp was surrounded by a wire barrier about 2 meters high. At the corners, there were wooden guard towers, on which machine guns were mounted. One tower was also located inside the camp, near the barracks where the prisoners from the work details lived. I was assigned to guard the work details. A machine gun was sometimes mounted on this tower as well.

The camp was not intended to hold prisoners but was for the mass extermination of the Jewish population brought to the camp from various European countries. The camp was equipped with gas chambers in which people were put to death, using gas from a diesel motor. At first, only one gas chamber was in operation, which I believe had a total of three rooms. Then another was built, the capacity of which was much higher than the first. Sick and old Jews who were unable to walk to the gas chambers were also shot at the so-called "Lazarett."

During my first days at Treblinka, the gas chambers were not yet functioning. I remember this because during this period I had to participate in the shooting of a large group of Jews, approximately 150. This was under the following circumstances: Soon after our arrival, one day, one of the *Zugwachmänner*—I don't remember his name—came to our barracks. He ordered us to take our weapons and follow him. There were about twenty or more of us in the barracks, among which I remember Sergej Vasilenko, Vladimir Chernyavskij, Petr Shilov, Nikolai Shalayev, Vasili Shilov, Vasili Usov, and Nikolaj Skakodub. I have forgotten the others. We stood in formation next to the barracks, and the *Zugwachmann* told us that on the orders of the Germans, we were to take Jews into the woods and shoot them.

The Germans took a group of about 150 Jews out of the camp. There, we along with six or seven Germans surrounded them and headed down the road into the woods toward the Treblinka labor camp. At a pit dug in the woods, we and the Germans shot these people. We shot with our rifles, and the Germans shot with pistols. Among the Germans and *Zugwachmänner* who participated in this, I remember Franz, Schmidt, and Binnemann.

When the doomed people were escorted to the gas chamber, one or two Jews from the work detail, as a rule, walked in front of the group along the path and continued to reassure the victims that they were being taken to a "bathhouse." On both sides of the wire barrier interwoven with branches stood *Wachmänner* for the purpose of preventing escapes. Behind the people walking along the path to the gas chamber, the Germans, *Zugwachmänner*, *Oberwachmänner*, and *Wachmänner* followed with whips and weapons. If they sensed slowness or resistance by the people, they would hit them with whips and rifle butts, and sometimes they set dogs on them. The *Wachmänner* helped push people by force into the gas chamber. The people entering the gas chamber corridor were pushed into the chambers. This was done, as a rule, by the Germans and the motor operators Nikolai Shalayev and Ivan Marchenko, and also by *Zugwachmänner* Yeger, Binnemann, and others.

I personally did not have to force the people into the gas chambers. But I served at posts in the cordon during the unloading, along the path, and at the undressing area. From there I could see what occurred near the gas chambers, as well as inside them. Once the gas chambers were full, they were hermetically sealed, and then Nikolai Shalayev and Ivan Marchenko started the motor from which gas was fed into the chambers. After about fifteen to twenty minutes they opened the doors, and the Jewish work detail began unloading the bodies. Before taking the bodies to the pits, rings were removed from them and gold teeth were pulled out. The bodies were thrown into the pits dug by an excavator. They were later burned.

Trains with people arrived regularly for a period of about two months. About two or three trains arrived per day. Trains then began arriving less often. On days when two or three trains arrived, the gas chamber worked from morning until night. During my service in Treblinka death camp, many thousands of Jewish people who were guilty of nothing were exterminated in the gas chambers and by shooting. Among these were men, women, and children.

In the camp there was not a single German, *Zugwachmann*, *Oberwachmann*, or *Wachmann* who did not participate in unloading railcars, escorting the people into the undressing area and the gas chamber, and shooting people at the "Lazarett." This was what our duties mainly consisted of, and no one could avoid performing these duties. These duties were performed by everyone, though it is possible that some did it more often and others less often, but not a single person could avoid it.

As a rule, the *Wachmänner* participated in the extermination process in a drunken state. They could do anything to the victims that they wanted to, because the Germans did not punish us for being cruel. Quite the opposite; they rewarded it.

The interrogation protocol was read to me. The statement was correctly recorded from my words. I do not have any remarks about the protocol. [Signature] Ryabtsev
Interrogated by senior investigator of the KGB for the Krasnodar District, Captain Pavlyukov
Note: The original document is located in criminal file #4, charging N. Matvienko and others. Senior investigator. [Signature] K. N. Pavlyukov

Protocol of Interrogation, Mikhail Laptev[27]
February 27, 1965
City of Krasnodar

I, senior investigator with the KGB for Krasnodar District, Captain Pavlyukov, interrogated the following person as a witness in compliance with the requirements of Articles 158 and 160 of the Criminal Code of the Russian Soviet Federated Socialist Republic: Mikhail Ivanovich Laptev, born 1919 in Saratov region. He is Ukrainian, has no party affiliation, and has six years of education. He works as a forger on a collective farm. He has no prior convictions. He resides in Dnepropetrovsk region. He possesses a passport issued in 1938 by the Vasilkovo District Police Department. He is married and has a daughter born in 1952.
The witness was advised of his responsibilities as stipulated in Article 73 of the Criminal Code of the Russian Soviet Federated Socialist Republic, and was warned of his criminal liabilities under Article 182 of the Criminal Code for refusing to give a statement or evasion, and under Article 181 of the Criminal Code for knowingly giving false statements.

In response to the questions posed, the witness M. Laptev stated the following: Until 1945, I was known by the last name Lapot. In 1945, after being released from a screening camp, I named myself Laptev, and since that time I have identified myself with this last name. I was drafted into the Red Army in December 1939 by the Sinelsk District Military Commissariat, Dnepropetrovsk region, and was sent to the city of Leningrad. There, I underwent three months of training. After that, I was transferred to the city of Baku, where I served in an antiaircraft artillery unit. I served in Baku until the start of the Patriotic War. In winter 1941, we were sent to Kerch to protect the port from attacks by German aircraft. It was there that in May 1942, I was captured by the Germans.

From Kerch, I was taken to a POW camp in Rovno. One day in summer 1942, an SS officer and a *Zugwachmann* arrived in the camp. They selected about 200 POWs. I was among those selected. They told us right there that we were going to serve in the German army. We were each given a loaf of bread and a piece of sausage and loaded into large tarp-covered cargo vehicles. The vehicles brought us to the town of Trawniki in Poland, to the

SS training camp located there. We were issued black uniforms and equipment, a bowl, and a spoon. Then, each of us was summoned to the camp office, where a form was completed on us, and they took our fingerprint. They photographed us and had us sign a commitment to serve Germany. We were then assigned to companies and platoons and began to undergo training. I was assigned to the first platoon, first company. The following persons underwent training with me in the same platoon:

Fedor Dmitrenko: born in Odessa region, arrested and convicted
Viktor Kurskij
Anatolij Getzman: born in Krasnodar District
Stepan Statsenko
Nikolaj Kvach
Pavel Grichanik
Mikhail Yankovskij: visited me at my home in 1957 and told me he was living in
    the city of Krasnyj Luch and working as an engineer in a mine
Ivan Yastrebov

We underwent training for about two months. We were trained in drill, German commands, singing German songs, and how to perform guard duty. We also got rifle training. As part of that training, some of us shot a few elderly Jews on three or four occasions. I did not personally participate in these shootings, but I did witness them.

Our platoon commander was a *Zugwachmann*, a Pole; I do not remember his name. Our squad commander was Oberwachmann Mikhail Yankovskij. From what he told me in 1957, after helping suppress the Warsaw ghetto uprising he escaped from the SS to the partisans and was decorated with the Red Star medal.

After completing training in late summer 1942, I was sent with a group of *Wachmänner* to a village in the Lublin District to confiscate bread from peasants and landowners for the German army. With our unit were two *Oberwachmänner*; one was from Estonia, and the other was a Volksdeutscher from Russia. There was also an SS officer.

In October or November 1942, I was sent with a *Wachmänner* squad to guard a lumber mill from attacks by partisans. Among those with me were Dmitrenko, Kurskij, and Getzman. We remained there until spring 1943.

In April 1943, all of us in Trawniki were sent by rail to Warsaw to help move Jews out of the Warsaw ghetto to the death camps. In the morning, we were led in formation through the streets to the ghetto. When we approached, people from the windows of the buildings began throwing burning bottles with flammable liquids at us. These people were also armed with grenades and other weapons. We were thrown in to suppress this uprising, and there were also German military units, and even tanks. The suppression and liquidation of the ghetto took about a month.

We had rifles and grenades. We broke into the houses where the Jews were residing. We shot all of the men, women, and children. We surrounded houses from which there was resistance, set them on fire, threw grenades into the windows, and then fired through windows and doors, not allowing anyone inside an opportunity to come out alive. We gathered the men, women, and children who had run out of the houses together; took them into the ruined houses; lay them facedown on the floor; and shot them.

People hid in the basements and attics, and we found them. Those who resisted were shot on the spot. In some cases, smoke grenades were used to flush the people from their hiding places.

During the suppression of the uprising, a very large number of Jews were shot. I cannot state, however, the exact number. During the operation, I personally killed approximately thirty-four people, including men, women, and children.

From among the *Wachmänner* who participated with me in suppression of the uprising in the Warsaw ghetto, I remember the following: Anatolij Getzman, Stepan Statsenko, Nikolaj Kvach, Pavel Grichanik, Viktor Kurskij, Fedor Dmitrenko, Vasili Kravchuk, Ivan Yastrebov, and Mikhail Yankovskij, who, just as I did, shot the Jews who participated in the uprising, including men, women, and children. After suppression of the uprising, many Jews remained alive. Along with the Germans, we loaded these people into freight railcars and sent them by train to the death camps. On one occasion, I personally served as an escort on a train carrying about twenty railcars full of Jews to the Treblinka death camp. Along with another *Wachmann* I guarded the roofs of the railcars along the way. During the journey, one Jew escaped from the train while it was moving. We opened fire on him, but I do not know whether or not we killed him, because the train did not stop.

An SS officer was in charge of the convoy. I do not remember his name. The railcars were guarded by *Wachmänner*, among whom I remember Statsenko, Getzman, and Yastrebov. The train was also escorted by *Zugwachmänner* and *Oberwachmänner*, but I do not remember their names.

After the liquidation of the Warsaw ghetto, I was sent with a *Wachmänner* platoon to Krakow to guard the Plaszow labor camp for Jews. In my unit were Getzman, Statsenko, Yastrebov, and Kovalchuk. I served at Plaszow for about one year.

In the summer of 1944, along with my *Wachmänner* platoon, I was sent to the city of Hamburg to guard the Neuengamme camp. It was located about 20 miles from Hamburg. I remained there until the end of the war and upon the arrival of American forces.

Besides the *Wachmänner* I already named, I also remember Petr Krasnobaj as having served with me at Plaszow camp. In 1943, he escaped along with a group of sixteen others. During the night of the escape, he invited me to join in the escape. He and I, however, did not come to a definitive agreement, and during the night he did not wake me up. Thus, I remained in the camp. The escapees included Lukjanchuk, Lysak, Ivan Gubenko, and a *Gruppenwachmann*. I do not remember the names of the others.

During my service at the Plaszow camp, on three or four occasions I had witnessed other *Wachmänner*, *Oberwachmänner*, *Gruppenwachmänner*, *Zugwachmänner*, and Germans shoot Jews in the camp at a pit located near the central gates. The Jews were brought to the camp in vehicles, in groups of ten to fifteen and more. I cannot state exactly when these shootings were carried out. I believe it was summer 1943. Others may have occurred in 1944. I did not have occasion to participate in these shootings. Just before one of these shootings was carried out, several *Wachmänner* and I were assigned as second guards in the watchtowers in order to reinforce camp security. After the shooting, we were relieved of these posts.

In 1945, upon the approach of American forces, the Germans moved the prisoners out of the Neuengamme camp, where we were serving guard duty. We were sent to the front, which was along the Elbe River. We remained for one night in trenches. In the morning, we were captured by the Americans. After that, we were sent to Hamburg under escort, and there we were released. In Hamburg, I changed into civilian clothes and went to a civilian camp. There, before being sent to the Motherland, the Americans invited those who wanted to remain to stay with them. I did not want to remain with the Americans, so they handed me over to the Soviet authorities along with other Soviet citizens.

After returning to the Motherland, I underwent screening, where I concealed my service in the SS forces. After that, I was sent to the Donbass, Donets region, to work on the restoration of farms that had been destroyed. I worked there for a year and a half, and in early 1947 I was released to return home.

Q: Did you know the following persons from having served in the SS forces: Alexander Fedchenko, Petr Demidenko, Nikolaj Stankov, Nikolaj Svetelik, Ivan Nikiforov, Nikolaj Matvienko, Ivan Zaitsev, Fedor Tikhonovskij, Roman Savchuk, Anatolij Denisenko, Vasili Podenok, and Vasili Belyakov?
A: I do not remember any of those names, and therefore I cannot state whether I served with any of them. I have already named the persons I remember from service in the SS.
Q: Do you have any additions, clarifications, or remarks for the protocol?
A: Having personally read the protocol of interrogation, I state that everything I have stated is reflected correctly in the protocol, and therefore I have no additions, clarifications, or remarks. I have read the protocol; the statement was recorded from my words correctly. [Signature] Laptev

Interrogated by senior investigator with the KGB for the Krasnodar District, Captain Pavlyukov

Protocol of Interrogation, Vasili Podenok[28]
March 18, 1965
City of Krasnodar
I, senior investigator of the Investigations Department of the KGB in Dnepropetrovsk region, Captain Shkonda, complying with the requirements of Article 141, 142, 150, and 151 of the Criminal Code of the Russian Soviet Federated Socialist Republic, interrogated the following defendant: Vasili Efimovich Podenok, born 1919. Other personal information on him is available in the case file.

Q: What is the reason you requested to be called for examination on such short notice?
A: I addressed one of the superintendents of the confinement cell, where I am currently being detained, with a request to ask the investigator if he could urgently call me in for examination. I filed a request for this motion due to the following circumstances. Yesterday, during the interrogation, I testified that during the period of my service as a *Wachmänner* in the SS unit at Belzec camp, there was someone who served there with me, by the name of Lazorenko, whom I knew very well. During questioning, I also gave brief testimony about the crimes that were committed by Lazorenko during his service at Belzec.

During my interrogation, a face-to-face questioning took place with an individual, in regard to whom I stated that I did not know him. This person identified himself as Alexei Lazorenko. However, during the face-to-face questioning, the person next to me did not appear as the Wachmann Lazorenko that I knew.

After the face-to-face questioning, I was able to recall in my memory the appearance of that Lazorenko who served with me in Belzec, and I ascertained that I had made a mistake. The person I was confronted with yesterday was indeed that same Lazorenko from Belzec. I wanted to clarify this issue.

The record has been read to me and is understood by me. It is documented from my words correctly. [Signature] V. Podenok
Interrogated by senior investigator of the Investigations Department of the KGB in the Dnepropetrovsk region, Captain Shkonda

Verified: Senior secretary of the Military Tribunal of the Northern Caucasus Military District Major of Administrative Services Bezrukov
Note: The original document is located in the investigation case on charges against Matvienko, et al. (volume 5, pp. 145–146).

Protocol of Interrogation, Ivan Tkachuk[29]
March 25, 1965
City of Krasnodar
I, senior investigator of the KGB for Krasnodar District, Captain Pavlyukov, in accordance with Articles 158 and 160 of the Criminal Code of the Russian Soviet Federated Socialist Republic, interrogated the following person as a witness: Ivan Kondratyevich Tkachuk, born 1909 in Khmelnitskij region, Ukraine. No party affiliation, a group III invalid, tried in 1950 under Article 58-1b of the Russian Soviet Criminal Code, and sentenced to twenty-five years in a labor camp. Was released on December 3, 1955, by a decree on September 17, 1955.

The witness was notified of his responsibilities in accordance with Article 73 of the Criminal Code. He was also warned about his liability for refusing to testify or for evasion from testifying under Article 182 of the Criminal Code, and for knowingly giving false testimony under Article 181 of the Criminal Code.

On the subject matter raised in questioning, the witness testified as follows: While at the front during the Patriotic War, around August 1941, I was taken prisoner by the Germans and put in a POW camp in the town of Chelm (Poland), where, among other POWs, I was sent to do carpentry work. Then in January or February 1942, I was brought to the town of Trawniki and put in a military training camp of the SS forces. There, we went through military training. This training lasted until spring 1942. We wore German military uniforms, were given German rifles, and we took an oath to serve Nazi Germany.

We were then sent to the city of Lublin, where we guarded a cemetery and then the belongings of Jews. I remained there until summer 1942. In summer 1942, my *Wachmänner* platoon was sent to guard the Warsaw ghetto. I was there for just one day and then boarded a train for Treblinka, where I would serve as a guard. This was a death camp where Jews were brought to be suffocated in gas chambers and shot by firing squad. Among these Jews were men, women, and children.

At first, I served in a platoon commanded by *Zugwachmann* Rogoza or *Zugwachmann* Robertus, and later, in the platoon of *Zugwachmann* Yeger. I served at Treblinka until summer 1943 and then, with the help of a Polish female acquaintance, obtained false civilian documents and escaped from the camp. The woman escaped with me. We stayed in the city of Lublin. Later, we moved to the city of Gdynia, where my woman friend had a house. We lived there until 1950, and then I was exposed as a former SS man by the Polish government and was handed over to the Soviet authorities.

At the camp, the executions were carried out by an armed group of *Wachmänner*, *Oberwachmänner*, and *Zugwachmänner*. This group consisted of over 100 men, under the guidance of Germans, of whom there were twenty to twenty-five. I know the name of only one of them, the camp commandant Franz, who almost always walked around with a large dog.

Almost daily, new trains with victims would arrive in the camp. All *Wachmänner* and *Oberwachmänner* not on guard duty were assigned to take part in unloading the train cars and sealing off the area. The *Wachmänner* and *Oberwachmänner* were assigned their posts by the *Zugwachmänner*. The extermination operations were supervised by the camp commandant Franz and by other Germans. The *Wachmänner*, *Oberwachmänner*, *Zugwachmänner*, and Germans forced the victims to the undressing area. Then under the pretext of going to a bathhouse for washing, the victims were taken through a barbed-wire passage that was guarded by *Wachmänner*. The victims were pushed to the gas chambers and shoved inside. The doors were then closed, a motor would turn on, and in a few minutes, everyone inside would suffocate. Then a work group would unload the bodies from the chamber.

I personally had to take part in this extermination and also observed it from the watchtowers while on duty. I did not have to participate in firing-squad duty at the "Lazarett" because I asked my commanders not to assign me to this since I could not tolerate helpless people being executed, including small children. I saw from the watchtowers how other *Wachmänner* executed people. Wachmann Voronkov, in particular, shot a lot of people at the "Lazarett." He seemed to always be on duty there. He even bragged about shooting Jews. At first, the bodies of the dead Jews were disposed of in pits that had been dug by excavators. Later, they were burned. During my service at Treblinka death camp, very many people were killed. Likely it was hundreds of thousands or several million, but what the exact number is, I am unable to tell; I just don't know.

Q: Who do you remember among the traitors to the Motherland who served with you at the Treblinka death camp?
A: *Zugwachmänner* Pilman (Bienemann) and Strebel, *Oberwachmann* Levchishin, the motor operators of the gas chamber Marchenko and Shalayev, and *Wachmänner* Sklyudov, Vedernikov, Shilov, Kulak, Dyachenko, and Ryabtsev.
Q: Did you know a Roman Savchuk from your service at Treblinka?
A: No, I do not know him.
Q: Prior to the war, did you know any of the following individuals who served with you in the SS forces: Alexander Fedchenko, Peter Demidenko, Nikolai Stankov, Nikolaj Svetelik, Ivan Nikiforov, Nikolaj Matvienko, Ivan Zaitsev, Fedor Tikhonovskij, Anatolij Denisenko, Vasili Podenok, and Vasili Belyakov?
A: I do not know them.

The interrogation protocol has been read to me by the investigator and has been recorded from my words correctly. [Signature] Tkachuk
Interrogated by senior investigator of the KGB for the Krasnodar District, Captain Pavlyukov
True copy
Note: The original of this document is located in criminal case #4, charging N. Matvienko and others.

Excerpt of Protocol of Interrogation, Vasili Orlovskij[30]
1965
I, interrogator of the Investigations Department of the KGB of Dnepropetrovsk region, Lieutenant Tschirkin, interrogated the following person: Vasili Orlovskij, born 1921 in Berdichev, Zhitomir region, Ukraine. He resides in Ryazan region, Russia. He works as a bookkeeper on a *sovkhoz* (state farm). He was convicted under Article 58-1b of the Criminal Code of the Russian Soviet Federated Socialist Republic in May 1953 and sentenced to twenty-five years of ITL (corrective labor camps). He was released in November 1955, on the basis of the September 1955 amnesty.

During the Patriotic War, I was taken prisoner by the Germans. I was then made to serve in the SS. I served as a *Wachmann* (guard) until the end of the war. I trained at the SS training camp at Trawniki and was then detailed to the Belzec death camp. I served there until March 1943. I was then assigned to Auschwitz concentration camp, and then to Buchenwald concentration camp in Germany until the end of the war.

From Belzec, I remember serving with the following *Wachmänner*: Schmidt, Schneider, Seibert, Alexejew, Lomow, Ivan Sissoj, Vasili Schuller, Vasili Popow, Kiril Prochorenko, Grigorij Logwinow, Bardaschenko, Netschajew or Netschaj, Zacharow, Pruss, Olejnik, Mamtschur, Zagrebajew, Zuev, Linkin, Lazorenko, Keresor, and Bessmertnj. I also remember a man named Woloschin.

I remember the following *Wachmänner* who deployed to Auschwitz with me: Alexejew, Lomow, Sissoj, Schuller, Popow, Logwinow, Bardaschenko, Netschajew, Zacharow, Pruss, Olejnik, Mamtschur, Zagebajew, and Zuev. Later they also served with me at Buchenwald. I remember that in March 1943, almost the entire guard unit was relieved in Belzec as the result of the flight of several *Wachmänner* from the camp. Only Schmidt, Schneider, Siebert, and Butschak remained.

Jews were brought to the camp in trains. They were exterminated with gas. First the bodies were buried, then, later, burned. All *Wachmänner* not on guard duty had to take part when the trains arrived in camp. A contingent of *Wachmänner* watched the trains. Another contingent accompanied the Jews to the undressing rooms. Other *Wachmänner* guarded the passage to the "soul destroyer" (gas chamber). *Wachmänner* also guarded the "soul destroyer" facility. I too had to take part in this work at different times.

Participation of the *Wachmänner* in the extermination of the Jews in Belzec consisted of watching the camp grounds to prevent any escape attempts, unloading the trains, escorting the people into the undressing rooms and into the "soul destroyer," and guarding the Jewish work detachment that burned the bodies. All the *Wachmänner* whose names I've mentioned arrived in Belzec before I did, with the exception of Zagrebajew. He and I arrived together in July or August 1942. Shootings took place in a grave behind the "soul destroyer." I myself was a witness to some of these shootings. Volksdeutsche commonly took part in these shootings. Among them were Schmidt, Schneider, and Siebert.

Q: Would you recognize your former comrades Zuev, Zagrebajew, Linkin, and Lazorenko if you saw them?
A: Yes, I believe so.
Q: Do you know the following other men: Boris Babin, Albert Braun, Vasili Kotelewetz, Vasili Guntschenko, Ivan Berdnik, Vasili Grebelnj, and Valentin Bogdan?
A: All of these names are known to me. However, the only one I specifically remember serving with in Belzec is Grebelnj.

Attorney-general of the USSR

Excerpt of Protocol of Interrogation, Petr Browzew[31]
August 1965
City of Dnepropetrovsk
I, interrogator of the Investigations Department of the KGB for Dnepropetrovsk region, Lieutenant Tschirkin, interrogated the following person: Petr Browzew, born 1921 in Kalinin region, Russia. He resides in Leningrad and works as a machine fitter / metalworker. He was convicted in 1947 under Article 58-1b of the Criminal Code of the Russian Soviet Federated Socialist Republic and was sentenced to fifteen years of ITL (corrective labor camps). He was released in 1955.

I was detailed to the Belzec death camp. I was there until early March 1943 and thereafter fled to the partisans. At Belzec, I, like the other *Wachmänner*, participated directly in the extermination of the Jews. We took them from train cars and chased them into an undressing barracks. We then drove them into a passage that was fenced in with barbed wire. This passage led to the "soul destroyer" (gas chamber). All the *Wachmänner* in Belzec had to perform the same duties. We rotated duty between guarding the camp and participating in the extermination process. The guard commanders I remember are Schmidt, Schneider, and Seibert. *Wachmänner* that I remember include the following: Taras Olejnik, Zuev, Petr Alexejew, Podcnok, Ivan Dozenko, Kotscherga, Ivan Zakarov, Scheremeta, Pokatilo, Gerassim Pavlenko, Vasili Chomko, Naumenko, Ivan Voloschin, Mikhail Korshikow, Nikolai Leontev, Ivan Baskakow, Petr Litus, Netschaj, Lomow, Prochorow, Sabat, Komarow, Ivan Khabarov, Davydov, Kustychin, Timoshenko, Alexander Duchno, Popow, Nikolaj Zhuravlev, Kiritschenko, Medvedev, and Alexander Bogdanov. Schmidt, Schneider, and Siebert were always occupied with the extermination process and led it. They were always in charge of shooting the old and sick people.

Q: From your service in the SS at Belzec, do you remember the following men: Boris Babin, Albert Braun, Ivan Zagrebajew, Vasili Kotelezew, Grigorij Linkin, Alexej Lazorenko, Nikita Mamtschur, Vasili Guntschenko, Yakov Keresor, Ivan Bessmertnj, Vasili Grebelnj, and Valentin Bogdan?
A: I can no longer remember if I knew those names.

Attorney general of the USSR

Protocol of Interrogation, Kiril Prochorenko[32]
September 1965
City of Dnepropetrovsk
I, interrogator of the Investigations Department of the KGB of Dnepropetrovsk region, Captain Shkonda, interrogated the following person: Kiril Prochorenko, born 1912 in Smolensk region, Russia. Resides in Dhzankoj District, Crimean region. Works as a driver on a *sovkhoz* (state farm). He was convicted in 1949 by a military district court in Tawritschesk, under Article 58-1b of the Criminal Code of the Russian Soviet Federated Socialist Republic, and sentenced to twenty-five years of ITL (corrective labor camps). He was released in September 1955 on the basis of an amnesty issued that same month.

Q: You have been subpoenaed as a witness in proceedings against persons who served in the SS during the Patriotic War. These persons served in camps in Trawniki, Belzec, Auschwitz, and other locations. What can you say in this matter?
A: I too served in the SS during the Patriotic War. I was assigned as a *Wachmann* (guard) to Trawniki, Belzec, Lublin, and Samostje [Zamosc?]. I was not, however, at Auschwitz.
Q: Tell us about Belzec.
A: I went to Belzec in spring 1942. I arrived there with about forty other *Wachmänner* in two trucks. I was assigned to drive a truck in the camp. I was subordinate to a German named Dybala. Some *Wachmänner* worked in the barracks, the stables, or the kitchen. The rest guarded the camp. I served in Belzec until spring 1943. I worked the whole time as a driver and delivered parts for the barracks. Sometimes, I also delivered heating material, food, etc. The following persons served with me at Belzec:

Emil Kostenko: worked in carpentry
Ivan Orlovskij
Ivan Woloschin
Timoschenko: shot in the camp by the Germans
Alexej Lazorenko: sometimes took part in dismantling the barracks and transporting barracks parts
Korshikow
Nesmejan
Siebert: a Volksdeutscher
Mawrodij
Akim Zuev
Kutichin: shot in the camp by the Germans
Schmidt: a Volksdeutscher
Schneider: a Volksdeutscher
Profirij Schpak: drove around barracks parts with me

As a driver, I often left the camp. However, when I was at the camp I was able to observe the Jews being brought in in trains. They were taken to a barracks, undressed, and were then killed in gas chambers. All the men that I have named took part in this.

During the first five or six months, the bodies were thrown into giant graves. By fall 1942, a dredger was brought to the camp. With this dredger, the bodies were removed from the graves and burned on a bonfire. I don't know how many Jews were exterminated during my service at Belzec. There were very many.

As a driver, I transported parts for the barracks. These barracks were built by the Germans in 1939–1940. They were commonly located along country roads in the vicinity of Tomaschew, Lublin, and other settlement areas. The Germans later decided to disassemble them. We were tasked with this. Taking part in this with me were Mawrodij, Kostenko, Orlovskij, Zuev, and other *Wachmänner*. Kostenko and Lazorenko came with me most often because they were carpenters by trade. We brought the barracks parts to the train depot in Belzec, and they were loaded on train cars and sent off somewhere. Jews also took part in disassembling barracks.

Kostenko and Lazorenko did construction work in Belzec. I saw them build a horse stable next to the camp commandant's residence. I also saw them build barracks in the camp. But they also did ordinary guard duty when they were not occupied with other activities. When trains with Jews arrived, they took part in unloading the trains and escorting the Jews into the undressing barracks.

A group of *Wachmänner* fled from the camp in spring 1943. I remember two of them: Woloschin and Korshikow. So far as I recall, they fled at night. After the escape was discovered, all the *Wachmänner* were assembled in the dining hall. The building was surrounded by guards armed with machine guns. Some *Wachmänner* were taken for questioning. They were asked about those who had fled. Two trucks came to the camp in the morning. About fifty *Wachmänner* were returned to Trawniki. I remained in Belzec along with Kostenko, Lazorenko, Schmidt, Schneider, and Siebert. A new *Wachmänner* unit was brought in, about fifty men strong. I remained at the camp for about one more month. I then transferred to Lublin. Kostenko, Lazorenko, Schmidt, Schneider, and Siebert remained in Belzec after I left.

Attorney-general of the USSR

Protocol of Interrogation, Vasili Litvinenko[33]
January 19, 1968
City of Lvov
I, senior investigator with the KGB of the Lvov region, Captain Malykhin, interrogated the following person regarding the case in which he was previously convicted. The interrogation took place at the KGB duty office: Vasilij Nikiforovich Litvinenko, born 1918. Other information on him is contained in the protocol dated January 18, 1968.

Q: During interrogation on January 18, you stated that while carrying out a punitive operation against citizens in the town of Biala Podlaska, you escorted physically healthy men in vehicles to the Majdanek death camp. You also stated that when you returned to Biala Podlaska, the remaining citizens had already been shot in the woods. During the trial proceedings against Prikhodko, Minochkin, Pankratov, and others in December 1966, you stated the following: "We were deployed from Lublin on a punitive operation to a local town, where we forced the Jewish citizens out of their homes and into a square. I escorted people to a shooting site, escorted them to the Majdanek camp, and stood in a cordon. The people were tied together with rope to prevent anyone from escaping. The people were escorted into the woods. A pit had already been dug there. We led the people to the pit in groups. The Germans then shot them." Describe how this occurred.

A: I did in fact participate, in April 1943, in a punitive operation against Jewish citizens in Biala Podlaska. I personally escorted male detainees in vehicles to the Majdanek camp. I made four such trips with prisoners that day. I escorted about 100 Jewish male detainees to the camp. I did not escort the other people, including women and children, to the shooting site. I did see other *Wachmänner* escorting these people into the woods. I stood in a cordon to make sure none of these people escaped as they were being escorted to the woods to be shot. Along with other *Wachmänner*, I forced the people to the pit, and the Germans shot them. The people were also shot by *Wachmänner* Yarosh, Vatrich, and others whose names I cannot remember. When I was interrogated as a witness in December 1966 during the trial of Pankratov, Minochkin, and others, I stated the same testimony as I am stating here.

Q: You were interrogated as a witness in Lvov on April 15, 1966. On that occasion you stated that while carrying out the punitive operation in Biala Podlaska, you escorted about 150 people about 1 mile from the town into the woods where they were shot. What caused you to change your statement today?

A: I do not wish to conceal anything from the investigation organs, and I wish to clarify my statement on this issue: I escorted about 100 men to Majdanek. Then, having returned, the other *Wachmänner* and I pushed along the people to a pit. I cannot explain why I stated during previous interrogations that during the conduct of the punitive operation in Biala Podlaska, I only escorted detained men to the Majdanek camp.

Q: State who served with you in the *SS Wachmänner* detachment that guarded the Janowska camp in Lvov.

A: I remember Pankratov, Lemeshev, Gordejew, Matvienko, Minochkin, Kovalev, Stankevich, Dmitriev, Butenko, Malov, Razanov, Belyakov, Melnik, and Beseda. All of them participated in escorting the prisoners of the camp to the shooting site in the ravine, just as I did. The shooting site was called "Piaski." This occurred during a three-day shooting of prisoners that was carried out in early June 1943. I remember that Pankratov shot five prisoners with his rifle while escorting them to the shooting site. The prisoners had been walking too slowly and slowing up the rest of the column. I personally shot an elderly female prisoner while escorting a group of prisoners to the shooting site. She was walking too slowly.

Q: How many prisoners were shot during this three-day shooting?

A: I cannot state the number. The prisoners were shot without interruption from morning till night. In December 1966, during the trial against former *SS Wachmänner* Minochkin, Pankratov, and others, the defendants and some of the witnesses stated that about 15,000 prisoners in Janowska camp were exterminated during the three-day shooting.

Q: It has been established that about 4,000 prisoners were shot in one day at the Janowska camp in summer 1943. After some time, another 400 prisoners were shot. State what you know about these shootings.

A: I was in the Janowska camp from May to August 1943. I participated only in the abovementioned three-day shootings. I learned that the Germans carried out several more mass shootings of prisoners in the camp only during the 1966 investigation into the criminal activities of former *SS Wachmänner* Minochkin, Pankratov, and others.

Q: Why did you conceal your criminal activities as an *SS Wachmänner* during the investigation into your own case in 1949?

A: Because I feared harsh punishment

Q: Tell us more about your service in the SS forces.

A: Regarding the three-day shooting operation in Janowska camp, I escorted prisoners to the shooting site. Along the way, I told the people that they were going to be shot and that if they had any valuables in their possession, that they should give them to me. Some of the prisoners gave me their gold and paper money. I exchanged these valuables and money for vodka and began to drink heavily. It had gotten to the point that I had sold my uniform pants for vodka. *Zugwachmann* Malov locked me in a cellar for about a week for this. In early August 1943, I was sent back to Trawniki and issued a new uniform. As I remember, Wachmänner Kurdenkov, Melnik, and Vetrigan arrived back in Trawniki along with me from Janowska. On October 1, 1943, I was sent in an eighty-man *Wachmänner* detachment for service in Flossenburg concentration camp.

In fall 1944, I was sent with a twenty-five-man *Wachmänner* detachment to Komutau/ Chomutov, near Prague in Czechoslovakia. There, we guarded a castle in which imprisoned members of the Romanian government were held. There were about thirty of them held there. In late January 1945, we returned to Flossenburg. In March or April 1945, the Germans began to send us *Wachmänner* to serve in the so-called Russian Liberation Army, which was commanded by the traitor to the Motherland Vlasov. Wachmann Beseda and I arrived in the city of Goldberg, where the Vlasov units were located. We did not want to join these units, so we escaped and ran to Austria. I found work for a farmer in Grieskirchen. On May 7, 1945, American forces entered Grieskirchen. Representatives of the Red Army command arrived in this city in the same month. I concealed the fact that I had served for the SS from the Soviet organs, and I was called up to serve in the Red Army. In December 1945, I was demobilized and arrived home to my family in Kiev region.

I have read the protocol. Is is recorded from my words correctly. [Signature] V. Litvinenko Senior investigator with the KGB of Lvov region, Captain Malykhin

Protocol of Interrogation, Yakov Klimenko[34]

May 19, 1968

City of Novomoskovsk

I, senior investigator of the Investigations Department of the KGB for the Lvov region, Captain Kharitonov, interrogated the following witness at the duty office of the KGB: Yakov Timofeyevich Klimenko, born 1917 in Zaporozhe region, Ukraine. He has no party affiliation, has seven years of education, and is married. Was convicted on January 19, 1955, under Article 58-1b of the Criminal Code of the Russian Soviet Federated Socialist Republic and sentenced to twenty-five years of ITL (corrective labor camps) for serving as a *Wachmann* in the SS forces and his participation in punitive activities. He was released on May 3, 1966. He works as a strap operator for the Novomoskovsk housing-construction trust. He lives in the city of Novomoskovsk, Tula region.

The witness was advised of his responsibilities as provided under Article 73 of the Criminal Code of the Russian Soviet Federated Socialist Republic. He was also warned of his criminal liabilities under Article 182 of the Criminal Code for evading or refusing to provide a statement, and under Article 181 of the Criminal Code for knowingly providing false statements.

When given the opportunity to make a statement regarding the matters at hand, the witness stated the following: In the period from summer 1942 to April 1945, I had to serve as a *Wachmann* and later as an *Oberwachmann* in the German SS forces. I guarded prisoners in concentration camps. Other former POWs and I were given military training in summer and fall 1942 at the Trawniki training camp of the SS. I remember the following people as having been trained along with me: Minochkin, Sagach, Shutov, Kovalev, and Naboka. I also remember *Zugwachmann* Malov from Trawniki. Malov trained *Wachmänner* in the camp.

On two occasions, I was part of a *Wachmänner* detachment deployed to settlements near Trawniki to round up Jews that were brought to Trawniki. In fall 1942, I was sent with a *Wachmänner* detachment to Lublin. The senior member of the detachment was Zugwachmann Malov. Other *Wachmänner* who served with me in Lublin included Kovalev, Zipochkin, Shutov, Nechayev, Tarasov, and Sagach.

On a particular occasion, I and other *Wachmänner* were deployed to a settlement about 15 miles from Lublin. We stood in a cordon around the settlement. The Germans pushed 700–800 Jews into the local square. The Germans then separated about 200 sick and elderly and children from the gathered people. These 200 were shot in a ravine nearby. The *Wachmänner* participated in the shooting. The *Wachmänner* pushed the people into the ravine and shot them on orders from the Germans. I do not believe that I personally shot anyone on this occasion. The remaining people were brought to Lublin and sent to Majdanek, and others to the Lublin concentration camp.

In May 1943, I was transferred with other *Wachmänner* in Lublin to the Janowska camp in Lvov. The following *Wachmänner* who had served with me in the Lublin Detachment were also sent with me to Janowska: Kovalev, Minochkin, Shutov, Nechayev, Tarasov, Sagach, and Malov.

During the first days of service at Janowska, I met Oberwachmänner Shirgaliev and Stankov, and *Wachmänner* Lemeshev, Lobyntsev, Skorokhod, Solomka, Naryzhnyj, Butenko, and Zazhirko.

I served at the Janowska camp until November 1943. After leaving Lvov, I served until April 1945 in a *Wachmänner* detachment that guarded a subcamp of Buchenwald camp. The prisoners in this camp were Poles who worked in a brick factory.

Q: Do you know the following former *Wachmänner* from the SS forces: Ivan Kitsenko, Alexander Fedchenko, Nikolaj Svyatelik, Petr Demidenko, Vasilij Litvinenko, Andrej Ostapenko, Alexander Kirelacha, and Sergej Lebedev? All of them, with the exception of Svyatelik, served in 1943 with you in the Janowska camp.
A: I certainly knew all of the *Wachmänner* just mentioned, although some of the names I can just barely remember.

I have read the protocol. It was recorded from my words correctly. [Signature] Klimenko
Senior investigator with the Investigations Department of the KGB of the Lvov region,
Captain Kharitonov
Note: The original interrogation protocol is located in case file #1-16136 on E. Lobyntsev.

Protocol of Interrogation, Alexander Fedchenko[35]
November 23, 1968
City of Lvov
Senior investigator of the KGB for the Lvov region, Captain Malykhin, at the KGB Investigations
Department, interrogated the following person in compliance with the requirements of
Articles 143, 145, and 146 of the Criminal Code of the Ukrainian Soviet Socialist Republic:
Alexander Zakharovich Fedchenko, born 1914 in Rostov region, Russia. He has no party
affiliation, he has four years of education, he comes from a peasant background, he is
married, and he is an unemployed pensioner. He resides in Rostov region and has no prior
convictions. His identity has been established by a passport / personal ID booklet issued
by the Zimovniki District Police Department in 1956.

Q: You have read the charges being presented to you under Article 56 of the Criminal Code
of the Ukrainian Soviet Socialist Republic, which are explained in the declaration. Do you
understand what you are being charged with, and do you acknowledge your guilt?
A: I have carefully read the declaration, and I understand what I am being charged with. I
fully acknowledge my guilt. I wish to state the following on the substance of the charges
against me: I worked and lived in Baku before the start of the Great Patriotic War. I was
called up to serve in the Red Army on June 22, 1941. I served in the 400th Rifle Division.
During the summer of 1941, our division was sent to Crimea, where I served with the rank
of private as a machine gunner in an air defense artillery unit. On May 20, 1942, other
troops and I were surrounded and captured by German forces near the city of Kerch. I was
sent to a camp in Dzhankoj. I was later sent to the POW camp in Rovno. German officers
came to the camp in June 1942. All of us POWs were placed in formation. The Germans
walked around us and selected physically healthy-looking men. A total of about 100 POWs
were selected, including me. As I recall, we were told that we were going to be sent to work.
We were loaded onto vehicles and taken to the town of Trawniki (Poland).

When we arrived, the Germans told us that we were going to serve in the SS guard
forces. I didn't object to this, thus giving my silent consent to serve the Germans. Each of
us was issued a black military uniform, and a form was completed on each of us. We were
also photographed. My fingerprint was placed on the form below the photograph, and I
signed a commitment to serve the Germans. This was the Trawniki SS training camp. We
underwent drill training. We all became *SS Wachmänner* (guards).

In late summer 1942, my sixty-man *Wachmänner* detachment was sent to a town 12
miles from Trawniki. Once there, a German SS officer told us that we were going to round
up and detain Jews. We were to go through buildings to force the Jews out into the town
square. If any of them showed resistance or tried to escape, we were ordered to shoot them
on the spot. We were to use force to move the people out to the square as quickly as possible.
I personally did not shoot anyone, but others did. The Jews were taken away in vehicles. I
do not know where they were taken.

In mid-May 1943, a 100-man *Wachmänner* detachment, including myself, was assigned
to guard duty in the Janowska camp in Lvov. I remember the following persons who served
with me there: Litvinenko, Sergienko, Derkach, Dundukov, Bogdanov, Lemeshev, Malov,

Matvienko, Yermilov, Pankratov, and Ostapenko. There was an occasion in late May 1943 when some of the prisoners were sent out of the camp to be exterminated. Several railcars were brought to the freight station. The *Wachmänner* and Germans stood in a cordon. The prisoners were then escorted from the camp to the railcars. The prisoners were forced to undress next to the railcars. They were then forced naked into the overcrowded railcars. I stood in the cordon near the railcars. I remember the following *Wachmänner* as having participated in this operation: Naryzhnij, Matvienko, Litvinenko, and Sergienko.

In summer 1943, soon after some of the prisoners had been sent away from Janowska, the Germans organized a mass shooting in the camp. This shooting went on for three days. Many prisoners were exterminated, and the shootings were carried out from morning to night. I participated in the shooting on two of the three days. While participating, I escorted about 2,000–3,000 prisoners to the shooting site. Columns of prisoners numbering about seventy to eighty were led at a time. They were escorted into a ravine. A large pit had been dug in the ravine. The pit measured about 50 × 20 meters. I do not know how deep it was. Each column of prisoners was escorted by *Wachmänner* and two or three Germans. Seeing that they were being taken to be shot, some of the prisoners fell and begged for mercy. Such people had to be beaten with rifle butts so that they walked faster and did not delay the movement of the column. I also beat prisoners. Other *Wachmänner* shot the prisoners. I remember the following *Wachmänner* as escorting prisoners to the shooting site: Litvinenko, Sergienko, Matvienko, and Derkach. A boy tried to escape by running into the bushes. Litvinenko and Matvienko shot him. We ordered the prisoners to stop and sit on the ground as they neared the pit. Then, on orders of the Germans, we stood people up and forced them to undress. We then brought the naked people to the pit and pushed them into the German field of fire. I did not personally shoot any prisoners.

There was another incident in summer 1943 in which prisoners in the camp were shot. The shooting lasted all day. I stood guard on this occasion. In late September 1943, I was sent to Flossenburg in Germany. There was a concentration camp there. I guarded prisoners there and escorted them to work. I served there until March 1945. Then a group of *Wachmänner*, including myself, were sent to serve in the so-called Vlasov army. We underwent training for about one month. We then deployed to a city whose name I do not recall, and all of us scattered. When Soviet forces occupied this city, I stated to a representative of the Soviet organs that I had been a POW of the Germans. I concealed the fact that I had served in the SS forces.

I have read the protocol. It was recorded from my words correctly. [Signature] Fedchenko
Senior investigator of the KGB for Lvov region, Captain Malykhin

State attorney Dr. Klockner as interrogator
Protocol of Interrogation, Roman Pitrow[36]
1962
Roman Pitrow, born 1916 in Chelm, Poland, resides in Bad Kissingen and works as a hotel doorman.
In response to questioning regarding the matter at hand, the witness stated the following:
When the war started in 1939, I served in the Polish army. Later, I was discharged because I was a Volksdeutscher, and in 1940 I worked at the German municipal headquarters in Chelm. There, I worked within the framework of resettlement, and I also worked as a trainer of the *Selbstschutz* (self-defense force). In 1941, I transferred from Chelm to Trawniki

training camp together with twenty men of the Selbstschutz. In Trawniki, I received training and was then employed training Ukrainians. I had the rank of *Oberwachtmeister*. I was assigned to Trawniki until September 1, 1943. At that time, unreliable Ukrainians and Russian Volksdeutsche were withdrawn from Trawniki. It occurred here and there that unreliable men deserted and went over to the partisans. Therefore, the attempt was made to pull unreliable men farther back into Reich territory.

On September 1, 1943, I, together with a company of Ukrainians and Volksdeutsche, was assigned to Flossenburg concentration camp. To replace the Ukrainians, about twenty-five to thirty Waffen-SS men were pulled from Flossenburg and transferred to Trawniki.

The *Selbtschutz* in Chelm was commanded by *SS-Oberscharführer* Majewski. He came from Upper Silesia. He spoke perfect Polish and German. Later, he also became a trainer at the Trawniki camp.

I remember the names of the following SS and police members who were detailed to Trawniki:

(1) Streibel: The camp commandant. I always had the impression he was not happy about the Jewish operations. He would always get drunk either before or after them. As far as I was told, the Jewish operations were ordered by telephone from Lublin. The orders by telephone were usually given to Policemeister (Sergeant-Major) Drechsel, who sat in the clerk's office and functioned as Streibel's right-hand man. I assume that Drechsel also determined which units were to carry out these operations.

In response to the question of whether Streibel ordered Ukrainians to be shot in the camp, I state that on one occasion there was a large escape of twenty-three Ukrainians who took along weapons from the weapons room, including heavy weapons. Eleven of these men were recaptured. They were then shot. I believe the order for this was personally signed by Globocnik. In the subsequent period, it happened several times that individual Ukrainians deserted. When they were recaptured again, they were shot. During my time, there might have been about forty Ukrainians who were shot in connection with desertions. The camp would assemble, and a death sentence would be read. As far as I know, these death sentences were signed by Streibel. The executions were carried out by members of the NCO class. I remember one case in particular in which a Ukrainian was shot for a very trivial reason. He must have fallen asleep on duty, and his weapon had disappeared. A few days later, he was called into the clerk's office, locked up in a cellar, and shot the following day. If Herman Reese stated that these Ukrainians were shot without court proceedings, then that is correct. There were no court proceedings, but before a shooting, a verdict was always read aloud.

(2) Schwarzenbacher: Commander of 1st Battalion. He led the unit during the so-called Jewish uprising in the Warsaw ghetto. I know this because I myself was in Warsaw at the time. Reese was then the battalion *Spiess* (top sergeant).

(3) Franz: commander of 2nd Battalion

(4) Rolixmann: For a time, he conducted the NCO course. He often participated in Jewish operations. When detachments were formed and deployed, he frequently took charge of these detachments.

(5) Baltzer: He was an *SS-Unterscharführer* and a company commander. I believe he also served at the Poniatowa labor camp.

(6) Reese: A member of the NCO class. He was a quiet and decent man.

(7) Kollaritsch: A member of the NCO course. He often participated in Jewish operations. During the Warsaw ghetto uprising, he shot members of the Jewish Council on orders from Stroop. There were four of them. They were driven in a car to the *Umschlagplatz* (deportation collection point) and shot across from Stawki Hospital. I saw the shooting myself. He shot each one of them in the back of the neck. He also shot two Ukrainian guards in Trawniki after he caught them trying to steal clothing from the storage warehouse. He was later shot by a member of his company during a deployment. The Ukrainian who shot him then deserted.

(8) Koziol: He was a *Zugwachtmeister* of the Schupo and a platoon commander in the NCO course.

(9) Pentziok: He was an *Oberwachtmeister* of the Schupo [Schutzpolizei] and a company commander. He participated in several Jewish operations, including in Parczew, Lubartow, and Szezebrzeszyn.

(10) Bieniek: He was a *Wachtmeister* of the Schupo and came from Upper Silesia. Among the Ukrainians, he had the nickname "Kaczka," which means "duck." He was the most hated man in all of Trawniki. He was a friend of Pentziok and took part in several Jewish operations. More than anything else, I remember that he was in Izbica.

(11) Basener: He was a policemeister and was commander of the Lublin Detachment. This unit participated in the clearing of the Lublin ghetto, as well as in the Jewish operations in Opole, Bilgoraj, and Rejowiec. This unit also provided the guard detachment at Majdanek camp.

(12) Drechsel: He was an older man and distinguished. He was essentially Streibel's right-hand man. He sat in the clerk's office and received telephone orders. I believe he also was responsible for assigning detachments.

(13) Erlinger: He was an *SS-Oberscharführer*. I believe he was assigned to Sobibor and Belzec.

The first Jewish operations took place in the area surrounding Trawniki, in Lublin District. These operations served to bring Jews to the Sobibor and Belzec extermination camps. As soon as these two camps began operating, detachments of Ukrainians were detailed to them. When these Ukrainians went on leave, word soon spread about what was happening to the Jews. The Ukrainians from these two camps always had a lot of money and drank an enormous amount. For this reason alone, people talked about where these Ukrainians got the money. Every German in Trawniki camp knew from the very beginning what the extermination camps were all about. If anybody wants to claim that he did not know, he is certainly lying.

There were also antipartisan operations. They were mostly prompted by reports from external Gendarmerie stations. On the whole, the success of these deployments against partisans was relatively small, since the partisans had usually already departed when the detachments from Trawniki arrived. Here and there, there were also firefights. The deployments were often organized more for show than for any real success that might have resulted. I myself was often deployed in such operations.

I can say little about the major ghetto-clearing operation in Warsaw in 1942. I do know, at any rate, that almost all the Ukrainians from Trawniki camp took part in the Warsaw operation. As far as I remember, [Willi] Franz led the Ukrainian detail. In addition, the Ukrainians participated in the clearing of the Rzeszow ghetto. The Ukrainians were also deployed to Krakow. At that time, the Jews were taken to the Jewish labor camp in Plaszow.

The Ukrainian detachment that carried out the clearing of the Krakow ghetto then remained in Plaszow camp as a guard detachment. Finally, I know that Ukrainians from Trawniki also participated in the clearing of the Bialystok ghetto. Franz was with the Ukrainians in Bialystok. It now also occurs to me that the Ukrainians were also deployed to Czestochowa. It gradually became known that the Ukrainians were very useful in such operations, and they were often requested from outside Lublin District.

I was present in Warsaw when the so-called ghetto uprising broke out. Some 300 Ukrainians were sent from Trawniki. It was said that 10,000 work Jews had to be brought out of the Warsaw ghetto. The Ukrainian detail was unloaded in Wola, a suburb of Warsaw. It was quartered in a school next to the trolley depot there. The next day, the detail then deployed. The NCO trainees deployed to the ghetto gate in trolley cars. The rest of the Ukrainian detail was sent to cordon off the ghetto. Behind the ghetto gate, we were called to attention in a square, and a high-ranking SD officer informed us that 10,000 Jews had to be brought out of the ghetto as laborers. As the officer spoke to us, we came under machine gun fire. Everything was chaotic. Our NCO trainees suffered about twenty losses. The NCO trainees were deployed to the *Umschlagplatz*. The rest of the Ukrainians who were supposed to be detailed to guard the ghetto were now deployed into the ghetto itself and had to act as assault and reconnaissance troops.

After that, I was no longer directly involved in the ghetto battles themselves. During the next few days, we had a schedule of twenty-four hours on duty and twenty-four hours off duty at the *Umschlagplatz*. Already on the first day of the operation, the first Jews showed up on Stawkiplatz and were loaded into the railway cars. These Jews were transported to Poniatowa camp. Following this, small and large groups of Jews constantly arrived at the *Umschlagplatz* and were housed in a large building until it was time to leave on a transport.

During the operation, Stroop utilized me as a translator for captured Jews, since I spoke perfect Yiddish. On the basis of statements made by those captured, certain hiding places were then uncovered. In response to questioning, it is correct that the Ukrainians behaved very badly at the *Umschlagplatz*. They searched the Jews who arrived there and took their money. With this money they then obtained alcohol and got drunk. In their drunken condition, they then did all kinds of things there. As far as I know, this behavior took place at night, not during the day. At the *Umschlagplatz*, the Ukrainians were commanded by Voss and Kollaritsch. Reese was also there, serving as the *Spiess* in the quarters next to the trolley depot. Also deployed in the ghetto was Oberwachtmeister Bieniek and SS-Unterscharführer Burkhardt. Burkhardt was assigned to the *Umschlagplatz*. The railroad transports that left Warsaw were escorted by Trawniki men.

The interrogation was dictated in my presence. The recording was played back to me, and what I said corresponds to the truth. Signed, Dr. Klockner.

Excerpt of Testimony of Karl Streibel, January 1973, Streibel Trial, Hamburg[37]
When I arrived in Trawniki, Globocnik told me that I was to take over the administration of the camp. When I arrived, Police *Oberwachtmeister* Drechsel was already there. There were Volksdeutsche, former Russian POWs, in the camp. I was tasked with increasing the personnel strength of the camp and establishing construction platoons to improve the major logistics support routes. At Trawniki, two battalions with four companies each were established. We had Balts, Ukrainians, Belorussians, and Poles in the camp, as well as Crimean Tatars.

Personnel were to be used for site protection, guarding estates, and the motor pool.

Vehicle mechanics were needed for the motor pool. Personnel were also needed to reinforce the SS and police bases. The personnel would be armed with captured weapons: Russian rifles. When I had visited the POW camps, I told recruits that they would enter German service and be deployed for construction assignments such as improving streets and supply routes. However, I never ended up establishing construction platoons.

When I arrived in Trawniki, I considered myself a member of the Waffen-SS. I received tabs with SS runes for my uniform. Camp personnel included members of the Waffen-SS, Allgemeine-SS, police, and police reserve. I did not choose this staff. They were assigned to me. There may have been ten to twelve police personnel. There was rivalry among the Germans in the camp due to their membership in either the Waffen-SS or Allgemeine-SS. The men in the Waffen-SS felt superior. I tried to mediate rivalries.

My personnel were supposed to build supply bases and support combat forces. They were needed for security reasons, including antipartisan operations. Detachments were used to guard estates and bridges and to evacuate ghettos. I thought that repair of supply routes would proceed, such as the construction of the trench works on the Bug River.

The majority of the personnel in the camp were Ukrainian. One company was made up of Balts. They felt superior to the other non-German nationalities in the camp. Everyone knew that Jews were being killed. It was not possible to keep it secret. I had asked Hofle if it was true that the Jews were being killed. He told me they were being gassed. Hofle was in charge of anti-Jewish operations. I did not get along with him. He felt I was too soft. He felt himself answerable to no one. He undermined my discipline. I am ashamed that it went so far. We and the Ukrainians were misused. I estimate that about 2,000 men went through the Trawniki camp. My job was to fight partisans and protect facilities. Anti-Jewish operations were a misuse that didn't belong to our mission. Anti-Jewish operations did not play a great role in our operations. My personnel were used more for other things.

Protocol of Interrogation, Prokofij Businnij[38]
November 18, 1974
Kiev
The senior investigative officer of the KGB of the Ukrainian Soviet Socialist Republic for the Kiev region, Captain Berestowskij, of the Office of the State Attorney of the USSR, in connection with legal-assistance proceedings of the judicial authorities of the Federal Republic of Germany, in compliance with the requirements of Articles 85, 167, and 176 of the Code of Criminal Procedure of the Ukrainian Soviet Socialist Republic, interrogated Prokofij Businnij, born 1912 in Kiev region, Ukraine. He is married, has three years of education, works on a state farm, and lives in Kiev region.

In accordance with Article 167 of the Code of Criminal Procedure of the Ukrainian Soviet Socialist Republic, the duties of a witness were explained to Businnij, and he was instructed regarding the criminal consequences of refusing to testify pursuant to Article 179 of the Criminal Code of the Ukrainian Soviet Socialist Republic and of giving deliberately false testimony under Article 178 of the Criminal Code.

At the start of the Great Patriotic War, I was conscripted into the Red Army and sent to the front. About two months later, in August 1941, I was captured by the Germans. I was taken with others to a POW camp in Chelm. I was weak under the severe conditions in this camp and so declared myself willing to enter service with the Germans. I went to the training camp in Trawniki.

In summer 1942, I was sent to serve at the Sobibor concentration camp, where I served as a guard for a few months, maybe even a year. From there, I transferred to service at the Auschwitz (Oswiecim) concentration camp, and I was there until nearly the end of the war. The Sobibor camp was intended for the annihilation of Jewish people. There were about fifty Jews who lived in the camp to do labor. About twenty of them worked as tailors and shoemakers for the Germans. The other thirty received incoming transports of Jews who arrived at the camp, and herded them in groups to the gas chambers, where they were killed. They then brought the bodies out on dump trucks and threw them into pits that were dug by excavators.

I guarded the outside of the camp with about thirty other guards. I saw with my own eyes how, under orders from the Germans, the Jewish labor detail led groups of fifty people at a time into the gas chamber. Then the engine was turned on, and after a while the bodies were taken out. The people went into the chamber without resistance because they were told that they were going to bathe. During my service at Sobibor, the Germans killed many thousands of Jewish people, men, women, elderly, and children, in the gas chamber. I cannot provide the exact number killed. The German administration of the camp consisted of about fifteen men. I remember only one of them, an *SS-Obersturmführer* by the first name of Franz. He was young, with blonde hair, and tall. I remember him because he supervised the guards more often than any of the other German staff. I no longer remember the camp staff member, named to me as Hubert Gomerski, so I cannot say anything about him.

The protocol was read aloud to me, at my request, by the investigating officer and has been recorded accurately from my words. [Signature] Businnij
Senior investigations officer of the KGB of the Ukrainian Soviet Socialist Republic for the Kiev region, Captain Berestowskij
Attesting accuracy:
State attorney for the Kiev region, State Judicial Counselor 3rd Class Bogatschew
Office of the State Attorney of the USSR
Office of the State Attorney for the Kiev region of the Ukrainian Soviet Socialist Republic
May 8, 1975, Frankfurt am Main
Certified translation
Vera Kapkayev: Sworn interpreter and translator of Russian for the Higher State Judicial District of Frankfurt am Main
Office of the State Attorney
regional Court Hamburg
Ms. Barthel: official inspector, Judicial Service, August 12, 1998

CHAPTER 5

Some Soviet Trials and Case Records

Chief of Counterintelligence Department
People's Commissariat of Defense, "SMERSH"
37th Guards Rifle Division
Major Kovsar

Prosecutor
37th Guards Rifle Division
Captain of Justice Zabludovskiy

August 20, 1944
Order for Arrest
I, an authorized operative of "SMERSH," Counterintelligence Department, People's Commissariat of Defense, 37th Guards Rifle Division, Guards 1st Lieutenant Taran, have reviewed the information received on the criminal activities of Pavel Kozlov, born 1923 in Novosibirsk Province, Krasnoyarsk region.

Findings: Kozlov served in the Red Army and surrendered to the Germans on May 25, 1942, in the Kerch Strait region. He was sent to Rovno POW camp until July 1942. He then volunteered for German service and was sent to Trawniki to become a guard. He served as a guard at the Lublin concentration camp, then later, in spring 1943, at Treblinka labor camp. During his guard service there, March 1943–July 25, 1944, he beat and killed Jewish prisoners. Two civilians, Abram Katz and Geni Tratch, have testified against Kozlov.

Ruling: Pavel Kozlov is to be searched and arrested.
Authorized operative of "SMERSH"
Counterintelligence Department
37th Guards Rifle Division
Guards 1st Lieutenant Taran

Chief, Counterintelligence Department
"SMERSH"
65th Army
Guards Colonel O. Los

October 15, 1944
INDICTMENT[1]
Investigation Case #94, against
(1) Ivan Shevchenko
(2) Mikhail Shkarupa-Poliszuk
(3) Pavel Kozlov
(4) Grigorij Sirota
(5) Valentin Rozhansky
(6) Nikita Rekalo

Under Article 1 of the Decree of the Presidium of the Supreme Soviet of April 19, 1943

In August 1944, the above-named guards of the Treblinka camp were detained and arrested by the SMERSH section of the 65th Army, in the Warsaw region. They participated in mass killings of the Jewish population.

Investigation in this case has concluded that while serving in the Red Army during the war, the six defendants surrendered to the Germans and became POWs in 1941–1942, after which they voluntarily served the German occupation forces, trained to be guards at the Trawniki training school, and then served as guards at the Treblinka camp.

The indicted individuals were arrested on August 21, 23, 28, and September 7, 1944, and have been detained in the preliminary detention cell of the SMERSH section of the 65th Army.

Criminal case was filed, August 21, 1944
Case was accepted for prosecution, August 21, 1944
Indictment was issued, September 3–20, 1944
Investigation was completed, October 12, 1944

Senior investigator
Counterintelligence Department
"SMERSH"
65th Army
Captain Tyukhty
Affirming
Chief of Department of Counterintelligence
People's Commissariat of Defense, "SMERSH"
of Military Division 49572
Guards Major Vdovoukhin

April 14, 1945
BILL OF INDICTMENT OF SERGEJ VASILENKO[2]
On investigation case #9

Against Vasilenko, Sergej
under Article 58-1 B of the Criminal Code of the Russian Soviet Socialist Republic

Vasilenko, Sergej, a former serviceman of the Red Army, has been arrested by the Department of Counterintelligence, "SMERSH," on March 25, 1945, and is being prosecuted for treason.

The investigation process has established the following: On June 25, 1941, Vasilenko, Sergej, was conscripted into the Red Army and served in an antiaircraft artillery regiment of the 6th Army. On August 17, 1941, he was captured by the enemy in the vicinity of the city of Kanev and was held in POW camps in Rovno and Chelm. In March 1943, while in captivity, he voluntarily joined the SS-Totenkopf guard units and completed four months of training. Upon completion of training, he earned the rank of *SS-Rottwachmann*. He was trained to guard military facilities. He was assigned to guard the Stutthof concentration camp and was awarded a bronze medal for his excellent service in the SS guard units.
To the charges presented, Vasilenko has pled guilty.

Vasilenko, Sergej, born 1917, in Zhitomir Province, Ukrainian nationality, of peasant ancestry, no party affiliation, fourth-grade education, not married.

Preliminary investigation in this case is to be considered as completed, and the obtained evidence is sufficient to bring the defendant to trial. Investigation case #9 shall be forwarded, through the military prosecutor, to the military tribunal for proceedings.

The bill of indictment has been prepared, April 14, 1945.
Investigator, Department of Counterintelligence
People's Commissariat of Defense, "SMERSH"
Military Division 49572
Guards 1st Lieutenant Rodionov

Information Sheet
(1) Date of arrest: March 25, 1945
(2) There is no material evidence in the case.
(3) There are no personal documents.
(4) Crime was committed during the period March 1943–March 1945.
(5) Criminal case was initiated March 24, 1945.
(6) The case was accepted for prosecution by Investigator Rodionov, March 24, 1945.
(7) The indictment was issued April 13, 1945.
(8) Preliminary investigation was completed April 13, 1945.

Investigator, Department of Counterintelligence
People's Commissariat of Defense, "SMERSH"
Military Division 49572
Guards 1st Lieutenant Rodionov

Record of Court Session[3]
April 15, 1945
The Military Tribunal of the 1st Guards Tank Army, at a closed judicial session, consisting of the presiding judge, Guards Major of Justice Ovsyannikov
Members: Guards Major of Justice Koryukin and Guards Major of Justice Korostelev
Before the judicial secretary: Guards Captain of Justice Yakushkin
The presiding judge opened the court session and announced the charges against Vasilenko, Sergej, under Article 58-1 B of the Criminal Code of the Russian Soviet Socialist Republic.
     The judicial secretary announced to the court that the defendant Vasilenko has been brought to the court under escort. The presiding judge explains to the defendant Vasilenko concerning his rights during the court session, announces the officials present at the trial, and clarifies the rules of challenging the officials.
     Defendant Vasilenko stated: "My rights during the court session are understood. I have no requests or challenges to the court."
     The presiding judge announces the verdict and asks the defendant whether he understands the charges brought against him, and whether or not he pleads guilty.
     Defendant Vasilenko stated: "I do understand the charges and consider myself only partially guilty."

Affirming
Chief of Department of Counterintelligence
People's Commissariat of Defense, "SMERSH"
Military Division 49572
Guards Major Vdovoukhin

April 14, 1945
BILL OF INDICTMENT OF IVAN TEREKHOV[4]
On investigation case #11

Against Terekhov, Ivan
Under Article 58-1 B of the Criminal Code of the Russian Soviet Socialist Republic

Terekhov, Ivan, a former military serviceman of the Red Army, was arrested by the Department of Counterintelligence, "SMERSH," on March 25, 1945, and is being prosecuted for treason.

During the investigation it has been determined: In September 1940, Terekhov, Ivan, was conscripted into the Red Army and served in a heavy artillery regiment. In August 1941, he was captured by the enemy in the vicinity of Belaya Tserkov and was held in a POW camp in Chelm. In July 1943, while in captivity, he voluntarily joined the SS-Totenkopf guard units and completed a three-month training course. He served as a guard at the Stutthof concentration camp.

To the charges presented, Terekhov has pled guilty.

Terekhov, Ivan, born 1922 in Kursk Province, Russian nationality, of peasant ancestry, seventh-grade education, not married.

Preliminary investigation in this case is to be considered completed, and the obtained facts are sufficient for bringing the defendant to trial. Investigation case #11 shall be forwarded, through the military prosecutor, to the military tribunal for proceedings.

The bill of indictment was prepared, April 14, 1945.
Investigator, Department of Counterintelligence
People's Commissariat of Defense, "SMERSH"
Military Division 49572
Guards 1st Lieutenant Rodionov

Information Sheet
(1) Date of arrest: March 25, 1945
(2) There is no material evidence in the case.
(3) There are no personal documents.
(4) Crime was committed during the period July 1943–March 1945.
(5) Criminal case was initiated March 24, 1945.
(6) The case was accepted for prosecution by Investigator Rodionov, March 24, 1945.
(7) The indictment was issued April 13, 1945.
(8) Preliminary investigation was completed April 13, 1945.

Investigator, Department of Counterintelligence
People's Commissariat of Defense, "SMERSH"
Military Division 49572
Guards 1st Lieutenant Rodionov

Record of Court Session[5]

The military tribunal of the 1st Guards Tank Army, at a closed judicial session, consisting of the presiding judge, Guards Major of Justice Ovsyannikov

Members: Guards Major of Justice Koryukin and Guards Major of Justice Korostelev
Before the judicial secretary: Guards Captain of Justice Yakushkin

The presiding judge opened the court session and announced the charges against Terekhov, Ivan, under Article 58-1 B of the Criminal Code of the Russian Soviet Socialist Republic.

The judicial secretary reported to the court that the defendant Terekhov has been brought to the court under escort. The presiding judge explained to the defendant Terekhov about his rights during the court session, announces the officials present, and clarifies the rules of challenging the court officials.

Defendant Terekhov stated: "My rights during the court session are understood. I have no motion for pardon or challenges to the court."

The presiding judge announces the verdict and asks the defendant Terekhov whether he understands the charges brought against him and whether or not he pleads guilty.

Defendant Terekhov stated: "I do understand the charges and am pleading guilty. I request the court send me to the battlefront for expiation of guilt."

The tribunal broke for recess, for deliberation to determine the verdict. Thirty-five minutes later, the presiding judge announces the verdict: The military tribunal has ruled to keep the defendant Terekhov in custody. The presiding judge announces that the court session is now closed.

Presiding judge: Ovsyannikov
Judicial secretary: Yakushkin

INFORMATION SHEET ON THE ARREST, TRIAL, AND CONVICTION OF ALEXANDER DUKHNO, MIKHAIL KORZHIKOW, AND IVAN VOLOSHIN[6]

Archived investigation case #6981 against Alexander Dukhno, Mikhail Korzhikow, and Ivan Voloshin

Dukhno was arrested on January 21, 1947; Voloshin was arrested on March 12, 1947; Korzhikow was arrested on March 25, 1947: they all served at the Belzec death camp.

Dukhno was born in Kharkov region and lives in Sverdlovsk (Yekaterinburg). He is a student at the Sverdlovsk Mining Institute.

Korzhikow was born in Chkalov (Orenburg) region and lives in the Chkalov region. He is an instructor at the Kuvandyk Land Department.

Voloshin was born in Dnepropetrovsk region and lives in Novo-Yarychev, Lvov region. He has been a member of the VLKSM since 1937, completed two years of law school, and works as an investigator at the prosecutor's office in Novo-Yarychev.

Dukhno served in the Red Army and was captured by the Germans in July 1941. He was held in Chelm POW camp and then recruited for Trawniki service in September 1941. In May 1942 he was assigned to Belzec death camp. On at least one occasion he closed the doors leading into the gas chambers. He convoyed people into the gas chambers. Twice he took part in raids, in combat against partisans, and guarded the site of firing-squad executions.

Dukhno served at Belzec until March 3, 1943. On that date, he, along with Voloshin, Korzhikow, Khabarov, and others, escaped from the camp and joined a partisan unit. In the partisan unit he became a platoon commander. He served in the partisan unit "Vershigory" until May 1944. He was awarded with a "Red Star" decoration while in the partisan unit.

During interrogation, Dukhno admitted that on two occasions he took part in killing Jews by firing squad. The first time he shot one person, and the second time he shot three. From his SS service Dukhno recalls the following comrades:

(1) *Zugwachmann* Schmidt, in Belzec
(2) *Oberwachmann* Rogosa, in Treblinka II
(3) Peter Krasnobaj
(4) Lysak, in Belzec
(5) Derkach
(6) Yermak
(7) Nikolai Plekhov, in Belzec
(8) Andrei Brodovoy, in Lublin; escaped and joined the partisans

In Belzec, the following men served with Korzhikow:

(1) Alexander Dukhno
(2) Ivan Voloshin, participated in executions; led to the partisans
(3) Ivan Zakota, fled to the partisans
(4) Mikhail Gavrimchuk, fled to the partisans
(5) Peter Litous, fled to the partisans
(6) Piotr Browzew, fled to the partisans
(7) Dimitri Prokhin, fled to the partisans
(8) Viktor Kirillov, fled to the partisans
(9) Vladimir Kozlov, executed people
(10) Oberwachmann Zibert, executed people
(11) Zugwachmann Schmidt, forced people into the gas chambers
(12) Zugwachmann Schneider, forced people into the gas chambers

Voloshin was captured by the Germans in October 1941. In February or March 1942, he was recruited for Trawniki service from the Chelm POW camp. In summer 1942, he was assigned to Belzec death camp. Voloshin was confronted with his codefendants Korzhikow and Dukhno, who identified him as having taken part in executions in the camp. Voloshin did not confirm their testimony.

Voloshin remembers the following comrades from service:

(1) Nikolai Leontev, in Belzec. In March 1943, fled to the partisans.
(2) Ivan Guba, in Belzec. He was a patrol guard in the camp.
(3) Nikolaj Stetsenko, in Belzec. He was in charge of the arms depot.

An ID card (trophy document) belonging to Alexander Dukhno was added to the case evidence. It indicates that his assignment to Belzec began on May 4, 1942.

During court session, Dukhno, Korzhikow, and Voloshin confirmed the testimony given during the preliminary investigation.

Dukhno testified: "I took part in the mass execution process from start to finish: from unloading the trains to escorting people to the gas chambers." He further stated: "I had to serve on all sorts of guard posts in the camp, including the undressing room, the hair-cutting room, near the path to the gas chambers, and near the fire pits where bodies were burned."

On June 5, 1947, the military tribunal of the Ural Military District, under Article 58-1b of the Russian-Soviet Criminal Code, sentenced Dukhno, Korzhikow, and Voloshin to twenty-five years each in a labor camp.

Dukhno pled guilty to his involvement in executions: unloading the train cars, escorting people to the undressing room, escorting people to the gas chambers, and closing the doors to the gas chambers. He also participated in killing people by firing squad.

Korzhikow escorted people from the trains to the undressing room and then to the gas chambers. He also participated in raids against partisans. Voloshin helped unload people from the trains, escorted them, and did guard duty. He also participated in killing five children by firing squad. Dukhno filed an appeal, asking that his case be reexamined in light of the severity of his punishment. Korzhikow pointed out that the charge of escorting people to the gas chambers had not been supported by evidence. During appeal, Voloshin indicated that when assigned to Belzec death camp, he had been under the impression before he got there that he was being sent there for routine labor. He requested a mitigation of his punishment and that he not be deprived of his government awards.

The court did not take into account the fact that the defendants had fled to the partisans, had served in a partisan unit, and that at least one of them was awarded a "Red Star" decoration.

On August 16, 1947, the Military Collegium of the Soviet Supreme Court affirmed the sentences and denied the appeals.

On July 24, 1954, the regional Commission on the Review of Appellate Cases in the city of Sverdlovsk (Yekaterinburg) denied the appeal in the case of all three convicts.

Investigation case #6981 is stored in the KGB Archive Sverdlovsk (Yekaterinburg) region. Chief, Investigations Department, KGB, Dnepropetrovsk region, Lieutenant Colonel Markin

October 1, 1965
City of Dnepropetrovsk

SENTENCING OF ALEXANDER ZAKHAROV[7]
IN THE NAME OF THE UNION OF SOVIET SOCIALIST REPUBLICS
August 19, 1947
The military tribunal of the MVD forces of the Moscow region, at a closed court session, including the following officials:
Presiding judge: Colonel of Justice Shaikov
Associate judges: Police Lieutenant Nikonov and Senior Sergeant Smirnov
Secretary: Lieutenant Alexeyev

Examined the case against Alexander Zakharov, for crimes committed under Article 1 of the Decree of the Presidium of the Supreme Soviet of April 19, 1943 (*Ukaz 43*).

On the basis of a judicial investigation by the military tribunal, it has been determined that defendant Zakharov became a POW of the Germans while serving in the Red Army in 1941. He betrayed his country by serving with the SS and passed himself off as a German under the last name of "Pruss." He served as a guard at the Belzec extermination camp, where he participated in the execution of Jews in gas chambers. In addition, Zakharov participated in capturing partisans who attempted to hide in the forests near the city of Lublin. He also participated in arresting and escorting Jews from Lublin. During the judicial investigation, Zakharov pled guilty and fully confessed to the charges against him. The military tribunal finds that the criminal charges against Zakharov have been proven. He is found guilty.

Ruling: Under Article 1 from April 19, 1943 and by decree of the Presidium of the Supreme Soviet from May 26, 1947, Alexander Zakharov is sentenced to twenty-five years in a labor camp and suppression of his civil rights for five years.

The sentence can be appealed through procedure to the military tribunal of the MVD forces of the Moscow region in the next three days since the handing of the copy of the sentence to the defendant.

Presiding judge, Shaikov
Associate judges, Nikonov and Smirnov

Verified: chief of the Administrative District of the KGB of Dnepropetrovsk region, Lieutenant Colonel Tyutrin
Note: The original document of the sentencing is located in criminal case #365, against A. Zakharov, which is stored in the KGB administration in the city of Moscow and Moscow region.
September 4, 1965

PROTOCOL OF TRIAL PROCEEDINGS, IVAN KONDRATENKO[8]
Case #0033
March 22, 1948
City of Kiev
The military tribunal of the 17th Air Army, in a closed trial proceeding, which consisted of the following:
Presiding judge: Major of Justice Sukhanov
Associate judges: Major of Justice Khlystun and Captain Alfimov
Secretary: Senior Lieutenant Gulov

There was no participation of government accusers or defense.

Examined the case that charges a former POW, Junior Sergeant Ivan Emelyanovich Kondratenko, with crimes stipulated under Article 54-1b of the Criminal Code of the Ukrainian Soviet Socialist Republic.

The secretary reported that the defendant was being held in custody in an internal jail of the MGB for the Kiev region, and that he had been brought to the trial proceeding under escort. No witnesses were being summoned in this case.

The defendant provided the following answers to questions posed by the court: I am Ivan Kondratenko, born 1923 in Brovarsk District, Kiev region, which remains my permanent residence. I am Ukrainian by nationality. I come from an average educated peasant family. In 1940 I finished a ten-year education, and in 1941 I completed courses at the Kiev Pedagogical School. I was going to work as a teacher, but instead I was summoned to serve in the Red Army. I was not a member of the Communist Party. From 1941 to May 1942, I was a member of the VLKSM (All-Union Leninist Communist Youth League). At the time of my capture in May 1942, I hid my Komsomol (Communist Youth League) ID booklet among the rubble in a cellar. At the present time, I have no party affiliation. I have never been convicted or under investigation before now.

I was summoned to serve in the Red Army in July 1941 by the Volnovakh District Military Commissariat, Stalino region, and I served until May 1942, when I surrendered to the Germans. I was mobilized to serve in the Red Army a second time in June 1945 by a field military commissariat in the town of Oswiecim (Auschwitz) and served in an evacuation hospital until August 1946, when I was demobilized from service. After demobilization, I worked in Cherkasy on a peat farm as a technician.

During the war, I served in the 156th Rifle Division as a squad commander with the rank of junior sergeant. I participated in combat against the Germans on the Crimean front along the Kerch Peninsula, December 1941–May 1942. I did not sustain any wounds. I was awarded the "Victory over Germany" medal. I lost the medal, and the certificate that was issued with it was taken from me when I was arrested.

I have been provided with copies of the indictment and the findings from the preliminary hearing of the military tribunal of the 17th Air Army on March 18, 1948. I have been detained in conjunction with the current case against me since February 9, 1948.

The presiding judge explained to the defendant his right to ask for the removal of any member of the court. The defendant responded, "I do not request that any member of the court be removed."

The presiding judge asked the defendant whether he had any applications to make before the court regarding the summoning of witnesses, any request for evidence, or the addition of any documents he may have in his possession for the case.

The defendant responded, "I have no applications to make before the court."

Judicial inquiry: The presiding judge read the indictment and the findings of the preliminary hearing of the military tribunal, explained the substance of the charges to the defendant, and asked him whether or not he understood the charges that had been presented to him, whether or not he acknowledged his guilt, and whether or not he desired to provide testimony to the court on the substance of the charges against him.

The defendant responded: "I understand the charges presented to me. I acknowledge my guilt in having betrayed the Motherland. I wish to testify before the court."

In response to questions posed by the presiding judge and the other members of the court, the defendant provided the following testimony on the substance of the case: On July 7, 1941, I was evacuated from the city of Kiev along with the rest of the young people to Stalino region, in order to work gathering grain on a collective farm. At the end of the month, I was summoned to serve in the Red Army. I was sent to a camp located near the city of Tbilisi (Georgia). In this camp, I swore a military oath and served there until October 1941. I was then sent to the 156th Rifle Division, located in the Kuban region. I completed the school for junior commanders in this unit, and was assigned as a squad commander with the rank of junior sergeant.

In February 1942, I was sent to the Kerch Peninsula, where my regiment had taken up a defense near the city of Kerch. In May 1942, the Germans fought their way into the city of Kerch. My regiment retreated in disarray and scattered. Some soldiers were taken away by ship to Novorossijsk, while I and several other soldiers hid in a local cellar. I still had my rifle and some ammunition.

In mid-May 1942, when the Germans captured Kerch, they began searching houses and cellars looking for Soviet soldiers. The Germans found us in the cellar and captured us. We were sent to a POW camp. Before capture, I buried my rifle and my Komsomol ID booklet in the ground.

Within a few days, the Germans transferred all of us to Dzhankoj, where there was another POW camp. Up to 15,000 of us were held there. Days later, I and other POWs were transferred to a POW camp in Rovno. There we worked at a railroad station unloading lumber and other construction materials from railcars.

In mid-June 1942, several Germans arrived in the Rovno camp and began selecting young, healthy POWs. Up to 300 were chosen, including me. I did not know why we had been selected. The Germans did not say anything about this to us at the time. The next day, we were given medical exams by a doctor and then taken in vehicles to the town of Trawniki (Poland). In Trawniki was an SS training camp, and about 1,500 POWs, like myself, had already been trained there.

We were assigned to companies commanded by Germans, and we were summoned to the staff headquarters of the camp, where a German wrote up a form that listed our autobiographical data. We were then provided with a written commitment to faithfully serve the German military, which I signed. We were then dressed in German military uniforms, issued a rifle with ammunition, and assigned a personal ID #. Mine was #1909. I was photographed with this number. The Germans trained us in weapons, drill, and how to perform escort and guard duties. We were told that upon completion of training, we were to serve in camps as *Wachmänner* (guards). We also got political training, which included lectures on the Aryan people, Hitler's biography, and the reasons why the Jews were to be hated.

Training lasted about three months. Then, in September 1942, I was assigned with a *Wachmänner* unit to the city of Lublin to serve at a clothing-sorting facility. Trains with eight to ten railcars full of clothing arrived every day at this facility from Majdanek. These were the possessions that had been removed from the Jews and Poles who had been killed. Our task was to guard Jews who were to sort this clothing, and to prevent them from escaping. I guarded this facility for about eight to nine months, then returned to Trawniki.

In April 1943, I was assigned to the Treblinka punitive camp. There, I guarded and prevented the escape of Jews and Poles. This camp was called a punitive camp because Jews and Poles were exterminated here by extreme physical labor and starvation. They were forced to work nearly around the clock, but they were not provided any food, and as a result they died of starvation and punitive labor. The bodies of the dead were thrown into pits.

A team of *Wachmänner* and German SS men staffed the camp. With sticks, they killed Jews and Poles who could no longer work. I saw the Germans kill fifteen to twenty emaciated Jews. I personally did not participate in the extermination of Jews and Poles, but I saw this done by the Germans and other *Wachmänner*.

When the Red Army advanced on the area, the Germans began to retreat and liquidated the camp. At the time of the liquidation, about 300 Jews were still alive in the camp. On the day of the liquidation, I stood guard at the entrance to the prisoner barracks. Several Germans began taking the Jews in groups of thirty to forty at a time and shot them within the camp. I personally did not participate in this shooting. The Germans shot all 300 Jews. We *Wachmänner* were forced to throw the bodies into a pit.

After the liquidation, we left with the Germans in vehicles and departed for the area around Krakow. After arriving, all of us were transferred to the SS "Streibel" Battalion. This unit worked on the construction of military fortifications in Poland. We went to nearby villages to gather the population and escort them to locations where they were to build military defensive fortifications.

In January 1945, we were sent to Dresden, where we did not do anything. The front was nearing, and all of us scattered in April 1945. Five other *Wachmänner* and I went to a village, and there I joined a Czech partisan detachment and participated in combat against the Germans, for which I received a recognition award from the unit. In June 1945, we joined up with units of the Red Army, and I was mobilized for a second time into the ranks of the Red Army. I served as a private in an evacuation hospital.

There had been opportunities to escape from the Germans, but I was afraid I would be caught and shot, and therefore I decided to serve until the end. I assumed that no one would find out about my service in the German military. When called up to serve in the Red Army a second time, I concealed my service in the German military, since I knew that this constituted a serious crime and that I would have to answer for it before the Motherland.

The presiding judge announced that the judicial inquiry was completed, and the defendant was provided an opportunity to have the last word, in which he stated: "I am clearly guilty. I was young back then, and I did not understand the consequences of my crimes. I ask the court to sentence me in accordance with the law." The court retired to confer on the sentence. An hour later, the presiding judge read the sentence and explained the substance of it to the convict. Having discussed the means of detention, the court decided that the means of detention regarding the convict, his detention under guard, should remain unchanged.

The presiding judge declared the trial proceedings closed.

Presiding judge, Major of Justice Sukhanov
Secretary, Senior Lieutenant Gulov

PROTOCOL OF COURT HEARING, NIKOLAJ GUTSULYAK[9]

June 25, 1948
Before the military tribunal of the MVD forces in Stanislavov region, in the city of Stanislavov, in a closed court session with the following:
Chairman: Lieutenant Colonel of Justice Musichuk
Associate judges: Lieutenant Colonel of Justice Kostenko and Lieutenant Kuznetsov
Secretary: 1st Sergeant Kovan
Without the participation of the prosecution or the defense

The chairman announced the case #____ would be examined. It charges Nikolaj Stepanovich Gutsulyak with committing a crime under Article 54-1b of the Criminal Code of the Ukrainian Soviet Socialist Republic.

The chairman verified the identity of the defendant, who stated the following: I, Nikolaj Gutsulyak, born 1923 in Stanislavov region, come from a middle-class peasant background; I am scarcely literate and am a former member of the VLKSM (All-Union Communist-Leninist Youth League). I am married and have two children, ages one and three years old. I did not serve in the Red Army. I was arrested on May 12, 1948, and I was familiarized with the summary of the charges and the findings of the preliminary hearing on June 17, 1948.

The chairman introduced the members of the court and informed the defendant of his right to reject any member. The defendant stated: I do not reject any members of the court. The chairman informed the defendant of his procedural rights and asked him if he understood his rights and whether or not he would like to submit a petition to the court.

The defendant stated: I understand the procedural rights and petition the court to call the witness Vasilij Yakipanchuk, who will state that the witness Grigorchuk is telling falsehoods about me by stating that I allegedly participated in the extermination of Jews when I was wounded.

The chairman announced the summary of charges, explained to the defendant the substance of the charges, and asked him whether he understood the charges against him, whether he acknowledged his guilt, and whether he wished to give a statement to the court. The defendant stated: I understand the charges against me, I acknowledge my guilt, and I wish to provide a statement to the court.

The military tribunal interrogated the defendant. The defendant stated: I lived in Kolomya District, Stanislavov region, and worked on my own farm. In February 1943, all males in my village born between 1920 and 1923 were summoned for service with the German punitive organs. We went before a medical commission, which would certify us as fit for military service. We were sent from Kolomya to the town of Trawniki. There, I was enlisted at the SS police training camp. I swore an oath of loyalty to the Germans. After training, I was given the rank of *SS Wachmann*. Until May 1943, I performed guard duty at Trawniki over imprisoned Jews.

In May 1943 I went to Warsaw, where I also guarded a camp with imprisoned Jews. I wanted to go home, so I deliberately shot myself in the hand. I was then sent to a hospital. After recovery, I was released from German service and went home.

The defendant answered questions from the tribunal: In the three months I spent at the SS police training camp Trawniki, I was trained in special SS police service regulations. I received a salary of 30 Polish zloty per month for my service with the Germans. In Warsaw, I guarded arrested Jews but did not take part in their extermination. Vasilij Yakipanchuk served with me in the SS. I concealed my service with the German punitive organs and did not report it to anyone. In 1945 I joined the VLKSM, but I was dismissed due to my responsibility in this case.

The chairman asks the defendant if he objects to ending the hearing in the absence of the witness Yakipanchuk. The defendant stated: If the tribunal believes me that I did not take part in the shooting of the arrested Jews in Warsaw, we can close the proceedings, but if the court does not believe me, than I persist in my petition of summoning the witness Yakipanchuk.

The tribunal deliberated in place and decided that the proceedings would continue without the witness.

The chairman asks the defendant if he has anything else to add to the court inquiry. The defendant did not. The chairman allows the defendant the last word.

The defendant responded: I ask the tribunal to lessen my punishment. The tribunal retired to the deliberation room. Twenty-five minutes later the tribunal returned, and the chairman read the sentence and explained to the defendant the nature of the sentence and the term and procedure for appeal.

The tribunal decided: Custody measures regarding the defendant will remain the same (i.e., he is to be kept in custody).

The chairman declared the court hearing closed.

Chairman, Musichuk
Secretary, Kovan

PROTOCOL OF TRIAL PROCEEDINGS, VLADIMIR TERLETSKIJ[10]

On, June 29, 1948, the military tribunal of the MVD for the Stanislavov region, in the city of Stanislavov, met in closed trial proceedings, which consisted of the following:
Presiding judge: Captain of Justice Tkachenko
Associate judges: Major Sotnikov and Captain Chelnokov
Secretary: Junior Lieutenant Gromanov
Without the participation of the prosecutor and defense

The presiding judge announced that case #_____ would be examined, which charges Vladimir Ivanovich Terletskij under Article 54-1b of the Criminal Code of the Ukrainian Soviet Socialist Republic.

In accordance with Article 245 of the Criminal Code of the Ukrainian Soviet Socialist Republic, the presiding judge established the identity of the defendant, who provided the following responses to questions posed during the inquiry: I am Vladimir Terletskij, born 1922 in Lisets District, Stanislavov region, Ukraine. From an average peasant background, eight years of education; none of my relatives serve in the Soviet army, and I have no prior convictions. I was arrested in regard to this case and familiarized with a copy of the indictment and findings of the preliminary hearing.

In accordance with Article 246 of the Criminal Code, the presiding judge announced the composition of the court and explained to the defendant his right to challenge any members of the court. The defendant stated: I understand my right to declare a challenge to any member of the court. I do not declare a challenge to any member of the court.

In accordance with Article 258 of the Criminal Code, the presiding judge explained to the defendant his procedural rights during the judicial inquiry. The defendant stated: I understand my rights during the judicial inquiry. I do not present any petitions to the court before the judicial inquiry begins.

Judicial inquiry: The presiding judge read the indictment and asked the defendant whether he understood the charges presented to him, whether he acknowledged his guilt, and whether he desired to make a statement to the court.

The defendant stated: I understand the charges presented to me, I acknowledge my guilt, and I desire to provide a statement. On the substance of the case, the defendant stated: During the German occupation, I resided in the Lisets District, Stanislavov region, and worked on my own farm. In February 1942, the Germans mobilized me to work at the reconstruction of destroyed railroad tracks. I worked in the city of Stanislavov repairing rail lines until February 1943. Then, other citizens and I were transported to the town of Trawniki (Poland). On arrival at Trawniki I went before a medical commission, which determined me to be suitable for service in the German military. I was summoned to the staff headquarters of the SS police, where I swore an oath to serve the Germans faithfully and was recruited into the SS police. I was issued a Russian rifle and received the clothing of a German soldier.

In Trawniki, I underwent military training and guarded Jews in the camp. In April 1943, along with a group of soldiers from the SS police, I was sent to the city of Warsaw, from where I escorted Jews to the city of Lublin. For about two months, I guarded Jews held in the Lublin death camp. In August 1943, I returned to Trawniki. That same month, I was sent to Poniatowa, where I guarded Jews. Also that month, I went to the city of Bialystok to escort Jews to Lublin. In Bialystok, Jews were loaded into trains and escorted to Lublin.

In September 1943, I was granted leave and went home. After going home, I did not return to Trawniki. In response to an offer from a regional leader of the OUN (Organization of Ukrainian Nationalists), Mikhail Luchkiv, I joined the UPA (Ukrainian Partisan Army) in October 1943 and performed the duties of a scout for the UPA. I was armed with a pistol and grenades.

In response to questions posed by the tribunal, the defendant stated: I did not shoot any Jews held in the camp. I only escorted them from one camp to another. Upon the arrival of Soviet units in our village, I was already a member of the UPA and continued to reside illegally. In summer 1944 I turned myself in, out of a sense of guilt, to the regional office of the MVD. I served for the Germans in the capacity of a *Wachmann* (guard).

In accordance with Article 287 of the Criminal Code, the presiding judge offered the defendant an opportunity to have the last word. The defendant stated: I ask that the term of punishment be reduced.

The military tribunal retired to confer in the conference chamber to determine the sentence.

Thirty minutes later, the tribunal returned and the presiding judge read the sentence and explained the substance of the sentence to the defendant, and the method to appeal it.

The military tribunal determined that the mode of detention for the defendant should remain the same; that is, confinement in the MGB prison in the city of Stanislavov until the period of the sentence comes into effect.

The presiding judge then declared the trial proceedings closed.

Presiding judge, Tkachenko

PROTOCOL OF TRIAL PROCEEDINGS, FILIP BABENKO[II]

On December 24, 1948, the military tribunal of the Kiev Military District, in a closed trial proceeding held in the city of Kiev, consisted of the following:
Presiding judge: Major of Justice Nelupov
Associate judges: Major Kurilov and Major Glotov
Secretary: Captain of Justice Pogachuyev
Other participants: advocates for the prosecution and defense

The presiding judge announced that the tribunal was to examine the file that charges Filip Pavlovich Babenko with crimes stipulated under Article 54-1b of the Criminal Code of the Ukrainian Soviet Socialist Republic.

The presiding judge established the identity of the defendant, who provided the following statement about himself: I am Filip Babenko, born 1905 in Rzhishchev District, Kiev region, Ukraine, from a poor peasant background; collective farmer, no party affiliation, education level of only one year, no prior convictions. I am married. I do not own any property. I served in the Red Army from May to July 1941 and served again from June to October 1945. I participated in combat at the front. I did not sustain any wounds or receive any decorations. I was provided a copy of the charges on December 18. I have been held in custody since November 12.

The presiding judge announced the composition of the court and advised the defendant of his right to ask for the removal of the entire court or any member or the secretary. Defendant did not make a request to this affect.

The presiding judge advised the defendant of his right to present petitions, to summon witnesses, to request additional documents, or to add any documents to the file.

The presiding judge advised the defendant of his procedural rights during the trial proceedings to provide explanations to the substance of the overall case, and to explain any particular circumstances in the case, at any time during the judicial inquiry.

The presiding judge read the charges and the findings of the preliminary inquiry and explained to the defendant the substance of the charges. He then asked the defendant if he understood the charges that were presented to him, whether he acknowledged his guilt, and whether he desired to testify before the court.

Defendant Babenko replied: I understand the charges presented to me, I fully acknowledge my guilt, and I desire to testify before the court.

Testimony of defendant Babenko: Before being mobilized for military service, I performed manual labor on a collective farm. In May 1941, I was summoned to an assembly point by the Rzhishchev District Military Commissariat and was sent to a camp, where I underwent training until June 1941. Around June 10, 1941, our unit went on a march. I don't remember what area we were in, but we were in the woods. We stopped and spent several days in the woods. On June 22, 1941, our unit commander told us that Germany had begun a war against our country. We were given combat equipment, rifles, and ammunition, and our unit moved toward the front. We arrived at the city of Lyubar, where we took up a defensive position. We remained there until July 1941. On July 9, our unit was surrounded by German forces, and they began to fire on us with mortars. We did not return mortar fire; we just fired with our rifles. After heavy firing, the Germans attacked us. At that time, I was in a foxhole. I had my rifle but no ammo left. The Germans approached me and captured me. I placed my rifle onto a stack of rifles, as ordered by a German soldier. I did not resist when captured. I was then sent to the city of Shepetovka to a camp for Soviet POWs. I remained there for several days, after which I was sent to the town of Chelm (Poland) to a camp for POWs.

In December 1941, all the prisoners in the camp were put in formation. The Germans began to select physically fit men and led them out of the formation. They selected about 100 people, and I was among them. After this, the Germans put us in vehicles and drove us away. We did not know where we were being taken. We were brought to Trawniki camp, where we were told that we would undergo training in the school for SS police forces to guard camps. I completed a form that I had to sign, provided a fingerprint, and was photographed with the ID #869. The next day, I was given clothing and equipment, including a tunic, greatcoat, pants, service cap, and boots. The clothing was black, the color of the German police uniform.

I underwent training at the Trawniki SS police school from December 1941 to March 1942. We learned the rules for performing guard duty, the German language, and weapons. We were also provided tactical training for fighting partisans, and we were also given anti-Soviet lectures. Upon completion of the police school, I swore an oath to serve the German forces faithfully, and I was given the rank of *Wachmann* (guard, private).

In March 1942, the Germans sent me to Poniatowa to guard the Jewish camp there. In July 1942, I was transferred to guard duty at the Belzec death camp, where I remained until October 1943. In this camp, there were two working gas chambers for the extermination of people. The chambers were serviced by special work details consisting of Jews. Seven to eight railcars of Jews were brought to the camp each day or every other day. Newly arrived people were undressed and escorted into the gas chamber as if going into a bathhouse. Then, a motor was started and gas was pumped in. After fifteen to twenty minutes, the people were dead. After this, the bodies were thrown into a pit and were later burned. Gold teeth were removed from the bodies. Several tens of thousands of Jewish people were exterminated in this camp.

In October 1943, I was sent to Flossenburg, where I continued to serve as a *Wachmann* until April 1945. In this camp, we led people to perform various types of work. In April 1945, American forces liberated me, and after some time they handed me over to Soviet forces. There, I was enlisted into a reserve regiment. In fall 1945, I was demobilized from the Red Army. I then returned to working on a collective farm.

In response to questions posed by members of the court, the defendant Babenko replied: I surrendered to the Germans voluntarily because our unit had been surrounded. When we did guard duty in the camp, we were given orders not to allow anyone to leave the camp alive, and to shoot escapees. I did not try to escape from the Germans. I had opportunities to escape from the camp, but I feared the Germans would capture and shoot me. I saw how the gas chambers were equipped. I entered them several times and looked around.

The presiding judge declared the judicial inquiry to be completed.

The presiding judge gave the defendant an opportunity to say the last word. Defendant Babenko, in his last words, stated: "I fully acknowledge my guilt in having betrayed the Motherland, and I ask the court to hand down a fair sentence." The court recessed to confer on the sentence.

Approximately an hour and fifteen minutes later, the presiding judge read out the sentence and explained the substance of the sentence to the convict, and the methods for appealing the sentence. The tribunal decided that the means of detention for the convict Babenko, should remain the same (i.e., that he should remain in custody). The presiding judge declared the trial proceedings closed.

Presiding judge [Signature] Nelupov
Secretary [Signature] Pogachuyev
Affirming
Head of the Ministry of State Security, Dnepropetrovsk region, Colonel Surkov

November 2, 1949
BILL OF INDICTMENT OF FEDOR RYABEKA, MIKHAIL ANDREYENKO, AND TERENTIJ GORDIENKO[12]
(On investigation case #6491)
On charges against Ryabeka, Fedor; Andreyenko, Mikhail; Gordienko, Terentij

For crimes under Article 54-1 B of the Criminal Code of the Ukrainian Soviet Socialist Republic.

In October 1949, the following individuals were arrested by the Ministry of State Security of the Dnepropetrovsk region and will be prosecuted as defendants in this case: Ryabeka, Fedor; Andreyenko, Mikhail; and Gordienko, Terentij.

The investigation has concluded: The defendants, at the beginning of the Great Patriotic War, having been mobilized into the Red Army, and while serving on the battlefront, surrendered to the enemy and were taken prisoner in August–September 1941; Ryabeka, in the vicinity of the city of Zhitomir, and Andreyenko and Gordienko in the vicinity of the city of Korsun-Shevchenko. Confirmed by the defendants' own admissions, located in the case file.

While being held in a POW camp for Soviet prisoners in the town of Chelm (Poland), all the aforementioned defendants, in October 1941, betrayed their country and joined the German SS forces and security police. They were trained at the SS military school in the town of Trawniki, which trains punitive personnel for service at mass extermination camps. Confirmed by the defendants' own admissions, located in the case file.

In April 1945, defendants Ryabeka and Andreyenko were captured by American troops on German territory and returned to the USSR as repatriates.

In the following indictment, Ryabeka, Andreyenko, and Gordienko have pled guilty. Their pleas are located in the case file.

For their criminal activity they were convicted by evidence and by in-person questionings. The following persons are indicted:

(1) Ryabeka, Fedor, born 1906 in Dnepropetrovsk Province of working-class background, with a primary education; no party affiliation, works as a driver, has no government awards. Prior to his arrest, worked as a freight handler/loader. Lives in Amur-Lower Dnepr town of Ordzhonikidze. As a serviceman of the Red Army, having surrendered to the enemy to become a POW, he betrayed his country and joined the German SS forces and security police. He gave a written oath to serve Nazi Germany and went through training at an SS school. Upon receiving the rank of *Wachmann*, he carried out service in mass extermination camps and concentration camps. While guarding people doomed to death, he participated in their killings. He escorted labor groups of prisoners at the death camps of Sobibor and Auschwitz, and the concentration camp in the city of Lublin. He also took part in the construction of the Belzec death camp. These are crimes under Article 54-1 B of the Criminal Code of the Ukrainian Soviet Socialist Republic.

(2) Andreyenko, Mikhail, born 1912 in Likhovka region, Dnepropetrovsk Province, of midlevel peasant background, Ukrainian nationality; no party affiliation, primary education, no criminal record, has no government awards. Prior to his arrest, worked as an accountant.

PROTOCOL OF TRIAL PROCEEDINGS. GEORGIJ SKYDAN[13]

On May 26, 1950, the military tribunal of the Belorussian Military District met in closed trial proceedings in the city of Baranovichi. The tribunal consisted of the following:
Presiding judge: Major of Justice Agafonov
Associate judges (Jurists): Captain Dementev and Lieutenant Vorobev
Recording secretary: Junior Lieutenant Greznev
Other participants: assistant military procurator for the Belorussian Military District, Lieutenant Colonel of Justice Moskalenko, and attorney Altshulery, a defense attorney from the Baranovichi regional Collegium of Attorneys.

The presiding judge announced that the case will be examined, charging Georgij Alexandrovich Skydan for crimes stipulated under Article 63-2 of the Criminal Code of the Belorussian Soviet Socialist Republic.

Statement of the defendant Skydan: On June 24, 1941, I was drafted to serve in the Red Army, by the Duryansk District Military Commissariat, and was sent to serve in the 878th Artillery Regiment. I was assigned as a crewman. In August 1941, my unit participated in combat against the Germans near the Taganga railroad station. We suffered heavy personnel losses. Later, some of us were surrounded by German motorcyclists and tanks. I became scared and surrendered. I had my rifle but I did not resist.

We were sent to a local village where the Germans were collecting POWs. We were marched to Belaya Tserkov. From there, we were loaded into railcars and transported to the town of Chelm, in Poland. There we were placed in a POW camp. The prisoners in the camp numbered about 75,000 people. The living conditions in this camp were very bad. Each day we were given only 200 grams of bread and half a liter of millet soup. Over the course of the two or three months I spent in this camp, about 50 percent of the prisoners died of starvation or disease.

After about three months, I was one of about 100 POWs transported to work in an alcohol factory near Warsaw. They gave us only 150 grams of bread per day, but we also had access to potatoes. In January 1942, some Germans came to see us with a doctor. On their orders, the entire work detail stood in formation. The healthy men, including me, totaling thirty-six, were taken by vehicle to the town of Trawniki and housed in barracks.

The Germans made us weave footwear for about a month. The Germans here gave us up to 500 grams of bread per day. The Germans issued us German uniforms and equipment. I was given a gray German coat, boots, and a service cap, and I was assigned to the third Russian company. We began two weeks of drill training. Our unit was part of the Trawniki school for *Wachmänner* of the SS forces. After initial training, we were summoned to the staff headquarters, where forms were completed on each of us and fingerprints were taken. Two days later, we were photographed with our personal ID numbers, which we held to our chests before being photographed. We then continued drill training for another 2.5 months and were then assigned to the city of Lublin. As *Wachmänner*, we guarded the Jewish ghetto there. It was a row of city blocks surrounded by barbed wire.

About one month after our arrival in Lublin, the Germans moved the Jews out of the ghetto. They numbered about 40,000–50,000 people. I do not know where they were sent. I remained in Lublin and guarded the possessions that were left behind in the ghetto. I simply guarded the ghetto, nothing else. In August 1942, after a one-week stay in Warsaw, two companies, including mine, were sent to the Treblinka death camp. In Warsaw, we conducted only military training. We were assigned to guard Treblinka.

Besides guarding Treblinka, I also served as a stable hand for three months in the camp. I cared for horses and brought produce for the Germans and *Wachmänner*. I lost this assignment after it had been discovered that the two Jews who had worked with me in the stables had concealed some gold coins. I was blamed for not having watched them closely enough to notice this. They were shot.

I stood guard both outside and inside the camp. People were brought to the camp for the purpose of mass extermination. Trains arrived, and the people inside were taken off and brought into the camp. The people walked into a building that looked like a bathhouse. After the "bathhouse" was filled to capacity with people, the doors were closed. It was only then that the people locked inside realized that they had been sent into a gas chamber. People screamed, beat on the door, and tried to get out. *Wachmänner* Shalayev and Marchenko then turned on the diesel motor, which fed exhaust gas into the gas chamber. After about fifteen minutes, the people inside were dead. The dead were carried out to some pits by special work details, who threw the bodies into the pits.

There were occasions when those people arriving learned the true intent of the "bath" from members of the work detail or the *Wachmänner*. They resisted entering the gas chamber. In such cases, so-called *kapos*, under strict supervision, forced people into the gas chamber with whips. Besides using sticks to force people into the gas chamber, the Germans also used dogs that lunged at the naked people. The *Wachmänner* participated in shooting prisoners right along with the Germans. *Wachmänner* also took part in standing guard along the path enclosed by barbed wire near the gas chamber, in order to prevent escapes. I personally stood guard several times along the path enclosed by barbed wire that led to the gas chamber. No prisoners tried to escape while I was standing guard.

I personally participated in shooting prisoners three times on orders from the Germans. The first time, I shot two people; the second time, one person. On the third occasion, I was escorting two people to be shot, but Wachmann Ratchenko took them from me and shot them himself, on his own initiative.

At the camp, the Germans received two or three trains per day carrying people of various nationalities. Most of them were Jews. At first, only one gas chamber was in use. After some time, the Germans built a second gas chamber because the first one could not keep pace with the daily number of people brought for extermination. Work details piled the bodies from the gas chamber in pits and destroyed them by burning. The Germans forced them to clean up the ashes from the bodies, and they collected the ashes in special bags and then buried them in the ground. After the bodies had been burned, not all of the bones had been destroyed. Bones that did not burn were dug up from the pits with an excavator and were milled and ground into a flour-like powder and then reburied. During my time at the camp, the Germans exterminated up to several thousand people per day.

In fall 1943, for reasons unknown to me, the Germans began to destroy all traces of the mass extermination. The pits in which the Germans burned the bodies were filled in with dirt. All camp structures and buildings were blown up. Ashes and bones were buried deep in the ground by excavators. The camp surface was leveled, the ground was plowed, and rye was planted. They built a house for Yeger and his wife to occupy. The liquidation of the camp was complete by November 1943. The *Wachmänner* were transferred back to Trawniki. Then, I was sent, along with thirty to forty other *Wachmänner*, to Oranienburg, near Berlin. The SS staff headquarters in Oranienburg then deployed us to East Prussia, to Stutthof, where we guarded a concentration camp.

We arrived in Stutthof in November 1943 and remained there until January 1945. There were about 50,000 prisoners in Stutthof. In January 1945, our *Wachmänner* unit was transferred to Pelz. There, we guarded a camp and I escorted prisoners to work. In April 1945, we were sent to the city of Hamburg and then, two days later, to the city of Neu Ulm. We were sent westward on foot. At this time, we heard rumors that Hitler was dead. As a result, we scattered. I dropped my rifle, destroyed my ID card, and was soon captured by the British. I was sent to a camp with a column of Germans. All of us were searched, including other *Wachmänner* who were with me, including Liskovskij, Nikolai Sennikov, and Ivan Machulin. One day, we found Soviet uniforms in the attic of a barracks in which we were held. We put these uniforms on, left the camp, and reached Hamburg on foot. From Hamburg, the British took us to Neu Ulm. We were later handed over to Soviet forces.

Presiding judge [Signature]
Secretary [Signature]
True copy: senior investigator for OVD (Especially Serious Cases), Investigations Department, KGB, Crimean region, Lieutenant Colonel A. Glushchenko
Note: The original protocol is located in archival criminal file #8309, charging G. Skydan.

PROTOCOL OF CLOSED TRIAL PROCEEDINGS AGAINST NIKOLAI SHALAYEV[14]
December 20, 1951

Protocol of closed trial proceedings of the military tribunal of the Voronezh Military District Consisting of the following: presiding judge, Colonel of Justice Kishkurno
Associate members: Lieutenant Colonel of Administrative Services Makhajlov, and Major Komolov
With secretary: Senior Lieutenant of Justice Afanaseva
Additional participants: deputy military procurator of the Voronezh Military District, Lieutenant Colonel of Justice Vodopyanov, and attorney Ognerubov

The presiding judge announced that the court was going to examine the case charging Nikolai Shalayev under Article 58-1b of the Criminal Code of the Russian Soviet Federated Socialist Republic.

The defendant Shalayev testified as follows: I was called up to serve in the Red Army in October 1940 by the Yasenov District Military Commissariat, Kursk region. I was sent to the town of Zabolote, Stanislavov region, where I was enrolled as a student in the regimental school of the 126th Sapper Battalion. As soon as the war against Germany began, I retreated along with my unit toward Kiev. I was captured by German forces along with other members of my unit on July 3, 1941, in the area of the village of Ternovka, near Belaya Tserkov. They sent me to a camp in Chelm, in Poland. I escaped from this camp, but I was detained and again sent to the camp. In November 1941, a camp interpreter told me that the Germans were gathering a group of forty POWs in the camp. I told the interpreter that I wanted to join this group. We were not told where we were going or for what purpose. In December 1941, we were taken to the town of Trawniki. There, I learned that we had been selected for enlistment into the SS guard force. There were many other Russians who were former POWs in the camp. We were divided into companies and began training. We did drill and rifle training. We trained for about two months. In February 1942, I deployed to Lublin to guard the Jewish ghetto. There, we formed a cordon around one-quarter of the city.

In late June 1942, I was sent with a thirty-to-thirty-five-man detachment to guard the Treblinka death camp. At first, I stood guard outside the camp. I was then transferred by the Germans to serve at the bathhouse or so-called gassing facility, where I served for twenty days as the motor operator of the gas chambers. Two Jews, two Germans, another Ukrainian, and I were assigned to the motor of the bathhouse. The Ukrainian and I guarded the Jews and supervised their work. The Jews serviced and started the motor that fed exhaust gas into the death chambers. The motor was turned on, and gas went into the chambers. The people inside lost consciousness in about two minutes and were dead after about five minutes. The motor was powerful, 90 horsepower. The people were then pulled out and carted away on a rail cart to pits. The bodies were buried there. Later, the Germans exhumed the bodies from the pits, stacked them, and burned them. By doing so, they eliminated their crimes.

About 5,000–6,000 Jews were killed during the period of my service as a guard-supervisor at the motor, and not 70,000 as listed in the indictment. In the motor room I supervised the work of the Jews, and sometimes I opened the pipe that allowed exhaust gas to flow into the gas chambers. I did not beat or shoot anyone in the camp. The Germans forbid us from beating the Jews, and they did not beat them either. They treated them well and wanted to hide from them the fact that they were going to die. I also did not force Jews into the gas chambers. During the investigation I stated that I had driven Jews into the chambers, but this is not true. I made this statement at the insistence of the investigator. I told the investigator that I had not done this, but he did not believe me.

I served as a guard-supervisor in the motor room for only twenty days. I was then transferred to serve as a guard-supervisor at the generator, which was located in the same facility. I served in this capacity until July 1943. The generator provided lighting for the entire camp. This generator was serviced by two Jews, and I guarded them and supervised their work. I was not assigned to this duty by anyone. I traded places with another *Wachmann* named Marchenko at my own initiative. I traded positions because I did not want to work with the motors at the gas chambers. Marchenko wanted this job, so he and I traded jobs.

In July 1943 I was sent to the city of Trieste (Italy). At first I served as a member of a captured material-exploitation company. I was then sent with a guard detachment to guard the roads between Trieste and Fiume, Trieste and Udine, Trieste and Pola, and Trieste and Ljubljana.

We did not have a jail, per se, at our police detachment in Trieste. We only had a transit point. Local residents spent two or three days at this transit point and were then sent to perform work on defensive positions or to repair roads. We guarded these people at the transit point. As a member of the police detachment, I guarded various points along the roads that I mentioned, and I guarded German officers who frequently traveled from Trieste along these roads to other cities and settlements. I was never deployed on roundups of partisans; however, I frequently participated in firefights with Italian and Yugoslav partisans while serving at guard posts along roads, or when escorting officers.

In April 1945, I left Italy along with the Germans and went to Austria. On May 7, 1945, I surrendered to the British. In May 1945, the British handed me over to the Soviet authorities in Austria. I concealed my criminal activities when being questioned at a screening point. I was then redrafted into the Red Army, and I served until I was demobilized in August 1946.

Presiding judge [Signature]
Secretary [Signature]
True copy: senior investigator of the Investigations Department, KGB, Crimea region, Captain Linnik
Note: The original of this document is held in archival criminal case file #17214.

Deputy director of the Files Directorate
Procurator's Office of the USSR, E. F. Vladimirov
Xerox copy made from a copy located in the criminal file charging Fedorenko, vol. 15, pp. 150–15?

Case #0858

PROTOCOL OF TRIAL PROCEEDINGS, IVAN SHVIDKIJ[15]

January 12, 1952

The military tribunal of the Kiev Military District, in a closed trial proceeding in the city of Stalino consisting of the following:
Presiding judge: Guards Lieutenant Colonel of Justice Kolomijtsev
Associate judges: Major Loktionov and Senior Lieutenant Shmykov
Secretary: Senior Lieutenant of Justice Petryayev
Other participants: the deputy military procurator of the Kiev Military District, Colonel of Justice Marudov and attorney Mizun

Examined criminal file #0858
The presiding judge declared that the court was to examine the file that charges Ivan Danilovich Shvidkij with committing crimes as stipulated under Article 54-1b of the Ukrainian Soviet Criminal Code.

From among the witnesses who have been summoned in this trial proceeding, the prisoners V. Elenchuk and G. Gapienko will be brought in one at a time.

The following persons have been summoned as witnesses: M. Lysak, sentenced to death and held in jail in the city of Dnepropetrovsk, and N. Pogrebnyak, sentenced to twenty-five years' imprisonment in corrective labor camps, and also held in Dnepropetrovsk.

The presiding judge established the identity of the defendant, who stated the following about himself:

I am Ivan Shvidkij, born in 1909 in Ukraine, Dzerzhinsk District, Stalino/Donetsk region. My father works on a collective farm. My mother resides in the same place. I am single. I have a brother, Mikhail, born in 1922. He serves in the Soviet army, with the rank of captain. He now serves in Izmailovo region, where an aviation unit is located. I do not have any relatives who served for the Germans and were subsequently repressed by Soviet authorities. My education level is about two years. I have no party affiliations, and no prior convictions.

Before the war, I worked as an ore loader in a mine, and before my arrest I worked as a loader in the transportation section of the Dzerzhinsk Coal Trust. I served in the Red Army after being called up by the Dzerzhinsk District Military Commissariat on June 28, 1941. I served until August 3, 1941. I served a second time from March to October 1945. I served as a private on both occasions. I participated in combat in 1941. I was not wounded. In April 1945, I was lightly wounded in the elbow by shrapnel from a mine in the area of Danzig (Gdansk) while taking up a defense. I was decorated with the medal "For Victory over Germany." I was arrested on June 12, 1951, and was shown the indictment on January 5, 1952.

The presiding judge announced the composition of the court and the last names of the persons participating in the case. He then explained to the defendant his rights and possible reasons to ask for the removal of any member of the court on grounds stipulated in Articles 38, 40, 42, and 44 of the Code of Criminal Procedure of the Ukrainian Soviet Socialist Republic. He then asked both sides if they desired the removal of any member of the court. They did not.

In response to questions posed by the presiding judge, the defendant stated: I do not object to having attorney Mizun defend me. The presiding judge asked for opinions from both sides on the possibility of hearing the case in the absence of the witnesses, Lysak and Pogrebnyak.

Procurator: I believe it is possible to hear the case in the absence of the witnesses. The statements they provided during the preliminary investigation should be read.

Defendant: I also believe it is possible to hear the case in the absence of the witnesses.

The tribunal determined that the case would be heard in the absence of the witnesses, but that the statements they provided during preliminary investigation would be read.

The presiding judge explained to the defendant that he had the right to present petitions, to summon new witnesses, to request documentary evidence from the case file, or to add documents available to him to the case file.

The presiding judge explained to the defendant his right during the judicial inquiry to ask questions of witnesses, and to provide explanations both to the substance of the case in general, as well as regarding any specific circumstances of the case, at any time during the judicial inquiry. He then explained to the defendant his right to say the last word, and asked him if he understood his rights.

Judicial inquiry: The presiding judge read the statement of charges and the findings of the preliminary hearing of the military tribunal. He explained to the defendant the substance of the charges presented against him, and then asked him if he understood what he was being charged with, whether or not he acknowledged his guilt, and whether or not he wanted to testify before the court.

Defendant: I understand the charges. I acknowledge my guilt to having betrayed the Motherland. I desire to testify before the court.

The tribunal determined that examination of the materials in the case will begin with the questioning of the defendant, after which the statements of Lysak and Pogrebnyak will be read, and the witnesses Elenchuk and Gapienko will then be questioned.

Testimony of the defendant Shvidkij: On June 28, 1941, I was called up to serve in the Red Army. I was sent by the District Military Commissariat with my unit to Mariupol. From there, we went to Belaya Tserkov. There, we took up defensive positions. In August 1941, I was captured near the village of Mironovka. The Germans brought me to Belaya Tserkov, and then to the town of Chelm. In December 1941, as a POW, I was selected and taken to Trawniki, where we were trained. In March 1942, we deployed to Lublin to guard the Jewish ghetto. In July 1942, we guarded the Jewish ghetto in Warsaw. I was then assigned to Treblinka, where prisoners were put to death in gas chambers. In Treblinka, I guarded prisoners as they were being herded naked into the gas chambers to be asphyxiated with exhaust gas. I also did shooting duty in the "Lazarett" on four or five occasions. I had to shoot old, crippled, and sick people there. I shot them in the head or chest. Sometimes we were forced to shoot fifteen to twenty-five people. I shot up to 120 people. From August 1942 to October 1943, I helped send 250,000–300,000 people into the gas chamber.

In October 1943, I was transferred to Stutthof. There I guarded a camp in which Russians, Poles, and Germans were imprisoned. In February 1945, during the approach of Soviet forces, we scattered. When Soviet forces arrived, I ended up at an assembly point. There, I underwent screening, after which I was once again called up to serve in the Red Army.

The defendant (in response to questions posed by the presiding judge): In August 1941, when I surrendered to the Germans, my unit had been surrounded. The Germans approached us. We did not show any resistance because there were many of them and we were afraid. They walked up to me, took my rifle, and threw it on the ground. I went on to serve the Germans because we were threatened that if we ran away, our families would be killed.

I guarded the exterior of the Treblinka death camp. I also forced naked people into the gas chamber. We beat people with rifle butts when they did not want to proceed into the gas chamber. Each time, I forced up to 150 people into the gas chamber. I forced up to ten such groups of prisoners per day. There were forty Germans in the camp. There were more than 100 of us *Wachmänner*.

The defendant (in response to questions posed by the attorney): After Soviet forces arrived, I spent three days in screening. However, I concealed my service as a *Wachmann*.

The defendant (in response to questions posed by the presiding judge): I believe that I surrendered to the Germans. I surrendered on August 3, 1941, near Mironovka, Kiev region. When we arrived at Trawniki, I learned that we had been enlisted in the SS forces. In January 1942, I swore an oath to the Germans. We were issued German clothing, which was gray in color. In Treblinka, we were given clothing that was black in color. I was also issued a rifle. I was paid a salary in German marks.

There were no prisoner riots in the Treblinka camp. A Jew ripped the gold teeth out of prisoners' mouths after they had been killed. The gold teeth were then taken to the camp staff headquarters. I did not take for myself the valuables of the people who had been killed. I did not exchange stolen property from those killed for vodka.

The defendant (in response to questions posed by the presiding judge): I confirm these statements. I took watches, rings, and money from among the possessions of those who had been killed. I drank away these possessions and money in the local villages, but this was not often. Having left the Red Army and gone home, I did not tell anyone of my crimes. I did not attempt to report this to the MGB, because I was afraid. I do not remember the personal ID # assigned to me in Trawniki.

The defendant (in response to questions posed by the presiding judge): Yes, I was assigned personal ID #1357. I provided a fingerprint when I swore an oath to the Germans.

The witness, Vlas Elenchuk, born 1918, under investigation in accordance with Article 54-1b of the Criminal Code of the Ukrainian Soviet Socialist Republic.

The presiding judge explained to the witness his criminal liabilities under Article 89 of the Criminal Code for knowingly providing false testimony.

Testimony of the witness Elenchuk: After I was captured by the Germans, I ended up in a camp in Rovno. In October 1942, I and about 150 other men were selected and transported to the camp in Trawniki. There, we were given a German uniform and underwent training. Three months later, I was sent to the Treblinka camp. I remember the last name Shvidkij, but I do not know what he looks like, and I know nothing about his criminal activities.

The defendant (in response to questions posed by the procurator): I met Elenchuk in Treblinka, both on duty and in the barracks, from spring or summer 1942 until October 1943.

The witness Elenchuk (in response to questions posed by the presiding judge): I served in Treblinka from March to May 1943. Yeger was the commander of our platoon.

The defendant (in response to questions posed by the presiding judge): Elenchuk and I served in the same platoon under the command of Yeger. Elenchuk also forced people into the gas chamber. I do not remember whether or not he shot people.

The witness Elenchuk (in response to questions posed by the presiding judge): I did not force people into the gas chamber, and I did not know that people had been burned in the camp.

The witness Grigorij Gapienko, born 1918, under investigation in accordance with Article 54-1b of the Criminal Code of the Ukrainian Soviet Socialist Republic.

The presiding judge explained to the witness his criminal liabilities under Article 89 of the Criminal Code for knowingly providing false testimony.

The witness Gapienko (in response to questions posed by the procurator): I served in Trawniki, Treblinka, and Osventsim (Auschwitz). I did not know Shvidkij in any of these camps.

The defendant (in response to questions posed by the procurator): I served with Gapienko in Treblinka in 1943. He served in the first platoon. I served in the second platoon. I saw him in the camp.

The witness Gapienko (in response to questions posed by the presiding judge): I served in the Treblinka camp and participated in forming a cordon around the trains that arrived within the camp. I also participated in the cordon around the area through which the prisoners proceeded to the gas chamber.

People were buried in pits. I did not take possessions from those who had been killed, but I took money and went to drink vodka in the local villages. I knew Yeger. He was the commander of the other platoon. I served in Treblinka for about five months in 1943.

The presiding judge declared the judicial inquiry closed, and the court proceeded to hear arguments from both sides.

The procurator was offered a chance to speak. Colonel of Justice Marudov stated in his presentation that the charges presented against the defendant had been completely proven and demonstrated as applicable in accordance with Article 54-1b of the Criminal Code of the Ukrainian Soviet Socialist Republic.

The procurator recommended that Shvidkij be sentenced to death by firing squad.

In order that the interests of the defendant be protected, the attorney Mizun was offered an opportunity to speak. He stated that the defendant's guilt had been proven, but that the defendant had admitted his crimes and acknowledged his guilt. The attorney asked the court to consider sparing Shvidkij's life.

The presiding judge declared the arguments of both sides to be concluded, and provided the defendant an opportunity to say the last word. The defendant stated: "I submit to your will."

The tribunal retired to confer on the sentence. An hour and a half after conferring, the tribunal returned from the conference room. The presiding judge read the sentence and explained the substance of it to the convict. He then explained the term and procedures for appealing the sentence to the Military Collegium of the Supreme Court of the USSR. He also explained to the defendant his right to appeal for clemency to the Presidium of the Supreme Soviet of the USSR.

The trial proceeding was closed. January 19, 1952.

Presiding judge [Signature] I. Kolomijtsev
Secretary [Signature] M. Petryayev

BACKGROUND INFORMATION SHEET ON THE ARREST, TRIAL, AND SENTENCE OF VASILI SHULLER[16]

Archived criminal case #6636, against Vasili Shuller (a.k.a. Vasili Kobylyatskij)
Arrested September 9, 1954, by the KGB in Zaporozhe region, for treason.

During preliminary investigation, Shuller pled guilty to the charges brought against him.

He became a POW of the Germans while serving in the Red Army in 1941. He joined the SS. He served in Lublin and the Belzec death camp until March 1943. He participated in the mass extermination of Jewish civilians in gas chambers.

The following documents were included as evidence in the case against Shuller:

(1) Captured document (trophy document): *Personalbogen* #223, a photo ID of Shuller filled out on October 23, 1941
(2) Transfer roster of March 29, 1943, indicating Shuller's assignment as an *SS-Gruppenwachmann* to Auschwitz concentration camp
(3) Bulletin of the Main Investigation Commission in Poland in 1947, which investigated the Belzec camp
(4) Copy of the record of interrogation of the following persons: Piotr Browzew, November 1947 and November 1954; Vladimir Lomov, May 1950; Alexander Zakharov, November and December 1954; Alexei Zhukov, May 1953, and review of the investigation case against Zhukov; Vladimir Belinskij, November 1954
(5) Excerpts from the record of the court session of the case against Piotr Browzew, December 20, 1947, and a copy of the sentencing decision in the Browzew case
(6) Excerpts from the record of the court session of the case against Vladimir Lomov and G. Chernikov, September 19, 1950
(7) Excerpts from the court session record of the case against Alexander Dukhno, Mikhail Korzhikow, and Ivan Voloshin from June 5, 1947, and review of the investigation case of those individuals
(8) Review of the investigation cases #365, against Alexander Zakharov; #406, against Peter Sergeyev; and #5276, against Mitrofan Klotz
(9) Copy of the sentencing decision on the case against Taras Olejnik
(10) Copy of the sentencing decision on the case against Vladimir Belinskij, March 31, 1950
(11) Review of the investigation case on charges against Akim Zuev, and the investigation case on charges against Vasili Popov

The witnesses Vladimir Lomov, Alexei Zhukov, Piotr Browzew, and Alexander Zakharov have testified that Shuller served in the German SS forces. Browzew and Zakharov also testified that Shuller participated in the mass extermination of Jews in Belzec death camp. Three civilian witnesses testified that Shuller also served at Buchenwald concentration camp. Three civilian witnesses gave testimony on characterizing Shuller during his time working in a bread production factory in the city of Stalino (Donetsk).

The case against Shuller was examined by the military tribunal of the Tavrichesky Military District on December 30, 1954, under Article 54-1b of the Criminal Code of the Ukrainian Soviet Socialist Republic. The case was heard on January 12, 1955. At the court session Shuller pled guilty.

The military tribunal found Shuller guilty with the following findings: In October 1941, Shuller betrayed his country and, under the name Wilhelm Shuller, joined the German SS-Police force at Trawniki. He served at Belzec camp, Auschwitz camp, and Buchenwald camp until April 1945.

Shuller is sentenced to twenty-five years in a labor camp, followed by suppression of his civil rights for five years.

On January 14, 1955, Shuller filed an appeal with the Soviet Supreme Court and confirmed that he did betray his homeland but that he did so for the purpose of getting out of the POW camp he was incarcerated in, in order to avoid starvation. He therefore requests a reexamination of his case and a reduction of his sentence. A similar appeal was filed with the Military Collegium of the Soviet Supreme Court on January 15, 1955, by attorney

Chernaya, at Shuller's request. The Military Collegium of the Soviet Supreme Court reaffirmed Shuller's sentence on April 2, 1955, and his appeal was denied.

Excerpts from a report from an August 20, 1956, committee meeting of the Presidium of the Supreme Soviet discussed proceedings of cases on individuals who are serving sentences for political, official, and economic crimes at the Dubrava penal camp of the MVD. The report illustrates that Shuller demonstrated good behavior and faithful work ethic while imprisoned. He requested that his sentence be reduced to ten years' imprisonment.

No findings are available in the case with regard to when Shuller was released from imprisonment.

Background information has been compiled for inclusion in the criminal case against Akim Zuev and Taras Olejnik.

Criminal case #6636, against V. Shuller, is stored at the KGB Registration Archive in Zaporozhe region.
This background information sheet was prepared by senior investigator, Investigations Department, KGB, Dnepropetrovsk region, Major Moroz.
August 7, 1965, city of Dnepropetrovsk

BACKGROUND INFORMATION SHEET ON THE ARREST, TRIAL, AND SENTENCE OF NIKOLAJ SKAKODUB[17]
Archived investigation case #25190, against Nikolaj Skakodub
Arrested November 14, 1960, and prosecuted
KGB, Vinnitsa region
Skakodub, who was interrogated at the court session, pled guilty and made a full confession regarding his service with the SS at Treblinka, Auschwitz, and Buchenwald. He has betrayed his country. His criminality is also confirmed by the testimony of witnesses presented at his trial:

(1) Ivan Safonov
(2) Ananij Kuzminsky
(3) Filip Levchishin
(4) Sergej Vasilenko
(5) Nikolaj Senik
(6) Prokofij Ryabtsev

On February 3, 1961, by a decision of the military tribunal of the Carpathian Military region, Skakodub was sentenced to fifteen years' imprisonment, under Article 1 of the law "On Criminal Responsibility for State Crimes." The sentence was not appealed and has become legally effective.
Investigation case #25190, against N. Skakodub, is stored at the KGB Archive, Vinnitsa region.
Senior investigator, Investigations Department, KGB, Kaliningrad region, Shabanov

SCHULTZ TRIAL[18]
Shortly before the "Schults" trial in 1962, the chairman of the Presidium of the Supreme Soviet, Leonid Brezhnev, signed a resolution that suspended the principle of "*Lex prospicit, non respicit*" ("The law looks forward, not back"). As a result, a military tribunal sentenced the twelve accused to death, on the basis of expired laws dating back to World War II and despite a legal prohibition on the death penalty for crimes committed more than fifteen

years earlier. In this way, the Soviet judicial system suspended the principle, recognized in Europe since Roman times, that any law increasing punishment for a crime should not be retroactive.[19] A 1962 resolution of the Presidium of the Supreme Soviet of the Soviet Union allowed the military tribunal in Kiev to sentence the defendants to death in the "Schults" trial. This resolution was contained in the twenty-eighth volume of the record of the previously secret trial.[20]

During the "Khrushchev Thaw" of 1953–1964, the Soviet government frequently proclaimed a return to "socialist legality," which had been violated under Stalin. Nevertheless, for this case, it enacted a "Resolution of the Presidium of the Supreme Soviet of the USSR," with a suspension of Article 6 and 41 of the "Fundamental Principles of Criminal Legislation of the Soviet Union" for the following defendants: Emanuel Schults (a.k.a. Emanuel Vinogradov), Filip Levchishin, Sergei Vasilenko, Samuel Pritsch, Ivan Terekhov, Yakov Karpliuk, Dimitri Borodin, Alexei Govorov, Fedor Ryabeka, Ivan Kurennoi, Mikhail Gorbachev, and Evdokim Parfinyuk:[21]

> Imprisonment shall be substituted with the death penalty if, in reviewing the case, the court establishes that the defendants committed punitive acts and personally participated in the torture and murder of Soviet citizens during the Great Patriotic War (World War II), and if the death penalty could have been applied to those crimes at the time they were committed.
>
> Chairman, Presidium of the Supreme Soviet, Leonid Brezhnev
> Secretary, Presidium of the Supreme Soviet, Mikhail Georgadze
> Moscow, Kremlin
> February 8, 1962

The defendants were charged under Article 56 of the Soviet-Ukrainian Criminal Code (equivalent to Article 58 of the Soviet-Russian Criminal Code for Treason). The "Schults" trial record contains a total of thirty-six volumes of material. The investigation of the defendants, in preparation for trial, was conducted by the Ukrainian KGB between February and November 1961 (see USHMM, RG 31.018M). The case was tried by the military tribunal of the Kiev Military District. The trial was completed on March 31, 1962, and all twelve defendants were sentenced to death. All the defendants were former Red Army POWs who had become Trawniki guards and had served at Treblinka and Sobibor.[22] Seven of the defendants were Ukrainian, four were Russian, and one was a Volksdeutscher from Russia (Schultz).

There was one court session of the military tribunal of the Kiev Military District, in closed proceedings in Kiev, presided over by Colonel Zakharchenko, assisted by Captain Kononov and Supreme Court member Klimenchuk. The prosecution was conducted by Senior Assistant Military Procurator Arikchyajnets.[23]

Former Sobibor prisoner Alexander Pechersky appeared as a prosecution witness at the trial. (Almost all publications about Sobibor mention his presence at the trial, often implying that he was the main prosecution witness. In fact, this was not the case: His role as a witness has been greatly exaggerated. This mistake was enabled by the fact that the trial was closed to the public. It was mentioned only once in the Soviet press, in the April 13, 1963 issue of the newspaper *Krasnaia Zvezda* [*Red Star*].)[24]

The evidence against the defendants consisted mainly of testimony from other former Trawniki guards in this and other cases, and the defendants' own admissions. For example, the number of Jews some of the defendants admitted to shooting during their service at Treblinka II were as follows: Sergei Vasilenko, ten to fifteen; Yakov Karpliuk, ten; Ivan

Kurinnoi, six; Emanuel Schults/Vinogradov, three; and Ivan Terekhov, three.[25]

During the war, the Presidium of the Supreme Soviet issued a *Ukaz* (order) on April 19, 1943, for the punishment of spies, traitors, and accomplices of the Germans. The penalty was death by hanging, or exile and hard labor. In 1955, the Presidium of the Supreme Soviet issued an amnesty order for those Soviet citizens who had collaborated with the Germans during the war. However, this amnesty was not to apply to those convicted of torture and murder.[26]

One of the defendants, Mikhail Gorbachev, had been sentenced by a military tribunal of the Urals Military District in 1951 to twenty-five years' imprisonment, under Article 58-1b of the Soviet-Russian Criminal Code (Treason), because he had volunteered to serve as a Trawniki guard. He was released during the amnesty in 1955. However, during investigations in 1961, evidence emerged that he had participated in mass murder at Treblinka II. As a result, the Military Collegium of the Soviet Supreme Court ordered that he be reinvestigated.[27]

In the late 1950s, Soviet criminal law reduced the maximum sentence for serious crimes from twenty-five years of imprisonment to fifteen years of imprisonment. The defendants in the "Schults" trial probably expected to get fifteen years minus time previously served.[28]

As chairman of the Presidium of the Supreme Soviet, Leonid Brezhnev was the highest official of the Soviet government, although the country was actually ruled by the chairman of the party's Central Committee (Nikita Khrushchev). Brezhnev's state position (though not his party position) was largely nominal. Decisions with important legal implications, such as that in the "Schults" case, were always signed by the chairman of the Presidium of the Supreme Soviet. The resolution signed by Brezhnev predetermined the deaths of the defendants in the trial. Apparently the resolution signed by Brezhnev and Georgadze had been adopted on the initiative of KGB chairman Vladimir Semichastnyi. The resolution was never made public, nor were the defendants aware of it, and it was not included in the trial transcript or in the sentence.[29]

Under the Soviet Constitution, courts were considered independent, formally subordinate only to the law. If they received orders "from above" regarding how to rule on particular cases (so-called "telephone" law), hard evidence has not yet emerged. In this regard, the resolution by Brezhnev in the "Schults" case is unusual. On its basis, the court was instructed to pass a more severe punishment than prescribed by the laws then in effect, applying instead a law that had been revoked in 1958.[30]

The defendants were shocked when the prosecutor asked the court to sentence them to death. For example, the main defendant, Schults, wrote a letter appealing to Khrushchev: "After the trial, the attorney could not explain why the court, in defiance of the law, passed a sentence of death against us." Five months later, an official from the State Prosecutor's Office told Schults that the court had had "some sort of special permission to exceed the law." Said Schults, "My nerves were frayed by the overly prolonged investigation. I accepted the fact that I was going to get more than I deserved."[31]

The trial record reflects that Schults contested every piece of evidence against him, including the charge that he whipped prisoners. He admitted that he had been promoted to the rank of *Zugwachmann* (his Trawniki ID # was 55), but insisted that he rarely took part in executions personally while serving at Treblinka II. During the trial, he stated, "Being a Soviet citizen, I should have tried to escape from Treblinka, but my consciousness had not yet matured to the point of acting with honor."[32]

The last words of the other defendants in the case were full of excuses to elicit sympathy from the court: difficult childhoods, upbringings in working-class or peasant families, achievements as good workers, postwar volunteer work they did, and the harsh conditions they endured in German POW camps with hunger and cold. The conditions experienced in POW camps had merit. Most of the defendants had been held in Stalag 319 in Chelm: bare ground under open sky with meager amounts of food and water: bread and turnips. In extreme cases, hunger sometimes led to cannibalism. Diseases in the camps included cholera, typhus, and dysentery. Up to early 1942, two million Soviet POWs died in German captivity.[33]

All the defendants in the "Schults" case appealed their death sentences. Only one of them was successful: Ivan Terekhov. A secret resolution of the Presidium of the Supreme Soviet, dated November 1962, reduced his death sentence to fifteen years' imprisonment, with a further reduction for time served in his previous conviction: meaning he would serve about five years.[34]

The sentence against the other defendants was carried out. As of 1962, the rules for carrying out the death penalty (which were altered in the early 1980s) were regulated by secret instructions of the KGB and MVD: executions were carried out by personnel from both, in each case by order of the Soviet Supreme Court. (The head of the Supreme Court at the time was Alexander Gorkin, and the head of the Military Collegium of the Supreme Court was V. Borisoglebskiy.) These orders were issued only after the Presidium of the Supreme Soviet had reviewed any appeals for pardon.[35]

In 1965, a decree by the Presidium of the Supreme Soviet ruled that there was to be no "statute of limitations" on the prosecution of those guilty of Nazi war crimes. Similarly, a UN Convention stated that there was to be no "statute of limitations" on trying persons for war crimes and crimes against humanity.[36]

It remains unclear why the Soviet government decided to override its own law in the "Schults" case. Perhaps it was a show of good faith to the West that the Soviet Union could harshly punish Nazi collaborators. Perhaps it was the KGB showing that it was still a powerful organization that could mete out punishment regardless of the law (it didn't have the power and status under Khrushchev that it had had under Stalin).[37]

Of particular note is that the indictment in the "Schults" case had been confirmed not by the state prosecutor, whose task it was under the law to do so, but by the chairman of the Ukrainian KGB (who at that time was Vitaliy Nikitchenko), with no legal basis. The absence of the prosecutor's signature on the indictment was a violation of Soviet judicial practice. Ordinarily, without this signature the sentence could not have been carried out. But in this case the court was following "orders from above."[38]

List of Indicted Individuals[39]
Held in detention in the KGB remand prison of the Ukrainian Soviet Socialist Republic:
(1) Gorbachev, Mikhail
(2) Vasilenko, Sergej
(3) Pritsch, Samuel
(4) Govorov, Alexei
(5) Terekhov, Ivan
(6) Karplyuk, Yakov
(7) Levchishin, Philip
(8) Kurinnyj/Kurennoy, Ivan
(9) Borodin, Dimitri
(10) Parfinyuk, Evdokim
(11) Ryabeka, Fedor
(12) Shultz/Vertogradov, Emanuel

Witnesses:

(1) Kuzminsky, Ananij: lives in Yefimovka, Vinnitsa Province
(2) Senik, Nikolai: held in the KGB remand prison of the Ukrainian Soviet Socialist Republic
(3) Saphonov, Ivan: held in the KGB remand prison of the Ukrainian Soviet Socialist Republic
(4) Ryabtsev, Prokofij: held in the KGB remand prison of the Ukrainian Soviet Socialist Republic
(5) Tkachuk, Ivan: lives in Slavutskij region, Khmelnitskj Province
(6) Skakodub, Nikolaj: held in the KGB remand prison of the Ukrainian Soviet Socialist Republic
(7) Andrienko, Mikhail: lives in Verkhne-Dneprovsk region, Dnepropetrovsk Province
(8) Businnyj, Prokofij: lives in Tarashenskj region, Kiev Province
(9) Solonina, Anton: lives in Kiev-Svyatoshin region, Kiev Province
(10) Korovnichenko, Fedor: held in the KGB remand prison of the Ukrainian Soviet Socialist Republic
(11) Pechersky, Alexander: lives in the city of Rostov-on-the-Don
(12) Noga, Vasili: lives in Dobrovelichkovskj region, Kirovograd Province
(13) Vetols, Yanis: lives in the city of Riga

Senior investigator of major cases of the KGB Investigations Department, Ukrainian Soviet Socialist Republic, Lieutenant Colonel Lysenko

Attachment
November 24, 1961
Information
The following individuals are connected with criminal case #14, on the indictment of E. Schultz and others:

(1) Gajdich, Vasili: was convicted, December 13, 1950, by the military tribunal of the Moscow Military District, under Article 58-1 B of the Criminal Code of the Russian Soviet Socialist Republic, and sentenced to death.
(2) Goncharov, Petro: was convicted, June 27, 1951, by the military tribunal of the Kiev Military District, under Article 54-1 B of the Criminal Code of the Ukrainian Soviet Socialist Republic, and sentenced to death.
(3) Sherbak, Nikolaj: was convicted, June 27, 1951, by the military tribunal of the Kiev Military District, under Article 54-1 B of the Criminal Code of the Ukrainian Soviet Socialist Republic, and sentenced to death.
(4) Machoulin, Ivan: was convicted, June 27, 1951, by the military tribunal of the Kiev Military District, under Article 54-1 B of the Criminal Code of the Ukrainian Soviet Socialist Republic, and sentenced to death.
(5) Korotkikh, Dmitri: was convicted, September 21, 1951, by the military tribunal of the Kiev Military District, under Article 54-1 B of the Criminal Code of the Ukrainian Soviet Socialist Republic, and sentenced to death.
(6) Shevchenko, Ivan: was convicted, October 21, 1944, by the military tribunal of the 65th Army of the 1st Belorussian Front, under Article 1 of the executive order of April 19, 1943, and sentenced to death.
(7) Leleko, Pavel: was convicted, March 19, 1945, by the military tribunal of the 2nd

SOME SOVIET TRIALS AND CASE RECORDS

Belorussian Front, under Article 1 of the executive order of April 19, 1943, and sentenced to death.

(8) Shalayev, Nikolai: was convicted, December 20, 1951, by the military tribunal of the Voronezh Military District, under Article 58-1 B of the Criminal Code of the Russian Soviet Socialist Republic, and sentenced to death.

(9) Yeger, Alexander: was convicted, September 9, 1952, by the military tribunal of the Kiev Military District, under Article 54-1 B of the Criminal Code of the Ukrainian Soviet Socialist Republic, and sentenced to death.

(10) Streltsov, Anton: was convicted, June 9, 1950, by the military tribunal of the Kiev Military District, under Article 54-1 B of the Criminal Code of the Ukrainian Soviet Socialist Republic, and sentenced to death.

Senior investigator of major cases of the KGB Investigations Department, Ukrainian Soviet Socialist Republic, Lieutenant Colonel Lysenko

The following persons are accused:

(1) Schultz, Emanuel, a.k.a. Vertogradov, born 1919 in the city of Bryansk; of Russian nationality, no party affiliation, working class, seventh-grade education, no prior convictions, married, resides in the city of Pechora, Komi Autonomous Soviet Socialist Republic. Occupation: engineer in labor and earnings at the Pechora forest combine.

   While in captivity in fall 1941, he betrayed his country and began service with the Germans. During training at the Trawniki SS training camp, he took part in raids on the Jewish population and took an oath to serve Nazi Germany. From summer 1942 through fall 1943, he served in the SS-Sonderkommando at the Sobibor and Treblinka death camps, where he was involved in mass killings of the civilian population by executions in gas chambers and by firing squad. From fall 1943 through the end of the Great Patriotic War, he served in SS-Police units in Italy and took part in punitive actions against anti-Fascist guerrilla units.

   These are crimes under Article 56 of the Criminal Code of the Ukrainian Soviet Socialist Republic.

(2) Levchishin, Philip, born 1913 in Tulchinsk region, Vinnitsa Province; of Ukrainian nationality, peasant ancestry, no party affiliation, fifth-grade education, married. On April 18, 1952, was convicted by the military tribunal of the Carpathian Military District, under Article 54-1 B of the Criminal Code of the Ukrainian Soviet Socialist Republic, and was sentenced to twenty-five years in a penal camp. Released in 1956 with full exoneration. The April 18, 1952, sentence was overturned due to newly discovered evidence by a July 25, 1961, decision of the military tribunal of the Carpathian Military District. On August 12, 1961, he was indicted in this case. Occupation: disinfector at the Tulchinsk regional hospital, Tulchinsk region, Vinnitsa Province.

   He served in the Soviet military and was taken prisoner by the Germans. He betrayed his country by joining the SS, where he served until April 1945. He took an oath to serve Nazi Germany. After completing training at the Trawniki SS training camp, he served as a *wachmann* at the Treblinka death camp from summer 1942 through fall 1943 and was involved in mass killings of the civilian population by suffocation in gas chambers and by firing squad. He served as a troop sergeant and was in charge of overseeing his subordinate *Wachmänner*.

From fall 1943 through April 1945, as part of the SS-"Totenkopf," he carried out guard duties at the Stutthof concentration camp by escorting prisoners to their places of hard labor.

These are crimes under Article 56 of the Criminal Code of the Ukrainian Soviet Socialist Republic.

(3) Vasilienko, Sergej, born 1917 in Radomyshl region, Zhitomir Province; Ukrainian nationality, no party affiliation, with a primary education. On April 15, 1945, he was convicted under Article 58-1 B of the Criminal Code of the Russian Soviet Socialist Republic and was sentenced to ten years in a penal camp. Released on June 6, 1952, with credit for days worked. On May 19, 1961, the previous sentence was overturned by the Primorsky Military District, due to newly discovered evidence, and on June 1, 1961, he was indicted in this case. Married. Occupation: worked on a collective farm.

In fall 1941, he betrayed his country and began serving the Germans until March 1945. During training at the Trawniki SS training camp, he took an oath to serve the Germans and participated in raids on the Jewish population and in escorting prisoners to Trawniki camp. During service in the SS in Lublin, he took part in raids and arrests of Jewish citizens, guarded the Jewish ghetto, and transported the Jewish population from the Lublin ghetto to the death camps. From summer 1942 to fall 1943, served in the SS-Sonderkommando at the Treblinka death camp, where he was involved in mass executions in gas chambers and by firing squad.

As part of the SS-"Totenkopf," carried out guard duties at the Stutthof concentration camp and escorted prisoners to their places of hard labor.

These are crimes under Article 56 of the Criminal Code of the Ukrainian Soviet Socialist Republic.

(4) Pritsch, Samuel, born 1913 in Kiev Province; Ukrainian nationality, of peasant ancestry, no party affiliation, primary education, married. On June 29, 1950, was convicted by the military tribunal of the Kiev Military District, under Article 54-1 B of the Criminal Code of the Ukrainian Soviet Socialist Republic, and was sentenced to twenty-five years in a penal camp. Released in 1955 with full exoneration. As determined on June 6, 1961, by the military tribunal of the Kiev Military District, due to newly discovered evidence, on June 21, 1961, was indicted in this case. Occupation: works on a collective farm.

While serving in the Soviet military and then being held in German captivity, he betrayed his country and joined the German SS, where he served until April 1945. He took an oath to serve Nazi Germany. After completing training at the Trawniki SS training camp, from summer 1942 through fall 1943 he served as a *Wachmann* at the Treblinka death camp, where he was involved in mass killings of the civilian population by suffocation in gas chambers and by firing-squad executions.

He was promoted to the rank of *SS-Oberwachmann* for his obedience, good disciplinary record, and diligence during his service at Treblinka death camp. From fall 1943 through April 1945, as part of the SS-"Totenkopf," he carried out guard duties at the Stutthof concentration camp, escorting prisoners to their places of hard labor.

These are crimes under Article 56 of the Criminal Code of the Ukrainian Soviet Socialist Republic.

(5) Terekhov, Ivan, born 1922 in Kursk Province; Russian nationality, no party affiliation, seventh-grade education, married, from a Kulak family. Was tried on April 15, 1945, by the military tribunal of the 1st Guards Tank Army, under Article 58-1 B of the Criminal Code of the Russian Soviet Socialist Republic, and was sentenced to ten years in a penal camp. Released on August 30, 1953, with credit for days worked. The April 15, 1945, sentence was overturned by military tribunal decision on May 16, 1961, due to newly discovered evidence, and on July 16, 1961, he was indicted in this case. Occupation: automobile park dispatcher at a mine in the Oymyakonskij region, of the Yakut Autonomous Soviet Socialist Republic.

As a POW of the Germans, in fall 1941, he betrayed his country and began service in the German SS, where he served until March 1945.

After completing training at the Trawniki SS training camp, he took an oath to serve the Germans. In Lublin, he took part in guarding the Jewish ghetto, through the summer of 1942, and participated in raids and escorting prisoners to the death camps.

As a *wachmann* in the SS-Sonderkommando at the Treblinka death camp, from summer 1942 through fall 1943, he was involved in mass executions by gas chamber and by firing squad. He participated in the firing-squad execution of a labor team of 150 people and consistently shot people in the so-called "Lazarette" in the camp.

As part of the SS-"Totenkopf," carried out the guarding of prisoners at the Stutthof concentration camp, escorting them to their places of hard labor.

These are crimes under Article 56 of the Criminal Code of the Ukrainian Soviet Socialist Republic.

(6) Karplyuk, Yakov, born 1916 in Novograd-Volynsk region, Zhitomir Province; Ukrainian nationality, of midlevel peasantry, fourth-grade education, no party affiliation, married. On September 28, 1949, was convicted by the military tribunal of Military Installation #77757, under Article 54-1 B of the Criminal Code of the Ukrainian Soviet Socialist Republic, and was sentenced to twenty-five years in a penal camp. Released February 26, 1956. By a May 19, 1961, decision of the military tribunal of the Carpathian Military District, the September 28, 1949, sentence was overturned due to newly discovered evidence, and on June 7, 1961, he was indicted in this case. Occupation: worked on a collective farm in the village of Tokarev, Novograd-Volynsk region, Zhitomir Province.

As a POW of the Germans during the war, he betrayed his country and joined the German SS in fall 1941, where he served until the end of the war. He completed training at the Trawniki SS training camp, where he took an oath to serve the Germans. From summer 1942 through fall 1943, he served as a *Wachmann* at the Sobibor and Treblinka death camps, where in addition to guarding the camp, he was involved in mass killings of the civilian population, in gas chambers and by firing squad.

From fall 1943 until the end of the war, he served as an armed guard in German concentration camps, escorting prisoners to their places of hard labor, and he also participated in fighting against British and American forces.

These are crimes under Article 56 of the Criminal Code of the Ukrainian Soviet Socialist Republic.

(7) Borodin, Dmitri, born 1918 in Volovsk region, Tula Province; Russian nationality, seventh-grade education, of poor peasantry, no party affiliation, married. Was

tried in 1948 under Article 1, by decree of the Presidium of the Supreme Soviet "On Criminal Responsibility for Embezzlement of State and Public Property." Released in 1953, under amnesty. Occupation: shop steward for road construction in the city of Zheleznogorsk, Kursk Province.

As a POW of the Germans, in fall 1941 he betrayed his country and began serving the German SS, where he served until the end of the war.

After completing training at the Trawniki SS training camp, he took an oath to serve the Germans. In Lublin, he guarded the Jewish ghetto and participated in raids and escorted apprehended individuals into the ghetto.

As a *Wachmann* in the SS-Sonderkommando at the Treblinka and Sobibor death camps, from June 1942 to March 1943, he was involved in mass executions by suffocation in gas chambers and by firing squad. He participated in the firing-squad execution of a labor team of 100 people and consistently shot people in the so-called "Lazarette" in the camp. He also carried out guard duties in the Auschwitz and Buchenwald concentration camps and escorted prisoners to their places of hard labor.

These are crimes under Article 56 of the Criminal Code of the Ukrainian Soviet Socialist Republic.

(8) Govorov, Alexei, born 1916 in Krasnozorensky region, Orel Province; Russian nationality, seventh-grade education, no party affiliation, married. Was tried in 1949 by a court in the Krasnozorensky region and sentenced to three years' probation, under Article 74 of the Criminal Code of the Russian Soviet Socialist Republic, and in 1950 was sentenced to twenty-five years' imprisonment under Article 58-1 B of the Criminal Code of the Russian Soviet Socialist Republic. Released in 1955, under amnesty. On July 25, 1961, the sentence was overturned due to newly discovered evidence, and on August 17, 1961, he was indicted in this case. Occupation: collective farmer on an agricultural peasant cooperative known as "40 Years of the October Revolution," in Orel Province.

As a POW of the Germans, in fall 1941 he betrayed his country and joined the German SS, where he served through the end of 1944.

After completing training at the Trawniki SS training camp, he took an oath to serve the Germans. In Lublin he carried out guard duties at the Jewish ghetto and escorted prisoner trains with Soviet citizens who were sent to hard labor in Germany.

In June 1942, he took part in unloading and executing people taken in trains from Lublin to the Trawniki camp.

As a *Wachmann* of the SS-Sonderkommando at Treblinka death camp, he was involved in mass killings of the civilian population by suffocation in gas chambers and by firing squad. In March 1943, he served as a *Wachmann* in the SS-Sonderkommando at Sobibor death camp, also taking part in mass killings.

As of March 1943, carried out armed guard service at the Auschwitz, Buchenwald, and Dora concentration camps.

Was promoted to the rank of SS-*Oberwachmann* for his diligent service in the SS.

At the end of 1944, began serving in the so-called RLA (Russian Liberation Army).

These are crimes under Article 56 of the Criminal Code of the Ukrainian Soviet Socialist Republic.

SOME SOVIET TRIALS AND CASE RECORDS

(9) Ryabeka, Fedor, born 1906 in Dnepropetrovsk Province; Ukrainian nationality, fourth-grade education, married, of poor peasantry, no party affiliation. In 1949, was tried under Article 54-1 B of the Criminal Code of the Ukrainian Soviet Socialist Republic and sentenced to twenty-five years in a penal camp. Released in 1955, under amnesty. On June 6, 1961, the previous sentence was overturned by decision of the military tribunal of the Kiev Military District due to newly discovered evidence, and on June 21, 1961, he was indicted in this case. Occupation: guard at a secondary school in the city of Dnepropetrovsk.

As a POW during the Great Patriotic War, in fall 1941 he betrayed his country and joined the German SS, where he served through the end of the war. He completed training at the Trawniki SS training camp and took an oath to serve the Germans, after which he deployed to the Lublin and Warsaw ghettos for armed-guard service.

In June 1942, he participated in escorting prisoner trains to Treblinka death camp. As a *Wachmann*, then later as an *Oberwachmann* of the SS-Sonderkommando at Treblinka death camp, he participated in mass killings of the civilian population by suffocation in gas chambers and by firing-squad executions.

In March 1943, as an *SS-Wachmann* at the Sobibor death camp, he also was involved in the mass killings of people. From March 1943 until the end of the war, he carried out guard service at the Auschwitz and Buchenwald concentration camps, escorting prisoners to their places of hard labor.

These are crimes under Article 56 of the Criminal Code of the Ukrainian Soviet Socialist Republic.

(10) Kurinnyj, a.k.a. Kurinnoy, Ivan, born 1921 in Petropavlovka, Gorodishenskj region, Cherkassy Province; Ukrainian nationality, of poor peasantry, seventh-grade education. In 1954, was excluded from candidate Communist Party membership; married, no prior convictions. Occupation: senior railway switchman at a train station. Received two medals: "For Victory over Germany in the Great Patriotic War" and "30 Years of the Soviet Armed Forces."

During the Great Patriotic War, was held captive by the Germans and betrayed his country. In summer 1942, began serving with the German SS, where he served through April 1945. Completed training at the Trawniki SS training camp and took an oath to serve Nazi Germany. He performed armed-guard duties in the Jewish ghetto in Warsaw, escorting prisoner trains to the Treblinka death camp.

From August or September 1942 through March 1943, served as a *Wachmann* in the SS-Sonderkommando at the Sobibor and Treblinka death camps, where he was involved in mass killings of the civilian population by suffocation in gas chambers and by firing-squad executions.

From summer 1943 through April 1945, guarded the Auschwitz and Buchenwald concentration camps, escorting prisoners to their places of hard labor. In early 1944, he was promoted to the rank of *SS-Oberwachmann* for his diligent service.

These are crimes under Article 56 of the Criminal Code of the Ukrainian Soviet Socialist Republic.

(11) Gorbachev, Mikhail, born 1922 in Yelatomsky region, Ryazan Province; Russian nationality, midlevel peasant, ninth-grade education, married, no party affiliation. Was tried on August 5, 1947, by a court in Kirov region, in the city of Ivanovo, under Article 1 of the decree of the Presidium of the Supreme Soviet "On Criminal Responsibility for Embezzlement of State and Public Property" and sentenced to

ten years in a penal camp. On June 23, 1951, was also sentenced by the military tribunal of the Ural Military District under Article 58-1 B of the Criminal Code of the Russian Soviet Socialist Republic to twenty-five years in a penal camp. Released October 7, 1955, under amnesty. The June 23, 1951, sentence was overturned due to newly discovered evidence by a July 25, 1961, decision of the Military Department of the Soviet Supreme Court, and on August 23, 1961, was indicted in this case. Occupation: plumbing technician in the city of Angarsk, Irkutsk region.

While in German captivity during the Great Patriotic War, he betrayed his country and in summer 1942 joined the German SS, where he served through April 1945. Completed training at the Trawniki SS training camp and took an oath to serve Nazi Germany. Carried out armed-guard duties at the Jewish ghetto in Warsaw, escorting prisoner trains to the Treblinka death camp. From August or September 1942 through March 1943, served in the SS-Sonderkommando at the Treblinka and Sobibor death camps, where he was involved in mass killings by suffocation in gas chambers and by firing-squad executions.

From spring 1943 through April 1945, he guarded the Auschwitz and Buchenwald concentration camps, and a concentration camp in the city of Leipzig. He escorted prisoners to their places of hard labor. In early 1944, he was promoted to the rank of *Oberwachmann* for his diligent service.

These are crimes under Article 56 of the Criminal Code of the Ukrainian Soviet Socialist Republic.

(12) Parfinyuk, Evdokim, born 1910 in Ternovka, Novograd-Volynsk region, Zhitomir Province; Ukrainian nationality, no party affiliation, married, midlevel peasant, third-grade education. Was tried August 23, 1952, by the military tribunal of the Carpathian Military District, under Article 54-1 B of the Criminal Code of the Ukrainian Soviet Socialist Republic, and sentenced to twenty-five years in a penal camp. On February 19, 1955, the sentence was reduced to ten years' imprisonment. Released on December 1, 1955, under amnesty. The August 23, 1952, sentence was overturned due to newly discovered evidence by a July 25, 1961, decision of the Military Department of the Soviet Supreme Court. On August 10, 1961, he was indicted in this case. Occupation: bricklayer on a collective farm.

As a POW in German captivity, he betrayed his country in fall 1941 and began serving in the German SS, where he served until spring 1945. Completed training at the Trawniki SS training camp and took an oath to serve Nazi Germany. Served as a *Wachmann* at the Treblinka death camp, summer 1942 to spring 1943.

As a *Wachmann*, was involved in the mass killings of the civilian population by suffocation in gas chambers and by firing-squad executions. Carried out armed-guard service at the Auschwitz and Buchenwald concentration camps, escorting prisoners to their places of hard labor.

These are crimes under Article 56 of the Criminal Code of the Ukrainian Soviet Socialist Republic.

In accordance with Article 225 of the Criminal Code of Procedure of the Ukrainian Soviet Socialist Republic, criminal case #14, against Shultz, a.k.a. Vertogradov; Kurinnoy, a.k.a. Kurrinyj; Borodin; and others, is to be forwarded to the military prosecutor of the Kiev Military District.

The bill of indictment was prepared on November 17, 1961, in the city of Kiev.
Senior investigator of major cases of the KGB Investigation Department, Ukrainian Soviet

Socialist Republic, Lieutenant Colonel Lysenko
Agreed: head of the KGB Investigation Department, Ukrainian Soviet Socialist Republic,
Colonel Nizovarets

Shultz, Emanuel, a.k.a. Vertogradov: "My correct name is Shultz. When I was in Italy in April 1945, I joined the Yugoslav guerrillas. I changed my German last name to the Russian last name Vertogradov, which was mother's maiden name. I am a Russian national, born in 1919 in the city of Bryansk. My father was a German national, but he was born in Russia and died in 1930. My mother was a Russian national. I was a member of the All-Union "Leninist Young Communist League" (VLKSM) from 1933 until the day of my German captivity. Since 1946, I have worked at the Pechora forest combine as an engineer in labor and salaries. From February through May 1946, I was in a filtration camp in the city of Kishinev, from where I was then sent to a camp in the city of Pechora. After being released from the camp, I remained in Pechora. I was conscripted by the Bryansk Military Recruitment Center into the Red Army in November 1939 and served until being taken captive by the Germans in July 1941. I sustained no wounds and received no government awards. I have been in custody since February 17, 1961, and have received the bill of indictment and court-martial charges."

The presiding judge asks the prosecutor and the other attorneys whether they have any questions for the defendant Shultz. Responding to the attorney Karpenko's questions, the defendant Schultz stated: "I have a deaf-mute brother who has a wife and three children, ages three to ten. He lives in the city of Bryansk. My wife is ill. I have received a number of commendations for my work. In 1958, for my work, I received an award: a merit certificate."

Levchishin, Philip: "I had a brother who was killed in 1943 in the defense of the city of Odessa. I served in the Red Army, 1935–1937, by conscription, then again from July 7 to 14, 1941, when I was taken prisoner by the Germans. After the war, I worked at the Tulchinsk regional hospital as a manual laborer, then as a disinfector. On April 18, 1952, I was convicted and sentenced to twenty-five years' imprisonment but was released under amnesty in 1956. On August 12, 1961, I was arrested in this case. I have received the bill of indictment and the court-martial charges."

Responding to the presiding judge, the prosecutor and the other attorneys indicated that they do not have any questions for the defendant Levchishin.

Vasilenko, Sergej: "I served twice in the Red Army: by conscription of the Radomyshlsky regional military recruitment center in Zhitomir Province, with service from 1938 to 1940, and then again June 24 to August 1941, when I was taken prisoner by the Germans. I was arrested on June 1, 1961, in this case. I have received the bill of indictment and court-martial charges."

The presiding judge asks the prosecutor and the other attorneys whether they have any questions for the defendant Vasilenko. Responding to the attorney Maximenko's questions, the defendant Vasilenko stated: "When I was released from imprisonment in 1952, I went home and worked on a collective farm as a wagon boy. I was a shock worker and was awarded two medals for my good work. I'm married with three children; the youngest is four years old."

Pritsch, Samuel: "I have four children, aged thirteen to twenty-four years old. I served twice in the Red Army, 1938–1940, and then again May–August 1941, when I was captured by the Germans. On June 29, 1950, I was convicted and was sentenced to twenty-five years' imprisonment. I was released November 21, 1955, under amnesty. After release, I worked on a collective farm. On June 21, 1961, I was arrested in this case. I have received the bill of indictment and court-martial charges."

Responding to the presiding judge, the prosecutor and the other attorneys indicated that they do not have any questions for the defendant Pritsch.

Terekhov, Ivan: "I was a member of the VLKSM from 1939 until the day I was captured by the Germans. My occupation is driver (chauffeur). I am married with two children, twins of age three. I had two brothers and a sister who were killed on the battlefronts. I was conscripted into the Red Army in March 1941 and served until taken prisoner by the Germans in August 1941. I have no government awards and was wounded in the leg and in the head during the war. I was awarded with a merit certificate for good work in the Nelkan mines, where I work. I have received the bill of indictment and court-martial charges."

Responding to the presiding judge, the prosecutor and other attorneys have indicated that they do not have any questions for the defendant Terekhov.

Karplyuk, Yakov: "I have three children, ages four through fourteen years old. Prior to the war, I worked as an arsenal specialist at the Novograd-Volynsk Timber Procurement Establishment. I was conscripted into the Red Army by the Novograd-Volynsk Military Recruitment Center on May 30, 1941. I went into German captivity on July 4 or 5, 1941. I have no government awards and no wounds. I have received the bill of indictment and court-martial charges."

The presiding judge asks the prosecutor and the other attorneys whether they have any questions for the defendant Karplyuk. Responding to the attorney Nikolayev's questions, defendant Karplyuk stated: "In 1952 I got a head injury, and since then I've had head illnesses. I also have heart and liver problems."

Borodin, Dmitri: "I was a member of the VLKSM from 1935 until I was captured by the Germans. I have completed five school grades and also completed a two-year accounting course. I was drafted into the Red Army in November 1939 by a military recruitment center in Tula Province and served until I was captured by the Germans on June 26, 1941. I am married and have no children, but I am taking care of a seven-year-old girl. I was convicted on December 24, 1948, by the Bogoroditsk People's Court of Tula Province, under Article 1 of the 1947 Decree of the Presidium of the Supreme Soviet 'On Criminal Responsibility for Embezzlement of State and Public Property.' I was sentenced to seven years' imprisonment while working as a bookkeeper at the highway department of the Bogoroditsk district executive committee, in Tula Province. I was released in April 1953, under amnesty. One of my brothers was killed at the battlefront during the war. Until I was arrested in this case, I worked as a shop steward in road construction and received twelve commendations in this job. I have no government awards and no wounds. I received the bill of indictment and court-martial charges."

The presiding judge asks the prosecutor and other attorneys whether they have any questions for defendant Borodin. Responding to the prosecutor's questions, defendant Borodin stated: "During the war, I served in artillery and was a sergeant."

Govorov, Alexei: "I was a member of the VLKSM from 1934 until I was captured by the Germans. I am a collective farmer, my parents were peasants, and I am married with three children. One of my brothers was killed on the battlefront during the war. I was conscripted into the Red Army by the Oktyabrskiy regional military recruiting center in the city of Moscow, in 1937, and then remained on reenlistment. From 1947 to 1949 I worked as the head of a collective farm. In 1949, I was convicted by a people's court in Orel Province, under Article 74 of the Criminal Code of the Russian Soviet Socialist Republic, and was sentenced to three years' probation. I was also convicted on December 25, 1950, by the military tribunal of the Voronezh Military District, under Article 58-1 B of the Criminal Code of the Russian Soviet Socialist Republic, and sentenced to twenty-five years' imprisonment. I was released in October 1955, under amnesty. I have no government awards. On July 9, 1941, I was wounded. There are three explosive fragmentation splinters in my lungs. I have no documentation of the wound. Prior to my arrest in this case, I worked on a collective farm called '40 Years of the October Revolution.' I received the bill of indictment and the court-martial charges."

Responding to the presiding judge, the prosecutor and the other attorneys have indicated that they do not have any questions for defendant Govorov.

Kurinnij, Ivan: "In 1946, I worked as a security guard at a penitentiary camp in the city of Kiev. In 1951 through 1954, I was a candidate member of the Soviet Communist Party. I was excluded from the party in fall 1954 for deceit, because I had failed to disclose that I had served the Germans during the war. In 1951, I completed the Kaliningrad Officer Cadet School of the paramilitary security service of the Ministry of Internal Affairs (MVD). I am married with three children, ages six to ten years old. One of my brothers was killed on the battlefront in 1944. I was conscripted into the Red Army in 1940 by the Gorodishensk regional military recruitment center and served until I was captured by the Germans on May 18 or 20, 1942. After the war, I worked for two years in a camp in the city of Kiev, where I guarded prisoners, then for a year and a half I worked as an inspector in the Kiev Province penitentiary camp. After completing the Officer Cadet School of the MVD, I was assigned to work in the city of Norilsk until September 1954. That's when I was excluded from the party and dismissed from the MVD. I then moved to the city of Bagrationovsk, Kaliningrad Province, where I worked as a craftsman, then as a highway department technician, then as a railway switchman at the Bagrationovsk train station. I have two government awards: 'For Victory over Germany in the Great Patriotic War of 1941–1945' and '30 Years of the Soviet Armed Forces.' I received the bill of indictment and court-martial charges."

The presiding judge asks the prosecutor and the other attorney whether they have any questions for the defendant Kurinnij. Responding to the prosecutor's questions, Kurinnij stated: "After completing the Officer Cadet School of the MVD, I received the rank of 2nd Lieutenant of the Internal Service."

Gorbachev, Mikhail: "I was a member of the VLKSM from 1938 until May 17, 1942, when I was captured by the Germans. I am married. My wife is handicapped. I have one child, born in 1949. I was mobilized into the Red Army on August 11, 1941, by the Ivanovo regional committee of the VLKSM and was deployed to the Kerch Peninsula, where I was captured by the Germans. While on the battlefront, I was wounded in both legs, but I have no documentation of this. I have no government awards. I was convicted in August 1947 in the city of Ivanovo, Kirov Province, under Article 1 of the 1947 Decree of the Presidium of the Supreme Soviet "On Criminal Responsibility for Embezzlement of State and Public Property," and sentenced to ten years' imprisonment. I was also convicted on June 23, 1951, by the military tribunal of the Ural Military District, under Article 58-1 B of the Criminal Code of the Russian Soviet Socialist Republic, and sentenced to twenty-five years' imprisonment. I was released in October 1955, under amnesty. I received the bill of indictment and court-martial charges."

The presiding judge asks the prosecutor and the other attorney whether they have any questions for the defendant Gorbachev. Responding to the attorney Glabai's questions, defendant Gorbachev stated: "My wife is a group II invalid."

Parfinyuk, Evdokim: "I am married. My wife is an invalid. I have four children. I served in the Red Army twice, first in 1932–1934, then again from June 22 to the end of July 1941. I had been conscripted by a military recruitment center in Zhitomir Province. I was convicted on August 23, 1952, by the military tribunal of the Carpathian Military District, under

Article 54-1 B of the Criminal Code of the Ukrainian Soviet Socialist Republic, and was sentenced to twenty-five years' imprisonment. I was released December 1, 1955, under amnesty. I have no government awards. In 1941, I was wounded but do not have documentation of this. I received the bill of indictment and court-martial charges."

The prosecutor and the other attorneys have no questions for the defendant Parfinyuk.

The presiding judge announces the officials present at the trial and declares that the senior assistant of military prosecutor of the Kiev Military District, Lieutenant Colonel Arikyash, will be the representative of the government's case. The defendants' interests will be defended by attorneys from the regional collegium of attorneys of Kiev Province: Glabai, Nikolayev, Grekhov, Smolenskij, Bolkhovitinov, Maximenko, and Karpenko. Lavrinenko and Chepelyuk will serve as the judicial secretaries.

The presiding judge then explained to each defendant his vested rights to reject or challenge the present officials, including the defense attorneys, prosecutor, and secretaries.

ZUEV TRIAL[40]
VERDICT # ____
IN THE NAME OF THE UNION OF SOVIET SOCIALIST REPUBLICS

February 24, 1967
City of Dnepropetrovsk

Military tribunal of the Kiev Military District, consisting of the following:
Presiding judge: Colonel of Justice A. Bushuyev
Associate judges: Lieutenant Colonel M. Lopata and Major G. Grechukh
Secretary: I. Povoroznik
Also with the involvement of the representative of the deputy prosecutor of the Kiev Military District, Colonel of Justice I. Bochkaryov, and assistant military prosecutor of the Kiev Military District, Lieutenant Colonel of Justice L. Sorokin
Defense attorneys: M. Shish, G. Shevchenko, Lipatov, B. Boyko, and V. Lotarev
In open court proceedings in Dnepropetrovsk Province, the following are indicted:

(1) Zuev, Akim, born 1912 in Byshevsky region, Kiev Province; Ukrainian nationality, fifth-grade education, no party affiliation, married; prior to arrest worked as a stockkeeper at a summer camp. Served in the Red Army, June–July 1941. Was tried February 18, 1950, under Article 54-1 B of the Criminal Code of the Ukrainian Soviet Socialist Republic, and sentenced to twenty-five years' imprisonment. Released October 1955 by the September 17, 1955, decree of the Presidium of the Supreme Soviet, "On Amnesty . . ." Sentencing from the first case was overturned by the Military Collegium of the Soviet Supreme Court due to newly discovered evidence.

(2) Olejnik, Taras, born 1910 in Dnepropetrovsk region, Dnepropetrovsk Province; Ukrainian nationality, poor-level peasant by social origin, poorly literate, no party affiliation. Served in the Red Army, May–July 1941. Married; prior to arrest worked as a plumbing-pipe handler in a repair-and-construction company. Was tried February 20, 1950, under Article 54-1 B of the Criminal Code of the Ukrainian Soviet Socialist Republic, and sentenced to twenty-five years' imprisonment. Released November 1956 by the September 17, 1955, decree of the Presidium of the Supreme Soviet, "On Amnesty . . ." Sentencing from the first case was overturned by the Military Collegium of the Soviet Supreme Court due to newly discovered evidence.

(3) Mamchur, Nikita, born 1906 in Tulchinsk region, Vinnitsa Province; Ukrainian nationality, of poor-level peasant by social origin, poorly literate. Prior to arrest worked as a horseman on the "Zhdanov" collective farm. Served in the Red Army, June–October 1941. Was tried on November 10, 1947, under Article 4 of the 1947 decree of the Presidium of the Supreme Soviet, "On Criminal Responsibility for Embezzlement of State and Public Property," and sentenced to twelve years' imprisonment.

4) Lynkin, Grigorij, born 1910 in Alexandrovsk region, Donetsk Province; Ukrainian nationality, of poor-level peasant social origin, with uncompleted secondary education, no party affiliation. Served in the Red Army, July–September 1941. No prior convictions. Prior to arrest, worked as an animal technician on a collective farm in Dnepropetrovsk Province.

(5) Lazorenko, Alexei, born in Sumskaya Province; Ukrainian nationality, of poor-level peasant social origin, fourth-grade education, no party affiliation. Was tried on July 28, 1949, under Article 54-1 B of the Criminal Code of the Ukrainian Soviet Socialist Republic, and sentenced to twenty-five years' imprisonment. Released October 1955 by the decree of September 17, 1955, of the Presidium of the Supreme Soviet, "On Amnesty..." The sentence in the first case was overturned by decision of the Military Collegium of the Soviet Supreme Court due to newly discovered evidence. Prior to arrest, resided in the city of Ordzhonikidze, Dnepropetrovsk Province, and worked as a timberman at a mining plant. Served in the Red Army, May–August 1941.

All five defendants are charged with crimes under Article 56 of the Criminal Code of the Ukrainian Soviet Socialist Republic.

Having reviewed all the materials in this case, the military tribunal

HAS FOUND

During the Second World War, the German invaders, fulfilling their ominous program of mass extermination of the civilian population in the occupied territories, built a death camp in the town of Belzhets (Poland), where they systematically murdered Jewish civilians from the occupied regions of the Soviet Union, Poland, Czechoslovakia, and other European countries, from early 1942 to March 1943.

Mass killings of civilians were done by suffocation in gas chambers (*Dushegubka*) by an SS-Sonderkommando comprising Germans and *Wachmänner* (guards) trained at the SS training camp in Trawniki (Poland).

The people doomed to die were brought into the camp by railroad trains. During unloading, in order to conceal the true intent of the camp, the civilians were told that they had to go through a decontamination process, after which they would be sent to work. Under this pretense, the Germans and *Wachmänner* brought the people into undressing rooms, where they had to undress and hand in their valuables. Women also had their hair cut off. Then the people were led through a barbed-wire passage and forced into gas chambers, where they were killed by exhaust gases from an internal combustion engine.

The dead bodies were removed by a work group of prisoners, thrown into large pit trenches, then later burned using special machinery. Those unable to walk on their own to the gas chambers were brought by the Germans and *Wachmänner* to the pits, where they were executed by a firing squad.

The defendants Zuev, Mamchur, Olejnik, and Lynkin testified that since the first day of their assignment in Belzhets camp, they learned that the camp was intended for mass extermination of the civilian population, and they understood that by convoying the people into the gas chambers, the defendants were participating in the killings.

Thus, the court has found that the criminal activity of the defendants has been demonstrated in this case. Therefore, and by decree of the Presidium of the Supreme Soviet of March 4, 1965, the statute of limitations in regard to the criminal liability of all the defendants is not applicable.

Based on the information given, the military tribunal has found Lazorenko, Zuev, Mamchur, Olejnik, and Lynkin guilty of betraying their Motherland; that is, in committing crimes under Article 56 of the Criminal Code of the Ukrainian Soviet Socialist Republic.

Given the fact that the defendants Lazorenko, Zuev, Mamchur, and Olejnik were heavily active participants of the mass killings, and these crimes were extremely harmful, the military tribunal has found it necessary to apply an exceptional measure of punishment in regard to the defendants: the death penalty.

Criminal actions by Lynkin were not as harmful because his involvement in those crimes was not as active, and during the court hearings he expressed deep regret for his actions. Therefore, the court finds it possible not to impose the death penalty, but to order him to serve a prison term.

In accordance with Articles 323 and 324 of the Criminal Code of Procedure of the Ukrainian Soviet Socialist Republic, the military tribunal of the Kiev Military District

HAS RULED

Zuev, Lazorenko, Mamchur, and Olejnik, under Article 56 of the Criminal Code of the Ukrainian Soviet Socialist Republic, shall all be sentenced to death: execution by firing squad, with confiscation of their belongings.

In accordance with Article 56 of the Criminal Code, Lynkin shall be sentenced to fifteen years in a maximum-security correctional labor facility, with confiscation of his belongings, and a five-year exile.

In accordance with Article 42, part 3, of the Criminal Code of the Ukrainian Soviet Socialist Republic, two years of imprisonment sentence from the December 19, 1949, judgment, previously served by Lynkin, shall be credited toward his sentence in this case. The final term of imprisonment that Lynkin is due to serve is therefore thirteen years. The start of his imprisonment, taking into account his preliminary detention, was June 25, 1966.

The sentence may be appealed and protested in a procedure through the Kiev Military District's military tribunal and the Military Collegium of the Soviet Supreme Court within seven days from the day of sentencing.

Approved: Presiding judge in this case,
Colonel of Justice A. Bushuyev

CHAPTER 6

JUDGMENT IN THE TRIAL OF FRANZ SWIDERSKY

Franz Swidersky was born on April 10, 1921, in Selz, near Odessa, Ukraine
He was arrested on October 30, 1968, on the basis of an arrest warrant of the State Court in Dusseldorf, and was held in pretrial detention in the Dusseldorf prison.
Charges: murder and aiding and abetting murder
Presiding judge: Oder
Six jurors: 3 businessmen, a housekeeper, an upholsterer, and an administrative employee
State prosecutors: Chanteaux and Tapper
Decision: Seven years imprisonment, with three years off for time already served in pretrial confinement
Defendant, fifty years old, was accused of cruelly and intentionally killing, out of "base motives," an unknown number of prisoners, as a member of the Trawniki guard unit at Treblinka labor camp (hereafter referred to as Treblinka I), between March 12, 1943, and July 23, 1944.

Swidersky is a Volksdeutscher. His ancestors were farmers who emigrated from Germany to the Odessa region in Ukraine around 1800. Until 1928, his father ran a farm. Starting in 1928, the farm was gradually confiscated under the Soviet policy of "collectivization." Thereafter, hard times fell on the Swidersky family, as it did on other people living in the region. Food rations provided by the *kolkhozes* (collective farms) were inadequate, and people began suffering from malnutrition and starvation. Swidersky's grandfather died of starvation. People did what they had to survive, including catching mice to eat. Swidersky himself suffered from malnutrition. Gradually, conditions improved and the collective farm began providing adequate rations of corn, potatoes, and milk provided by a cow on the farm.

Swidersky attended elementary school and learned some German and Russian. However, he went to classes irregularly because of a lack of proper winter clothing and footwear. In 1936, he contracted malaria. He left school without being able to adequately read, write, or do arithmetic. Even in adulthood his academic skills were average at best. He worked on a collective farm and laying railroad tracks.

In 1941, he was drafted into the Red Army and assigned to an artillery unit. His basic training lasted about six to eight weeks, during which time he barely even got proper rifle training.

In June 1941, his unit deployed to the Soviet western border region and was wiped out during initial battles with German forces. Swidersky had slight wounds from shrapnel to his chest, legs, head, and right eye. He was captured by the Germans and became a POW. When it became known that he was a Volksdeutscher, he was taken for medical attention to a military hospital in Warsaw. Some of the shrapnel fragments were removed with magnets. His eye, however, had to be removed due to the injury it had sustained. He began wearing an eye patch. In 1943, he was able to get a glass eye in Warsaw, and he wore it at least sometimes from then on.

Following his medical treatment, he was returned to a POW camp. It was located near Bialystok. Rations there were generally inadequate. In fall 1941, he was recruited for Trawniki service because he was a Volksdeutscher. By fall 1942, he was promoted to *Gruppenwachmann*. In December 1942, he was assigned to Lublin concentration camp (Majdanek). There, he performed administrative duties as a quartermaster. This included providing rations to the rest of the guards stationed at the camp.

In February or March 1943 he returned to Trawniki and was assigned to Treblinka I on March 12, 1943. In 1944 he was promoted to *SS-Zugwachmann*. In late July 1944, some of the Trawniki guards at Treblinka I fled westward in a truck, including Swidersky, to escape the approaching Soviet forces. They met up with and joined the SS-"Streibel" Battalion in Lodz. The unit was sent to build fortifications along the Vistula River. In February 1945, the battalion went to Dresden and then, by April 1945, to Prague. By then the war had ended.

Swidersky obtained civilian clothing and mixed in with Polish and Russian laborers and reached Chemnitz. There he avoided capture by Soviet forces and headed for the Upper Palatinate region. He was taken prisoner by American forces near Hof. He feared being repatriated to the Soviet Union. He adopted the false name of Franz Zerr when questioned. Four days later the Americans released him.

In the Wunsiedel Rural District, a priest found him work with a local farmer and wood merchant. He met a local woman and married her in 1948, still using the false name Franz Zerr. His wife's parents owned a rope-making business, and Swidersky learned the skill of rope making. He trained in this vocation and became a master rope maker. He had two sons, Hermann and Reinhard.

Swidersky got the address of two of his relatives, his uncle and his younger sister, still living in the Soviet Union, and wrote to both of them, using his false name. He kept in touch with his sister until about 1961. The German Red Cross informed him that he might be able to get visas for his family living in the Soviet Union so that they could move to West Germany. Apparently the letters he wrote to his relatives were intercepted by Soviet authorities (who monitored the mail), and attention was drawn on Swidersky. Soviet authorities provided German authorities with documents pertaining to Treblinka I and Swidersky's service there. Following an extensive investigation, a warrant for Swidersky's arrest was issued by the Dusseldorf court in October 1968. He was arrested ten days later.

Swidersky is considered a Volksdeutscher. But he had never acquired German citizenship. "Even though the 'Decree Concerning the Acquisition of German Citizenship through Employment in the Wehrmacht, Waffen-SS, the German Police, or the Todt Organization,' dated May 19, 1943, provided for such collective naturalization, the 'Implementation Order of May 23, 1943,' stated" that a determination had to be made by the Central Immigration Office on the basis of an evaluation of the individual seeking the citizenship. There is no evidence that Swidersky went through this process.

Also, "The Law Governing the Ruling on Citizenship, of February 22, 1955," states that service in the abovementioned organizations alone does not automatically guarantee German citizenship: in addition, a declaration notice of citizenship must be issued by a certified office. Swidersky's having lost his Soviet citizenship because of his German collaboration, and his failure to obtain legal German citizenship, resulted in the court considering him a "stateless person."

Treblinka I was established in late 1941. It was under the authority of the SS and police commander of the Warsaw District. First the camp held only Polish political prisoners, but then Jews were brought in as well. Jews were expected to die in the camp through overwork and exhaustion.

Treblinka I was located about 1 mile from Treblinka II. It was surrounded by barbed-wire fence that was 3–4 meters high. The camp contained the following buildings: an administrative barracks, a house for the camp commandant, a food storage barracks, a garage, a gas station, a small farm, barracks for the SS staff, barracks for the Trawniki guards, barracks for the prisoners, a kitchen, a laundry room, prisoner workshops, a bathroom, a wood storage shed, and a wood storage yard. The camp also had three or four wooden watchtowers, each about 4 meters high. A water well was the sole source of water for the camp.

The camp was divided into three sections: the Jewish camp, the Polish camp, and the women's camp. The camp contained an area known as the "sanitorium." It was the same area that was known in the "Reinhard" death camps as the "Lazarette." It was an execution pit used for shooting prisoners no longer capable of work, although sometimes prisoners were killed by being bludgeoned to death. The camp also had mass graves.

The camp staff consisted of about fifteen SS men and fifty to sixty Trawniki guards. The camp commandant was *SS-Hauptsturmführer* (Captain) Van Eupen, and his deputies were SS-Sergeant Prefi and SS-Sergeant Heinbuch. In charge of the Trawniki guard unit was *SS-Unterscharführer* (Junior Sergeant) Stumpe. Later he was replaced by SS-Unterscharführer Roge. The SS staff were armed with pistols and whips.

The camp included skilled Jewish prisoners including carpenters, bricklayers, cobblers, tailors, and mechanics. The man who supervised these Jews was SS-Unterscharführer Schwarz.

Commandant Van Eupen was shot by partisans toward the end of the war. Cases against former SS men Prefi, Heinbuch, and Roge were pending in the State Court Dusseldorf. Heinbuch died in the meantime. Proceedings against the other two were dismissed due to their age and ill health.

In Treblinka I, the Trawniki guards were divided into four squads, each led by a *Zugwachmann* or *Gruppenwachmann*. The *Wachmänner* had rifles and bayonets. The *Zugwachmänner* and *Gruppenwachmänner* had pistols. In addition to guard duty in and around the camp, the Trawniki guards also formed firing squads to shoot prisoners at the "sanitorium," under the command of the SS.

Swidersky led one squad. The other squads were believed to have been led by Liudas Kairys, Wilhelm Baltschys, and a third man whose name is not known.

The number of prisoners held in Treblinka I at any given time fluctuated between 500 and 1,800. Jews made up the largest portion.

Prisoners got half a liter a day of water for washing, shaving, and drinking. Unhygienic conditions existed in the camp. Prisoners were dirty, and there was a lice problem in the prisoners' barracks. Food for prisoners was 1 liter per day of soup made from beets, flour, or potatoes, and bread with jam and coffee. Prisoners rarely got fat or protein in their diets. A few ounces of margarine were given to each prisoner, and it had to last a week. Meat was available only if local cattle died from natural deaths. Prisoners could be beaten or shot as punishment for stealing additional food to supplement their meager diets. Polish prisoners and the skilled Jewish workers were allowed to wear their own civilian clothing. The rest of the prisoners wore striped prisoner clothing.

The prisoners were to be destroyed through labor. Apparently, according to the commandant's orders, it was up to each guard's own discretion how to treat the prisoners. According to Swidersky, nothing was forbidden; the guards could behave as they pleased. Any beating or killings committed were to be the responsibility of the German leadership, according to SS-Unterscharführer Stumpe.

Each morning in the camp, roll call was conducted of the prisoners. It was supervised by the SS staff. Then the prisoners went to their respective worksites. Female prisoners did laundry. Male prisoners other than the skilled workers either worked in the gravel pit, engaged in farming, chopped wood, built fortifications along the Bug River, loaded materials at the railroad station, or built roads. The largest group of prisoners worked in the gravel pit, and Swidersky supervised them there. Prisoners were also assigned to draw water from the camp well and distribute it to the other prisoners, and to dig graves and bury dead prisoners. The prisoners worked from dawn till dusk, 7 a.m.–6 p.m. Because of malnutrition and exhaustion, prisoners occasionally collapsed and even died at work. At the end of the day, other prisoners had to carry them back so that the SS could account for them. They were usually then taken to the "sanitorium" to be shot.

At the "sanitorium," prisoners had to climb into the pit and lie facedown. They were then shot from above by a firing squad armed with rifles, standing at the edge of the pit. The executions were often supervised by SS-Unterscharführer Stumpe. The bodies were then covered with soil. When the graves filled up to the top, they were covered up and leveled. According to Stumpe, two or three and sometimes up to eight or nine prisoners were shot each day at the execution pit. Sometimes prisoners were also transferred to Treblinka II to be gassed.

Among the prisoners, Swidersky had a reputation for being cruel. He was feared to such an extent that prisoners gave each other warning signals when he came around. He occasionally took part in the prisoner roll calls and at least twice a week led prisoners to their worksites.

On August 2, 1943, a prisoner uprising took place at Treblinka II. A similar action was allegedly planned in Treblinka I and was uncovered. A Jewish boy who reportedly knew the ringleaders of the plot was questioned and tortured; however, he revealed nothing. Nevertheless, a group of prisoners were shot to serve as a deterrent, according to Stumpe.

Final liquidation of the camp: German authorities may have decided as early as spring 1944 to destroy the camp upon approach of the Red Army and to liquidate the remaining prisoners in order to eliminate witnesses. In spring or summer 1944, many of the Trawniki guards fled to the partisans in the nearby forests. For example, Zugwachmann Munder fled two or three months before Treblinka I was to be liquidated, and with him went an entire squad or platoon of Trawniki guards. Later, Swidersky's own guard squad also fled, but Swidersky himself did not because his comrades had not confided in him with the escape plan.

On July 23, 1944, Commandant Van Eupen received a code word over the telephone or teletype. "It probably transmitted the order of the SS and police commander of Warsaw District to liquidate the camp and shoot all the Jewish prisoners."

The Jewish prisoners were led to the woods just outside the camp. In groups of fifteen to twenty, they were led away, guarded by SS men and Trawniki guards. To prevent anyone trying to escape, the prisoners were ordered to drop their pants down below their knees as they walked with their hands raised. In the forest were prepared pits. Along the edge of the pits, the prisoners were lined up in small groups and shot. Group after group was led to the mass grave and shot. The killing lasted several hours in the afternoon.

One prisoner survived by pretending to be dead after being hit by two bullets: one in the arm and one in the neck. At night, he crawled away, bandaged himself with strips of clothing, and found shelter in a nearby house. Another prisoner, a woman, survived. At night, she pulled herself out of the mass grave and fled to the woods. She was found unconscious by local farmers. Another man survived and later emerged from the mass grave.

Swidersky took part in escorting the prisoners to the mass grave and shooting them. The number of prisoners shot during the camp's liquidation was believed to be between 300 and 700. The court favored the lower number.

The Polish prisoners were mostly released. The few that were shot had been political prisoners sent to the camp by the Security Police and SD in Sokolow.

The basis of facts in the case came from several sources:
(1) Swidersky's own testimony
(2) Sworn testimony of several Polish and Jewish survivors of the camp, and former Trawniki camp commandant Karl Streibel
(3) Sworn testimony of a former Trawniki guard from Treblinka I, Vladas Amanaviczius
(4) Unsworn testimony of former Trawniki guards from Treblinka I: Alexei Kolgushkin, Alexander Moskalenko, Ivan Zvezdun, Semen Kharkovskij, and Fedor Vilshun

(5) Unsworn testimony of former SS staff from Treblinka I: Stumpe, Prefi, Heinbuch, and Roge

(6) Expert testimony of Dr. Wolfgang Scheffler and Dr. Hans-Gunther Seraphim, senior librarian and university lecturer, retired

"The defendant was especially marked by his black eye patch, since he was the only man in the camp who wore one." The court was of the opinion that there was a possibility that perhaps, because of this physically memorable trait of the defendant, some witnesses might have attributed to him certain acts that may have actually been committed by other guards. For example, one witness who had originally attributed the stabbing to death of a prisoner to Swidersky later recanted and identified the guard Munder as the perpetrator.

The witness, Kaim, stated that he saw several killings at the wood storage area of the camp and identified SS-Sergeant Schwarz as the man who did the killing there with a wooden hammer.

The totality of witness testimony suggested that one Trawniki guard in particular had the "specialty" of killing prisoners with a wooden hammer. Although Swidersky was identified as this man in some cases, most witnesses identified the guard named Olschanikow. For example, "The witness Chodzko stated that Olschanikow was known as a particularly brutal and wild murderer. He was called the 'killer with the wooden hammer.' On several occasions the witness himself saw Olschanikow beat prisoners to death with a wooden hammer." The witness Scheinberg remembered Olschanikow: "He took great pleasure in beating prisoners to death with a hammer." And witness Szejnberg spoke of *Zugwachmann* Munder, who carried a knife or bayonet: "He did a lot of stabbing with it. Stabbings were always done by Munder, not by others."

Following the Treblinka II uprising on August 2, 1943, a similar plot was uncovered in Treblinka I, and Swidersky allegedly took part in retaliation measures against prisoners at the "sanitorium." He denied involvement in any such retaliation measures. The witness, Lewit, spoke of a roll call of the prisoners following the uncovering of the planned revolt. "A Jewish youth who had stolen keys to the ammunition depot and had had duplicates made of them was beaten bloody during the roll call and later taken away. About five or six prisoners, perhaps even ten, were led away and shot."

Former Trawniki guard Amanaviczius claimed no knowledge of retaliatory measures because of a planned uprising at Treblinka I and stated only that as a result of the uprising at Treblinka II, the guards were reinforced, but no additional measures were taken.

Swidersky, both alone and together with other Trawniki guards, mistreated prisoners, beat prisoners, and hastened their deaths by means of forcing them to work to the point of exhaustion. In general, he denied committing atrocities at the camp, but this had been disproven by the court. For example, former Trawniki guard Kolgushkin said he saw Swidersky beat prisoners with punches, kicks, and objects. Another guard, Moskalenko, saw Swidersky hit prisoners with a wooden cane at the gravel pit. Said the witness, Anglik: "He was considered a particularly dangerous guard: we prisoners were warned about him." Another witness, Sypko, stated: "He was a sadist." And the witness Sterdyner stated: "It was said that Swidersky was the worst guard in the camp." Witness Rzepka said: "He always looked for a reason to beat someone. In my opinion he did this to gain the approval of his superiors."

On orders from SS-Unterscharführer Stumpe, Swidersky beat four prisoners to death with a wooden pole in the summer of 1943. This was confirmed by the guard Zvezdun, who witnessed it while on guard duty in a watchtower near the wood storage yard.

Regarding the number of prisoners killed with Swidersky's participation within the framework of the camp, no definite figure could be determined from the differing testimonies of the witnesses. The court therefore assumed, as a minimum, seventy-one. This was calculated according to the amount of time Swidersky served at the camp and the minimum number of times he escorted prisoners on work details, and it assumed that at least one prisoner per week died because of his actions.

In addition, during the liquidation of the camp on July 23, 1944, Swidersky and his squad of Trawniki guards took several groups of prisoners to a mass grave in the forest and, together with the SS, shot them. At least 300 prisoners were shot that day. Various witnesses saw Swidersky personally escorting the prisoners to the execution site and taking part in the shootings. For example, Moskalenko stated that on the day of the liquidation, additional guards were put in the watchtowers. He himself was in the watchtower. The Germans chased the prisoners out of their barracks and lined them up in groups of thirty each. They were then led into the woods. The first group was escorted by the SS along with Swidersky and his group of guards. Moskalenko heard gunfire in the woods. Later, he came down from the watchtower and saw Swidersky and other Trawniki guards and SS men shooting prisoners at the mass grave in the forest.

The guard Kolgushkin also stated that Swidersky was among the camp personnel who escorted prisoners to the mass graves. Kolgushkin also witnessed this from a watchtower, as Moskalenko had. The guard Zvezdun recalled having seen several Trawniki *Gruppenwachmänner* and *Zugwachmänner* in the woods during the shooting: Franz Swidersky, Karl Mattus, Liudas Kairys, and Heinrich Stieben. In the evening, Zvezdun himself went into the woods with the last group of prisoners to be shot.

The Trawniki guards were often under the influence of alcohol. Alcohol was almost always available, either legally or smuggled in.

Swidersky and the other Trawniki guards feared that as soon as all the prisoners were liquidated, it would then be their turn at the hands of the SS. This was a concern that the guards spoke about with each other in their off-duty hours.

Culpability: The leaders of the Nazi state—Hitler, Goring, Himmler, and Heydrich—were considered the originators of the "annihilation through work" policy carried out in Treblinka I, as well as the mass shootings that took place when the camp was liquidated. They and the senior SS and police commanders "must be considered principal perpetrators of the crimes." "The behavior of Hitler, Goring, Himmler, Heydrich, Globocnik, and Wirth constituted complicity in committing murder" according to German law. They acted intentionally and out of base motives with cruelty.

The "Final Solution" was classified as a "top-secret matter" by its implementors, "who recognized its unlawful nature and, as far as circumstances permitted, prepared and executed it with the greatest possible secrecy."

Genocide "violates every right under natural law, which has an elemental central core of human rights that is untouchable by the laws of the state and the power of the state, and it also violates the generally acknowledged principles of international law."

Evaluation of Swidersky's behavior under German criminal law: because of his blind obedience, he willingly collaborated in the atrocities of the camp, including murder.

The problem of making a distinction between a perpetrator and an accessory had gained new significance in light of examining the mass crimes of the Holocaust. Are those who carry out state-mandated crimes to be considered actual perpetrators or merely as accessories? According to the Dusseldorf court in this case: "The inner attitude of the defendant is decisive. Thus, he may be considered merely an accessory as long as his intention was only to lend support to" the actions of his superiors. However, in this case, Swidersky's inner attitude was not known. The court determined he was "a simple man with a low-level of intelligence who did not have a personality that was capable of resisting" orders from his superiors.

"The defendant appeared to be a compliant, authority-oriented recipient of orders, and this spoke against his being a perpetrator." On the other hand, he appeared to carry out his orders with zealousness. "The defendant aided" in carrying out murder, "but not out of base motives."

"Given the defendant's simple personality," it couldn't be determined that he consciously identified with the racial hatred of the Nazi regime, and because of this, base motives on his part could not be proven for a conviction as a perpetrator, only as an accessory.

The killings in Treblinka I were unlawful. "The so-called Führer Order was therefore not capable of providing grounds to justify the actions of the defendant."

Mitigating circumstances: exculpatory grounds under section 47 of the Military Criminal Code: defendant may not claim exculpatory grounds under this code, which went into effect on October 10, 1940. It read, "If, in carrying out an order in the line of duty, a criminal law is violated, the authority issuing the order is solely responsible. The obeying subordinate, however, can be punished as an accomplice if he exceeded the order, or if he was aware that the order was illegal."

"On the basis of section 3 of the 'Decree of Special Jurisdiction in Criminal Matters for Members of the SS and Police,' dated October 17, 1939, in conjunction with the 'Provisional Disciplinary Regulations for Police Troops,' issued April 19, 1940, by Himmler, the defendant was subject to the regular disciplinary provisions applicable for German police personnel. Thus, the provision of section 47 of the Military Criminal Code was applicable to him.

However, "the defendant must be punished as a participant since the narrow prerequisite defined in section 47 of the Military Criminal Code, for the situation that the superior has sole responsibility, does not pertain here. This is because the orders given to the guards at Treblinka I were vague and general, as opposed to specific and precise. The guards had considerable discretion and leeway in their behavior toward the prisoners."

The court was convinced that the defendant had knowledge of the criminal purpose of the order to kill prisoners in Treblinka I. The defendant cannot excuse his conduct by citing duress or compulsion to obey orders in the sense of section 52 or 54 of the German Criminal Code, because this would assume that he was in fear for his life if he didn't obey. There is no reason to assume he felt duress or compulsion to follow his orders.

"The killings in Treblinka I occurred unlawfully, even though they were based on a secret order of the Führer for the 'Final Solution of the Jewish Question.' Hitler's law-making competence in the Nazi state cannot make them lawful." To this end, the court relied on thoughtful testimony from Dr. Wolfgang Scheffler. For several years he conducted research into the organization and history of the Jewish policies of Nazi Germany and systematically searched all available sources in existing archives. On the basis of evaluation of this material, he reached the conclusion that none of the sources gave any indication that those in German service were threatened with death if they refused to participate in atrocities. The organization, operation, and structure of the SS and police courts confirm this conclusion.

Swidersky signed a statement, contained in his Trawniki personnel file (*Personalbogen*), on June 2, 1943, that in criminal matters he was subject to the "Provisional Disciplinary Regulations for German Police Troops," dated April 19, 1940, and that as such, he would be judged and tried by SS and police courts for any crimes committed by him. Himmler held authority to confirm death sentences when they were imposed.

The defense's expert, Dr. Seraphim, was of the opinion that in practice, reality was quite different, and that anyone who refused to obey orders could not count on a proper court procedure because such matters were handled discreetly by means of secret execution. But the court did not agree with this opinion, because Dr. Seraphim was unable to cite any specific, convincing examples of this. Conversely, Dr. Scheffler did cite known cases relevant to his argument. For example, Dr. Scheffler pointed out that summary judgment of military crimes and implementation of a sentence pronounced immediately thereafter "was possible only in special instances, determined by circumstances. This was restricted to divisions on the front lines when they found themselves in particularly difficult combat situations." Even then, justification had to be reported for the carrying out of an execution. "Had there been any on-the-spot shootings for disobeying orders in connection with mass crimes," this would have been reflected in personnel records, most of which have survived. Not even Dr. Seraphim contested that in this regard the "Dirlewanger unit was in quite an exceptional position and that it cannot be assumed that other commanders had been granted similar special rights." "There is no historical evidence of court-martial shootings for refusal to participate in mass executions."

Even Dr. Seraphim admitted that there were a number of instances in which individuals were successful in avoiding execution duty. "His added observation, however, that one would then have been charged with 'demoralizing of the troops,' the court considered theoretical and unconvincing due, once again, to a lack of documented examples.

Dr. Scheffler cited a publication by Herbert Jäger titled *Verbrechen unter Totalitarer Herrschaft* ("Crimes in totalitarian regimes") that contains over 100 individual cases of men who resisted carrying out criminal orders without being threatened with death.

Dr. Seraphim did not convincingly demonstrate to the court that there existed an "administrative channel—a second legal channel—that led to an internal conviction of those who refused to obey orders." Dr. Seraphim contradicted himself as soon as it came to the issue of jurisdiction. First he stated that the Gestapo had responsibility for this practice, but then later stated that this "second legal channel" was used by everyone but the Gestapo.

The court declared that the idea of an "administrative channel" having had authority to administer death sentences could not have been the case, because SS disciplinary procedures as well as civil service disciplinary procedures "were held to firm rules, and therefore neither could have created a situation" in which an individual would fear imminent death for disobeying an order to take part in killings.

Dr. Seraphim believed that for reasons of secrecy alone, the "administrative channel" of conviction without trial would have been necessary, but the court did not accept this to be correct. Certain German courts were well aware of the extermination of the Jews at the time, and criminal proceedings took place in connection with it, as Dr. Scheffler explained to the court.

In addition, when the Holocaust was nearing completion, "such complete secrecy," by necessity, would have led to the liquidation of those who took part in the mass murder: a measure that was not implemented. "Neither research nor numerous court proceedings nor investigations by state attorneys' offices has yielded any evidence of any such 'secret proceedings.'" Although these concepts applied more to members of the actual SS, Dr. Schefffler could not come to any "essentially different conclusions for the defendant" as an SS auxiliary.

Dr. Seraphim's source material was very unclear, and it was one of the reasons the court accepted the opinions of the much more convincing Dr. Scheffler. Evidence shows that anyone unwilling to participate in mass murder was simply transferred to other assignments.

In Treblinka I, witness Lewit reported: "When there was a man with a heart, he did not stay long." Similarly, witness Szejnberg cited two specific instances in which transfers took place because Trawniki guards did not agree with what was going on there.

Though evidence showed that some Trawniki guards were shot, the circumstances had nothing to do with refusing to take part in killings. Witness Levy remembered two guards being shot for theft, and the Trawniki commandant, Streibel, testified that Trawniki guards were shot for desertion. Amanaviczius, Zvezdun, Kharkovskij, and Kolgushkin, Trawniki guards at Treblinka I, all remembered a fellow guard there named Kudelja who was apparently shot for going AWOL.

Once an entire prisoner labor detail escaped, however, no disciplinary measures were taken against the guards who had been watching them; at least none of the witnesses mentioned it.

When the "Munder" group deserted, it resulted, as Swidersky said, merely in the remaining camp guards being put on lockdown. The same thing happened when some of Swidersky's own group fled. "The defendant had a real opportunity to avoid what took place in Treblinka I. It might have been feasible for him to have deserted to the underground or the partisans. After all, a large number of other Trawniki guards took this way out, even if not until 1944." He could also have carried out his orders with less zeal, but he chose to be hard on the prisoners, even when his superiors were not around. The defendant would have had to tell himself, in 1944 at the latest, that, all things considered, Treblinka I would have to be liquidated sooner or later. The evidence for it was strong: the dismantling of Treblinka II nearby in November 1943, the ever-approaching military front, and the desertion of many Trawniki guards up to that point.

"When section 47 of the Military Criminal Code is applied, mere doubts as to the legality of an order or imputable failure to recognize its illegality do not suffice for culpability; rather, definite knowledge is required."

"The application of the legal rulings developed for 'an erroneous attitude toward interdiction' is not excluded if the person subject to orders, even though he recognized the criminal purpose of an order, still believed that he had to carry it out, because for reasons of falsely understood duty to obey or to be loyal, he thought that even orders that require him to commit criminal acts are mandatory. An error of this type relates to a basis for justification not recognized by the legal system (West German Supreme Court, August 2, 1968: 4 StR 623/67, confirming finding of West German Supreme Court, April 22, 1955: 1 StR 653/54). "It cannot be entirely ruled out that the defendant acted in such a belief." This is especially true considering his apparent mindset of obedience to authority. All his life he made himself subordinate to authority: in the Soviet Union, to the "collective farm" on which he worked, then in the Red Army for a short period, then to the Germans as a collaborator. Nevertheless, the court holds the defendant responsible for his actions. Defendant is held accountable and convicted for aiding and abetting murder in the camp, including the minimum number of 300 prisoners shot during the liquidation of the camp.

The death penalty under section 211 of the German Criminal Code was abolished and replaced by life imprisonment. "According to this, an accomplice in murder can also, in principle, be punished by life imprisonment" unless mitigating circumstances are involved. The court decided that life imprisonment was not appropriate punishment in this case. "Even if the defendant exhibited great zeal in his acts, it must be taken into account that, in the whole context, he is not of the same status as the principal perpetrators, and he was merely a 'little cog in the apparatus of annihilation.'"

The court used section 44 of the German Criminal Code to arrive at a sentence range for the defendant of three to fifteen years' imprisonment. The court considered as mitigating circumstances the defendant's background: his harsh life growing up in the Soviet Union, his limited education, his obedience-to-authority mentality, the harshness of his stay in a POW camp, and his young age at the time he had been a Trawniki guard (early twenties). In addition, "The particularly unfavorable circumstances and the special situation of the Trawniki guards must be noted, especially the morally confusing command situation in which the defendant found himself by being placed involuntarily in the sphere of power and tension of two nations (i.e., Nazi Germany and the Soviet Union)." Furthermore, the defendant's unblemished conduct both before and after the war was weighed in his favor.

Conversely, the "senselessness and cruelty" of the defendant's crimes were considered aggravating circumstances. Also, during his trial, he had not shown any signs of remorse about his actions. When survivors testified about the horrors of those days, the defendant was visibly unimpressed. He only appeared to be moved when there was talk in the court of "his own unfavorable childhood situation."

The court sentenced Swidersky to seven years' imprisonment. Under section 60 of the German Criminal Code, he was given credit for time spent in pretrial detention (three years).

CHAPTER 7

OSI AND US CASES

OSI

In the 1970s, the public was shocked to learn that Nazi war criminals had settled in the US. There were calls for their expulsion, and laws were passed to facilitate their deportation.[1] By 1974, New York congresswoman Elizabeth Holtzman, a member of the House Subcommittee on Immigration, Citizenship, and International Law, determined that the Immigration and Naturalization Service (INS) was not working diligently to uncover suspected Nazi war criminals living in the US, so she proposed establishing a "War Crimes Strike Force" within the INS to remedy the situation.[2] Originally known as the "Special Litigation Unit" (SLU)[3], the name was soon changed to the "Office of Special Investigations," or OSI[4], in 1979, to handle such cases. It was moved from the jurisdiction of the INS to the US Department of Justice's Criminal Division. Since its founding, OSI has investigated approximately 1,500 individuals.[5] Most Nazis found in the US are discovered through the thorough review of Nazi-era documents. The work is done by multilingual OSI historians in archives around the world.[6]

OSI cannot file criminal charges against alleged Nazi perpetrators, because their crimes were committed on foreign soil against non-US citizens and therefore violated no US laws at the time they were committed. Any attempt to prosecute Nazi war criminals criminally in the US is barred by the "ex post facto clause" on retroactive punishment. As a result, the US government can bring only civil suits against Nazi suspects, seeking to strip them of their US citizenship and deport them.[7]

Prior to 1978, anyone ordered deported could request the US attorney general to prevent the deportation by arguing that the deportation could result in persecution in the country the defendant is being deported to, or by arguing that the deportation would cause personal or family hardship.[8] In 1978, Congress passed the so-called Holtzmann Amendment, named after Congresswoman Holtzmann. After this, if an immigration judge ordered deportation on the basis of participation in Nazi persecution, the attorney general is statutorily precluded from reversing the order. This amendment passed just prior to the founding of OSI and became an important factor in OSI's work.[9]

A convicted defendant may choose a country to be deported to. If that country is unwilling to accept him, he can be deported to his country of birth, the last country he resided in prior to coming to the US, or, if those countries won't accept him, then any country willing to accept him.[10] If no other designated country agrees to take a deportable individual, Germany agrees that it would be the receiving country, provided that the individual had assisted or participated in persecution while serving during World War II in a military, paramilitary, police, or auxiliary police unit under the direction or control of the German government.[11] As of 2006, twenty-three OSI defendants have gone to Germany. One was extradited, some fled during OSI proceedings against them, and others left the US as a result of settlements with OSI. As of 2008, sixteen former Trawniki guards have come under investigation and prosecution by OSI.

OSI prosecutes cases on the basis of a defendant's "assistance in persecution." But what does that entail? Does it, or should it, include unwilling assistance? And what about assistance willingly rendered, but only because the alternative might be death? Are policemen who rounded up Jews different from camp guards? Are there distinctions to be drawn among camp guards themselves? Should volunteers be treated differently from those who may not have served voluntarily?[12]

"Some historians speak privately about 'historical truth' vs. 'judicial truth' and express some frustration about the difference." One OSI historian basically stated that alleged perpetrators put on trial, for the purposes of gaining a conviction, will be made to be more sinister than they actually are: the prosecution, in other words, will "overemphasize the role of the individual because that's what the trial is about."[13]

Sometimes there was tension between investigators and historians. "Much of it related to status. Who was going to put the case together, the investigator or the historian? Who would decide which investigations to open and which witnesses should be interviewed? Who would accompany the attorney to the interview?[14]

In 1980, OSI director Allan Ryan decided that historians needed to be the main contributor to the cases in order to persuade judges to convict defendants. Ryan wanted OSI historians to develop the cases and then have outside "expert" historians testify during trial. OSI historians made contact with outside historians including Raul Hilberg, Christopher Brownig, and Charles Sydnor Jr. Hilberg and Sydnor would be the two experts most often used in OSI cases in court.[15]

OSI historians wanted, like the OSI attorneys and investigators, to be assigned to individual cases. They wanted to be briefed on case backgrounds and case strategy. Additionally, they also wanted to develop and maintain contact with other historical and archival experts and follow up on research leads. These suggestions were gradually all adopted, and some of the work usually delegated to investigators, such as locating defendants and witnesses, was increasingly handled by the OSI historians. The OSI's "Research and Development" program[16] was based on the research of the OSI historians and run by Dr. David Marwell until his departure in 1988, when Dr. Elizabeth White took over. All the historians collected documents on Nazi war crimes and the units and individuals that assisted in it. The chief historian then collected data from the documents to identify suspects, checked for US immigration records on those individuals, tracked them down if they were in the US, and conducted further research to determine if there was a basis for opening an investigation. For trial, OSI historians obtain certified copies of documentary evidence, ensure that it is accurately translated into English, draft historical portions of prosecution memos, and attend depositions and trials in order to assist the OSI attorneys with historical questions.[17]

Dr. Peter Black was the first formally trained historian hired by OSI, in 1980. He and other OSI historians spent most of their time in archives. They searched for rosters, identity documents, and testimony from hundreds of postwar trials held in Europe.[18] The first chief historian at OSI had been a translator at the Nuremberg trials and had then worked at the Center of Military History. By 1986, Dr. Black assumed many of the responsibilities of the chief OSI historian. He was formally named to that position in 1989, when the first OSI chief historian departed.[19] The chief historian is a deputy director and consults with the OSI director and principal deputy director on nearly all major case decisions. Staff historians work and strategize with the attorneys on cases.[20] In 1983, at its height, OSI had a staff of fifty-one, including twenty attorneys. As of 2006, OSI had a staff of twenty-six, including five attorneys. As of 2008, OSI had seven historians and one investigator. The chief OSI historian, first Dr. Black and then Dr. White, gave the other OSI historians their case assignments on the basis of each historian's area of expertise. Trial exhibits in OSI cases were selected from among historical documents used by the historians. Choosing which documents to incorporate into the trial record was a collaborative process between the OSI attorney and historian assigned to the individual cases.

During the Cold War, the most difficult hurdle was getting information from the Soviet Union. Congressman Joshua Eilberg and Congresswoman Elizabeth Holtzman (in 1975),

SLU director Martin Mendelsohn (in 1978), OSI director Walter Rockler and his deputy, Allan Ryan (in 1980), and Deputy Assistant Attorney General Mark Richard all made trips to the Soviet Union to discuss the issue. Attorney General Benjamin Civiletti also raised the matter in a meeting at the US Department of Justice with the chief justice of the Soviet Supreme Court.[21] As a result of these meetings, the Soviets agreed to allow questioning of Soviet citizens in accordance with US legal procedures. A Soviet prosecutor had to be present, but he would not have advance notice of the questions. OSI attorneys and defense attorneys could question and cross-examine the witnesses, and the questioning was to be videotaped. In 1989, Attorney General Richard Thornburgh, the first attorney general to visit the Soviet Union, signed a "memo of understanding" with the Soviet chief prosecutor, in which the US and the Soviet Union agreed to further their cooperation with regard to investigating suspected Nazi war criminals.[22] Additionally, a "Mutual Legal Assistance Treaty" facilitating closer law enforcement coordination between the US and Russia was approved by the US Senate, but not until late 2001.[23]

The US Department of Justice was promised that the US would have increased archival access. However, the Soviets had inadequate archival indexes and were not willing to grant access directly to Western scholars. OSI therefore had to rely on the Soviets themselves to do the research, and the task often went to prosecutors and police investigators rather than historians. The Soviet Union lacked the resources, both personnel and material, to accommodate many requests. It was not uncommon for responses to take up to a year.[24] Problems were often mundane: inadequate copying facilities, lack of toner or paper, and deteriorating records due to insufficient preservation methods (sometimes OSI would provide toner and paper or bring a portable copying machine.) Poland was the only eastern European country that allowed OSI historians direct archival access during the Cold War.[25] Soviet cases required proof only that a defendant had been a member of a certain unit in order to be prosecuted, whereas OSI required the historical context of the unit to bring a case to court.[26]

In 1990, OSI historian Dr. Peter Black gained access to Czech archives; specifically, the archive of the Ministry of Interior in Prague. There he found a collection of rosters from the SS-"Streibel" Battalion. The information from this material eventually led the OSI historians to the FSB (former KGB) Central Archive in Moscow, where they found a treasure trove of Trawniki documents: personnel files (*Personalbögen*) and deployment rosters. As part of OSI's research and case development, OSI historians have amassed the largest concentration of documents in the world concerning the Trawniki camp.[27]

In regard to the FSB Archive in Moscow, while OSI historians can view documents there, they cannot make reproductions or even request them on-site. All requests must be made in writing beforehand. The archive itself will not respond to requests: everything is done through intermediaries. Thus, the US embassy contacts the Russian procurator, who in turn deals with the FSB Archive. Two-year response times are not uncommon.[28]

When the US Holocaust Memorial Museum was founded in 1993, another Holocaust scholarly resource became available. However, because OSI had by then attained stature as an international repository of Holocaust scholarship, there was no question of its being supplanted by the museum. Together, OSI and the museum have provided expertise and manpower on several Holocaust issues, including the "Interagency Working Group," which oversees the "Nazi War Crimes Disclosure Act."[29]

Under OSI director Eli Rosenbaum, OSI established the so-called OSI Bank, which holds "exhaustively indexed documents, pleadings, reports, judgements, and memos."[30] Documentation based on scholarship by OSI historians is accessible in court files. Complete records, including court exhibits, of several early OSI trials have been microfilmed and donated to the archive of the Yad Vashem Museum in Jerusalem. Attorney General Smith presented them to the Israeli ambassador to the US in 1984.[31] Once OSI has completed its Nazi cases, it will likely turn over similar materials from more-recent trials to the US Holocaust Memorial Museum and Yad Vashem.[32] DOJ is committed to making its historical material available, "as far as possible, consistent with privacy and national security concerns," so that others may use it for their own scholarly and educational pursuits. Once OSI has completed its Nazi cases, DOJ hopes to disclose much of OSI's litigation material.[33] Most of OSI's historical documents, including wartime records and postwar interrogations, come from German and Soviet archives. These are now open to outside scholars.

The methods in which OSI organized the material, in various databases, will assist researchers.[34] This includes OSI's massive collection of investigative records: suspect interrogations, witness interviews by OSI personnel, historians' reports, prosecution memos, depositions, etc.[35] Additionally, as a repository of World War II knowledge, OSI has been requested by other government agencies to write reports and to assist in nonlegal matters concerning the Holocaust. For example, with assistance from attorneys, OSI historians have written "exhaustive reports" on controversial subjects, such as Josef Mengele and Klaus Barbie. They also contributed significantly to a US State Department report on Nazi gold.[36]

In 2004, OSI's expenditures were $5,869,000.[37] The organization's name has since changed to the Human Rights and Special Prosecutions Section (HRSP), and it now prosecutes other cases of human rights violations and not just Nazi war criminal cases.

As of 2006, because of OSI's work, eighty-three Nazi war criminals have been stripped of US citizenship and sixty-two have left the country.[38] Over twenty defendants died while their cases were pending. In a few cases, the defendants were not deported because no country was willing to accept them.[39] Over 90 percent of OSI defendants have been non-German Nazi collaborators.[40]

Individuals who served as OSI directors included Walter Rockler, Allan Ryan, Neal Sher, and Eli Rosenbaum.

US VS. FEDORENKO

This was the US Department of Justice's seminal case. Fedor Fedorenko was a Ukrainian drafted into the Red Army. He was captured by the Germans in 1941 and held in several POW camps. He was then recruited for Trawniki service and served as a guard in the Lublin ghetto, Treblinka II, and Stutthof.

Fedorenko believed that his wife and children had died during the war, and he immigrated to the US in 1949. He falsely stated on his US visa application that he had been born in Poland and had spent the war years there as a farmer and a factory worker. He remarried in the US and became a US citizen in 1970. Later, he learned that his family had survived the war after all and were still in the Soviet Union. He visited them in 1972, 1973, and 1976. During his 1973 trip there, he was questioned by Soviet authorities regarding his whereabouts during the war. He was released after authorities concluded that he was "not criminally liable" for anything.[41]

The INS started an investigation in 1975, after an article in a Ukrainian newspaper identified Fedorenko as a war criminal. At the request of the INS, Israeli authorities interviewed several Treblinka survivors. Most picked Fedorenko from a photo spread and recalled him as a guard who had beat prisoners.

Under INS questioning, Fedorenko admitted serving at Treblinka but claimed he had served there under duress and had not personally killed anyone. The US Attorney's Office in southern Florida filed a "denaturalization" complaint against him in 1977. He was accused of committing war crimes and committing fraud on his visa application.

A trial against Fedorenko lasted two weeks. Six Treblinka survivors testified that he had beaten or shot prisoners at the camp.[42] He testified on his own behalf. He claimed that his Trawniki service had not been voluntary and that he had served at Treblinka only as a perimeter guard and had not participated in any atrocities. He admitted shooting in the direction of fleeing prisoners during the Treblinka uprising but claimed he hadn't planned on actually hitting anyone. He told the court that he had listed Poland as his birthplace on his visa application in order to avoid being repatriated to the Soviet Union.

The judge found Fedorenko to be a good US citizen with no criminal record in the United States.[43] The crux of the case was whether or not Fedorenko's Trawniki service had been voluntary. The court concluded that it had not been. The judge disagreed with the prosecution that Fedorenko should have risked his life and deserted if his service had not been voluntary. Furthermore, the court determined that there was no specific evidence that Fedorenko had personally participated in atrocities. The court also concluded that Fedorenko had reasonably viewed himself as still being a POW rather than a German auxiliary. The court focused on his exemplary twenty-nine years in the US and thus refused to revoke his US citizenship.[44]

The Department of Justice and the INS recommended to the US solicitor general that the ruling should be appealed. Attorney General Benjamin Civiletti argued the Fedorenko case before the US Supreme Court. The Supreme Court reexamined the language of the "Displaced Persons Act," under which Fedorenko had entered the US. The Supreme Court took the opposite view of the original court ruling: therefore, those who had assisted in persecuting civilians during the war were automatically ineligible for a US visa, regardless of whether or not their Nazi service had been voluntary. Fedorenko's US citizenship was revoked. Two of the justices dissented. Justice Stevens believed that voluntariness, or lack thereof, was the key issue. "Without the distinction of voluntariness there can be no difference between someone like a *kapo* and a guard."[45]

Fedorenko was ordered deported in 1983, and he chose the Soviet Union as his destination. The US embassy recommended that Fedorenko be told of the possible risks he faced if deported there. The Department of Justice chose not to inform him in light of the fact that he had not been arrested when he had visited his family there several times in years past. He was deported in 1984.[46]

In 1985, the US embassy in Moscow announced that Fedorenko was living in Crimea and had applied for pension benefits. However, in 1986 the Soviet government put Fedorenko on trial for war crimes for deserting the Red Army and participating in mass executions.

His fate was determined by a judgment dated June 19, 1986, before the Court Collegium for Criminal Matters of the Crimea regional court, with Judges M. Tyutyunik and S. Demidobaya presiding. The public assessor was V. Mikhajlov, and the prosecutor was Z. Tesak. Fedorenko's defense attorney was A. Viktorov. Y. Andreyev gave expert testimony.[47]

Fedorenko was found guilty and sentenced to death. He was shot by firing squad in 1987.[48]

By focusing on conduct rather than intent, the Fedorenko case made it possible to prosecute camp guards without showing that their service was voluntary, a showing that in most cases could not easily be made.[49]

It is unknown why the Soviet government changed its mind on Fedorenko's wartime culpability and decided to put him on trial.[50]

US VS. KAIRYS[51]

In the US District Court of Northern Illinois, on December 28, 1984, the US government sought to "denaturalize" Liudas Kairys under 8 U.S.C., 1451 (a), on grounds that he had obtained US citizenship by misrepresentation and concealment of his Trawniki service, which legally barred him from entering the United States. The government case was brought by OSI attorneys Norman Moscowitz and Michael Wolf.

Kairys had served as a Trawniki guard at Treblinka labor camp (a.k.a. Treblinka I). Treblinka I was under the administration of the SS. Labor carried out there by prisoners was strenuous, including loading coal at a railroad station, breaking stones at a quarry and transporting them, chopping wood, paving and repairing roads, and loading sand from the banks of a nearby river. Prisoners worked six days a week, from early morning until evening. The death of the prisoners from disease and exhaustion was a weekly and sometimes daily occurrence. Prisoners too weak to continue working were killed by the SS or Trawniki guards. Several thousand Jews died at the camp during its existence, 1941–1944. In addition to the SS personnel, the camp had four platoons of Trawniki guards that guarded the camp perimeter and the prisoner worksites.

In July 1944, the camp closed down as the Red Army approached the area. Over 300 remaining Jewish prisoners were shot by the SS or Trawniki guards. The Trawniki guards from the camp were then absorbed into the SS-"Streibel" Battalion. The unit went to Dresden for clean-up duties in February 1945 and ended the war in Czechoslovakia in April 1945.

Liudas Kairys was born in Lithuania and served in the Lithuanian army, which was absorbed into the Red Army in 1940. He was captured by German forces in 1941 and taken to Hammerstein POW camp in Pomerania. The US government contended that Kairys was recruited from the POW camp in 1942, by the Germans, for Trawniki service. In July 1942 he was assigned to the Lublin Detachment, from March 1943 to July 1944 he was assigned to Treblinka I, and from August 1944 to April 1945 he was assigned to the SS-"Streibel" Battalion.

Kairys claimed on his US visa application that he resided in Lithuania until 1944 and then Czechoslovakia. After the war, he lived and worked with a farmer near Regensburg, Germany. He continued working as a farm laborer through 1946 and early 1947. In 1947, he joined the US Army labor service, a civilian auxiliary force consisting of displaced persons that carried out various tasks for the US occupation forces. In 1949, Kairys immigrated to the US and settled in Chicago. In 1957, he applied for and was granted "naturalization." He got married, had two children, and was employed in a blue-collar job.

The US government prosecution team from OSI submitted as evidence against Kairys his Trawniki *Personalbogen* (personnel file). Kairys claimed that the document was not authentic and that it should not have been admissible as an "ancient document" because it was not "self-authenticating," that it did not come within the "public document exception" because it was a foreign document, and SS documents were not public, and that there was insufficient foundation laid by a custodian. He also argued that it did not bear his signature.

Kairys introduced evidence that the photo on the *Personalbogen* may have been torn off or replaced, that the signature could not be conclusively established as his, that the chemical composition of the paper demonstrated that it could have been produced postwar, and that the thumbprint on the document was not made with normal ink. Thus, Kairys claimed that the document was either a forgery or that it referred to a person other than him. The implication was that the forged document was part of a program of disinformation by the Soviet Union.

The court heard expert testimony on all aspects of the *Personalbogen*. Regarding the thumbprint, Kairys did not deny that it was his, and expert testimony demonstrated conclusively that it was his. No expert testified that the document was not authentic or that it was a forgery. The most that could be said is that certain aspects of the document were open to certain questions. When that evidence was combined with the fact that the document was certified as having come from a Soviet archive—the repository of nearly all SS documents recovered in Poland during the war as the result of the Red Army overrunning the region—and the fact that other individuals who served as Trawniki guards at Treblinka I verified their own *Personalbögen* in similar form, these led to the indisputable conclusion that Kairys was the person identified on his *Personalbogen*, and that it was a genuine document. Thus, the court admitted it as an "ancient document."

Also submitted into the prosecution's evidence was the Trawniki deployment roster for Treblinka I for March 22, 1943, which indicated that *Oberwachmann* Liudas Kairys had served there and was assigned Trawniki ID #1628.

Kairys disputed the testimony of several witnesses (former Trawniki guards) and the identification by some of the photo from his *Personalbogen* as being a photo of him. These included

(1) Ivan Zvezdun: his deposition was taken, and he identified Kairys as his platoon commander at Treblinka I and had in 1980 stated to Soviet authorities that he recognized Kairys's photo.
(2) Vladas Amanaviczius: he gave a deposition in Belgium, where he was living, and recalled Kairys as his platoon commander at Treblinka I and also identified Kairys's photo.
(3) Vladas Zajanckauskas: he testified under immunity in Massachusetts that he recalled there being a Kairys with him at the Hammerstein POW camp and also at Trawniki.
(4) Semen Kharkovsky and Fedor Vilshun both testified that Kairys was at Treblinka I, but neither of them was able to identify his photo.

Kairys argued that the photo spread was impermissibly suggestive and that the passage of time made any photo identification questionable. However, the court concluded that the photo spread was not suggestive, and it was admitted as evidence.

The 1944 statement of Nikita Rekalo, the 1968 and 1971 statements of Franz Swidersky, and the statements at the Swidersky trial that Liudas Kairys was a guard at Treblinka I substantially undercut any idea that Kairys's presence at Treblinka I was a fabrication by the witnesses as part of a Soviet disinformation campaign.

None of the survivors recalled any specific conduct by Kairys. Swidersky, who had also served at Treblinka I, was convicted of war crimes before a West German court in 1968. The witnesses at that trial, including survivors, vividly recalled Swidersky's individual acts of brutality and sadism. Such testimony was absent in the Kairys case.

The US Congress passed the "Displaced Persons Act" (DPA) of 1948. It relaxed immigration quotas from 1948 to 1952 to permit the immigration of over 400,000 displaced persons. However, the Constitution of the International Refugee Organization (IRO) excluded from this those who had "assisted the enemy in persecuting civilian populations during the war," and this exclusion generally applied to war criminals.

The administrative procedures established to screen displaced-person applicants were described in *US vs. Fedorenko*, 449 U.S. 490, 101 S. Ct. 737, 66 L. Ed. 2d 686 (1981). US officials in the field would determine whether an applicant was qualified to immigrate to the US under the "Displaced Persons Act." It is beyond dispute that former Trawniki guards were not eligible for US visas under the DPA. The US Supreme Court expressly stated so in *US vs. Fedorenko*.

Kairys claimed that illegal procurement of his US visa couldn't serve as a basis for revoking it, because revocation was not included in the law at the time of Kairys's "naturalization." It's true that in 1957, when Kairys was "naturalized," 8 U.S.C., 1451 (a), did not list illegal procurement of a US visa as a basis for revoking it. However, Kairys's case wasn't brought to court until 1980, well after enactment of an amendment to that law.

Kairys's nationality or allegiance changed several times, both before, during, and after the war: he was a Polish national, a Lithuanian national, a Lithuanian soldier, a Soviet national, a Soviet soldier, a German collaborator (as a Trawniki guard), and, finally, a US "naturalized" citizen. His status as a Soviet national and Soviet soldier was involuntary (Lithuania was forcibly annexed to the Soviet Union in 1940). One cannot be sure whether his Trawniki service was voluntary or involuntary.

In 1986, the US Court of Appeals affirmed his "denaturalization." Kairys complained that in his case, both the district court and the appellate court refused to address a criticism that he had made concerning the Soviet-provided Trawniki *Personalbogen*. The Soviets had refused to allow Kairys's document experts to clip a fiber from the thumbprint on the document, for testing. The fact that the appellate court did not discuss the extent to which this evidence should have been deemed impeached by the Soviets' failure to allow chemical analysis of a fiber hardly resulted in unfairness or inadequacy in the proceedings. "Procedural fairness does not require an appellate court to discuss every issue raised by an appellant."

Kairys also argued that the Soviet Union had given the DOJ evidence for use in his case as part of an unwritten, secret, unratified, and therefore illegal "Moscow agreement" between the OSI director and the Office of the Soviet Procurator-General. Supposing this was true, the appellate court deemed the issue irrelevant: the evidence obtained from the Soviet Union is neither more nor less reliable, because it was obtained by an agreement that may not have complied with US law that concerns not the reliability of evidence, but "the relations within and between the executive and legislative branches of the federal government." "To prevent the evidence, despite its reliability, from being considered, as a sanction for improper government behavior, would be inconsistent with the US Supreme Court's decision not to apply the 'exclusionary rule' of the 4th Amendment in deportation proceedings" (*INS vs. Lopez-Mendoza*, 468 US 1032, 1050, 1984).

With the collapse of the Soviet Union, it was acknowledged that the KGB had employed accusations of collaboration with the Nazis to discredit Soviet political opponents. An article from the Lithuanian press reported on the contents of a KGB file found in Lithuania. The file contained a recommendation, made in 1980, that the KGB, "to impede the anticipated consolidation of Zionist and Lithuanian émigré nationalist organizations, and to sharpen the enmity between them," provide the American Jewish community with information regarding certain Lithuanian emigrants, including Liudas Kairys, who resided in the United States. Kairys, who was active in the Lithuanian nationalist movement in the US, and thus a logical target for Soviet disinformation, asked the appellate court to believe that the KGB had framed him to impede the Lithuanian nationalist movement and cause friction between it and Zionism.

Of course the KGB was not above using forgeries to discredit state enemies. However, the KGB had an even-greater interest in using genuine information about Nazi collaborators to foment distrust and hostility between Lithuanians and Jews than in forging evidence of such collaboration. Kairys argued throughout his case that the Soviet Union had forged the evidence against him and thus was trying to frame him. The district court and the appellate court considered this possibility but rejected it.

Regarding the issue of whether Kairys's service as a Trawniki guard at Treblinka I made him deportable under the "Holtzman Amendment" because of his assistance in the persecution of Jewish prisoners: his assistance in that persecution, whether or not he committed any specific atrocities, was settled in an appellate court already in *INS vs. Schellong*, supra, 805 F. 2d at 660-61. If the operation of a camp such as Treblinka I "were treated as an ordinary criminal conspiracy," the Trawniki guards, "like the lookouts for a gang of robbers, would be deemed co-conspirators, or if not, certainly aiders and abettors of the conspiracy": no more should have been required to satisfy the provisions of the "Holtzman Amendment," which "makes assisting in persecution" grounds for deportation. Kairys's argument that he had been coerced to serve as a Trawniki guard did not ring true with the court, on the basis of the fact that he had been promoted by the Germans to *Gruppenwachmann*. Two promotions do not indicate evidence of having served under coercion.

In 1987, a US immigration judge ordered him deported, a decision affirmed by the US Board of Immigration Appeals in 1989. Just prior to his deportation, the US Supreme Court denied Kairys's petition to have his case reviewed by that court (called a "writ of certiorari"). Kairys designated Germany as the country to which he wanted to be deported if his deportation order was upheld, and Germany agreed to take him. On April 9, 1993, the US Department of Justice announced that Kairys, at age seventy-two, was deported to Germany for his role as a Trawniki guard during the war. The deportation was carried out by the INS in Chicago.

In Germany, investigation proceedings were initiated against Kairys in Darmstadt, for aiding in murder at Treblinka I. That investigation was suspended in 1999. Kairys had died in the meantime.

US VS. HAJDA[62]

Bronislaw Hajda was born in 1924 in Jordanov, Poland. His nationality was Goralian (an ethnic group from the Goral Mountains of southern Poland). In the 1930s and up to 1942, he had worked for his father as an apprentice shoemaker/cobbler.

On March 22, 1943, he and fifty-four other Trawniki guards were assigned to Treblinka I, and he served there until the evacuation of the camp on July 22, 1944, when the Red Army arrived in the area. Following orders, the guards helped the SS kill all of the camp's Polish political prisoners, and they released the nonpolitical prisoners. The next day, they forced all of the camp's Jewish prisoners to lie facedown in the camp. The guards then took them in groups of about twenty to mass graves in the nearby woods, where they were shot, totaling 300–700 people.

By July 24, 1944, the guards fled westward, away from the advancing Soviet forces. Trawniki was evacuated around the same time as Treblinka I, and its remaining guard force became the SS-"Streibel" Battalion. Other Trawniki guards, including the ones fleeing from Treblinka, also joined the battalion.

The battalion forced Polish civilians to construct fortifications against the Red Army's advance. The battalion headquarters was located in Zlota, then in November 1944 it moved to Pinczow. The battalion was subordinate to the SS-Special Staff "Sporrenberg," led by a former SS and police commander of the Lublin District, SS-General Jakob Sporrenberg. Sporrenberg's headquarters was located in Jedrzejow.

In February 1945, the SS-"Streibel" Battalion retreated toward Dresden, and by April 25, 1945, the battalion had dissolved in the face of the Red Army.

Hajda had been recruited by the SS for Trawniki service in the fall of 1942. He trained at Trawniki starting in January 1943. Other former Trawniki guards who had been assigned to Treblinka I made statements to Soviet authorities during interrogations that Hajda had beat and shot prisoners and took part in the massacre on the last day before the guards fled the camp.

In April 1945, once the "Streibel" Battalion disbanded, Hajda lingered near Dresden and mingled in with a sea of refugees. In 1945, Hajda's family was tried by a Polish court for collaborating with the Germans in their hometown of Jordanov. They all were acquitted.

Also in 1945, Hajda got a job as a civilian guard for a Polish military unit working with the US Army. He went to the US under the "Displaced Persons Act," on a visa in 1950. He became a US citizen in 1955, settled in a Chicago suburb, and got a job as a factory worker at the Container Corporation of America.

In 1994, the US Department of Justice's OSI filed a "denaturalization" action against him. His US citizenship was revoked. He appealed the decision on the grounds that the DOJ had the wrong man. In 1998, his appeal was denied.

Hajda's Trawniki personnel file (*Personalbogen*) wasn't available for his trial. Soviet authorities had it, and in 1950 they gave it to officials in Ukraine, who took measures to locate Hajda and other former Trawniki guards until 1959. In 1992, authorities in Ukraine destroyed the personnel file because the time period they had set for keeping it in storage had expired. However, Soviet authorities had copied down the information contained in the file before they had given it to the officials in Ukraine. That information was provided for Hajda's US trial. Also introduced into evidence were the Trawniki guard deployment rosters for Treblinka I for March 22, 1943, and April 6, 1944, which contained Hajda's name, birthdate, and birthplace.

US VS. KWOCZAK[53]

In June 2002, the US District Court for Eastern Pennsylvania heard a case to revoke the citizenship of Fedor Kwoczak. The OSI accused him of obtaining his US citizenship illegally by procuring an immigration visa to which he was not entitled. OSI alleged that he had concealed his service as a Trawniki guard at Trawniki, in the Warsaw Detachment, in the Bialystok Detachment, Poniatowa, and in the SS-"Streibel" Battalion and, as such, had assisted in persecuting civilians and had participated in a movement hostile to the United States and its democratic form of government.

For the prosecution team were Scott Coffina, assistant US attorney for Philadelphia, and Eli Rosenbaum, Edward Stutman, and Jonathan Drimmer, all OSI attorneys. The government's burden of proof in such a case is "clear, convincing, and unequivocal evidence" (see *US vs. Fedorenko*). In the case, the government relied on the testimony of Charles W. Sydnor Jr., a historian specializing on the Nazi period.

In February 1943, there was a recruitment drive for Trawniki service among civilian Ukrainians in the Galicia District. Kwoczak was among them, and he received Trawniki ID #3222. During his service he was promoted to *Oberwachmann*.

In January 1946, he was issued a "displaced-persons registration card" by a branch of the International Red Cross.

Among the wartime documents offered into evidence against Kwoczak were Trawniki deployment rosters for the Warsaw Detachment, April 17, 1943; Poniatowa, June 1943;

the Bialystok Detachment, August 14, 1943; Poniatowa, September 1943; and the SS-"Streibel" Battalion, August 1944–April 1945, all of which included Kwoczak's name and Trawniki ID number.

The Trawniki unit deployed to the Warsaw ghetto to help suppress the Jewish uprising was not used in the assault on the Jewish insurgents, but in guarding the periphery of the ghetto to make sure no one escaped, and in overseeing the transport of the ghetto residents to Treblinka II.

In Poniatowa, the Trawniki guards manned watchtowers, patrolled the camp perimeter, guarded prisoner worksites, and guarded the camp entrance.

During the Bialystok ghetto uprising, the Trawniki guards oversaw the removal of ghetto residents from their homes and their transport by train to Treblinka, Majdanek, and Auschwitz.

Kwoczak remained in Poniatowa from September 1943 until sometime between March and July 1944. That means he would have been present in the camp when 12,000–14,000 Jews were shot there on November 4, 1943, in an operation known as *Erntefest* (Harvest Festival), but there is no proof that the Trawniki guards in the camp took part in it, only that Germans did.

The SS-"Streibel" Battalion guarded civilian forced laborers who constructed fortifications along the Nida and Vistula Rivers in 1944 to try to slow down the advance of the approaching Red Army. In February 1945, the battalion helped clear rubble near the bomb-damaged areas of Dresden. The battalion ended the war in April 1945 in the vicinity of the German-Czech border region.

In 1949, Kwoczak applied to immigrate to the US under the "Displaced Persons Act." He was interviewed by the US Army Counterintelligence Corps (CIC) and made no mention of his Trawniki service. Asked about his wartime whereabouts, he stated that he had worked on his father's farm in Tysmienica, Galicia District, and then was sent as a forced laborer to Germany in April 1944.

Also in 1949, Kwoczak filed an immigrant visa application with the US consulate in Munich, and his visa was issued soon thereafter. He came to the US, arriving in New York, and then settled in Pennsylvania.

In 1957, he filed an application for "naturalization" with the INS but was advised to reapply when his English-speaking skills were better. He reapplied in 1966 and his "naturalization" was granted by a judge at the US District Court for Eastern Pennsylvania.

Under the "Displaced Persons Act" of 1948, the US Congress made immigration visas available to "eligible displaced persons," allowing for immigration to the U.S., for war refugees, in excess of normal quota limitations.

The OSI contended that Kwoczak was ineligible to enter the US under the "Displaced Persons Act" because he made willful, material misrepresentations on his visa application (by lying about his wartime whereabouts and activities) and assisted in the persecution of civilians (as a Trawniki guard), both of which are violations of the "Displaced Persons Act."

Kwoczak argued that the US government had presented no proof of specific instances of his personal and direct participation in persecution actions. However, the court found the evidence presented by the government was sufficient to establish that Kwoczak had served as an armed Trawniki guard at multiple locations and on multiple occasions. Therefore, no further evidence than that was required. "There need be no personal participation by the defendant in the commission of physical atrocities" (see *INS vs. Naujalis* and *INS vs. Kalejs*).

In considering to deport a defendant from the US under the Holtzman Amendment, a court "may infer one's assistance in persecution from the general nature of the person's role in the war," and "atrocities committed by a unit may be attributed to an individual based on [*sic*] his membership and seeming participation."

Kwoczak also argued that his Trawniki service had not been voluntary and was undertaken out of fear of possible reprisals by the SS against him and his family if he didn't collaborate. The argument was not accepted by the court. In *US vs. Fedorenko*, the court "declared itself unable to find any basis for an 'involuntary assistance' exception": an individual's service as an armed camp guard—whether voluntary or involuntary—made him ineligible for a US visa (*US vs. Fedorenko*, 449 US at 512, 101 S. Ct. 737).

The court's decision in the case: Kwoczak's US citizenship was rescinded and his "certificate of naturalization" was canceled. Kwoczak died in 2003 while he was appealing the "denaturalization."

MYCHAILO FOSTUN[54]

Mychailo Fostun, a Ukrainian from the Galicia District, according to Trawniki deployment rosters, had served at Trawniki, the Warsaw Detachment, starting on April 17, 1943, and the Bialystok Detachment, in August 1943. He was issued Trawniki ID #3191. During the Warsaw ghetto and Bialystok ghetto uprisings that took place while Trawniki units were assigned to these locations, over 60,000 men, women, and children were killed in both operations combined.

In 1944, Fostun left Trawniki service to join the 14th SS Division "*Galicia*," where he rose to the rank of corporal (*Waffen-Rottenführer*). The division, or a detachment of it, has been accused of committing atrocities in several Polish villages during the war, including Huta Pieniacki, where it allegedly killed about 500 civilians.

Days before the end of the war, in 1945, the division became part of the "Ukrainian National Army" (UNR) under General Pawlo Shandruk and surrendered to the British in Austria.

After the war, Fostun is believed to have lived in West Germany, the US, and Canada before settling in Great Britain. He apparently earned a doctorate in international law from an American university. It is not known exactly when he finally moved to Great Britain, but it is known that it was decades ago. He worked in London for a Ukrainian newspaper. He had a wife, but no children. He also became general secretary of the "Association of Ukrainian Former Combatants in Great Britain," the veterans organization for former members of the 14th SS Division "Galicia."

Stephen Ankier, a British citizen whose parents are Polish Jewish immigrants, has been investigating former Nazi collaborators living in Great Britain for some time, although he doesn't like being labeled a "Nazi hunter," since he feels that that title sensationalizes what he does. Years ago, he uncovered the fact that one of his relatives, Chaskiel Ankier, had been on the famous "Schindler's List." Chaskiel survived the war and immigrated to Israel, but he reportedly was too traumatized by his wartime experiences to talk about them when Stephen wanted to meet him and talk to him about it.

Ankier made detailed inquiries and studied lists of former guards. He also received anonymous tip-offs. One of these was a "brown paper envelope" put through his door, which listed the names of former Trawniki guards and gave him a great deal of leads. "That's all I can say about how I got it, but it's quite genuine, and this sort of thing does happen from time to time." Mychailo Fostun's name was on that list in the "brown envelope."

As of 2003, Fostun had been living under the name Dr. Swiatomyr Mychailo Fostun, in Wimbledon, southwestern London. That year, at seventy-eight years old, his Trawniki service was uncovered and brought to public attention. Lord Janner, former secretary of the "House of Commons" War Crimes Group and chairman of the Holocaust Educational Trust, called for an investigation: "If Fostun is a British citizen, then immediate steps must be taken to strip him of his nationality. He should either be prosecuted here or deported for prosecution."

Fostun admitted being a Trawniki guard but denied having taken part in atrocities. He was never prosecuted. "He died mysteriously in Ukraine, in a car crash, in 2004," said Ankier. "The press was hounding him, his case had been brought up in the House of Commons, and the British police had taken an interest in his background. I was assured the car crash was genuine, but it seemed very convenient," Ankier said.

US VS. SAWCHUK[55]

In 1999, Dmytro Sawchuk, who lived in New York, appeared at the US consulate in Frankfurt, Germany, to relinquish his US citizenship. The US Attorney's Office in Manhattan had been seeking to have him deported. Rather than face trial, he fled the country. A complaint against him had been filed in federal district court in Manhattan.

Sawchuk was Ukrainian, born in the Kolomyja District of the Stanislavov/Ivano-Frankivsk region in 1924 or 1925. It is in present-day Ukraine, although at the time of his birth it had been part of Poland.

Sawchuk was recruited for Trawniki service. He served at Belzec, April 12–June 1943; at Poniatowa, June 1943; at the Bialystok Detachment, August 14, 1943; at Trawniki, October 3, 1943; and in the SS-"Streibel" Battalion, August 1944.

He immigrated to the US in 1952 and became a US citizen in 1957. On his US visa application, filed in Munich, he stated that he had been a farmworker in Poland and a sawmill worker in Germany during the war.

In 1999, once he fled to Germany and surrendered his US passport, the Public Prosecutor's Office in Heidelberg was assigned to his case. After three years of investigation, the case was terminated because Germany could prosecute him only if Poland, as the principal criminal investigative authority responsible for the case, dispensed with extradition. Poland investigated the case but later suspended that investigation. Sawchuk died in 2004.

US VS. REIMER[56]

In the US District Court of New York, before District Judge Lawrence McKenna, the US government sought, under 8 U.S.C., 1451 (a), to revoke the U.S. citizenship and to cancel the "certificate of naturalization" of Jack Reimer (formerly known as Jakob Reimer). Evidence justifying revocation of US citizenship must be "clear, convincing, and unequivocal" and not leave the issue in doubt. Reimer's defense attorney was Ramsey Clark, who had been the US attorney general under the Johnson administration. The US government submitted into evidence protocols of interrogations conducted by the KGB of three former Trawniki guards: Mikhail Korzhikow, for April 9 and 21, 1947, September 9, 1964, and October 17, 1968; Nikolai Leontev, for June 30 and August 17, 1964; and Piotr Brovtsev, for August 25, 1964.

The district court noted, "The role of the KGB in the Soviet government under Stalin, Khruschev, and Brezhnev, and its tactics, are well-enough known" (see *US vs. Kowalchuk*, 773 F. 2d 488, 503-05, 3d Cir. 1985). In an interview with Leontev conducted by DOJ attorneys on January 5, 1998, Leontev stated that KGB "investigators had you sign things, and you really don't know what you are signing."

Count I: Reimer's "naturalization" was unlawful because he was not lawfully admitted to the US. He was not eligible for the US visa he obtained in 1952 under the "Displaced Persons Act" (DPA) of 1948 because he had assisted in the persecution of people on the basis of "race, religion, or national origin."

Count II: Reimer was not eligible for his US visa under provisions of the DPA of 1948, which prohibits issuance of a visa to any person who "has been a member of any movement which has been hostile to the United States or the form of government of the United States."

The US government alleged that Reimer's service as a Trawniki guard, at Trawniki, and as a member of the SS-"Streibel" Battalion, "organizations which were part of the Waffen-SS, constituted membership or participation in a movement hostile to the United States and to the form of government of the United States."

Count III: Reimer was not eligible for his US visa under the DPA of 1948 because he had "willfully misrepresented material facts on his US visa application."

Jakob Reimer was born in 1918. He was a *Volksdeutscher* from Khmelnitsky, Ukraine. In the early 1930s, his family moved to the Caucasus region. He had studied to become a librarian in a state school in Pyatigorsk and spoke both German and Russian. In 1940, he was drafted into the Red Army and attended Officer Candidate School. He was commissioned as a lieutenant in January 1941. War with Germany began, and he was captured near Minsk in early July 1941. He was held in a POW camp in Biala-Podlaska, Poland, until early September 1941. He was then recruited by the Germans for Trawniki service.

When he arrived in the Trawniki camp, it was under the jurisdiction of the Order Police (Orpo), but by November 1941 it came within the jurisdiction of the SS. It was commanded by SS-Captain Karl Streibel.

A historical report on Operation *"Reinhard"* and the role of the Trawniki guards was submitted to the court by the US government's historical expert, Dr. Charles W. Sydnor Jr. The purpose of the report was to give the court a historical context for the issues at hand in the case.

Reimer's Trawniki personnel file (*Personalbogen*) was also submitted as evidence against him.

Reimer had been promoted to *Zugwachmann* on October 9, 1942, and to *SS-Oberzugwachmann* on April 17, 1945. In September 1944, he was awarded the War Service Cross Medal.

The evidence reflected that Reimer had spent a brief period assisting in the training of fellow Trawniki guards and then spent most of his Trawniki service in office clerical duties, involving logistics and payroll: supplying fellow Trawniki personnel with their food and salary. In November 1943, a document showed that he transferred from the Trawniki training camp to the SS-Garrison Administration Lublin, Trawniki Branch Office. The transfer didn't change his duties: he was still listed as an accountant for the Trawniki administration.

However, Reimer also was assigned to field deployments: in spring 1942, he briefly went to the Lublin ghetto. Both he and Leontev described an event in which a Trawniki detachment, which had included both of them, under the command of the SS, escorted several groups of Jews to a pit into which the Jews were pushed and then shot. Reimer denied having shot any of the Jews himself.

From September 19 to November 6, 1942, Reimer was assigned to the Order Police in Czestochowa for the clearance of the ghetto there. Its 40,000 Jews were deported to Treblinka II. Reimer claimed he knew of no atrocities that took place. US government witness Charles Sydnor Jr. could offer no proof of Reimer's duties in the Czestochowa assignment, but he suggested that it must have been more than just routine administrative work as Reimer claimed. Reimer had also likely led a group of Trawniki guards in helping to clear the ghetto.

In a similar situation, on April 19, 1943, Reimer's personnel file indicates that he was assigned to the Warsaw Detachment. Reimer claimed he had administrative duties there only, but once again Sydnor suggested that Reimer would likely have played an active role in helping to suppress the Warsaw ghetto uprising. However, nothing conclusive could specifically be proven.

In November 1943, Reimer was present in Trawniki camp when the Operation "*Erntefest*" (Harvest Festival) massacre was carried out, in which 6,000 Jews were shot in the camp in a single day. Reimer said he witnessed some of the killings and the subsequent burning of the bodies.

In July 1944, German forces retreated westward in the face of the Soviet advance. Remaining Trawniki guards in Trawniki camp formed into the SS-"Streibel" Battalion, including Reimer.

"It is clear that personal participation in atrocities is not required for one to have assisted in persecution: being an armed camp guard is sufficient enough" (see *US vs. Fedorenko*, 449 U.S. at 512).

Reimer argued strenuously that he had been, in essence, a POW, subject to being shot by the SS for the slightest reason. To the extent that this argument raised an issue as to whether he had become a Trawniki guard voluntarily, *US vs. Fedorenko* made clear that voluntariness, or not, in assistance of persecution is not relevant with respect to the "Displaced Persons Act" and its requirements for making a person eligible for a US visa.

Reimer's US visa application under the DPA was initiated in 1951. The US government presented testimony about the processing of these applications by the following:

(1) a former "Displaced Persons Commission" (DPC) case analyst
(2) a former US Army "Counterintelligence Corps" (CIC) visa screener
(3) a former vice consul of the US State Department assigned to the US embassy in Hamburg, Germany, who interviewed visa applicants, examined their files, and made decisions as to whether or not to issue visas.

Records show that Reimer had been investigated by the US Army CIC twice. A CIC report in November 1951 stated: "Subject was drafted into the Soviet Army, 1940, attended Officer Candidate School, and graduated 1941 as a 2nd Lieutenant of Infantry. He served in the Moscow area as a reconnaissance officer until captured by the German Army in August 1941. He then served as an interpreter for the German Army until 1944. Subject received German citizenship in February 1944."

In a second CIC interview, in March 1952, it was reported: "Subject stated that he had been assigned to a guard unit near Trawniki, and that his supervising officer was a member of the SS. He claimed that he himself had never been integrated into an SS unit, but was assigned as a paymaster in the guard unit."

As to his service in the SS-"Streibel" Battalion, Reimer wrote and signed a statement indicating the following: "In 1944, all units had to build fortifications on the Vistula River. When the Soviets broke through the front, we were transferred to Dresden to do clean-up work. In April 1945, we began marching toward Sudetenland and the war ended. In Carlsbad I went to a German discharge camp. I then went into a refugee camp."

Reimer claimed in his testimony in court that his way to the US may have been aided by a German girlfriend who had worked for US intelligence after the war. This may or may not have been true.[57] Reimer arrived in the US and settled in Brooklyn, New York, in 1952. He worked as a bartender, and eventually manager and part owner of a restaurant in Times Square. He also ran a potato chip company in Manhattan, got married, had two children, got divorced, and then remarried. His US citizenship was granted in 1959 by the US District Court of Eastern New York.

Reimer was originally interviewed in 1980 for the Demjanjuk case. In 1992, and now under investigation himself, Reimer met with Eli Rosenbaum and another DOJ-OSI official and stated: "I did not volunteer for Trawniki. I was ashamed of it. I didn't want to remember it. I have been a model citizen in this country (the US)."

The court ordered Reimer's citizenship revoked and his "certificate of naturalization" canceled, as of September 3, 2002. Reimer appealed this decision in August 2003. Appearing for the prosecution side at the appeal was James Comey, US attorney for the Southern District of New York; Eli Rosenbaum, director of OSI; and Jonathan Drimmer, trial attorney for the OSI. The appeal was denied in January 2004.

By 2005, Reimer had exhausted his appeals and was to be deported to Germany. However, he died before the deportation could be carried out. He was eighty-six years old.

As Eric Steinhart had noted, within his lifetime Reimer went from being a Volksdeutscher peasant in Ukraine, to a Red Army officer, to a Soviet POW, to a Nazi collaborator (Trawniki guard), to a refugee/displaced person, and finally to a model US citizen.

SAMUEL KUNZ[58]

Samuel Kunz was a Volksdeutscher born in the town of Sichelberg, a German settlement on the Volga River in southern Russia. He had served in the Red Army in 1941 and was captured. He volunteered for Trawniki service in order to get out of the Chelm POW camp, where he feared death. "Ten to twenty of our comrades were buried there every day."

Kunz was twenty years old when he began his Trawniki service. He served at Belzec, January 1942–July 1943; the Warsaw concentration camp, early 1944; and the SS-"Streibel" Battalion, August 1944–April 1945. He was promoted to the rank of *Zugwachmann* (sergeant/platoon commander) during his service.

His name had surfaced in past investigations, and recent allegations came up in Germany as prosecutors went through wartime documents in preparation for the Demjanjuk trial in Munich in 2009–2010. The investigation had prompted the Simon Wiesenthal Center to list Kunz as the world's third-most-wanted Nazi war criminal in the present day. He was to have testified in the Demjanjuk case but changed his mind after learning that he himself was now under investigation.

Kunz had testified as a witness in other Nazi war crimes trials in 1969 and 1975 (proceedings against Karl Streibel) and in 1980 (probably in proceedings against Liudas Kairys).

Kunz had long been ignored by the German justice system, with authorities in the past showing little interest in going after relatively low-ranking camp guards. However, in the last decade, a new generation of German prosecutors have begun pursuing all individuals suspected of involvement in Nazi crimes, regardless of rank.

After the war, Kunz had settled in Bonn, West Germany, and had worked as a low-level civil servant in the German government's Ministry of Construction, until he retired.

The "Central Judicial Office for the Investigation of Nazi Crimes" in Ludwigsburg had completed a preliminary investigation of him and produced an eighty-page report. The case was then handed over to the public prosecutor in Dortmund. State prosecutor Andreas Brendel, head of the Dortmund office for the investigation of Nazi war crimes, spent a year working on the Kunz case.

Kunz was under indictment by the state court in Bonn on allegations of involvement in mass murder. The indictment, filed in July 2010, charged him with ten specific counts of murder and 430,000 counts of accessory to murder as a Trawniki guard at Belzec. Prosecutors stated that he had been involved in the entire killing process in the camp: from unloading the trains, to escorting people to the gas chambers, to overseeing the disposal of bodies. Between May and July 1943, he was specifically accused of shooting ten Jews at the camp. His trial was to begin in early 2011.

He had admitted serving at Belzec, which is why he had been scheduled to testify in the Demjanjuk trial in Munich: "The bodies of the Jews gassed in the camp were buried in pits, and later burned, because we could no longer stand the stench."

Kunz died at the age of eighty-nine in November 2010 in his hometown of Wachtberg, near Bonn. German prosecutors launched an investigation into the circumstances of his death. An autopsy found that he may not have died of heart failure, as initially believed (he had a pacemaker), but from "unnatural hypothermia." Bonn prosecutor Robin Fassbender acknowledged that an autopsy had been completed. Another source stated this: "On a cold night in April 2011, assassins entered Kunz's home in Bonn, snatched him from his bed, and left him outside to die of hypothermia."[59]

US VS. ZAJANCKAUSKAS[60]

In March 2006, a decision was made in this appeal case. The prosecution team included Jeffrey Menkin, senior trial attorney, DOJ-OSI; William Henry Kenety V, senior trial attorney; Eli Rosenbaum, OSI director; Michael Sullivan, US attorney, Massachusetts; and Mark Grady, assistant US attorney, Massachusetts. The judges included Torruella, circuit judge; Stahl, senior circuit judge; and Howard, circuit judge.

In June 2002, the US government filed a civil action against Vladas Zajanckauskas, a resident of Millbury, Massachusetts, to revoke his US citizenship on the basis of his participation in the Nazi operation to clear and destroy the Warsaw ghetto during World War II, and because of misrepresentations on his US visa application.

Zajanckauskas illegally procured US citizenship, and it therefore had to be revoked according to 8 U.S.C., 1451 (a). In January 2005, a three-day bench trial in front of the district court determined that Zajanckauskas had made materially false statements on his US visa application. As a result, his US citizenship was revoked and his "certificate of naturalization" was canceled. Zajanckauskas appealed the decision of the district court. The appellate court confirmed the district court's decision.

Zajanckauskas was born in 1915 in Lithuania. In May 1939, he was drafted into the Lithuanian army. In 1940, the Soviet Union annexed Lithuania, and he was absorbed into the Red Army. In July 1941 he was captured by German forces and held in the Hammerstein POW camp in Pomerania. In mid-1942 he was recruited for Trawniki service by the Germans and received Trawniki ID #2122. In a short time, he was promoted to *Gruppenwachmann* (sergeant), and by April 1943 he also began training other Trawniki guards for promotion to NCO rank like himself.

Zajanckauskas's name and Trawniki ID # were contained on the roster of Trawniki guards deployed to help suppress the Warsaw ghetto uprising on April 17, 1943. The roster was submitted as evidence in court by the OSI.

Duties of the Trawniki guards during the Warsaw operation:

(1) standing in a cordon around the ghetto to prevent Jews from escaping
(2) guarding the transit square where captured Jews awaited rail transport to concentration camps, labor camps, and the Treblinka death camp

(3) escorting the trains to their destinations

(4) conducting house-to-house searches in the ghetto in search of hidden Jews

(5) skirmishing with resistance fighters

(6) capturing Jews hiding in bunkers

(7) shooting some of the captured Jews and guarding them in a cordon

Tens of thousands of Jews were killed during the operation, thousands more were sent to Treblinka II to be gassed, and thousands more were deported to concentration camps and labor camps.

In February 1944, Zajanckauskas married Vladislava Kowalcyk, a local woman from Trawniki. They would remain married for the rest of their lives (nearly seventy years). From August 1944 to March 4, 1945, Zajanckauskas had also served in the SS-"Streibel" Battalion.

In 1949 or 1950, Zajanckauskas sought a US immigrant visa under the "Displaced Persons Act" (DPA) of 1948. Zajanckauskas told US officials that he had lived and worked on his parents' farm in Lithuania until 1944, that he then fled to Dresden in November 1944, and that he then went to Austria and worked as a farmhand and laborer.

In 1950, Zajanckauskas filed an application for a US immigration visa with the US consulate in Salzburg, Austria. He stated on the application that he had been in Austria since March 1945. He was issued a US visa and entered the US the same year, 1950. In 1956, he applied for US citizenship. It was granted the same year by the Massachusetts Superior Court, which issued him a "certificate of naturalization."

In 2002, after an investigation, the US government filed a complaint against Zajanckauskas in US District Court in Massachusetts to revoke his citizenship:

Count I: He was not lawfully admitted to the US because of his participation in the liquidation of the Warsaw ghetto and because he had trained other Trawniki guards who took part in that operation: this constituted assistance in the persecution of the civilian population, thus making him ineligible for a US visa under the "Displaced Persons Act."

Count II: He misrepresented his wartime whereabouts and activities and was therefore ineligible for a US visa under the "Displaced Persons Act." Clear, convincing, and unequivocal evidence (the standard of proof required in such US civil cases) demonstrated that Zajanckauskas's US citizenship had been illegally procured.

In the proceedings before the district court, Zajanckauskas had based much of his defense on the so-called Stroop report, in particular the section in which SS-Brigadeführer Stroop wrote that the "average daily deployment" of Trawniki men in Warsaw was 335. Zajanckauskas attempted to use this figure to undermine the government's claim that he had been present in Warsaw during the ghetto liquidation. Zajanckauskas claimed there was a reasonable possibility that he was one of the sixteen men whose names were listed on the Warsaw deployment roster but who were not among the 335 sent to Warsaw. The deployment roster contained 351 names. The district court rejected Zajanckauskas's argument.

The court recognized that it could offer no definitive explanation of the numbers in the "Stroop report." This derived, in part, from the fact that there was no way to replicate Stroop's precise calculations. Several factors were unknown to the court, including the number of days Stroop had used to calculate the average in the report's "average daily deployment" and the exact criteria for declaring a Trawniki man "available" for duty. However, the court was confident that whatever the true meaning of the "Stroop report," under any acceptable interpretation of the document the deployment roster is reliable evidence that Zajanckauskas was deployed to Warsaw. The appellate court believed that this was a factual determination that the district court was able to make without the aid of any expert testimony.

"Expert testimony does not assist where the 'trier of fact' has no need for an opinion because it easily can be derived from common sense, common experience, the 'trier of fact's' own perceptions, or simple logic" (Charles Alan Wright and Victor James Gold, *Federal Practice and Procedure*, 62–64, 2005).

Zajanckauskas also admitted being present in the Trawniki camp at the time of Operation "*Erntefest*" (Harvest Festival), when about 6,000 Jews were shot in the camp. He stated that he had been in the camp canteen at the time and had been unaware of what was going on. The court found that unbelievable.

The appellate court affirmed the judgment of the district court. In 2010, a US circuit court upheld an order to deport the ninety-five-year-old Zajanckauskas. A federal appeals court in Boston said it lacked jurisdiction to review an immigration judge's decision to deport Zajanckauskas after his citizenship was revoked in 2005 for committing fraud on his US visa application.

On appeal, Zajanckauskas had argued that he was eligible for a waiver forgiving his fraud on the basis of his age, the amount of time he had lived in the US (sixty years), his health, and the large family he would be forced to leave behind if deported.

Immigration judge Wayne Iskra ordered that Zajanckauskas be deported to his native country of Lithuania. However, as of 2013, the then-ninety-seven-year-old Zajanckauskas was still living in Massachusetts, eleven years after US authorities had first begun legal proceedings against him, and even though he had exhausted his appeal process by 2010, because neither Lithuania nor any other country had been willing to accept him.

"Without any doubt, the greatest single frustration has been our inability, in quite a number of cases now, to carry out the deportation orders that we've won in federal courts. We can't carry them out because governments of Europe refuse to take these people back," said OSI director Eli Rosenbaum.

Zajanckauskas wrote a ninety-nine-page memoir about his childhood and wartime experiences, titled *My Bits of Life in This Beautiful World*. He died in Sutton, Massachusetts, on August 5, 2013, at age ninety-seven. His wife died the following year.

CHAPTER 8

THE DEMJANJUK CASE

John Demjanjuk entered the US from Germany under the "Displaced Persons Act" in 1952. He became a US citizen in 1958 and settled in Cleveland, Ohio, where he became an auto mechanic at the Ford auto plant. In 1975, Jacob Javits, a Republican senator from New York, received a letter from the editor of the New York–based *Ukrainian Daily News*, which listed the names of seventy alleged Ukrainian war criminals living in the US. The editor was Michael Hanusiak, a Ukrainian American Communist. Hanusiak had apparently received the list during a trip to Kiev and had gotten it from Moscow. At the time, the Soviet government was dealing with its own domestic issues, among which were Jews who wanted to immigrate from the Soviet Union and the agitation of Ukrainian nationalists. The Soviets wanted to deflect attention from their Jewish problem and simultaneously discredit the Ukrainian nationalists. Thus, the list of alleged war criminals provided to Hanusiak to pass along to US authorities was intended to portray Ukrainian nationalism as a movement of former Nazi collaborators, in order to invoke friction between Soviet Jews and Ukrainian nationalists. Senator Javits forwarded the list to the INS, and the seventy names were eventually narrowed down to nine, since the rest were either dead or no longer in the United States. Demjanjuk and Fedorenko were among the names that remained on the list. Also at this time, at the behest of New York congresswoman Elizabeth Holtzman, the INS began to more aggressively investigate suspected Nazi war criminals living in the US.[1] Hanusiak notified the INS that Demjanjuk had been a Trawniki guard at Sobibor during World War II.[2] A 1977 article in a Soviet newspaper showed a photo of Demjanjuk's Trawniki ID card (*Dienstausweis*). It was from this article that the US Department of Justice learned of the existence of the ID card. The article also contained a quote from Ignat Danilchenko, another Trawniki guard who served with Demjanjuk at Sobibor.[3] The INS contacted Israel about the alleged Ukrainian war criminals, and an Israeli police special unit showed photo spreads that included Demjanjuk and Fedorenko to Treblinka and Sobibor survivors in Israel. Up to ten Treblinka survivors pointed to Demjanjuk's photo as being of a guard that they recognized as having been in Treblinka.[4] The US Attorney's Office in Cleveland filed a "denaturalization" action against Demjanjuk in 1977.

Soon afterward, Nazi suspect cases in the US would transfer from the jurisdiction of the INS to the DOJ's Office of Special Investigations (OSI). It started out with a dozen criminal investigators, a dozen attorneys, and two professional historians.[5]

During the course of the "Fedorenko" case, the US government learned that the Soviet government had interviewed several Treblinka witnesses. The US Department of Justice sought to get reports of these interviews. The reports, called "protocols," were obtained by the US government after the Fedorenko trial was completed. They came to be known as the "Fedorenko protocols." The "protocols" were reviewed by the DOJ attorneys assigned to the Demjanjuk investigation. They included a statement made by Fedorenko while he had been visiting the Soviet Union. He recalled two gas chamber operators at Treblinka, Ivan and Nikolai. Another former Trawniki guard remembered them as Marchenko and Nikolai, and another recalled just one man, Nikolai Marchenko. OSI attorney Norman Moscowitz had possession of statements of former Trawniki guards who served at Treblinka, named Pavel Leleko and Nikolaj Malagon, who identified the guard Ivan Marchenko as the gas chamber operator at Treblinka. At the time, the statements seemed of little significance to him or the case, or at the least it was fragmentary information that he didn't know what to make of. Had a historian been assigned to assist Moscowitz at the time, perhaps something more could have been made of this evidence.[6]

Moscowitz asked the Soviet government for additional material, including new statements from Danilchenko, Leleko, and Malagon. Soviet authorities reinterviewed Danilchenko in 1979, and Malagon, while Leleko had been executed for war crimes in 1945. These new Soviet interviews became known as the "Danilchenko protocols." With regard to these Soviet protocols of interrogation, it is impossible to determine the conditions in which the interrogations had been conducted. OSI uses them only if their details are corroborated by historical documents, other Soviet interrogations, and interviews with witnesses. Some courts find the protocols reliable; others do not.[7] OSI conducted many interviews. Former *SS-Unterscharführer* Otto Horn, who had been a cremation supervisor at Treblinka, and eighteen Treblinka survivors identified Demjanjuk as "Ivan the Terrible," the nickname of the Trawniki guard who had run the gas chambers at Treblinka.

Demjanjuk had given his mother's maiden name as "Marchenko" on his US visa application: this made one OSI attorney assigned to the case hypothesize that Marchenko and Demjanjuk were one and the same person. But how could Demjanjuk be in two places at once? Sobibor and Treblinka?

In 1980, OSI attorney George Parker wrote a memo to the OSI director Walter Rockler and his successor, Allan Ryan, declaring that a review of the evidence in the Demjanjuk case suggested that it was so contradictory and inconclusive that proceeding with the case would raise ethical concerns. The memo was titled "Demjanjuk: A Reappraisal" and stated: "We may have the right man for the wrong act. Demjanjuk could not have been 'Ivan the Terrible' in Treblinka as well as the Demjanjuk known to Danilchenko in Sobibor. A reading of the *Canons of Ethics* persuades me that I cannot pursue this case simply as a Treblinka matter." Parker resigned soon after. Nevertheless, the case went to trial in 1981.[8] However, some continue to question the timing of the memo; at least one former OSI attorney, suspicious that it had been backdated, wished it could have been subjected to metadata analysis.[9]

The defense was not given the "Fedorenko protocols," the "Danilchenko protocols," the Otto Horn interview, or a partial roster of Trawniki guards assigned to Treblinka. The OSI trial attorneys said that they did not believe there was any significant or exculpatory material in the "Fedorenko" and "Danilchenko" protocols, or on the partial Treblinka roster. They also claimed that they had never seen the Horn interview.

The US government obtained Demjanjuk's Trawniki ID card (*Dienstausweis*) from the Soviet government and introduced it into evidence. It was the first Trawniki identity document ever seen by scholars, and it differed from many known German ID documents. Demjanjuk claimed that the ID was a KGB forgery made to frame him, a claim shared by many in the American Ukrainian community who were anti-Soviet. In fact, the alleged unreliability of Soviet-supplied evidence was the most common defense of OSI defendants for over a decade.[10] During the Cold War, neither OSI nor defense attorneys had direct access to Soviet archives. One could only request information and hope that the Soviet authorities would respond. Moreover, Soviet authorities searching for documents on behalf of the US were sometimes prosecutors rather than historians. They often relied on name-linked indexes that referenced only documents with a given subject's name. Additionally, not all Soviet archivists knew German or had sufficient knowledge of the captured records held by their archives.[11] Vladimir Grachev, second secretary to Anatoli Dobrynin, Soviet ambassador to the US from 1979 to 1986, assigned to Moscow, oversaw the Soviet response to OSI requests for evidence. During a 2003 meeting with OSI director Eli Rosenbaum, Grachev, then serving as principal officer to the UN secretary-general, was adamant that the Soviets had never fabricated documents for OSI cases, nor was there ever any attempt to frame anyone. According to Grachev, the Soviet government took cooperation on the issue "very, very seriously."[12] The two cases in which the issue of authenticity of wartime documents submitted as prosecution evidence was most thoroughly litigated were Demjanjuk and Kairys. As an interesting sidenote, Dr. Adalbert Ruckerl, who had been head of West Germany's "War Crimes Unit," had met with OSI director Allan Ryan and his deputy, Neal Sher, in 1982, and he told them at the time that West Germany had been using evidence from the Soviet Union in war crimes trials since 1963, yet the fabrication-of-evidence issue had never come up.[13] Demjanjuk claimed that he had never been a Trawniki guard, and that once he had become a POW, he joined General Pawlo Shandruk's "Ukrainian National Army," and then General Andrei Vlasov's "Russian Liberation Army." He admitted lying on his US visa application for fear of being repatriated to the Soviet Union. The court revoked Demjanjuk's US citizenship, concluding that he had been a Trawniki guard at Treblinka. In 1983, Israel issued a warrant for Demjanjuk's arrest and petitioned the US for his extradition (Israel had passed the "Nazi and Nazi Collaborator Punishment Law" in 1950). He was deported to Israel to face mass murder charges. Under the presiding judge, Dov Levin, he was found guilty and sentenced to be hanged for having been the gas chamber operator at Treblinka. He sat on death row for five years in Israel, 1988–1993, while his conviction was on appeal.

The Soviet Union collapsed during his appeal process, opening a treasure trove of material from Soviet archives that had a bearing on the case. Defense attorneys and prosecutors went to the former Soviet Union to examine the "Fedorenko protocols." The prosecutors examined the case files several times in Moscow and Kiev from 1990 to 1992. Records from Fedorenko's trial consisted of twenty-two volumes of material. Included were excerpts of transcripts from other cases of former Trawniki guards. For example, an interrogation statement from a former guard named Nikolai Shalayev, who stated that he and another man named Ivan Marchenko had been the two gas chamber operators at Treblinka, came to light.[14]

Other former Trawniki guards who had served at Treblinka had given similar statements, and they, along with several women who had also worked at the camp, picked Marchenko's picture out of a photo spread (the statements given by these former guards were contained in evidence in the "Schults" trial, 1961–1962, in Kiev). The defense had other evidence as well: statements from a Polish farmer and his wife that Ivan Marchenko, the gas chamber operator of Treblinka, had spent time in their nearby village. The farmer and his wife were interviewed on *60 Minutes* on CBS in 1990.

All this evidence demonstrated to Israeli prosecutors that the Soviet government had been investigating and prosecuting former Trawniki guards from late 1944 to the late 1960s (excluding Fedorenko, who was tried in 1986). It also demonstrated that Demjanjuk was not "Ivan the Terrible" and had not served at Treblinka. The Israeli Supreme Court reversed Demjanjuk's death sentence on the basis of the new evidence that the gas chamber operator at Treblinka had been the Trawniki guard Ivan Marchenko.

How did so many survivor eyewitnesses' identifications of Demjanjuk as the gas chamber operator of Treblinka turn out to be wrong? A likely answer is that the Israeli police had showed the witnesses a photo spread that had been unfairly suggestive. Demjanjuk's photo in the spread was larger and clearer than the rest of the photos, resulting in a biased appearance.[15] The Israeli court had relied too heavily on this witness identification when they had initially sentenced Demjanjuk to death. "All legal experts are familiar with both the power and the unreliability of eyewitness testimony."[16] "Ironically, the misidentification that nearly sent him to the gallows in Israel also possibly saved his life." If he hadn't been extradited to Israel, he may very well have been deported to the Soviet Union, as Fedorenko had been, and, like Fedorenko, might have been tried and shot.[17]

The Israeli Supreme Court still could have convicted Demjanjuk for his service at Sobibor even though it had exonerated him on the Treblinka charge. According to the Israeli Code of Criminal Procedure, a court may "convict the accused of an offense of which he is shown to be guilty, even though it is different from that of which he was convicted by the lower court." However, Israel opted not to bother with any more legal proceedings against him.[18] Demjanjuk returned to the US.

In 1987, at the OSI's request, the DOJ's Office of Professional Responsibility (OPR) opened an investigation into how the Demjanjuk defense team and the media had come into possession of OSI material. The media had gotten hold of classified and sensitive documents. In addition, Demjanjuk's defense counsel had gotten hold of internal OSI documents.

OPR determined that between 1985 and 1987, OSI personnel had "negligently discarded" sensitive and classified documents, which had then been retrieved from public trash bins (so-called dumpster diving) by persons sympathetic to those being investigated by OSI (although protocol at that time called for shredding or burning of sensitive material, much more care was put on this issue after this incident). The material included notes that had been taken by an OSI historian and an investigator. The notes suggested that Otto Horn, interviewed in Berlin, had had trouble identifying Demjanjuk in a photo spread, and he had done so only after being shown a second stack of photos that also had a picture of Demjanjuk. It implied that the photo spread had been unfairly suggestive.[19] Additionally, Assistant Attorney General Robert Mueller asked DOJ-OPR to investigate whether OSI had improperly failed to provide the "Fedorenko protocols" to the defense. OPR concluded in 1993 that there had been no prosecutorial misconduct.

Chief Judge Gilbert Merritt of the US Appeals Court asked the DOJ to investigate former OSI director Allan Ryan. Allegedly, Ryan had told a colleague that he would withhold exculpatory evidence from Demjanjuk's defense. If true, it was a case of prosecutorial misconduct. However, OPR found no merit to the charge.

In 1992, Merritt wrote to Assistant Attorney General Robert Mueller requesting copies of the interrogations of former Trawniki guards who had identified Ivan Marchenko as the notorious "Ivan the Terrible" of Treblinka. Merritt received no response. He then convinced other members of his circuit court to reopen Demjanjuk's case. Merritt was concerned that OSI may have engaged in professional misconduct by "concealing or withholding evidence in their possession." The appellate court appointed Thomas Wiseman, a federal judge from Tennessee, as a "special master" to report on the matter.[20] Publicity about this new evidence and alleged improprieties in OSI's handling of the case was extensive.[21] The DOJ announced it was reviewing the case. Over a six-month period in 1993, Wiseman reviewed more than 300 exhibits of evidence, heard testimony from six attorneys who had worked on the case, and reviewed depositions from nine other participants. He issued a 210-page unpublished report with his findings and conclusions.

As early as 1978, DOJ had received copies of statements from two former Trawniki guards, Pavel Leleko and Nikolaj Malagon, who had named Marchenko as the gas chamber operator at Treblinka. In 1979, the Polish "Main Commission for the Investigation of Nazi Crimes" had sent OSI a list of Trawniki guards known to have served at Treblinka. It wasn't a complete roster, but it did include about seventy names. Marchenko and Fedorenko were on the list, but Demjanjuk was not.

Wiseman pointed out that "OSI had failed to share its doubts with Israeli prosecutors, who only learned of the exculpatory material from their own investigations in former KGB archives."[22] Nevertheless, DOJ prosecutors in the case were excused from any wrongdoing. The judge found no prosecutorial misconduct. The judge affirmed Demjanjuk's "denaturalization" on the grounds that he had served at Sobibor.

A three-judge panel skeptically accepted Wiseman's finding that no OSI attorneys had deliberately withheld evidence from Demjanjuk's defense, or the court—information they believed they had a duty to disclose—but nevertheless found DOJ's conduct unacceptable: "The attitude of the OSI attorneys toward disclosing information to Demjanjuk's counsel was not consistent with the US government's obligation to work for justice." The panel believed that the DOJ should have given the defense the "Fedorenko protocols," the Horn interview, and the partial Treblinka roster. The panel found that the DOJ had "recklessly disregarded" its duty, and in so doing, it had perpetrated fraud on the court, without which Demjanjuk would not have been "denaturalized" and extradited. The appellate court accused the OSI of prosecuting Demjanjuk in order to "please and maintain very close relationships with various interest groups because their continued existence depended on it." This implied that OSI went forward with the Demjanjuk case even though it had doubts about his Treblinka service, in order to curry favor with the American Jewish community.[23] The Demjanjuk defense team, Congressman James Traficant, a Democrat from Ohio and Demjanjuk supporter, as well as family members, succeeded in getting the "Fedorenko" and "Danilchenko" protocols, via the Freedom of Information Act (FOIA).[24] Traficant proposed several remedies for OSI's alleged problems. These included appointing a special prosecutor to handle the Demjanjuk case and having a House committee investigate OSI's practices and behavior.[25] Traficant pointed to OSI conduct in the Demjanjuk case as one justification for an independent federal agency to investigate allegations of misconduct by DOJ personnel. He stated this in testimony before the House Judiciary Subcommittee on Administrative Law, under House Resolution 4105, the "Fair Justice Act," on July 27, 2000. However, none of Traficant's proposals were adopted.[26] The US Supreme Court denied a DOJ request to review the case. One of the reasons the solicitor general decided to seek Supreme Court review was to vindicate the OSI attorneys, who he felt had been "unfairly harmed."[27] Demjanjuk filed a $5 million suit against the US government, alleging that he was a victim of torture at the hands of the US. He contended that the government had falsely accused him of being a mass murderer, had mocked his refusal to confess, and caused him to be tried abroad in a "circus atmosphere" where he was held in solitary confinement and had been sentenced to death. The court dismissed the suit on jurisdictional grounds.[28] In 1999, OSI filed a new complaint against Demjanjuk. It had been done on the decision of OSI director Eli Rosenbaum. Demjanjuk's second "denaturalization" trial in the US District Court in Ohio, in 2000–2001, focused on additional wartime documentation that had not been available in the earlier trial: namely, forty Trawniki ID cards (*Dienstausweisen*) provided by the Russian government to establish the authenticity of Demjanjuk's own ID card. Additional new evidence was presented in a report prepared for OSI by historian Dr. Charles Sydnor Jr. His report, however, was actually the work of OSI historian Todd Huebner. The chief OSI prosecutor in the case was Edward Stutman, assisted by Jonathan Drimmer.

Among the prosecution witnesses called were the following:

Gideon Epstein: forensic document examiner, director of the INS Forensic Document Lab, 1980–2000; holds a master's in forensic science from Antioch School of Law, Yellow Springs, Ohio; completed a two-year resident training program in the forensic science of questioned document examination at the US Army Crime Lab, Fort Gordon, Georgia, 1967–1969; certified by the American Board of Forensic Document Examiners; member of the American Academy of Forensic Science, member of the American Society of Questioned Document Examiners; taught forensic document examination to US Army criminal investigators, and at the Federal Law Enforcement Training Center in Glynco, Georgia, and at the George Washington University

School of Forensic Science; published articles in the *Journal of Forensic Science*; worked on over 3,000 cases of questioned documents; examined the signatures and stamps on Demjanjuk's *Dienstausweis*, and conducted handwriting comparisons, stamp comparisons, and microscopic examination by using ultraviolet light, and certified the document as genuine, in his expert opinion. Epstein had originally examined the *Dienstausweis* back in 1981 at the Soviet embassy in Washington, DC. He examined it again in Jerusalem in 1987.

Larry Stewart: lab director for the US Secret Service and chief forensic examiner for document authentication; holds a master's in forensic science from the Antioch School of Law, Yellow Springs, Ohio; member of the American Academy of Forensic Science: he examined the ink and paper of Demjanjuk's *Dienstausweis* at his lab in Washington, DC, and certified the document as genuine in terms of the paper and photograph attached to it, in his expert opinion. He tested the *Dienstausweis* by using a process called "thin-layer chromatography" to determine the chemical composition of the paper. Subjects he was asked about in his testimony included the chemical test he did on the *Dienstausweis*, the proper handling and preservation of historical documents according to the book *Scientific Examination of Questioned Documents* by Ordway Hilton, and whether or not it was feasible to conduct a fingerprint analysis on the *Dienstausweis* (it was not done, for fear of causing undue damage to the document by using a chemical called ninhydrin, used to reveal latent fingerprints).

Tom Smith: a lead document examiner with the US Secret Service: he examined the typing on Demjanjuk's *Dienstausweis* and certified it as consistent with typing fonts from the 1940s.

Dr. Charles W. Sydnor Jr.: World War II historian with expert knowledge of German wartime documents (Judge Lewis Pollack, former dean of Yale Law School, stated, "There are only a handful of other scholars who have a comparable inventory of information and insights as Dr. Sydnor"), and author of *Soldiers of Destruction: The SS Death's Head Division, 1933–1945*, published 1977, which had been his PhD dissertation. The book is part of the standard curriculum of military history and modern warfare at the School of Advanced Military Studies, Fort Leavenworth, Kansas, and the US Military Academy at West Point. Holds a PhD in history and taught history at Ohio State University. Taught courses in modern German history and the Holocaust. Has done research in various archives in the US, Germany, Israel, and Russia. Reviewed the manuscript for Peter Black's biography of Ernst Kaltenbrunner, which was published in 1984. He was also a prosecution witness in other Trawniki-related cases: *US vs. Hajda*, in Chicago, 1995; *US vs. Reimer*, in New York City, 1998; and *US vs. Kwoczak*, in Philadelphia, in 1999. Reviewed Trawniki documents with OSI historian Dr. Steven Coe at the FSB Archive Moscow and spent three and a half months preparing a report on the Demjanjuk case in cooperation with the OSI. Subjects he was asked about in his testimony in the Demjanjuk case: his trip to the FSB Archive Moscow, the capturing of the Trawniki documents when Trawniki and Lublin were overrun by the Red Army in July 1944, Soviet poor handling of the Trawniki documents, Trawniki training camp and its purpose, the tasks of the Trawniki guards, Trawniki uniforms, and David Marwell, one of the first OSI historians and last director of the Berlin Document Center when it was still under US State Department jurisdiction.

Dr. Bruce Menning: Russian and Soviet military historian specializing in Soviet and German war planning, strategy, and operations on the Eastern Front in WWII; holds a PhD in modern Russian history, with an emphasis on Soviet military history; professor of strategy, US Army Command and General Staff College, Fort Leavenworth, Kansas; colonel (ret.), US Army Reserve, 1965–1996; training officer and military historian, US Army Center of Military History, 1972–1982; taught a course on Operation Barbarossa (1941) and Operation Blau (1942) and wrote a curriculum for a course on Operation Bagration (1944). Adjunct professor, University of Kansas, Department of Russian and East European Studies. Worked with OSI historians

Dr. Steven Coe and Dr. Todd Huebner in preparation for his testimony in the Demjanjuk case. Has done research in several military archives in the former Soviet Union, including the archive of the Russian Ministry of Defense; chairman of the editorial board of the *Journal of the Society of Military History*; member of the editorial advisory board of *Encyclopedia of Russian and Soviet History*. Subjects he was asked about in his testimony in the Demjanjuk case: the "Ukrainian National Army" (UNR) under General Pawlo Shandruk; the "Vlasov army"; the book *Soviet Opposition to Stalin*, by George Fisher; access to and the condition of Russian archives; the POW transit camp in Rovno; the POW camp in Chelm; problems caused by the failure of DOJ/OSI staff to hand over materials that should have been handed over in the earlier Demjanjuk case in the 1980s; the appropriateness of professional historians relying on secondary sources; and the criteria for peer review of historical publications.

Demjanjuk alleged that the US government had suppressed internal FBI documents created in the early 1980s. However, those FBI materials had set forth nothing more than the conjecture of two Cleveland FBI counterintelligence agents who had not been involved in any aspect of his case. The agents' theoretical concerns that the Soviets might have fabricated the Trawniki ID attributed to Demjanjuk, and the basis for that speculation, were disclosed more than twenty-five years earlier by one of the agents directly to Demjanjuk's then counsel. The FBI materials reveal that the agents' speculation was based on indisputably inaccurate and incomplete information, including the demonstrably inaccurate premise that the Soviets possessed a motive to discredit Demjanjuk because he was an anti-Soviet dissident living in the US. The FBI never examined Demjanjuk's Trawniki ID, and the agents had been seemingly unaware that the document had been forensically tested. By the time of the second denaturalization trial in 2001, Demjanjuk had largely abandoned his focus on the KGB forgery defense in the wake of the failure of his expert forensic witnesses in the trial in Israel to cast any doubt on the authenticity of the ID card, and the unearthing of numerous additional Nazi-era German documents in former Soviet and Western archives that both corroborated the Trawniki ID card and proved his Trawniki guard service at Sobibor and other camps. The FBI did not provide the materials in question to the Demjanjuk prosecution team, and the prosecution team was unaware of the document until after the judgment in the current case.

CLEVELAND FBI MATERIALS[29]

The FBI documents at issue in Demjanjuk's motion to get his case thrown out, dated from 1981 to 1985, were created by counterintelligence agents in the Cleveland FBI field office, and they never worked on any FBI matter involving allegations that the Soviet Union had forged documents for use in American legal proceedings, or on any investigation of an individual alleged to be involved in Nazi persecution. Moreover, they were written without examining any of the evidence and were prepared following meetings with persons working on behalf of the Demjanjuk defense. None of the materials generated by the Cleveland FBI were provided by the FBI to the prosecution team. They were, however, discussed with the defense. In 1981, having noticed press accounts of concerns voiced by some members of the Cleveland Ukrainian community regarding use of evidence from the Soviet Union in the Demjanjuk case, then FBI special agent Thomas Martin became interested in the Demjanjuk case shortly after he began working in Cleveland in 1981. There is nothing unusual about this; curiosity and theorization are what FBI counterintelligence agents were trained to do during the Cold War. Agent Martin prepared a 1981 memo seeking permission from FBI HQ to examine press coverage of the

Demjanjuk case and to develop contacts in the Ukrainian community to investigate the nature and extent of possible Soviet penetration of Ukrainian-American affairs and claims reported in the press that the KGB was furnishing fake documents in the Demjanjuk trial. FBI HQ responded by advising Cleveland that the Soviet Union had provided documentary evidence in US courts since the Nuremberg trials against persons accused of Nazi collaboration, and explained that the "Federal Rules of Evidence" governed authentication procedures for such foreign documents. Cleveland FBI was instructed to close the matter due to an absence of probable cause to believe that the evidence was not authentic. In 1984, however, Demjanjuk defense attorney Mark O' Connor began contacting FBI officials in an effort to persuade the FBI to investigate the defense's allegation that District Court Judge Battisti and the Demjanjuk prosecutors had participated in a KGB perpetration of fraud on the court by utilizing the Trawniki ID card as evidence. Additionally, that same year, Demjanjuk defense team member Jerome Brentar met with Cleveland FBI special agent George Arruda at the field office to complain about OSI and its purported use of evidence obtained from the Soviet Union against Demjanjuk. FBI HQ responded by memo, in 1985, that the Cleveland FBI office should close the counterintelligence file opened on the Demjanjuk case. Agent Arruda advised Storm Watkins, Washington FBI liaison officer, not to share with OSI the information reported by the FBI Cleveland office regarding the Demjanjuk case because of Brentar's complaints regarding OSI wrongdoing in conjunction with the KGB. Said Agent Arruda, "I advised Watkins that the Cleveland case on Demjanjuk was not for OSI consumption, since complaints received at the Cleveland office indicated KGB handling of evidence in the Demjanjuk trial and other wrongdoing that could possibly warrant a counterintelligence case." The FBI Cleveland counterintelligence agents were specifically asking that the prosecution team not be provided certain information.

In 1985, Agent Martin wrote a cover memo and a memo that were sent to Watkins from the Cleveland FBI office regarding the Demjanjuk prosecution. The cover memo inaccurately characterized Demjanjuk, without support, as a "prominent, anti-Soviet, outspoken dissident." The cover memo stated: "Cleveland speculates that the matter could easily have been initiated and controlled by the KGB as a means of intimidating Soviet émigrés who speak out against the Soviet regime." The memo, titled "John Demjanjuk, Foreign Counterintelligence–Russia," stated that investigation in Cleveland strongly indicated "Soviet utilization of the OSI to effect Soviet purposes." The memo concluded: "Cleveland speculates that this matter is an extension of Soviet active measures conducted by the KGB's First Chief Directorate (Foreign Intelligence), designed to demonstrate the long arm of the KGB in monitoring the activities of Soviet émigré dissidents, especially those actively engaged in anti-Soviet organizations or public expression."

Agent Martin's memo was based on the incorrect assumptions that Demjanjuk was an outspoken anti-Soviet dissident and that the Trawniki ID card had not been forensically tested. The memo was premised on inaccurate assumptions, a lack of information, or a misunderstanding of how the case against Demjanjuk had proceeded. Martin's information was derived from press accounts, from his background knowledge of Soviet practices involving dissidents, and from memos generated by Agent Arruda following discussions with Jerome Brentar. Agent Martin did no independent investigation, interviewed no witnesses, and reviewed no documents prior to writing up his memo. Although the cover memo stated that the attached memo was to be discussed with OSI, in coordination with counterintelligence, the memo was never provided by the FBI to the prosecution team, nor were the memos obtained by the prosecution team prior to Demjanjuk's second denaturalization in 2002.[30] The lack of investigation into this matter was not surprising, given that FBI HQ had twice directed Cleveland FBI counterintelligence agents not to pursue any investigation of the Demjanjuk matter.

The cover memo also recommended that Watkins arrange a meeting with OSI to suggest, among other things, that OSI "compare handwriting and fingerprints on anonymous letters and obtain originals or copies of Soviet documents introduced as evidence" in an attempt to prevent the DOJ from becoming a tool of the KGB. No such meeting ever occurred, nor was OSI otherwise contacted by anyone at the FBI to convey the concerns of the two Cleveland agents. Had OSI been contacted, or had the two FBI agents been aware of the published 1981 decision denaturalizing Demjanjuk, they would have learned that the original Soviet-provided Trawniki ID card had been examined by the court and forensically tested. Neither FBI agent conducted any investigation into the evidence against Demjanjuk, nor did they reach any conclusion regarding the authenticity of the Trawniki ID card. Neither FBI agent ever worked with OSI, the DOJ Criminal Division, or the US Attorney's Office on any investigation of alleged Nazi war criminals. Neither of them ever worked on any FBI matter involving allegations that the Soviet Union had forged documents for use in American legal proceedings. Neither agent was aware of any investigation by the FBI of Demjanjuk's wartime activities or his immigration to the US.

Between 2000 and 2002, some 4,100 files containing approximately 360,000 pages of documents, including copies of the FBI's Demjanjuk materials, were sent by FBI HQ to the National Archives and Records Administration (NARA) pursuant to the "Nazi War Crimes Disclosure Act." After processing, these documents were made available for review by OSI in 2002. OSI did not have possession of the FBI materials until 2009, at which time Demjanjuk had already been deported to Germany.

Demjanjuk defense attorney Mark O'Connor wrote letters to FBI director William Webster that were forwarded to the attention of OSI via the assistant attorney general of the DOJ's Criminal Division, which was OSI's supervising authority. O'Connor also wrote to the Soviet ambassador to the US in 1984.

Demjanjuk's attorneys became aware of and were given access to the FBI materials. On December 31, 2009, Demjanjuk's defense attorney John Broadley contacted OSI and asked for access to these materials. In January 2010, OSI director Eli Rosenbaum advised the NARA that he was waiving the statutory exclusion for these materials and that they could be made available for public release. Rosenbaum then informed Broadley that he, or any member of the public, could view the files at the NARA.[31]

The "Nazi War Crimes Disclosure Act" required that the US government "locate, identify, inventory, recommend for declassification, and make available to the public, all Nazi war criminal records." However, the act expressly excludes from release any records belonging to OSI or pertaining to any current or former subject of an OSI investigation, inquiry, or prosecution.[32] OSI senior historian Steven Rogers was tasked by OSI with reviewing the voluminous records sent to the NARA by federal agencies pursuant to the Nazi War Crimes Disclosure Act, to identify those that potentially fell within the statutory exclusion. In July 2002, Rogers received inventories from the NARA indexing all 4,100 FBI file transfers. The inventories included three files pertaining to Demjanjuk. Rogers submitted a request to the NARA to review the Demjanjuk files. Rogers reviewed the files and noted on the file containing the Cleveland FBI memo from 1985: "The large bulky dossier contains records concerned with the investigation of O'Connor's allegations that fraud had been committed in the government's case against Demjanjuk as a result of Soviet disinformation. There is also material dealing with the defense's claim of new evidence information available concerning the authenticity of the Trawniki ID card." Because Rogers was not part of the Demjanjuk prosecution team, he did not realize that the materials were not already in OSI's possession and were not known to the prosecution team. His notes on the files were forwarded to his supervisor, OSI chief historian Dr. Elizabeth White.

In October 2002, Dr. White contacted the NARA, identifying those FBI files, including those pertaining to Demjanjuk, that were statutorily excluded from release because they fell under the OSI exclusion to the Nazi War Crimes Disclosure Act. OSI director Rosenbaum was also contacted regarding this matter.

OSI did not view the FBI Demjanjuk files held at the NARA until after the publication of a story in *Focus*, a German online magazine, in May 2009, about "secret" FBI files on Demjanjuk that were located at the NARA. Shortly thereafter, Rogers was sent by OSI to the NARA to obtain digital photos of the files to send for review by the German prosecutor in Demjanjuk's trial in Munich. OSI director Rosenbaum reviewed the documents and believed that they contained only public-domain content and long-since-discredited and public claims made by Demjanjuk defense counsel Mark O' Connor and Demjanjuk supporters that the Trawniki ID card was a KGB forgery.

In 2011, former OSI director Neal Sher informed Rosenbaum that an AP reporter had provided him with copies of FBI documents, and Rosenbaum then became aware that Cleveland FBI agents had expressed concerns about some of the evidence used against Demjanjuk by the prosecution team in the 1980s, and had written up documents regarding those concerns.[33] Representatives from the US Attorney's Office went to the Cleveland FBI office and made copies of their files pertaining to Demjanjuk. Those copies were provided to the defense.

Because the FBI did not assist OSI with investigative work and the FBI was not part of the prosecution team in the Demjanjuk case, the prosecution team had no reason to suppose that Cleveland FBI agents had developed such concerns or had generated such material. Had the prosecution team known of the agents' concerns or the existence of the materials they had generated, it would have instituted a thorough investigation into the basis for the theories contained in the FBI materials, and sought to interview the FBI agents who held those concerns.[34] The FBI had not been part of the prosecution team at any time in the Demjanjuk litigation. Since OSI brings civil, not criminal, denaturalization and deportation actions, the FBI was not part of the OSI's litigation team and did not investigate Demjanjuk or any other suspected Nazi perpetrators in the US on behalf of OSI.[35] Demjanjuk knew as far back as 1985 the very information contained in the FBI memo, yet he apparently decided not to pursue it. Even if he was unaware that Agent Martin had put his concerns about Soviet forgery into writing, Demjanjuk could have deposed Agent Martin or called him as a witness at trial, but he chose not to do so. The US government did not violate the *Brady vs. Maryland* principle: Demjanjuk's claim that the government failed to meet its obligation under *Brady*, resulting in fraud on the court, has no basis in law or fact. *Brady* imposes a duty on the government to disclose to a defendant all evidence that is both favorable to him and material to his guilt or punishment (also known as "due process under the law"). Evidence is material only if there is a reasonable probability that it would have changed the outcome of the trial. The materials in the FBI files ultimately would not have been favorable to Demjanjuk because they were speculative, based on erroneous information, and were unpersuasive in the face of overwhelming evidence that Demjanjuk lied to US immigration officials to conceal his service as a Nazi camp guard. *Brady* is concerned only with cases in which the government possesses information that the defendant does not have. On the contrary, Demjanjuk's defense team had known of the contents of the FBI materials for decades. While the FBI is a government agency, its knowledge of the materials cannot be imputed to OSI or the US Attorney's Office because the FBI was not part of the prosecution team. The purpose of *Brady* is not to require the prosecutor to search out exculpatory evidence, but rather to divulge whatever exculpatory evidence he already has. There is no imposing of "a duty on the prosecutor's office to learn of information possessed by other government agencies that have no involvement in the investigation or prosecution at issue."

Demjanjuk's defense made the following argument: the court accepts the government's position that "because the internal FBI documents are merely speculative, they are not exculpatory." However, a determination like that cannot be made without a hearing where the evidence supporting and challenging that finding can be presented. Additionally, the OSI's attempt to compartmentalize itself away from the FBI was something the 6th Circuit Appellate Court prohibited, and the OSI promised the court it would not do it again. The government then dodged its obligation to produce a statement of an interview with Ignat Danilchenko that OSI itself requested in 1983 or 1984. It never denied having requested the interview or that it took place. Instead, the government claimed it already produced all of Danilchenko's statements that it possessed. Then why is the 1983–1984 statement missing? Since OSI requested the interview, OSI should know what happened to the resulting statement. The US government hides behind a ruling of a German court denying an apparent motion to compel production of the statement. But why is a ruling by a German court even relevant here when we are considering the US government's discovery obligations?

Additionally, the defense contended that "the court committed procedural errors by denying Demjanjuk's discovery motion without conducting any oral argument or a hearing, and without allowing any further discovery." The court did not see all the internal FBI documents at issue, did not ask the FBI agents who authored one of the documents whether the document in fact contained nothing more than conjecture, and did not ask anyone in the government whether such conjecture was in fact unsupported by investigation. The court reached the conclusion that the FBI material was not relevant, without subjecting a single FBI agent to cross-examination. This violated basic due-process rights and fundamental fairness, said the defense.

When Demjanjuk's defense counsel asked the court to throw out the case against him because of a claim that the US government had not shared all evidence with the defense, the government argued as follows: Even assuming the FBI documents could somehow qualify as suppressed *Brady vs. Maryland* materials, which they were not, their materiality would have to be evaluated in the context of all other evidence against the defendant. However, documents are material only when they undermine confidence in the judgment. When viewed against that evidence, Demjanjuk's claim that the speculative FBI materials would have affected the outcome of the proceedings must be rejected. Overwhelming and essentially unchallenged expert evidence from scientists who actually examined the Trawniki ID card and presented their conclusions at the 2001 denaturalization trial established that the ID card discussed in the FBI materials is authentic and that it pertains to Demjanjuk. Every court that has examined the ID card, in the US, Israel, and Germany, has found it to be authentic. The Soviet forgery theory requires that one accept the astonishing coincidence that the MGB listed on its "fake" Trawniki card a posting to Sobibor: the very same place where Demjanjuk would admit to Western immigration authorities in 1948 and 1951 that he had spent part of the war. The other captured German documents naming Demjanjuk were found in four different archives in former Iron Curtain countries, and in an archive in what was then West Germany. With the exception of the Trawniki ID card, all were discovered after the collapse of the Soviet Union. It defies logic that the KGB would go to the trouble of creating masterful forgeries capable of withstanding historical and forensic analysis, but then hide them in archives scattered across eastern Europe, hoping someone would stumble across them at some future date when the Soviet Union might collapse, Demjanjuk might still be alive, and those archives would be opened up to Western researchers and investigators.

Forensic testing authenticated the Trawniki ID card: The FBI counterintelligence agents' theory notwithstanding, Demjanjuk's Trawniki ID card is one of the most thoroughly forensically-tested documents in legal history. It was first examined by Gideon Epstein, a world-renowned handwriting expert, who testified that the signature of two SS officials on the ID card (Streibel and Teufel) matched known examples.[36] Demjanjuk has never offered any credible forensic testimony challenging the Trawniki ID card's authenticity. The court found that rather than suggesting forgery, minor inaccuracies on the ID card—such as different spellings of Demjanjuk's name—were actually indicative of authenticity because "if the Soviets had set out to create false documents, they would not have allowed the omissions and minor inaccuracies that occur in the trail of documents in this case."

The FBI agents' theory had been premised on the assertion that the Soviets would prevent any forensic testing of the ID card. That theory, however, is fundamentally at odds with the facts of this case. Demjanjuk cannot plausibly argue that the court would have found the FBI's speculation meaningful, in light of the expert forensic testimony, which likely would have satisfied the agents' concerns about the ID card's authenticity.

Other documents that identified Demjanjuk as being in Trawniki guard service included a disciplinary report from Majdanek concentration camp, dated January 20, 1943; a Sobibor roster dated March 26, 1943; a Flossenburg roster dated October 1, 1943; and a Flossenburg roster dated October 3, 1944.

Demjanjuk's speculative claims that the US government had either deliberately or negligently failed to disclose Soviet investigative file #1627 is another example of his attempt to use the discovery of the unrelated FBI materials to relitigate his rejected defenses.

Demjanjuk's US citizenship was revoked, for the second time, in 2002. He was ordered deported in 2004. The DOJ requested that Demjanjuk be sent to Ukraine, his country of birth, or, if it refused to accept him, Poland or Germany. Demjanjuk filed a motion to avoid being deported to Ukraine, arguing that he would be tried and tortured there. To support this claim, he submitted to the court some reports issued by the US State Department and Amnesty International, asserting that torture is common in Ukrainian prisons. In 2009, Demjanjuk was extradited to Germany to stand trial for his service as a Trawniki guard at Sobibor:

Prior to the Demjanjuk case, OSI generally turned over to the defense only those documents which had been requested as part of the discovery process. The law in civil cases called for no more. In 1992, OSI began providing potentially exculpatory material, whether or not there had been a request for it. Determining if something is potentially exculpatory is sometimes difficult to determine, however. Now, all material that is arguably relevant is turned over. The amount of material is staggering. In a typical case involving a former Trawniki guard, OSI produces eleven CD-ROMs with generic historical information, plus hard copies of documents relevant to the particular case. This gives the defense between 100,000 and 150,000 pages worth of documents. The enormous resource drain involved in assembling this material, by attorneys, paralegals, and historians, cuts into OSI's ability to investigate new cases. It also prolongs litigation. The defense requires a significant amount of time to go through this material. In the second Demjanjuk trial, the court initially granted one year. However, due to issues that arose over the material, an extension of several more months was granted.[37]

The Demjanjuk case ended reliance on victim eyewitnesses to identify defendants, since it was demonstrated that eyewitness memory so many decades later could be unreliable.

The Bar Association reviewed the conduct of OSI director Allan Ryan and OSI attorney Norman Moscowitz, who had been assigned to the Demjanjuk case. Both were cleared of any wrongdoing. The 6th Circuit Court particularly criticized former OSI director Ryan, including his professed policy of turning over exculpatory information. The court went so far as to suggest that Ryan had been co-opted by Jewish interests because the Anti-Defamation League (ADL) had sponsored a lecture trip by him to Israel. However, Ryan had left the OSI three years prior to that trip. Ryan and the ADL requested that the court remove the accusation from its ruling, but it refused. The court was also skeptical that trial attorney Norman Moscowitz had not read the accounts of the Horn photo identification, which would have alerted him to the fact that Otto Horn's trial testimony conflicted with those reports.[38] There were also five internal DOJ investigations of matters relating to the Demjanjuk case.[39] In 2002, the IPN in Poland began an investigation of Demjanjuk and other SS auxiliaries who had served on Polish soil during the war. However, by 2007 the investigation was suspended, "concluding that there was insufficient proof that Demjanjuk had personally participated in killings."[40]

DEMJANJUK CRIMINAL TRIAL, MUNICH, 2009

Unlike the OSI standard to "denaturalize" a convicted war criminal, which required showing only that an individual had served as a camp guard, in German court, "mere service" alone was not considered a crime. There had to be evidence that the individual had participated in a specific act or acts of murder. Thomas Walther and Kirsten Goetze, investigators from the "Central Office for the Investigation of Nazi Crimes" in Ludwigsburg, looked into the case. They wrote up an outline of the case in 2008.[41] The reasons remain unclear as to why Germany chose to try Demjanjuk. In the past, Germany had often been reluctant to try its own citizens for Nazi crimes, let alone try non-Germans for such crimes. Regardless, Walther and Goetze would help lay the groundwork for Demjanjuk's prosecution in Germany. Both of them were former judges.[42] In a report, Walther and Goetze pointed out that Sobibor had been a death camp: not a concentration camp or a labor camp, but a pure death camp. Its sole purpose of functioning was to murder Jews. The SS staff and Trawniki guards were present there exclusively to operate a killing machine. According to Goetze, this made Demjanjuk's specific acts at the camp irrelevant. The fact alone that he had been a guard there should have been able to prove his guilt. All Trawniki guards at Sobibor were accessories to murder. That was their job.[43] However, Demjanjuk was not a German citizen and his alleged crimes did not occur on German soil, and in the past German courts had concluded that they lacked jurisdiction over non-Germans accused of crimes outside Germany. Walther and Goetze then argued that as a Trawniki guard, Demjanjuk had essentially functioned as a German official and as a result came "under the jurisdiction of German law."[44] The German court accepted this. By early 2009, the Bavarian State Criminal Investigation Office, on the basis of Walther and Goetze's report, recommended prosecution. Shortly thereafter, a judge from Munich's district court issued an arrest warrant for Demjanjuk.[45] OSI arranged Demjanjuk's flight to Germany.

To qualify as a perpetrator under German law, one typically had to have killed or authorized killing without orders. Only then could a court conclude that one had the "inner conviction" required to be a perpetrator. In order to be found guilty of murder, one had to act as an *Exzesstäter* (excess killer). Those who met this standard were a select group of monsters and fanatics: sociopaths such a Kurt Franz, an SS officer at Treblinka II. The Ivan Marchenko who operated the gas chambers at Treblinka II also fit this model. The vast majority of deeply implicated killers could be convicted only as accessories, and thousands of lowly foot soldiers of genocide were never even prosecuted in the first place.[46]

Ivan Demjanjuk[47] was born in 1920 in the village of Dubovye Macharenzi, Vinnitsa region, Ukraine

Occupation: tractor driver on a collective farm (*kolkhoz*)

Drafted into the Red Army: 1940, in the Kiev area

He sustained an artillery shrapnel wound in his back in 1941 or 1942 and was sent to a military hospital. He returned to the front in 1942, in Kutaisi, near the Turkish border.

In May 1942, he became a POW during the Battle of Kerch, on the Crimean Peninsula, and was sent to a POW camp in Rovno (Stalag 360), then a POW camp in Chelm (Stalag 319).

He was accused of serving as a Trawniki guard at Sobibor: this included inner and outer guard duty at the camp, assisting with unloading of the train transports, and escorting victims from the trains to the undressing barracks, and then to the gas chambers.

He was charged with having assisted in mass murder, out of base motives:

(1) three transports of 1,100 people each
(2) three transports of 1,200 people each
(3) three transports of 1,900 people each
(4) three transports of 2,300 people each
(5) three transports of 2,800 people each

This included

April 1943: a transport from Izbica, with 200 people; 160 of them were immediately taken to the gas chamber, including the families of survivors Toivi Blatt and Filip Bialowitz, who were teenagers at the time.

April–July 1943: Fifteen transport trains coming from the Westerbork camp in Holland. The number of people in these transports totaled at least 29,500. Among them were at least 1,900 German Jews who had fled from Germany and Holland.

summer 1943: At least one transport with about 200 people coming from the Soviet Union. Most of them were taken to the gas chamber on arrival.

Demjanjuk's Trawniki *Dienstausweis* is genuine. This was shown to be the case by Dr. Dallmayer, an expert witness from the Bavarian Criminal Investigation Department (expert opinion given in proceedings, March 4 and 12, 2009).

Larry Stewart made a statement regarding the chemical and physical examination of the *Dienstausweis* (expert opinion given, September 22, 2000). He examined the ink and paper of the *Dienstausweis*.

The photo on the *Dienstausweis* is a photo of Demjanjuk. Richard Altmann, an expert witness, demonstrated this (expert opinion given, December 19, 1986).

Additional information about ink and paper forensic techniques comes from a recorded interview in 2003 with Dr. Antonio Cantu, a forensic ink specialist with the US Secret Service, as well as from "Analytical Methods for Detecting Fraudulent Documents," an article by Dr. Cantu published in the September 1991 issue of *American Chemical Society*.[48] The Demjanjuk Trawniki ID card had ink from multiple sources: fountain pen ink, stamp pad ink, typewriter ribbon ink, and printing ink. All were analyzed. Additionally, a defect in the stamp on the ID card was matched with the same defect on other documents.[49]

Witness statements were made available from other former Trawniki guards: Ignat Danilchenko, Ivan Ivchenko, Anatoli Gontscharenko, Nikolaj Svyatelik, Alexei Nagorny, and Sabat Badurtdinov.

Probably in early 1945, Demjanjuk and other Trawniki guards serving at Flossenburg concentration camp were recruited for the 2nd Division of the "Vlasov army," in Graz, Austria, via the Heuberg training area. However, the guards did not reach their destination but were instead captured by the US Army near Landshut. The former guard, Nagorny, could testify to this fact.

After the war, Demjanjuk registered as a "displaced person" with the US military administration and spent time in various refugee camps in Bavaria: Landshut, Regensburg, Ulm, Bad Reichenhall, and Feldafing.[50] In 1947 in Regensburg, Demjanjuk got married to a woman named Vinnya, five years younger than himself. In 1950, they had a daughter, Lydia. In 1951, he applied for a US entry visa. In 1952, he and his wife and daughter boarded a ship in Bremerhaven, bound for New York. In 1958, Demjanjuk applied for US citizenship, and it was granted three months later. He changed his first name from Ivan to John. They moved to Indiana, and later to Cleveland, Ohio. He found work as an auto mechanic at the Ford Motor Company. He and his wife had two more children, including a son, John Jr.

Demjanjuk's attorney, Ulrich Busch, sought to get the case dismissed on the grounds of prejudice: that the German legal system was trying Demjanjuk to attempt to make up for its pathetic past record of bringing Nazis to justice. He also pointed out that Demjanjuk was neither German nor high-ranking, nor had he been a full member of the SS. "What of all the SS higher-ups who were either acquitted or never even charged in the first place? Demjanjuk was taken as a POW by the Wehrmacht. The killing of Red Army POWs was the first Holocaust! The Trawniki guards had no more freedom of action than the Jews themselves!"[51] Busch's argument was that the whole case was an "exercise in displacement in which German guilt for the Holocaust was being shifted from the actual perpetrators onto a handful of foreigners, who themselves had been victims of the Germans." Said Busch, "How could a system that acquitted the SS commandant of Trawniki (Streibel) now convict Demjanjuk?"[52] "He was a victim of the Ukrainian famine in 1932–1933 and nearly became a victim in a POW camp."[53] Busch declared to the court that Demjanjuk had been a victim of the OSI and "its behind-the-scenes supporters: the World Jewish Congress and the Simon Wiesenthal Center." Busch's statement was like an echo of Hitler's theory of a "Judeo-Bolshevik world conspiracy."[54]

Busch argued that Demjanjuk's trial in Germany violated double jeopardy because he had already been acquitted of the same charges in Israel. This is incorrect, since double jeopardy usually does not apply if the accused is tried in another country's legal system.[55]

In 2011, Demjanjuk's defense stated that there was a file with the number "1627," and that it was "an ultra-secret KGB file" containing evidence that could exonerate Demjanjuk, including alleged proof that the Demjanjuk Trawniki ID was a forgery and proof that Ignat Danilchenko's statements that he had served with Demjanjuk were given under torture.[56] Demjanjuk wanted the court to obtain the file, which his attorney claimed was "critical defense evidence." However, most observers of the trial doubted that this mysterious file existed, but in fact it did, and "its existence had been known back at the time of Demjanjuk's second denaturalization trial in the US in 2001. Even then, Demjanjuk's attorney at the time, Michael Tigar, was excited about the possibility that such a file might be full of exculpatory material. However, file #1627, consisting of six volumes, ended up being a collection of noninvestigative materials, including Israeli government requests from Demjanjuk's trial in Jerusalem, Soviet field reports, twenty years' worth of DOJ requests, and internal Soviet/Russian inquiries and responses. "It would have been standard practice for the KGB to compile such a file and to refuse researchers access to its contents." Demjanjuk's defense attorney would never get his hands on it, but its inaccessibility served its purpose of fueling conspiracy theories.[57]

Demjanjuk's defense strategy was a contradiction. On the one hand he continued to insist, as he always had, that he had never been a Trawniki guard, at Sobibor or anywhere else. On the other hand, his attorney stated that if he had served as a guard, he had "no more choice than the Jews who worked at the camp." Demjanjuk could not have it both ways: one cannot deny something altogether and at the same time use a hypothetical "putative necessity defense," which is what Demjanjuk's attorney was trying to do. "Because Demjanjuk's first line of defense had always been denial, he foreclosed reliance on his own strongest argument," which would have been "putative necessity."[58] The prosecution, lacking evidence that Demjanjuk had personally killed anyone, developed a simple but logical theory regarding guard service at death camps, using deductive reasoning:[59]

(1) All Trawniki guards at Sobibor participated in the camp's killing process.
(2) Demjanjuk was a Trawniki guard at Sobibor.
(3) Therefore, Demjanjuk participated in the camp's killing process.

As historian Dieter Pohl explained to the court, all the Trawniki guards facilitated the camp's function of mass murder of Jews.[60]

The position of the prosecution was that mass murder or the aiding and abetting of mass murder cannot be justified by the fact that the orders were covered in laws and official regulations of the German government at the time. Injustice does not become justice by means of standardization. The accused cannot plead having executed a binding military order to justify his acts. As a principle, action upon order can be used as justification only if the ordered action is legal. Also, the accused cannot claim to have acted under superior orders in the sense of section 35, subsection 1, of the German Penal Code. The accused could have deserted, as many other Trawniki guards did. But had Demjanjuk served at Sobibor voluntarily? This is the one question that has never really been answered.[61]

In contrast to a pure "necessity defense," which must show that the defendant had no choice but to engage in a criminal act, a "putative necessity defense" must show only that the defendant believed that he lacked choice, and that this belief, even if erroneous, was reasonable under the circumstances. This defense is different from the "superior orders defense" that had been disallowed at the Nuremberg trials. In that defense, a defendant would argue that his actions were considered legal because they had been ordered by his superiors. On the other hand, the "putative necessity defense" assumes that the defendant knew the orders he received were criminal, but carried them out anyway because he reasonably believed he would be harmed or killed if he failed to obey.[62] In 1963, several German SS men who had served at Belzec were acquitted during a trial in which they used this defense. In 1966, German SS staff who had served at Sobibor used this same defense, and several of them were acquitted as a result.[63] "Over the years, however, as historians came to better understand SS culture and practices, German courts became far less receptive to the 'putative necessity defense.'" Historians failed to find a single case in which German personnel faced "dire punishment" for refusing to carry out killings.[64] Separate from German SS personnel, the "Central Office of Investigation of Nazi Crimes" in Ludwigsburg neglected investigating former Trawniki guards, on the assumption that they would always use the "putative necessity defense." This defense is supported by a statement made by Helga Grabitz, the woman who prosecuted Karl Streibel, when she said that the Trawniki guards had allowed themselves to be recruited by the Germans in order to escape death in the POW camps.[65]

Similarly, a judge named Hans-Robert Richthof, who had tried former Sobibor SS staff member Karl Frenzel in 1985, stated that he believed that the Trawniki guards had been in a "powerless position."[66] Demjanjuk's attorney, Ulrich Busch, stated that the Trawniki guards "were closer in status to their Jewish captives than to their SS overseers. Dr. Peter Black disagreed with this assessment, since his research suggested that the Trawniki guards were very much considered as part of the SS apparatus: they wore uniforms, they were armed, they had rank insignia and were eligible for promotion on the basis of their performance and loyalty, they were well fed, they were paid a salary by the Germans, and they were eligible for leave, all of which were indications that they had "status."[67] Alternatively, historian Angelika Benz stated that the Trawniki guards were "tragic figures" occupying a position somewhere in between the Jewish victims and the Germans.[68]

Witnesses were summoned for the trial via the DOJ-OSI, and OSI historian Dr. David Rich acted in an advisory capacity to Kirsten Goetze. Originally, the court considered summoning Dr. Peter Black as an expert witness. He is perhaps the world expert on the Trawniki guards. However, concern over Black's previous employment with the OSI resulted in the court deciding against calling on him, in case Demjanjuk and his defense counsel objected.[69] The same reasoning applied when the court considered calling on Dr. Charles Sydnor Jr. as an expert witness and then chose not to because of his previous relationship working with OSI and his apparent bias against Demjanjuk.[70]

Witnesses to be summoned for trial:[71] (note that not all would ultimately be called)
(1) Thomas Walter, former district court judge, Ludwigsburg
(2) K. Daumann, senior detective, Bavarian Criminal Investigation Office (BKA), Munich
(3) Reinhard Altmann
(4) Dr. Dallmayer, BKA, Munich
(5) Dr. Dieter Pohl, Institute of Contemporary History, Munich
(6) Dr. Gideon Epstein, forensic document examiner
(7) Dr. Larry Stewart, forensic document examiner
(8) Dr. Eli Rosenbaum, director of DOJ-OSI
(9) Edward Stutman, OSI attorney
(10) Norman Moscowitz, OSI attorney
(11) Thomas Blatt, survivor of Sobibor; Santa Barbara, California
(12) Jules Shelvis, survivor of Sobibor; Amstelveen, Holland
(13) Alexander Nagorny, former Trawniki guard; Landshut, Germany
(14) Ignat Danilchenko, former Trawniki guard; Tyumen, Russia (deceased as of 1985)
(15) Nikolaj Svyatelnik, former Trawniki guard; Lugansk region, Ukraine
(16) Ivan Ivchenko, former Trawniki guard; Yuzhnij, Kharkov region, Ukraine
(17) Nikolaj Gontcharenko, former Trawniki guard; unknown location
(18) Aglyamutdin Badurtdinov, former Trawniki guard; Irkutsk region, Siberia
(19) Prokofij Businnij, former Trawniki guard; Kiev region, Ukraine
(20) Samuel Kunz, former *Zugwachmann*, Trawniki Volksdeutscher; Wachtberg, Germany

Documents available for trial:[72]
Trawniki personnel files (*Personalbögen*)
Trawniki ID cards (*Dienstausweisen*)
Sobibor roster, March 26, 1943
Records of interrogations of former Trawniki guards
Other Trawniki documentation, including internal reports

MGB circular, "Information on Wanted Persons," 1948
MGB circular, "Information on Wanted Persons," 1952
Ivan Demjanjuk birth certificate
Ivan Demjanjuk US visa application, 1951
John Demjanjuk US citizenship application, 1958
Documents from Ludwigsburg: preliminary investigation against Kurt Bolender
    and others, Dortmund
Documents from Ludwigsburg: criminal proceedings against Kurt Bolender, Hagen
Documents from Ludwigsburg: criminal proceedings against Werner Dubois and
    others, Dortmund
Indictment against Hubert Gomerski, Frankfurt, 1950
Preliminary investigation against Karl Streibel, Hamburg
Documents from Ludwigsburg: proceedings against Karl Frenzel, Hagen
Judgement against Josef Oberhauser, Munich
Statements of Erich Bauer, former *SS-Oberscharführer*
Documents regarding "Request for Judicial Assistance," Department of Prosecution,
    Munich, inspection of the investigation files of the DOJ-OSI
Master report, US Court, #85-3435
Polish documents of investigation regarding Belzec and Trawniki
Examination of the witness Thomas Blatt, Sobibor survivor
Documents: US Holocaust Memorial Museum Research Institute, interview with
    Kurt Thomas, Sobibor survivor
Expert opinion of Dieter Lehner
Articles by Dr. Dieter Pohl
Sobibor: History of a Nazi Death Camp by Jules Shelvis, 2007
Sobibor: The Forgotten Revolt by Thomas Blatt, 2004

The court in Munich deliberated for about two hours. The judge announced that Demjanjuk had been found guilty as an accessory to the murder of at least 28,000 Jews at Sobibor.[73] The sentence: five years' imprisonment.[74] It was the first time in history that Germany had convicted a non-German for Nazi crimes.[75]

The trial and verdict in Munich "never would have happened without the stubborn exertions of the OSI and the "Central Office of Investigations of Nazi Crimes" in Ludwigsburg. Their historians and attorneys "worked tirelessly and creatively."[76]

Ivan/John Demjanjuk died in a nursing home in Bavaria on March 17, 2012, at the age of ninety-one, while his conviction in Germany was on appeal. His body was returned to his family in the US. Had he been tried in the Soviet Union, most likely he would not have lived so long. If at the end of the war or immediately afterward he had been on Soviet or Soviet-occupied territory, he could have been shot or hanged by order of a military field tribunal. Had he been discovered in the late 1940s or early 1950s like so many other former Trawniki guards, he would have been sentenced to up to twenty-five years of hard labor. In the mid-1950s, like other former Trawniki guards convicted in the Soviet Union, he would have been released under the amnesty, but in the 1960s he might have been retried on the basis of newly discovered evidence, like the defendants in the "Schults" trial, and could have been sentenced to death by firing squad.[77] By the time he died, Demjanjuk had spent the last thirty-four years of his life in and out of legal limbo, from 1977 to 2011.

Appendix A:
Trawniki Trials

INDIVIDUAL TRIALS BY SOVIET COURTS, WITH NAMES OF DEFENDANTS, YEAR AND LOCATION OF PROCEEDINGS, AND SENTENCES WHERE KNOWN

1945

Pavel Leleko, 2nd Belorussian Front, 1945: death sentence

Ivan Terekhov, 1st Guards Tank Army, April 15, 1945: ten years in corrective labor camps

Sergei Vasilenko, 2nd Belorussian Front, April 15, 1945: ten years in corrective labor camps

Unknown Years

Ivan Baskakov, Yaroslavl

Nikolaj Bondarenko, Kaluga

D. Datsenko, Kiev

Karl Diener, Blagoveshchensk, Omsk: death sentence

N. Dmitrenko, Kiev

Jakob Engelhardt: twenty-five years in corrective labor camps

Nikolaj Gordejew, Kalinin/Tver

Alexei Isaenko, Tashkent

Ivan Juchnowskij: twenty-five years in corrective labor camps

Petr Karnashnikov/Kornaschenkas, Vilnius

Alexander Kolgushkin, Yaroslavl

Petr Koval, Zaporozhe

Mikhail Lysak: death sentence

Wasyl Marticzuk, Stanislavov/Ivano-Frankivsk

Alexei Milutin, Voroshilovgrad/Lugansk

Nikolaj Nepejvoda, Stanislavov/Ivano-Frankivsk

Petro Niniowskij, Stanislavov/Ivano-Frankivsk

N. Pogrebnyak: twenty-five years in corrective labor camps

Vasili Popov

Hryzko Prymak, Stanislavov/Ivano-Frankivsk

Dimitri Rjasanow, Tula

Alexander Schafer, Komi Republic: death sentence

Peter Sergeyev

Wasyl Stoljarow, Chernigov

Fedor Tichonowskij (interrogated in Karaganda, 1955)

1946

Petro Kuschnir, Stanislavov/Ivano-Frankivsk

Ivan Tarasov, Kazan

1947

Petr Browzew, Leningrad: fifteen years in corrective labor camps

Alexander Byschkow: twenty-five years in corrective labor camps

Wasyl Chlopeckyj, Lvov

Vladimir Emelyanov, Sverdlovsk/Yekaterinburg

Ivan Grigorchuk, Stanislavov/Ivano-Frankivsk

Ivan Ivchenko, Kharkov

Dmytro Kobiletskij, Stanislavov/Ivano-Frankivsk

Josef Masuk, Stanislavov/Ivano-Frankivsk

Dmitri Modschuk, Stanislavov/Ivano-Frankivsk

Alexander Moskalenko, Lvov: twenty-five years in corrective labor camps; released, 1964

Nikolaj Olejnikov, Stalingrad/Volgograd

Wasyl Popeliuk, Stanislavov/Ivano-Frankivsk

Vladimir Pronin, Zaporozhe

Yakov Sagach, Simferopol, Crimea

Nikolaj Skorokhod, Lvov

Anton Solonina, Kiev

Alexander Volobuev/Kuris, Lutsk, Volhynia

Alexander Zakharov/Pruss, Moscow Military District: twenty-five years in corrective labor camps

Ivan Zvezdun, Novosibirsk: twenty-five years in corrective labor camps

1948

Filip Babenko, Kiev

Nikolaj Butenko-Sherstnev, Tashkent

Jurko Danilov, Lvov
Ivan Demkar, Stanislavov/Ivano-Frankivsk
Petr Didukh, Stanislavov/Ivano-Frankivsk
Vladimir Gadsicki: twenty-five years in
corrective labor camps
Ivan Gumenyuk, Stanislavov/Ivano-Frankivsk
Nikolaj Gutsulyak, Stanislavov/Ivano-
Frankivsk
Ivan Knysch, Stalino/Donetsk
Ivan Kondratenko, Kiev
Nikolai Leontev: fifteen years in corrective
labor camps; released 1956
Ivan Lukanyuk, Stanislavov/Ivano-Frankivsk
Kiril Lukyanchuk
Nikolaj Potyatynik, Stanislavov/Ivano-
Frankivsk
Vladimir Revyuk, Krasnoyarsk
Mikhail Rozgonjajew, Dnepropetrovsk
Vasili Shkarpovich, Stanislavov/Ivano-
Frankivsk
Fedor Tartynskij, Stalino/Donetsk
Vladimir Terletskij, Stanislavov/Ivano-
Frankivsk
Mikhail Titov, Stanislavov/Ivano-Frankivsk
Todor Turjanskij, Stanislavov/Ivano-Frankivsk
Zaki Tuktarov: twenty-five years in corrective
labor camps; released, 1955
Artymon Yatskiv, Stanislavov/Ivano-Frankivsk
Alexander Yeger, Kiev: death sentence
Jakob Zechmeister/Tsekmistro, Kharkov

1949
Nikolaus Belous, Lvov
Ivan Chornobaj, Lvov
Ignat Danilchenko, Kiev: twenty-five years
in corrective labor camps (the prosecutor
had recommended a death sentence)
Nikolaj Gontcharenko, Zaporozhe
Yakov Karpliuk: twenty-five years in corrective
labor camps
Wasyl Kartaschev, Ternopil
Semen Kharkovskij
Ivan Kozlowskj: twenty-five years corrective
labor camps; served his time at an ore
mine in Karaganda region, Kazakhstan
Alexei Lazorenko: twenty-five years in
corrective labor camps
Vasili Litvinenko, Kiev

Ivan Lysyj, Sverdlovsk/Yekaterinburg
Petr Madamov, Volhynia
Grigorij Nesmejan: twenty-five years in
corrective labor camps
Nikolaj Pavli, Stalino/Donetsk
Kiril Prochorenko: twenty-five years in
corrective labor camps
Alexander Semenov: twenty-five years in
corrective labor camps
Wasyl Shyndykevskij, Stanislavov/Ivano-
Frankivsk
Dimitri Yarosch, Rostov-on-the-Don &
Poltava

1950
Vladimir Belinskj
Vasili Bronov, Blagoveshchensk, Omsk
Grigorij Chernikov
I. Churin, Vladivostok
Vasili Gajdich, Moscow Military District:
death sentence
Alexei Govorov: twenty-five years in corrective
labor camps
Andrej Kuchma, Kiev
Ananij Kuzminskij: twenty-five years in
corrective labor camps
Vladimir Lomov
Ivan Mistyuk
Taras Olejnik: twenty-five years in corrective
labor camps
Wasyl Oleksiuk, Stanislavov/Ivano-Frankivsk
Vasili Pankov, Stalino/Donetsk
Samuel Pritsch, Kiev Military District: twenty-
five years in corrective labor camps
Grigorij Skydan, Baranovichi
Anton Streltsov, Kiev: death sentence
Ivan Tellman, Novosibirsk: death sentence
Ivan Tkachuk
Akim Zuev: twenty-five years in corrective
labor camps

1951
Mikhail Gorbachev, Urals Military District:
fifteen years in corrective labor camps
Fedor Gorun, Kiev
Peter Klemeshow
Mitrofan Klotz: twenty-five years in corrective
labor camps

Stefan Kopytyuk, Lvov
Dimitri Korotkikh, Kiev: death sentence
Vasili Pochwala, Lvov
Dmitrij Pundik, Prikarpatsky: twenty years
in corrective labor camps
Alexander Semigodow: twenty-five years in
corrective labor camps
Milko Sendetskij, Stanislavov/Ivano-Frankivsk
Nikolai Shalayev, Voronezh Military District:
death sentence
Ivan Slivka, Stanislavov/Ivano-Frankivsk
Romualdas Vilekas, Lithuania

1952
Alexei Kulinitsch, Moscow Military District
Filip Levchishin, Carpathian Military District:
twenty-five years in corrective labor
camps
G. Marusenko/Garus, Moscow Military
District
Anastasij Mavrodij, Odessa: twenty-five years
in corrective labor camp
Grigorij Napkhanko, Kiev
Evdokim Parfinyuk, Carpathian Military
District: twenty-five years in corrective
labor camps
Ivan Shvidkij, Stalino/Donetsk, Kiev

1953
Vasili Orlovskij: twenty-five years in corrective
labor camp
Alfons Slaitas, Lithuania
Alexei Zhukov

1955
Yakov Klimenko: twenty-five years in
corrective labor camps; released, 1966
Vasili Schuller, Tavrichesky Military District:
twenty-five years in corrective labor
camps

1961
Nikolaj Skakodub, Pre-Carpathian region:
fifteen years in corrective labor camps

1968
Alexander Kirelacha, Lvov

1971
Franz Swidersky, Dusseldorf: seven years'
imprisonment

1986
Fedor Fedorenko, Simferopol: death sentence

1987–1988, 1990, 2009–2010
Ivan Demjanjuk, Jerusalem: death sentence,
overturned on appeal; Munich: five years'
imprisonment

GROUP TRIALS. SOVIET COURTS

Shevchenko Trial, October 1944, 65th Army, 1st Belorussian Front
Ivan Shevchenko: death sentence
Nikita Rekalo: death sentence
Pavel Kozlov
Mikhail Poleszuk
Valentin Roshanskij
Grigorij Sirota

Ural Military District, 1947
Ivan Voloshin: twenty-five years in corrective
labor camps
Mikhail Korzhikow: twenty-five years in
corrective labor camps
Alexander Dukhno: twenty-five years in
corrective labor camps

Rjabtsev Trial, Voronezh, 1948
Prokofij Rjabtsev: twenty-five years in
corrective labor camps; released, 1962

Other defendants unknown
Yakov Iskaradov, Stalino/Donetsk, 1948
Fedor Duschenko, Kharkov, 1949
Dnepropetrovsk region, 1949
Fedor Ryabeka: twenty-five years in corrective
labor camps
Mikhail Andreyenko: twenty-five years in
corrective labor camps
Terentij Gordienko: twenty-five years in
corrective labor camps; died in captivity
serving his sentence

Goncharov Trial, Kiev Military District, 1951
Petr Goncharov: death sentence
Nikolaj Sherbak: death sentence
Ivan Machoulin: death sentence

Schults Trial, Kiev, 1961–1962
Emanuel Schults/Vinogradov: death sentence
Filip Levchishin: death sentence
Sergei Vasilenko: death sentence
Samuel Pritsch: death sentence
Ivan Terekhov: death sentence; commuted
    to fifteen years, with an additional ten-
    year reduction for time already served
    from 1945 to 1955
Yakov Karpliuk: death sentence
Dimitri Borodin: death sentence
Alexei Govorov: death sentence
Fedor Ryabeka: death sentence
Ivan Kurinnyj: death sentence
Mikhail Gorbachev: death sentence
Evdokim Parfinyuk: death sentence

Akkermann Trial, Krasnodar, 1963?
Andrej Akkermann: death sentence
Other defendants unknown

Matvienko Trial, Krasnodar, 1964–1965
Nikolaj Matvienko: death sentence
Vasili Belyakov: death sentence
Vasili Podenok: death sentence
Fedor Tichonowskij: death sentence
Ivan Nikiforov: death sentence
Ivan Zaitsev: death sentence

Zuev Trial, Dnepropetrovsk, 1965–1966
Akim Zuev: death sentence
Nikita Mamchur: death sentence
Alexei Lazorenko: death sentence
Taras Olejnik: death sentence; commuted to
    fifteen years' imprisonment
Grigorij Lynkin: fifteen years' imprisonment
Ivan Zagrebayev: fifteen years' imprisonment
    (his case was detached from the others,
    and he was tried separately for
    undetermined reasons)

Pankratov Trial, Lvov, 1966
Georgij Pankratov
Petr Prikhodko
? Minochkin

Litvinenko Trial, Lvov, 1966–1968
Vasili Litvinenko
Yegor Lobyntsev
Alexander Fedchenko
Ivan Kitsenko
Andrej Ostapenko

Streibel Trial, Hamburg, 1976
Karl Streibel: acquitted
Josef Napieralla: acquitted
Kurt Reinberger: acquitted
Michael Janczak: acquitted
Ernst Mitterach: acquitted
Theodor Pentziok: acquitted

POLISH COURTS

Wladyslaw Sliwinski
Stanislaw Michalak
Dymitr Holub
Jan Pawluczuk
Jan Martyniuk
Bazyli Dudziak
Dymitr Bartnik
Alexander Nawoznik
Ignacy Gardzinski: served at Treblinka II
Czeslaw Krzykocki
Franciszek Hajczuk: served at Treblinka II
Wlodzimierz Zinkiewicz
Eugeniusz Maytchenko

DOJ-OSI CIVIL PROCEEDINGS, UNITED STATES

(1) Walter Berezowskyj: served at Trawniki,
    Poniatowa, Sachsenhausen, and Maut-
    hausen
(2) Jaroslaw Bilaniuk: Trawniki, antipartisan
    deployments, and SS-"Streibel" Battalion
(3) Ivan/John Demjanjuk, Cleveland, Ohio:
    served at Majdanek, Sobibor, and
    Flossenburg

(4) Fedor Fedorenko, Fort Lauderdale, Florida: served in Lublin Detachment, Treblinka II, and Stutthof

(5) Bronislaw Hajda: Treblinka I and SS-"Streibel" Battalion

(6) Liudas Kairys, Illinois: served in Lublin Detachment, Trawniki, and Treblinka I

(7) Wasyl Krysa: served at Poniatowa and Mauthausen

(8) Andrei Kuras: served at Trawniki, Poniatowa, and SS-"Streibel" Battalion

(9) Fedor Kwoczak, Pennsylvania: served at Trawniki, Poniatowa, Warsaw Detachment, Bialystok Detachment, and SS-"Streibel" Battalion

(10) Wasyl Lytwyn: served at Trawniki, Warsaw Detachment, and SS-"Streibel" Battalion

(11) Ivan Mandycz: served at Trawniki, Poniatowa, and Sachsenhausen

(12) Jakiw Palij: served at Trawniki and SS-"Streibel" Battalion

(13) Jakob/Jack Reimer, New York: served at Trawniki, Warsaw Detachment, and SS-"Streibel" Battalion

(14) Dmytro Sawchuk: served at Belzec, Poniatowa, Bialystok Detachment, Trawniki, and SS-"Streibel" Battalion

(15) Mykola Wasylyk: served at Trawniki, Budzyn, and SS-"Streibel" Battalion

(16) Vladas Zajankauskas, Boston, Massachusetts: served at Trawniki, Warsaw Detachment, and SS-"Streibel" Battalion

DOJ-CANADA CIVIL PROCEEDINGS

Josef Furmanchuk
Jura Skomatchuk

Preliminary investigations initiated but charges not filed

Mikhail Fostun, Great Britain: served at Trawniki and Warsaw Detachment, 14th SS Galicia Division

Samuel Kunz, Germany, 2010: served at Belzec and SS "Streibel" Battalion

FORMER TRAWNIKI GUARDS WHO SERVED AS WITNESSES AT THE TRIALS OF OTHER TRAWNIKI GUARDS

Ivan Tarasov Trial, Kazan, 1946
A. Tikhonov

Nikolaus Belous Trial, Lvov, 1947
Ivan Zvezdun

Ivan Gumenyuk/Huminiuk Trial, Stanislavov/Ivano-Frankivsk
Petr Didukh

Ivan Knysch Trial, Stalino/Donetsk, 1948
Nikolaj Chernyshev
Viktor Klimenko
Ivan Stepanov
Vladimir Emelyanov
Andrej Sergienko

Yakov Iskaradov Trial, Stalino/Donetsk, 1948
Vladimir Emelyanov
Alexander Titievskij
Fedor Tartynskij
Viktor Bogomolov
Andrej Vasilega
Ivan Knysch

Nikolaj Butenko-Sherstnev Trial, Tashkent, 1948
P. Parkhomenko
Sabit Shirgaliev

Alexei Isaenko Trial, Tashkent, 1948
Rudolf Ittermann

Fedor Duschenko Trial, Kharkov, 1949
V. Zhuralayev

Grigorij Napkhanko Trial, Kiev, 1952
Nikolaj Akhtimijchuk, Krasnoyarsk, 1948

Schults Trial, Kiev, 1961–1962
Prokofij Businnyj

Ivan Tkachuk, Vinnitsa
Prokofij Ryabtsev, Vinnitsa
Nikolaj Skakodub
Ivan Juchnowskij
Fedor Korovnichenko
Jakob Engelhardt
Ananij Kuzminski
Nikolaj Senik
Ivan Safonov
Anton Solonina
Alexander Pechersky (former prisoner in
Sobibor)

Matvienko Trial, Krasnodar, 1964–1965
Mikhail Korzhikow
Nikolai Leontev
Ivan Kozlowskij
Boris Babin
Ivan Tkachuk
Prokofij Ryabtsev
Ananij Kuzminsky?
Mikhail Lapot/Laptev
Zaki Tuktarov
Nikolaj Gordejew
Alexander Zakharov/Pruss
Alexander Semenov

Zuev Trial, Dnepropetrovsk, 1964–1966
Vasili Shuller
Alexander Zakharov/Pruss
Kiril Prokhorenko
Fedor Gorun
Grigorij Kniga
Fedor Tichonowskij
Luka Bardachenko
Andrei Kuchma
Alexander Semigodow
Wasyl Gulyj
Ivan Voloshin
Petr Lukyanchuk
Grigorij Nesmejan
Dimitri Pundik
Petro Popeliuk

Josef Oberhauser Trial, Munich, 1965
(Interrogation protocols only; actual witnesses
not present)
Timofei Gurch

Vladimir Gadsicki
Piotr Brovzev
Alexander Byczkow
Mitrofan Klotz
Vasili Orlovskij
Kiril Prokhorenko
Grigorij Lynkin
Grigorij Nesmejan
Anastasi Mawrodij
Dimitri Pundik
Mikhail Greniuk
Taras Olejnik
Alexander Semigodow
Piotr Guzulak

Litvinenko Trial, Lvov, 1966–1968
Yakov Klimenko
Dimitri Yarosch
Vjacheslaw Dmitriev

Georg Michalsen Trial, Hamburg
Heinrich Schaefer, 1969

Kurt Franz Trial, Dusseldorf
Karl Streibel, 1969

Lothar Hoffmann Trial, Wiesbaden
Abram Thiessen, 1971
Hermann Reese, 1971
Karl Streibel, 1972

Franz Swidersky Trial, Dusseldorf, 1971
Ivan Zvezdun, Irkutsk, 1969; Moscow, 1971
Alexander Kolgushkin, Yaroslavl, 1969
Alexander Moskalenko, Nikolayev, 1969
Vladas Amanaviczius, Belgium, 1970
Semen Kharkovskij, Moscow, 1971
Fedor Vilshun, Moscow, 1971

Streibel Trial, Hamburg, 1976
Hermann Reese, 1962
Abram Thiessen, Hamburg, 1964
Erich Lachmann, 1969
Samuel Kunz, 1973
Kiril Prokhorenko, 1973
Semen Kharkovskij, Kharkov, 1973
Alexander Kolgushkin, Yaroslavl, 1973
Alexander Semigodow, Penza, 1973

Heinrich Schafer, Hamburg, 1973
Rudolf Reiss, Hamburg, 1973
Helmut Leonhardt, Hamburg, 1973
Prokofij Businnij, Kiev, 1975
Jakob Engelhardt, Leningrad / St. Petersburg, 1975
Piotr Brovzev, Leningrad / St. Petersburg, 1975

Liudas Kairys Proceedings
Ivan Zvezdun, Irkutsk, 1980
Semen Kharkovskij, Kharkov, 1980
Vladas Amanaviczius, Belgium, 1981
Paul Fessler, 1981

Fedor Fedorenko Proceedings
Nikolaj Malagon, Zaporozhe, 1978

Ivan/John Demjanjuk DOJ-OSI Proceedings, Cleveland
(Interrogation protocols only; actual witnesses not present)
Nikolaj Malagon, Zaporozhe, 1978
Ignat Danilchenko, Tyumen, 1979

Ivan/John Demjanjuk Trial, Jerusalem, 1987–1988
(Interrogation protocols only)
Rudolf Reiss, Hamburg, 1987
Written statements of defendants and witnesses from the Schults trial, Kiev, 1961–1962: Used by the Demjanjuk defense to demonstrate that Ivan Demjanjuk and Ivan Marchenko were two different Trawniki guards.

Ivan/John Demjanjuk Trial, Munich, 2009–2010
(Except for Nagorny, none of them testified)
Aglam Batartinov
Nikolaj Gontcharenko
Ivan Ivchenko
Alexei Nagorny, Landshut, 2009–2010
Samuel Kunz, Wachtberg, 2009–2010
Nikolaj Svyatelnik

Appendix B:
Trawniki Documents Used in Soviet Trials and DOJ-OSI Proceedings

The United States Holocaust Memorial Museum archive has copies of eighteen trials against former Trawniki guards prosecuted in Ukraine, two in Russia, five in Uzbekistan, and two in Kazakhstan.[1]

Soviet archives organized their files according to *fond* (collection), *opis* (finding guide), and *delo* (file).[2]

PERSONALBÖGEN

Alexander Yeger, TPF #14, Yeger proceedings, archive file #55402, vol. 1, p. 176, FSB Archive Molotov/Perm.

Franz Swidersky, TPF #26, RGVA-TsKhIDK (Russian State Military Archive), Moscow, fond 1367, opis 1, delo 239, pp. 1–5, *US vs. Hajda, US vs. Reimer.*

Franz Swidersky, TPF #26, Swidersky proceedings, State Attorney's Office Dusseldorf, 8 Ks 4/70, vol. 3, p. 133, *US vs. Kwoczak.*

Karl Diener, TPF #178, Diener proceedings, Blagoveshchensk, file #2271, pp. 200–204, FSB Archive Moscow.

Anatolie Rige, TPF #185, FSB Archive Moscow, vol. 8, pp. 185–189, *US vs. Hajda.*

Valerian Danko, TPF #206, FSB Archive Moscow, *US. vs. Reimer.*

Konstantin Demida, TPF #443, FSB Archive Moscow, vol. 24, pp. 116–118, *US vs. Demjanjuk,* Demjanjuk trial in Munich.

Anton Solonina, TPF #448, Solonina proceedings, case #5957, archive file #58322, fols. 50–51, SBU Archive Kiev, *US vs. Demjanjuk.*

Ivan Marchenko, TPF #476, original probably located at FSB Archive Moscow or SBU Archive Dnepropetrovsk, Demjanjuk appeal in Israel.

Alexei Milutin, TPF #548, Milutin proceedings, case #12457, archive file #19086, pp. 79–85, SBU Archive Lugansk/Voroshilovgrad, *US vs. Demjanjuk.*

Alexander Golub, TPF #619, SBU Archive Vinnitsa, archive file #28736, fols. 50–54, 60–64, *US vs. Demjanjuk.*

Konstantin Balabayev, TPF #748, FSB Archive Moscow, vol. 8, pp. 177–179, *US vs. Demjanjuk.*

Ivan Tscherkasow, TPF #774, FSB Archive Moscow, vol. 8, pp. 79–94, *US vs. Demjanjuk*, Demjanjuk trial in Munich.

Ivan Ivchenko, TPF #780, Ivchenko proceedings, archive file #21728, pp. 84, 84a, and 84b, SBU Archive Kharkov, *US vs. Demjanjuk.*

Philip Wergun, TPF #796, FSB Archive Moscow, vol. 8, pp. 170–172, *US vs. Demjanjuk*, Demjanjuk trial in Munich.

Jakob Zechmeister, TPF #838, Tsehkmistro proceedings, case #5969, archive file #21076, SBU Archive Kharkov.

Jakob Reimer, TPF #865, Zaporozhe regional archive, unknown sign., *US vs. Zajankauskas, US vs. Reimer.*

Mikhail Rozgonjajew, TPF #907, Rozgonjajew proceedings, archive file #5858, case #18828, p. 146, SBU Archive Dnepropetrovsk, *US vs. Demjanjuk.*

Samuel Pritsch, TPF #941, IPN Archive Warsaw, 903, sygn. 1, p. 4, *US vs. Demjanjuk.*

Nikita Rekalo, TPF #979, FSB Archive Moscow, vol. 8, pp. 139–143, *US vs. Hajda, US vs. Reimer.*

Viktor Bogomolow, TPF #984, Iskaradov trial, case #5734, archive file #37834, pp. 275–288, SBU Archive Donetsk, *US vs. Kwoczak, US vs. Demjanjuk, US vs. Reimer.*

Paul Garin, TPF #1075, file K-779, fond 16, opis 312 "e," delo 411, pp. 415–420, FSB Archive Moscow, *US vs. Demjanjuk, US vs. Reimer.*

Alexander Lazorenko, TPF #1126, Zuev trial, case #44, archive file #31232, vol. 11, pp. 2–8, SBU Archive Dnepropetrovsk, *US vs. Reimer, US vs. Zajankauskas.*

Yevgenij Prigoditsch, TPF #1159, FSB Archive Moscow, vol. 20, pp. 3–4, *US vs. Demjanjuk.*

Mikhail Korzhikow, TPF #1162, FSB Archive Moscow, vol. 20, pp. 19–20, *US vs. Reimer.*

Ivan Baskakow, TPF #1216, case against Baskakow, case #803, archive file #4200, FSB Archive Yaroslavl.

Wasyl Djomin, TPF #1242, FSB Archive Moscow, vol. 22, p. 148.

Nikolaj Soljanin, TPF #1277, FSB Archive Moscow, vol.?, p. 182, *US vs. Reimer.*

Vasili Schishajew, TPF #1280, IPN Archive Warsaw, 903, sygn. 1, p. 18, *US vs. Demjanjuk.*

Grigorij Yezhov/Jeschow, TPF #1351, FSB Archive Moscow, vol. 20, pp. 13–14, *US vs. Reimer.*

Stepan Mogilov, TPF #1402, FSB Archive Moscow, vol. 22, fols. 506–509, *US vs. Zajankauskas, US vs. Reimer, US vs. Kwoczak.*

Jurko Danilov, TPF #1408, Danilov trial, case #7054, archive file #10085, pp. 31–49, SBU Archive Lvov, *US vs. Demjanjuk.*

Fedor Duschenko, TPF #1450, Duschenko proceedings, archive file #27960, p. 122, SBU Archive Kharkov.

Vladimir Tcherniawskij, TPF #1504, IPN Archive Warsaw, 903, sygn. 2, p. 9, *US vs. Demjanjuk, US vs. Reimer.*

Wasyl Stoljarow, TPF #1513, Stoljarow proceedings, case #151, archive file #3537, SBU Archive Chernigov, *US vs. Demjanjuk.*

Vladimir Pronin, TPF #1515, Pronin proceedings, archive file #2667, case #449, SBU Archive Zaporozhe, *US vs. Demjanjuk.*

Vasili Rjaboschapka, TPF #1521, FSB Archive Moscow, vol. 23, pp. 199–206, *US vs. Reimer.*

Mikhail Poleszuk, TPF #1536, FSB Archive Moscow, vol. 23, pp. 127–129, *US vs. Hajda, US vs. Demjanjuk.*

Ivan Shalamov, TPF #1574, Knysch trial, case #5336, archive file #37099, SBU Archive Stalino/Donetsk, *US vs. Reimer.*

Liudas Kairys, TPF #1628, Central State Archive Vilnius, fond 1173, ap. 4, b. 51, pp. 1–4, *US vs. Hajda, US vs. Demjanjuk.*

Vladas Amanaviczius, TPF #1640, fond 1173, ap. 4, b. 55, pp. 3–5, Central State Archive Vilnius, *US vs. Hajda, US vs. Demjanjuk.*

Ivan Chapajew, TPF #1687, FSB Archive Moscow, vol. 20, pp. 50–54, *US vs. Demjanjuk,* Demjanjuk trial in Munich.

Vasili Pochwala, TPF #1716, Pochwala trial, case #10562, archive file #30326, folios 93–100, SBU Archive Lvov, *US vs. Demjanjuk.*

Paul Jurtschenko, TPF #1843, FSB Archive Moscow, vol. 13, pp. 344–346, *US vs. Demjanjuk,* Demjanjuk trial in Munich.

Valentyn Roshanskij, TPF #1870, FSB Archive Moscow, vol. 23, pp. 177–179, *US vs. Demjanjuk.*

Vasili Burljajew, TPF #1883, FSB Archive Moscow, vol. 13, pp. 51–54, *US vs. Demjanjuk.*

Ivan Knysch, TPF #1892, Knysch trial, case #5336, archive file #37099, pp. 355–363, SBU Archive Stalino/Donetsk, *US vs. Demjanjuk, US vs. Reimer,* Demjanjuk trial in Munich.

Nikolai Bondarenko, TPF #1926, Bondarenko proceedings, case #475, archive file #31138, pp. 279–283, FSB Archive Kaluga, *US vs. Demjanjuk.*

Alexei Schamordin, TPF #1961, Demjanjuk trial in Munich.

Ivan Kostinow, TPF #1989, FSB Archive Moscow, vol. 8, pp. 200-201, *US vs. Demjanjuk,* Demjanjuk trial in Munich.

Anatoli Rumjanzew, TPF #1996, FSB Archive Moscow, vol. 23, pp. 186–188, *US vs. Demjanjuk.*

Georgij Pankratov, TPF #2062, Pankratov proceedings, case #113, archive file #56911, vol. 14, p. 160, SBU Archive Lvov.

Nikolaj Timin, TPF #2116, FSB Archive Moscow, vol. 8, pp. 72–73, *US vs. Reimer.*

Vladas Zajankauskas, TPF #2122, Central State Archive Vilnius, fond 1173, ap. 4, b. 53, II. 1–5, *US vs. Zajankauskas.*

Grigorij Stoilow, TPF #2124, FSB Archive Moscow, vol. 8, pp. 67–69, *US vs. Reimer.*

Alexander Wisgunow, TPF #2133, FSB Archive Moscow, vol. 8, fols. 16–17, *US vs. Reimer.*

Ivan Tschornobaj, TPF #2147, Chornobaj trial, case #8010, archive file #13258, pp. 66–72, SBU Archive Lvov, *US vs. Zajankauskas, US vs. Reimer.*

Nikolaj Gordejew, TPF #2219, Gordejew proceedings, FSB Archive Kalinin/Tver, archive file #201, folios 82–84, *US vs. Demjanjuk,* Demjanjuk trial in Munich.

Ivan Filipow, TPF #2281, FSB Archive Moscow, vol. 23, pp. 409–413, *US vs. Hajda, US vs. Reimer.*

Nikolaj Skorokhod, TPF #2282, Skorokhod proceedings.

Rustambek Saitow, TPF #2540, FSB Archive Moscow, vol. 4, folios 89–99, *US vs. Kwoczak, US vs. Reimer.*

Myron Flunt, TPF #2804, FSB Archive Moscow, vol. 10, pp. 53–62, *US vs. Demjanjuk.*

Willi Stark, TPF #2910, FSB Archive Moscow, vol. 8, pp. 96–101, *US vs. Zajankauskas, US vs. Reimer, US vs. Kwoczak.*

Wyaczeslaw Malesza, TPF #2965, fond 3676, opis 4, delo 329, fols. 14–16, Central State Archive Kiev, *US vs. Hajda.*

Nikolaj Gutsulyak, TPF #3192, FSB Archive Moscow, vol. 2, fols. 73–78, *US vs. Reimer, US vs. Zajankauskas, US vs. Kwoczak.*

Wolodymyr Rewiuk, TPF #3246, procuracy of the Krasnoyarsk region, FSB Archive Krasnoyarsk, Rewiuk case, *US vs. Kwoczak.*

Ivan Gumenyuk/Huminiuk, TPF #3451, Gumenyuk proceedings, SBU Archive Ivano-Frankivsk.

Milko Sendezkij, TPF #3469, Sendetskij proceedings, SBU Archive Ivano-Frankivsk, investigative file #9213, archive file #11059, pp. 58–63 ob, *US vs. Kwoczak.*

Wasyl Martiszczuk, TPF #3475, Martiszczuk trial, case #5337, archive file #2585, p. 40, SBU Archive Ivano-Frankivsk, *US vs. Hajda, US vs. Kwoczak, US vs. Reimer.*

Wasyl Popiliuk, TPF #3481, Popiliuk trial, SBU Archive Stanislavov/Ivano-Frankivsk, archive file #680, p. 29, *US vs. Hajda, US vs. Kwoczak.*

Eugen Tymczuk, TPF #4659, FSB Archive Moscow, vol. 19, pp. 230–242, *US vs. Kwoczak.*

Ivan Saniuk, TPF #4819, fond 3676, opis 4, delo 330, fols. 7–12, Central State Archive Kiev, *US vs. Demjanjuk.*

Waclaw Reymann, TPF #4889, FSB Archive Moscow, vol. 4, pp. 14–18, *US vs. Kwoczak.*

DIENSTAUSWEISEN

Alexander Kirelacha, Dienstausweis #415, Kirelacha proceedings, case #18114, archive file #2041, vol. 1, pp. 16–17.

Dimitri Jarosch, Dienstausweis #749, Yarosh proceedings, case file #2028, archive file #19844, 3 vols., vol. 1, SBU Archive Poltava, *US vs. Demjanjuk.*

Ivan Juchnowskij, Dienstausweis #847, Demjanjuk trial in Israel, *US vs. Demjanjuk.*

Woldemar Wutke, Dienstausweis #862, FSB Archive Moscow, vol. 22, fol. 83, *US vs. Demjanjuk.*

Filip Babenko, Dienstausweis #869, Babenko trial, case #6937, archive file #58240, p. 43, SBU Archive Kiev, *US vs. Demjanjuk.*

Ignat Danilchenko, Dienstausweis #1016, file #6134, archive file #15437, fol. 2, SBU Archive Dnepropetrovsk, *US vs. Demjanjuk.*

Mikhail Titov, Dienstausweis #1040, Titov proceedings, case #5050, archive file #2528, SBU Archive Ivano-Frankivsk, *US vs. Demjanjuk.*

Ivan Kutschnijtschuk, Dienstausweis #1123, Zhitomir regional archive, fond 1151, opis 1, delo 1, I. 10, *US vs. Demjanjuk.*

Wasyl Kartaschew, Dienstausweis #1185, proceedings against Kartashev, investigative file #7858, archive file #10230, p. 86, SBU Archive Ternopil, *US vs. Demjanjuk.*

Ivan Wolembachow, Dienstausweis #1211, Demjanjuk trial in Israel, *US vs. Demjanjuk.*

Nurgali Kabirow, Dienstausweis #1337, FSB Archive Moscow, vol. 22, pp. 318–318v, *US vs. Demjanjuk.*

Ivan Demjanjuk, Dienstausweis #1393, Demjanjuk trial in Israel, *US vs. Demjanjuk* (probably originally located at FSB Archive Moscow or SBU Archive Vinnitsa).

Boris Odartschenko, Dienstausweis #1573, FSB Archive Moscow, vol. 24A, fol. 419, *US vs. Demjanjuk, US vs. Zajankauskas, US vs. Kwoczak.*

Vasili Slowjagin, Dienstausweis #1999, FSB Archive Moscow, vol. 20, fol. 62–62v, *US vs. Demjanjuk.*

Nikolaj Butenko, Dienstausweis #2059, SNB Archive Tashkent (Uzbekistan), case against Butenko-Sherstnev, case #208, archive file #24102, *US vs. Demjanjuk.*

Dimitri Rjasanow, Dienstausweis #2077, Ryazonov proceedings, archive file #5492, folio 47, FSB Archive Tula, *US vs. Demjanjuk.*

Ivan Zvezdun, Dienstausweis #2112, FSB Archive Moscow, vol. 22, p. 315, *US vs. Demjanjuk.*

Alexander Solontschukow, Dienstausweis #2537, FSB Archive Moscow, vol. 24A, fols. 567–571, *US vs. Demjanjuk.*

Josef Masyuk, Dienstausweis #3183, Masyuk trial, case #4501, archive file #891, SBU Archive Stanislavov/Ivano-Frankivsk, *US vs. Demjanjuk.*

Petro Popeliuk, Dienstausweis #3427, Popeliuk proceedings, FSB Archive Moscow, *US vs. Demjanjuk.*

Wasyl Chwaliuk, Dienstausweis #4188, fond 3676, opis 4, delo 331, fols. 23–23v, Central State Archive Kiev, *US vs. Demjanjuk.*

DEPLOYMENT ROSTERS

Majdanek Roster, February 15, 1943, file K-779, fond 16, inventory 312 "e," serial #410, p. 286, FSB Archive Moscow, *US vs. Kwoczak.*

Plaszow Roster, March 18, 1943, file K-779, fond 16, opis 312 "e," delo 411, pp. 53–54, FSB Archive Moscow, *US vs. Hajda.*

Plaszow Roster, August 9, 1943, file K-779, fond 16, inventory 312 "e," serial #410, p. 94, FSB Archive Moscow, *US vs. Demjanjuk.*

Sobibor Roster, March 26, 1943, Prikhodko trial, SBU Archive Lvov, *US vs. Demjanjuk.*

Sobibor Roster, March 26, 1943, file K-779, fond 16, opis 312 "e," delo 411, pp. 274–275, FSB Archive Moscow, *US vs. Demjanjuk*, Demjanjuk prosecution in Israel.

Sobibor Roster, September 16, 1943, file K-779, fond 16, opis 312 "e," delo 411, pp. 112–114, FSB Archive Moscow, *US vs. Demjanjuk*.

Sobibor Roster, March 30, 1944, Kopytyuk trial, SBU Archive Lvov, *US vs. Hajda*.

Belzec Roster, March 27, 1943, file K-779, fond 16, opis 312 "e," delo 411, pp. 280–281, FSB Archive Moscow, *US vs. Demjanjuk, US vs. Zajankauskas*.

Belzec Roster, April 12, 1943, file K-779, fond 16, opis 312 "e," delo 410, p. 242, FSB Archive Moscow, *US vs. Kwoczak, US vs. Zajankauskas*.

Auschwitz Roster, March 29, 1943, file K-779, fond 16, inventory 312 "e," serial #410, pp. 179–182, FSB Archive Moscow, *US vs. Zajankauskas*.

Auschwitz Roster, March 29, 1943, Zuev trial, case #44, archive file #31232, vol. 3, pp. 259–266, SBU Archive Dnepropetrovsk, *US vs. Hajda*.

Security Police Warsaw Roster, April 8, 1942, Provincial State Archive Warsaw, Warsaw District Governor's File, folder 61, p. 12, *US vs. Kwoczak*.

Warsaw Detachment Roster, April 17, 1943, file K-779, fond 16, opis 312 "e," delo 411, pp. 115–126, FSB Archive Moscow, *US vs. Zajankauskas*.

Warsaw Detachment Roster, April 17, 1943, Zuev trial, case #44, archive file #31232, vol. 3, pp. 276–284, SBU Archive Dnepropetrovsk, *US vs. Kwoczak*.

Warsaw Concentration Camp Roster, March 29, 1944, file K-779, fond 16, inventory 312 "e," serial #410, p. 267, FSB Archive Moscow, *US vs. Kwoczak*.

Lublin Detachment Roster, May 17, 1943, file K-779, fond 16, opis 312 "e," delo 411, pp. 257–259, FSB Archive Moscow, *US vs. Zajankauskas*.

Lublin Detachment Roster, March 21, 1944, file K-779, fond 16, inventory 312 "e," serial #410, pp. 311–312, FSB Archive Moscow, *US vs. Kwoczak*.

SS Garrison Administration HQ Lublin Roster, March 21, 1944, file K-779, fond 16, opis 312 "e," delo 410, p. 350, FSB Archive Moscow, *US vs. Kwoczak*.

SS Garrison Administration Lublin, Branch Office Zamosc Roster, November 7, 1943, file K-779, fond 16, inventory 312 "e," serial #410, p. 15, FSB Archive Moscow, *US vs. Zajankauskas*.

Poniatowa to Bialystok Detachment Roster, August 14, 1943, file K-779, fond 16, opis 312 "e," delo 411, pp. 85–87, FSB Archive Moscow, *US vs. Kwoczak*.

Lublin Detachment to Bialystok Detachment Roster, August 15 and 18, 1943, file K-779, fond 16, opis 312 "e," delo 411, pp. 85–87, 97, FSB Archive Moscow, *US vs. Kwoczak*.

Flossenburg Roster, October 1, 1943, file K-779, fond 16, opis 312 "e," delo 410, pp. 193–195, FSB Archive Moscow, *US vs. Demjanjuk, US vs. Zajankauskas*.

Poniatowa to Trawniki Roster, September 27 & October 3, 1943, file K-779, fond 16, opis 312 "e," delo 411, pp. 102–103, 105, FSB Archive Moscow, *US vs. Kwoczak, US vs. Demjanjuk*.

Poniatowa to Trawniki Roster, November 17, 1943, file K-779, fond 16, opis 312 "e," delo 411, pp. 135–137, FSB Archive Moscow, *US vs. Kwoczak*.

Sachsenhausen Roster, November 9, 1943, Schults trial, case #14, archive file #66437, SBU Archive Kiev.

Sachsenhausen Roster, November 20, 1943, file K-779, fond 16, opis 312 "e," serial #410, pp. 117–118, FSB Archive Moscow, *US vs. Demjanjuk*.

Sachsenhausen Roster, December 1, 1943, Zuev trial, case #44, archive file #31232, vol. 3, pp. 303–308, SBU Archive Dnepropetrovsk, *US vs. Hajda*.

Treblinka I Roster, April 6, 1944, file K-779, fond 16, opis 312 "e," delo 410, pp. 343–345, FSB Archive Moscow, *US vs. Hajda*.

SS "Streibel" Battalion Rosters, August 1944–
April 1945, Archive of the Ministry of
Interior, Prague, *US vs. Hajda, US vs.
Zajankauskas, US vs. Kwoczak.*

REPORTS AND MEMOS

Circular to all Trawniki detachments, from
Streibel, re: ranks and rank insignia,
October 19, 1942, IPN Archive Warsaw,
156/KdG Lublin, sygn. 77, pp. 82–83,
US vs. Hajda, US vs. Reimer.

Order signed by Streibel re: ranks and
uniforms, May 10, 1943, IPN Archive
Warsaw, RG 891, sygn. 5, fols. 149–150,
US vs. Zajankauskas.

Memo signed by Ehrlinger, Majdanek to
Trawniki, re: desertion of the guard
Kundishew, November 28, 1942, file
K-779, fond 16, inventory 312 "e," serial
#409, p. 247, FSB Archive Moscow, *US
vs. Demjanjuk*, Demjanjuk trial in Munich.

Report, commander of Majdanek (POW
Camp Lublin), signed by Ehrlinger, re:
the guards Krutij and Lasebnij leaving
the camp without permission, January
20, 1943, file I.f.5, SS-Totenkopf Battalion
correspondence, p. 17, Majdanek Museum
Archive, *US vs. Demjanjuk*, Demjanjuk
trial in Munich.

Report, commander of the SS-Totenkopf
Battalion, Majdanek (Waffen-SS POW
Camp Lublin), signed by Langleist, re:
hostile attitude of the Ukrainian guards,
January 24, 1943, Lithuanian State Archive,
Vilnius, *US vs. Demjanjuk, US vs. Reimer.*

Report, commander of the SS-Totenkopf
Battalion, Majdanek (Waffen-SS POW
Camp Lublin), signed Langleist, re:
desertion of the guard Platonow, January
24, 1943, file I.f. 5, SS-Totenkopf Battalion
correspondence, p. 37, Majdanek Museum
Archive, *US vs. Demjanjuk*, Demjanjuk
trial in Munich.

Report re: the desertion of five *Wachmänner*
from the agricultural estate "Olbiszyn,"
May 3, 1943, file K-779, fond 16, inventory
312 "e," serial #409, p. 106, FSB Archive
Moscow, *US vs. Reimer.*

Memo from deputy commandant of Sobibor
to inspector of the Aktion "Reinhard"
camps, re: desertion of two *Wachmänner*,
July 1, 1943, file K-779, fond 16, inventory
312 "e," serial #409, p. 42, FSB Archive
Moscow, *US vs. Demjanjuk.*

Report, "Desertion of Ukrainian Guards from
Auschwitz Concentration Camp," July
5, 1943, to the SS-WVHA / Office Group
D, Berlin, signed by Hoss, file K-779,
fond 16, opis 312 "e," delo 410, pp.
231–234, FSB Archive Moscow.

Report from Trawniki to SS and Police Court
VI in Krakow re: desertion of eight
Wachmänner, October 1, 1943, file K-779,
fond 16, opis 312 "e," delo 409, folio 120,
FSB Archive Moscow, *US vs.
Zajankauskas.*

Personnel status report of the Lublin
Detachment: desertion of nineteen *Wachmänner*, April 3, 1944, file K-779, fond
16, inventory 312 "e," serial #410, p. 263,
FSB Archive Moscow, *US vs. Kwoczak.*

Personnel report: missing members of the
SS-"Streibel" Battalion, January 12, 1945,
Archive of the Ministry of Interior,
Prague, *US vs. Hajda, US vs. Kwoczak.*

Investigation of three *Wachmänner* who were
captured after deserting: Kostinow,
Keliwnik, and Prigoditsch, May 1943,
FSB Archive Moscow, vol. 24, pp.
231–286, *US vs. Demjanjuk.*

Himmler order for the establishing of SS and
police bases in the East, May 15, 1942,
Globocnik SS File, Berlin Document
Center, *US vs. Reimer, US vs. Hajda.*

Secret memo, Himmler to SS-General Kruger,
February 16, 1943, re: the necessity to
destroy the Warsaw ghetto, RG 238,
document No-2494, NARA, *US vs.
Reimer, US vs. Kwoczak.*

Report, *The Jewish Residential Quarter in
Warsaw Is No More!,*" by the SS and police
commander of Warsaw District, Jurgen
Stroop (a.k.a. the "Stroop report"), May
16, 1943, RG 238, document 1061-PS,
NARA, Washington, DC, *US vs. Kwoczak,
US vs. Reimer, US vs. Zajankauskas.*

Top-secret memo from HSSPF Adriatic Coast, Globocnik, to RFSS, Himmler, January 5, 1944: concluding account of Aktion "Reinhard" assets, RG 238, document 4024-PS, NARA, Washington, DC, *US vs. Demjanjuk*, *US vs. Reimer*, *US vs. Hajda*.

Memo from HSSPF East, Koppe, to SSPFs, Sipo commanders, and Orpo commanders in Occupied Poland, re: construction of the San-Vistula Defense Line, July 17, 1944, Federal Archive Freiburg, *US vs. Hajda*.

Top-secret memo from Operations Section, Army Group "Northern Ukraine," to HQ of the 1st and 4th Panzer Armies, re: preparation for battle within the rear area, including the San-Vistula Line, July 20, 1944, Federal Archive Freiburg, *US vs. Hajda*.

SEARCH FOR WANTED PERSONS

MGB circular, "Information on Wanted Persons," August 1948, Lithuanian Special Archive, Vilnius, *US vs. Demjanjuk*.

MGB circular, "Information on Wanted Persons," December 1949, SBU Archive Kiev, *US vs. Reimer*, *US vs. Hajda*.

Appendix C: Lists of Information

INTERROGATIONS

Interrogation of Pavel Kozlov, August 24, 1944, Moskalenko trial, case #2871, archive file #11991, pp. 107–108, SBU Archive Lvov, *US vs. Hajda*.

Interrogation of Valentyn Roshanskij, August 28, 1944, Swidersky proceedings, file 8 Ks 4/70, Dusseldorf State Court, *US vs. Hajda*.

Interrogation of Pavel Kozlov, August–October 1944, Shevchenko proceedings, October 1944, SBU Archive Kiev.

Interrogation of Ivan Shevchenko, September 18, 1944, Shevchenko proceedings, case #94, archive file #13199.

Interrogation of Pavel Leleko, February 20, 1945, SMERSH, 2nd Belorussian Front; a copy is located at the 1st Deputy Procurator, Crimean region, Senior Counselor of Justice Kuptsov, January 1978, *US vs. Fedorenko*.

Interrogation of Sergej Vasilenko, March 19, 1945, FSB Archive Moscow, vol. 4, pp. 10–16.

Interrogation of Alexander Orubs, March 22, 1945, Talinn Archive, 1986/1/43705, pp. 15–25.

Interrogation of former SS-General Jakob Sporrenburg, February 1946, Lublin Court, Archive of the Main Commission for the Investigation of Nazi Crimes in Poland, Warsaw, IPN Archive Warsaw, *US vs. Reimer*, *US vs. Hajda*, *US vs. Kwoczak*.

Interrogation of Amon Goth, Krakow, August 1946, Supreme National Tribunal, Archive of the Main Commission for the Investigation of Nazi Crimes in Poland, Warsaw, IPN Warsaw, *US vs. Kwoczak*.

Interrogation of A. Tikhonov, September 1946, Tarasov proceedings, archive file #941, p. 134, FSB Archive Kazan.

Interrogation of Ivan Stepanov, September 1946, Knysch proceedings.

Interrogation of Nikolaj Olejnikov, January 1947, Olejnikov proceedings, FSB Archive Stalingrad/Volgograd, *US vs. Zajankauskas.*

Interrogation of Mikhail Korzhikow, April 1947, FSB Archive Moscow, *US vs. Reimer.*

Interrogation of Vladimir Pronin, April 1947, Pronin proceedings, case #449, archive file #2667, SBU Archive Zaporozhe.

Interrogation of Alexander Zakharov/Pruss, July 1947.

Interrogation of Josef Masyuk, August 1947, Masyuk trial, SBU Archive Stanislavov/Ivano-Frankivsk, *US vs. Reimer, US vs. Kwoczak.*

Interrogation of Vladimir Emelyanov, September 1947, Iskaradov trial, SBU Archive Stalino/Donetsk, *US vs. Demjanjuk, US vs. Zajankauskas.*

Interrogation of Ivan Zvezdun, September 1947, Zvezdun proceedings, criminal file #674, FSB Archive Novosibirsk.

Interrogation of Peter Karnashnikov, September 1947, Lithuanian Special Archive, Vilnius, fond K-1, ap. BB, B. 35639/3, 11. 16-17v.

Interrogation of Nikolaj Skorokhod, November 1947, Skorokhod proceedings, case #6075, archive file #11042, SBU Archive Lvov.

Interrogation of Alexander Moskalenko, November 1947, Moskalenko trial, case #2871, archive file #11991, SBU Archive Lvov, *US vs. Hajda.*

Interrogation of Piotr Browzew, November 1947.

N. Smirnov, November 1947, Lithuanian State Archive, 1986/1/l, 1607.

Interrogation of Ivan Bogdanov, December 1947, FSB Archive Moscow, vol. 13, pp. 286–301.

Interrogation of Yakov Sagach, December 1947, Simferopol, Sagach proceedings, case #11522, archive file #4546, SBU Archive Crimea, *US vs. Zajankauskas.*

Interrogation of Edward Chrupowitsch, December 1947, Chlopeckyj trial, case #6105, archive file #617, SBU Archive Lvov, *US vs. Reimer.*

Interrogation of Anton Solonina, December 1947, Solonina proceedings, case #5957, archive file #58322, SBU Archive Kiev.

Interrogation of Fedor Tartynskij, 1948, Stalino/Donetsk, Iskaradov trial, case #5734, archive file #37834, SBU Archive Donetsk, and archive file #58228 on Yurij Andreyev, SBU Archive Kiev, *US vs. Demjanjuk.*

Interrogation of Ivan Knysch, January 1948, Iskaradov proceedings, pp. 229–234, SBU Archive Donetsk.

Interrogation of Vasili Chlopeckyj, January 1948, Lvov, Chlopeckyj trial, case #6105, archive file #11043, SBU Archive Lvov, *US vs. Reimer.*

Interrogation of Nikolaj Chernyshev, January 1948, Stalino/Donetsk, Knysch trial, case #5336, archive file #37099, SBU Archive Donetsk, *US vs. Reimer.*

Interrogation of Viktor Klimenko, January 1948, Knysch trial, case #5336, archive file #37099, SBU Archive Donetsk.

Interrogation of Andrej Sergienko, February 1948, Knysch trial, case #5336, archive file #37099, pp. 198–206, SBU Archive Donetsk.

Interrogation of Ivan Kondratenko, February 1948, Kondratenko trial, SBU Archive Kiev, *US vs. Hajda.*

Interrogation of Vasili Shkarpovich, April 1948, Shkarpovich trial, archive file #32750, SBU Archive Ivano-Frankivsk, *US vs. Kwoczak.*

Interrogation of Ivan Lukanyuk, April 1948, Lukanyuk trial, SBU Archive Stanislavov/Ivano-Frankivsk, *US vs. Kwoczak.*

Interrogation of Petr Didukh, April 1948, Gumenyuk trial, SBU Archive Stanislavov/Ivano-Frankivsk, *US vs. Kwoczak.*

Interrogation of Alexander Yeger, April 1948, Yeger proceedings, archive file #55402.

Interrogation of Jakob Zechmeister, May 1948, Tsehkmistro proceedings, SBU Archive Kharkov.

Interrogation of Vladimir Terletskij, May 1948, Terletskij proceedings, SBU Archive Ivano-Frankivsk.

Interrogation of Alexander Titievskij, May 1948, Iskaradov trial, case #5734, archive file #37834, pp. 246–247, SBU Archive Donetsk, *US vs. Reimer.*

Interrogation of P. Parkhomenko, June 1948, Butenko-Sherstnev proceedings, pp. 97–99, SNB Archive Tashkent, copy in USHMM Archive, RG 75.001, microfiche 11–14.

Interrogation of Nikolaj Akhtimijchuk, September 1948, Napkhanko proceedings, case #12804, archive file #1958, SBU Archive Kiev; Shyndekevskij trial, case #6791, archive file #6392, SBU Archive Ivano-Frankivsk; *US vs. Zajankauskas, US vs. Kwoczak.*

Interrogation of Mikhail Rozgonjajew, September 1948, Dnepropetrovsk, Rozgonjajew proceedings, case #5828, archive file #1877, SBU Archive Dnepropetrovsk.

Interrogation of Filip Babenko, Rzhitsev, November 1948, Babenko trial, case #6937, archive file #58240, pp. 12–29, SBU Archive Kiev, *US vs. Reimer.*

Interrogation of Sabit Shirgaliev, December 1948, case #22560, archive file #185, pp. 14–30, SNB Archive Tashkent, copy in USHMM Archive, RG 75.001, microfiche 5–11.

Interrogation of Peter Koval, December 1948, Koval trial, case #8198, archive file #7338, SBU Archive Zaporozhe, *US vs. Hajda.*

Interrogation of Nikolaj Belous, 1949, Lvov, Belous trial, case #2391, archive file #27090, SBU Archive Lvov, *US vs. Hajda.*

Interrogation of Vasili Grigorev, 1949, Estonian National Archive, *US vs. Zajankauskas.*

Interrogation of Peter Madamov, 1949, Madamov proceedings, archive file #10012, SBU Archive Volhynia, *US vs. Zajankauskas.*

Interrogation of Ignat Danilchenko, March 1949, Danilchenko proceedings, case #6134, archive file #15457, pp. 47–68, SBU Archive Dnepropetrovsk, *US vs. Demjanjuk.*

Interrogation of Dimitri Yarosch, April 1949, Rostov-on-the-Don, Yarosch proceedings, case #2028, archive file #19844, SBU Archive Poltava, *US vs. Demjanjuk.*

Interrogation of Ivan Lysij, April 1949, Lysij trial, case #7070, archive file #504, pp. 29–37, FSB Archive Sverdlovsk/Yekaterinburg, *US vs. Reimer.*

Interrogation of Nikolaj Pavli, November 1949, Stalino/Donetsk, Goncharov proceedings, archive file #56434, vol. 2, pp. 118–121.

Interrogation of Andrei Kuchma, February 1950, Kuchma trial, case #7707, archive file #59446, SBU Archive Kiev, *US vs. Reimer.*

Interrogation of Anton Streltsov, March 1950, Kharkov; a copy is with the 1st deputy procurator, Crimean region, Senior Counselor of Justice Kuptsov, February 1976, *US vs. Fedorenko.*

Interrogation of Ivan Tkachuk, March 1950, Tkachuk proceedings, archive file #12074; Interrogation of Ivan Tkachuk, July 1954, Tkachuk proceedings.

Interrogation of Dimitri Korotkikh, April 1950, Voroshilovgrad/Lugansk.

Interrogation of Georgij Skydan, May 1950, Baranovichi, *Demjanjuk vs. Petrovsky, US vs. Reimer.*

Interrogation of Vladimir Lomov, May 1950.

Interrogation of Ivan Telman, September 1950, Novosibirsk, Telman trial, archive file #15382, FSB Archive Novosibirsk, *US vs. Reimer.*

Interrogation of Ivan Churin, September 1950, Churin proceedings, case #892, archive file #PU-6375, pp. 67–68, FSB Archive Vladivostok.

Interrogation of Vasili Bronov, October 1950, Blagoveshchensk, Bronov trial, case #217556, archive file #34, FSB Archive Omsk, *US vs. Zajankauskas.*

Interrogation of Vasili Pankov, October 1950, Stalino/Donetsk.

Interrogations of Nikolai Shalayev, Voronezh, November–December 1950, Shalayev trial, archive file #17214, fols. 15–34, *Demjanjuk vs. Petrovsky, US vs. Reimer.*

Interrogation of Stefan Kopytyuk, April 1951, Kopytyuk proceedings, case #4266, archive file #29805, pp. 34–41, SBU Archive Lvov.

Interrogation of Fedor Gorun, May 1951, Gorun trial, case #6035, archive file #4277, SBU Archive Kiev.

Interrogation of Ivan Shvidkij, July 1951, Shvidkij trial, case #7168, archive file #56433, pp. 16–20, SBU Archive Donetsk, *US vs. Reimer*.

Interrogation of Romualdas Valekas, October 1951, Lithuanian State Archive, K-1/58/20007/3.

Interrogation of Anastasij Mawrodij, 1952, Mawrodij proceedings, SBU Archive Nikolayev.

Interrogation of Alexei Tronko, January 1952, Tronko proceedings, case #10685, archive file #30804, SBU Archive Lvov.

Interrogation of Grigorij Garus/Marusenko, 1952, State Attorney's Office Dusseldorf, Swidersky proceedings, *US vs. Hajda, US vs. Kwoczak*.

Interrogation of V. Yalynchuk, July 1952, Yeger proceedings, archive file #55402, SBU Archive Stalino/Donetsk.

Interrogation of Grigorij Napkhanko, 1952, Napkhanko proceedings, case #12804, archive file #1958, SBU Archive Kiev.

Interrogation of Alfonsas Slaitas, January 1953, Lithuanian State Archive, K-1/58/ 20007/3.

Interrogation of Alexei Zhukov, May 1953.

Interrogation of Piotr Browzew, November 1954.

Interrogation of Vladimir Belinskij, November 1954.

Interrogation of Alexander Zakharov, November and December 1954.

Interrogation of Fedor Tikhonovsky, January 1955, Zuev trial, case #44, archive file #31232, vol. 6, pp. 95–99, SBU Archive Dnepropetrovsk, *US vs. Reimer*.

Interrogation of Georg Michalsen, 1961, Streibel proceedings, State Prosecutor's Office Hamburg, *US vs. Kwoczak*.

Interrogation of Sergei Vasilenko, March 19, 1945, Schults trial, vol. 14, pp. 18–20, case #14, archive file #66437, SBU Archive Kiev.

Interrogation of Petro Goncharov, 1951, Schults trial, vol. 33, pp. 206–215, case #14, archive file #66437, SBU Archive Kiev.

Interrogation of Emanuel Schults/Vertogradov, February 1961, Schults trial, case #14, archive file #66437, vol. 1, SBU Archive Kiev.

Interrogation of Ivan Juchnowskij, March 1961, Schults proceedings, case #14, archival file #66437, vol. 31, pp. 1–2, SBU Archive Kiev.

Interrogation of Jakob Engelhardt, March 1961, Schults proceedings, case #14, archive file #66437, vol. 31, pp. 26–30, SBU Archive Kiev.

Interrogation of Prokofij Rjabtsev, April 1961, Schults trial, case #14, archive file #66437, vol. 32, pp. 1–16, SBU Archive Kiev, *Demjanjuk vs. Petrovsky, US vs. Reimer*.

Interrogation of Dimitri Borodin, April 1961, Schults trial, Case #14, Archive file #66437, Vol. 3, pp. 44–45, SBU Archive Kiev.

Interrogation of Ivan Kurinnyj, May 1961, Schults Trial, case #14, archive file #66437, vol. 2, pp. 139–141, SBU Archive Kiev.

Interrogation of Alexei Govorov, September 1961, Schults trial, case #14, archive file #66437, vol. 14 or 27, pp. 36–48, SBU Archive Kiev, *US vs. Reimer*.

Interrogation of Ivan Terekhov, Schults trial, case #14, archive file #66437, vol. 18, pp. 23–31, SBU Archive Kiev.

Interrogation of Filip Levchishin, 1951, Schults trial, case #14, archive file #66437, vol. 19, pp. 17–33, SBU Archive Kiev.

Interrogation of Nikolaj Skakodub, 1961, Schults trial, case #14, archive file #66437, vol. 31, pp. 283–301, SBU Archive Kiev.

Interrogation of Ivan Tkachuk, 1961, Schults trial, case #14, archive file #66437, vol. 31, pp. 259–282, SBU Archive Kiev.

Interrogation of Fedor Korovnichenko, 1961, Schults trial, case #14, archive file #66437, vol. 31, pp. 140–152, SBU Archive Kiev.

Questioning of Alexander Pechersky, 1961, Schults trial, case #14, archive file #66437, vol. 31, pp. 120–139, SBU Archive Kiev.

Interrogation of Ivan Safonov, 1961, Schults trial, case #14, archive file #66437, vol. 32, pp. 17–21, SBU Archive Kiev.

Interrogation of Ananij Kuzminskij, March 7, 1961, Vinnitsa, Schults trial, case #14, archive file #66437, SBU Archive Kiev.

Interrogation of Evdokim Parfinyuk, October 1961, Schults trial, case #14, archive file #66437, vol. 24, pp. 145–151, SBU Archive Kiev.

Interrogation of Heinrich Gley, November 1961, Michalsen proceedings, State Prosecutor's Office, Hamburg, *US vs. Kwoczak.*

Interrogation of Hermann Reese, 1962, Streibel proceedings, vol. 17, pp. 3289–3291.

Interrogation of Kurt Reinberger, 1962, Streibel proceedings, vol. 19, p. 3630.

Interrogation of Karl Schluch, April 1962, Kurt Bolender proceedings, Zentrale Stelle, Ludwigsburg, *US vs. Kwoczak.*

Interrogation of Georg Wippern, April 1962, Lothar Hoffmann proceedings et al., State Archive, Wiesbaden, *US vs. Reimer.*

Interrogation of Gustav Hanelt, April 1963, State Archive, Detmold, *US vs. Kwoczak.*

Interrogation of Peter Klemeshov, July 1951, Matvienko trial, case #4, archive file #100366, vol. 4, pp. 104–111, FSB Archive Krasnodar.

Interrogation of Nikolai Leontev, June and August 1964, Matvienko trial, case #4, archive file #100366, vol. 10, pp. 49–58 and 72–75, FSB Archive Krasnodar, *US vs. Reimer.*

Interrogation of Ivan Voloshin, July 29, 1964, Dnepropetrovsk, Matvienko trial, case #4, archive file #100366.

Interrogation of Piotr Browzew, August 1964, Moscow, Zuev or Matvienko trial.

Interrogation of Alexander Semenov, September 1964, Matvienko trial, case #4, archive file #100366, vol. 10, pp. 169–174, FSB Archive Krasnodar.

Interrogation of Mikhail Korzhikow, September 1964, Matvienko trial, case #4, archive file #100366, vol. 10, pp. 118–128, FSB Archive Krasnodar, *US vs. Reimer.*

Interrogation of Ivan Kozlovskij, September 29, 1964, Matvienko trial, case #4, archive file #100366, vol. 9, pp. 22–29, FSB Archive Krasnodar.

Interrogation of Nikolaj Gordejew, December 1964, Matvienko trial, case #4, archive file #100366, vol. 7, pp. 199–205.

Interrogation of Vasili Shuller, December 1964, Krasnodar, Zuev or Matvienko trial.

Interrogation of Grigorij Kniga, December 1964, Krasnodar, Zuev trial, case #44, archive file #31232, vol. 1, pp. 133–138, SBU Archive Dnepropetrovsk.

Interrogation of Fedor Tikhonovskij, December 1964, Zuev trial, case #44, archive file #31232, vol. 6, pp. 104–110, SBU Archive Dnepropetrovsk.

Interrogation of Wasyl Gulyj, 1965, Zuev trial, case #44, archive file #31232, vol. 3, pp. 12–18, SBU Archive Dnepropetrovsk.

Interrogation of Andrei Kuchma, 1965, Zuev trial, case #44, archive file #31232, vol. 2, p. 217, SBU Archive Dnepropetrovsk.

Interrogation of Luka Bardachenko, January 1965, Zuev trial, case #44, archive file #31232, vol. 6, pp. 120–125, SBU Archive Dnepropetrovsk.

Interrogation of Alexander Zakharov/Pruss, January 9, 1965, Krasnodar, Zuev trial, case #44, archive file #31232, vol. 1, pp. 82–85, SBU Archive Dnepropetrovsk.

Interrogation of Boris Babin, January 1965, Matvienko trial, case #4, archive file #100366, vol. 13, pp. 83–94, FSB Archive Krasnodar.

Interrogation of Ivan Tarasov, February 1965, Matvienko trial, case #4, archive file #100366, vol. 13, pp. 83–94, FSB Archive Krasnodar.

Interrogation of Zaki Tuktarov, February 1965, Matvienko trial, case #4, archive file #100366, vol. 13, pp. 95–97, FSB Archive Krasnodar, *US vs. Demjanjuk.*

Interrogation of Prokofij Rjabtsev, February 1965, Matvienko trial, case #4, archive file #100366, vol. 13, pp. 21–24, FSB Archive Krasnodar, *Demjanjuk vs. Petrovsky, US vs. Reimer.*

Interrogation of Mikhail Laptev, February 1965, Matvienko trial, case #4, archive file #100366, vol. 13, pp. 115–123, FSB Archive Krasnodar, *US vs. Zajankauskas.*

Interrogation of Vasili Podenok, March 1965, Krasnodar, Matvienko trial, case #4, archive file #100366, vol. 5, pp. 145–146, FSB Archive Krasnodar.

Interrogation of Ivan Tkachuk, March 1965, Krasnodar, Matvienko trial, case #4, archive file #100366, *Demjanjuk vs. Petrovsky, US vs. Reimer*.

Interrogation of Nikolaj Butenko-Sherstnev, March 1965, Pankratov proceedings, vol. 8, pp. 114–117.

Statement of Alexander Byczkow, June 21, 1965, proceedings against Josef Oberhauser, State Archive Munich, StanW 33033/32.

Statement of Anastasij Mawrodij, June 27, 1965, Zuev trial, case #44, archive file #31232, SBU Archive Dnepropetrovsk.

Interrogation of Vasili Shuller, July 9, 1965, Zuev trial, case #44, archive file #31232, vol. 1, pp. 117–127, SBU Archive Dnepropetrovsk.

Statement of Alexander Semigodow, July 7, 1965, Zuev trial, case #44, archive file #31232, vol. 1, pp. 117–127, SBU Archive Dnepropetrovsk.

Statement of Mitrofan Klotz, August 9, 1965, Zuev trial, case #44, archive file #31232, vol. 1, pp. 117–127, SBU Archive Dnepropetrovsk.

Statement of Vasili Orlowskij, August 23, 1965, Zuev trial, case #44, archive file #31232, vol. 1, pp. 117–127, SBU Archive Dnepropetrovsk.

Statement of Dimitri Pundik, September 23, 1965, Zuev trial, case #44, archive file #31232, vol. 1, pp. 117–127, SBU Archive Dnepropetrovsk.

Statement of Kiril Prochorenko, September 27, 1965, Zuev trial, case #44, archive file #31232, vol. 1, pp. 117–127, SBU Archive Dnepropetrovsk.

Statement of Grigorij Nesmejan, September 28, 1965, Zuev trial, case #44, archive file #31232, vol. 1, pp. 117–127, SBU Archive Dnepropetrovsk.

Interrogation of Taras Olejnik, September 29, 1965, Zuev trial, case #44, archive file #31232, vol. 1, pp. 54–58.

Interrogation of Petro Popeliuk, February 1966, Zuev trial, case #44, archive file #31232, vol. 5, pp. 75–77, SBU Archive Dnepropetrovsk.

Statement of Vladimir Gadsicki, February 5, 1966, Zuev trial, case #44, archive file #31232, vol. 5, pp. 75–77, SBU Archive Dnepropetrovsk.

Statement of Piotr Guzulak, February 5, 1966, Zuev trial, case #44, archive file #31232, vol. 5, pp. 75–77, SBU Archive Dnepropetrovsk.

Statement of Mikhael Greniuk, February 7, 1966, Zuev trial, case #44, archive file #31232, vol. 5, pp. 75–77, SBU Archive Dnepropetrovsk.

Interrogation of Nikolaj Gordejew, April 1966, Pankratov proceedings, vol. 8, pp. 207–211, SBU Archive Lvov.

Interrogation of Fedor Gorun, May 1966, Zuev trial, case #44, archive file #31232, vol. 14, pp. 25–26, SBU Archive Dnepropetrovsk.

Statement of Taras Olejnik, July 23, 1966, Zuev trial, case #44, archive file #31232, vol. 14, pp. 25–26, SBU Archive Dnepropetrovsk.

Statement of Grigorij Linkin, July 27, 1966, Zuev trial, case #44, archive file #31232, vol. 14, pp. 25–26, SBU Archive Dnepropetrovsk.

Interrogation of Akim Zuev, August 1966, Zuev trial, case #44, archive file #31232, vol. 12, pp. 67–70, SBU Archive Dnepropetrovsk.

Statement of Piotr Browzew, August 2, 1966, Zuev trial, case #44, archive file #31232, vol. 12, pp. 67–70, SBU Archive Dnepropetrovsk.

Statement of Stepan Dejnek, December 18, 1966.

Interrogation of Ivan Mistyuk, January 1950, Litvinenko trial, vol. 9, pp. 114–122, SBU Archive Lvov.

Interrogation of Yegor Lobyntsev, April 1966, Litvinenko trial, vol. 10, pp. 80–87, SBU Archive Lvov.

Interrogation of Vyaczeslaw Dmitriev, October 1966, Litvinenko trial, vol. 9, pp. 235–239, SBU Archive Lvov.

Interrogation of Emil Gutarz, November 1949, Kurt Franz proceedings, BA-ZSt, 208 AR-Z 23/59, vol. 21, pp. 5649–5650.

Examination of archive file K-779, signed by Lt. Boechko, July 1966, Prikhodko trial, case #113, archive file #56911, vol. 21, pp. 42–47, SBU Archive Lvov, *US vs. Demjanjuk.*

Interrogation of Yakov Klimenko, May 1968, Litvinenko trial, case #158, archive file #57252, vol. 7, pp. 269–272, SBU Archive Lvov, *US vs. Reimer, US vs. Zajankauskas.*

Interrogation of Vasili Litvinenko, October 1968, Litvinenko trial, case #158, archive file #57252, vol. 1, SBU Archive Lvov.

Interrogation of Georgij Pankratov, November 1968, Litvinenko trial, case #158, archive file #57252, vol. 2, pp. 71–74.

Interrogation of Alexander Fedchenko, December 1968, Litvinenko trial, case #158, archive #57252, vol. 2, pp. 166–167, SBU Archive Lvov, *US vs. Demjanjuk.*

Interrogation of Franz Swidersky, Dusseldorf, January 1969, Kurt Franz proceedings, Zentrale Stelle, Ludwigsburg, *US vs. Hajda.*

Interrogation of Alexander Fedchenko, February 1969, Litvinenko trial, case #158, archive file #57252, vol. 2, pp. 184–187, SBU Archive Lvov, *US vs. Reimer, US vs. Zajanckauskas.*

Interrogation of Hermann Reese, March 1969, Georg Michalsen proceedings, Zentrale Stelle Ludwigsburg; State Archive Hamburg, collected statements concerning Lublin District, *US vs. Reimer.*

Interrogation of Ivan Zvezdun, Irkutsk, April 1969, Swidersky proceedings, State Court Dusseldorf, *US vs. Hajda.*

Interrogation of Alexei Kolgushkin, Yaroslavl, April 1969, Swidersky proceedings, State Court Dusseldorf, *US vs. Hajda.*

Interrogation of Alexander Moskalenko, Belgorod region, 1969, Swidersky proceedings, State Court Dusseldorf, *US vs. Hajda.*

Interrogation of Ivan Zvezdun, Moscow, September 1971, Swidersky proceedings, State Court Dusseldorf, *US vs. Hajda.*

Interrogation of Semen Kharkovskij, 1973, Kharkov, Streibel proceedings, Zentrale Stelle Ludwigsburg, *US vs. Reimer, US vs. Hajda.*

Interrogation of Prokofij Businnij, 1974, Kiev, Streibel proceedings, State Prosecutor's Office Hamburg, *US vs. Reimer.*

Interrogation of Piotr Browzew, Leningrad / St. Petersburg, August 1975, Streibel proceedings, Zentrale Stelle Ludwigsburg, *US vs. Reimer.*

Interrogation of Nikolaj Malagon, Zaporozhe, March 1978, *US vs. Fedorenko, US vs. Demjanjuk.*

Interrogation of Ignat Danilchenko, Tyumen, November 1979, *US vs. Demjanjuk, Israel vs. Demjanjuk.*

Interrogation of Ivan Zvezdun, Irkutsk, November 1980, with photo spread for identification purposes, *US vs. Kairys, US vs. Hajda.*

Statement of Rudolf Reiss, December 1987, Hamburg, *Israel vs. Demjanjuk, US vs. Reimer, US vs. Kwoczak.*

TRIAL RECORDS

Case against Ivan Shevchenko, Mikhail Shkarupa-Poleshuk, Pavel Kozlov, Grigorij Sirota, Valentin Rozhansky, and Nikita Rekalo, October 1944, 65th Army, 1st Belorussian Front, case #94, archive file #13199, SBU Archive Cherkassy.

Record of court session, case against Alexander Dukhno, Mikhail Korzhikow, and Ivan Voloshin, Ural Military District, June 5, 1947.

Case against Alexander Zakharov, case #365, Moscow region, August 19, 1947.

Record of court session, case against Piotr Browzew, Leningrad region, December 20, 1947.

Record of trial appearance, Ivan Kondratenko, March 22, 1948, SBU Archive Kiev, *US vs. Hajda, US vs. Kwoczak, US vs. Zajankauskas, US vs. Reimer.*

Record of court appearance, Nikolaj Gutsulyak, June 25, 1948, SBU Archive Stanislavov/Ivano-Frankivsk, *US vs. Kwoczak*.

Record of trial appearance, Vladimir Terletskij, June 29, 1948, SBU Archive Stanislavov/Ivano-Frankivsk, *US vs. Kwoczak*.

Record of court session, trial of Filip Babenko, Kiev, December 24, 1948, SBU Archive Kiev, *US vs. Reimer*.

Trial proceedings against Ignat Danilchenko, March 31, 1949, case #15457, SBU Archive Dnepropetrovsk (or Kiev) (interrogation took place in Dnepropetrovsk; trial took place in Kiev).

Trial against Fedor Ryabeka, Mikhail Andreyenko, and Terentij Gordijenko, November 2, 1949, case #6491, archive file #66437, SBU Archive Kiev.

Case against Vladimir Belinskij, March 31, 1950.

Trial record of Georgij Skydan, Baranovichi, May 1950, *Demjanjuk vs. Petrovsky*, *US vs. Reimer*.

Record of court session, case against Vladimir Lomov and Grigorij Chernikov, September 19, 1950.

Trial record of Nikolai Shalayev, Voronezh, December 20, 1951, archival file #17214, *Demjanjuk vs. Petrovsky*, *US vs. Reimer*.

Record of court session, trial of Ivan Shvidkij, January 1952, SBU Archive Stalino/Donetsk, *US vs. Reimer*.

Case against Alexei Zhukov, 1953.

Case against Emanual Schultz, Mikhail Gorbachev, Sergej Vasilenko, Samuel Pritsch, Alexei Govorov, Ivan Terekhov, Yakov Karplyuk, Filip Levchishin, Ivan Kurinnij, Dimitri Borodin, Evdokim Parfinyuk, and Fedor Ryabeka, February–November 1961, Kiev, case #14, archive file #66437, SBU Archive Kiev.

Case against Akim Zuev, Taras Olejnik, Alexei Lazorenko, Nikita Mamchur, and Grigorij Linkin, April–December 1966, Dnepropetrovsk, case #44, archive file #31232, SBU Archive Dnepropetrovsk.

Judgment of State Court Dusseldorf against Franz Swidersky, October 1971, file 8

Ks 4/70, State Prosecutor's Office, Dusseldorf, *US vs. Hajda*, *US vs. Reimer*.

Judgment against Lothar Hoffmann et al., March 1973, State Archive Wiesbaden, *US vs. Reimer*.

Streibel judgment, 1976, Hamburg.

THESE FORMER TRAWNIKI GUARDS WERE INTERROGATED BY THESE SOVIET INVESTIGATORS

Pavel Kozlov by deputy section chief, SMERSH, 65th Army, 1st Belorussian Front, Guards Captain Postovalov, August 1944; investigator, Lieutenant Kaluzhsky, SMERSH, 65th Army, 1st Belorussian Front, September 7, 1944; Operations Section, MGB, 1947.

Valentin Roshanskij by senior investigator, SMERSH, 65th Army, 1st Belorussian Front, Captain Tyukhtij, and deputy military procurator of the 65th Army, 1st Belorussian Front, Guards Major of Justice, Mazor, August 1944.

Ivan Shevchenko by investigator, SMERSH, 65th Army, 1st Belorussian Front, Lieutenant Kaluzhsky, September 18, 1944; a copy is stored with the 1st deputy procurator, Crimean region, Senior Counselor of Justice Kuptsov, April 1978.

Pavel Leleko by investigator, SMERSH, 2nd Belorussian Front, Lieutenant Eppel, February 20, 1945; a copy is stored with the 1st deputy procurator, Crimean region, Senior Counselor of Justice Kuptsov, January 1978.

Petro Kuschnir by case officer, Investigations Department, MGB, Lieutenant Vidryakov, Stanislavov/Ivano-Frankivsk region, 1946.

Nikolaj Olejnikov by section chief, Investigations Department, MGB, Major Stoyakin, 1947; Ministry of Foreign Affairs, Consular Department, Uzbekistan, 2001.

Alexander Volobuev/Kuris by deputy section chief, MGB, Lutsk, Volyn region, Captain Andreyev, 1947.

Mikhail Korzhikow by senior investigator, Investigations Department, MGB, Sverdlovsk/Yekaterinburg region, Captain [name deleted], 1947; senior case officer, MGB, Lieutenant Colonel [name deleted].

Vladimir Pronin by senior case officer, MGB, Zaporozhe region, Captain Shakovtsov, 1947; procurator, Department of Liaison and Extradition, International Legal Directorate; General Procuracy, Ukraine.

Wasyl Popiliuk by section chief, MGB, Guards Major Stromyadnikov, Stanislavov/ Ivano-Frankivsk region, 1947.

Josef Masyuk by department chief, MGB, Guards Major Stromyadnikov, Stanislavov/ Ivano-Frankivsk region, 1947.

Vladimir Emelyanov by investigator, MGB, Lieutenant Zaschlev, 1947; deputy department chief, Investigations Department, MGB, Sverdlovsk/ Yekaterinburg region, Guards Captain Klejmenov.

Alexander Zakharov/Pruss by senior investigator, MGB, Captain Dmitriyev, July 1947.

Ivan Zvezdun by deputy case officer, MGB, Lieutenant Shuvalov, 1947; chief, SBU Archive, Lvov region (Belous trial).

Ivan Grigorchuk by case officer, Investigations Section, MGB, Kolomya, Lieutenant Katayev, 1947.

Peter Karnashnikov/Karnaschenkas by deputy department chief, Investigation Section, MGB, Lithuania, Guards Lieutenant Colonel Belyakov, 1947.

Alexander Moskalenko by senior investigator of the OKR (Counterintelligence Department) of the MGB, 14th Air Army, Guards Captain Isayev, 1947.

Edward Chrupowitsch by senior operations officer, MGB, Lvov region, Lieutenant Proshin, 1947.

Vasili Chlopeckyj by chief of the Investigations Department, MGB, Lvov region, Captain Ustimenko, 1948.

Nikolaj Chernyshev by section chief, MGB, Stalino/Donetsk region, Major Stejmatskin, 1948.

Ivan Knysch by deputy department chief, Investigations Department, MGB, Stalino/ Donetsk region, Guards Captain Klejmenov, 1948 (Iskaradov trial).

Ivan Lukanyuk by department chief, MGB, Stanislavov/Ivano-Frankivsk region, Guards Major Stromyatnikov, 1948.

Petr Didukh by section chief, MGB, Stanislavov/ Ivano-Frankivsk region, Guards Major Stromyatnikov, 1948 (Gumenyuk trial).

Nikolaj Gutsulyak by case officer, MGB, Kolomya, Lieutenant Katayev, 1948.

Vladimir Terletskij by section chief, MGB, Stanislavov/Ivano-Frankivsk region, Guards Major Stromyatnikov, 1948; Procuracy, Ivano-Frankivsk region; General Procuracy, Ukraine.

Nikolaj Nepejvoda by assistant case officer, MGB, Stanislavov/Ivano-Frankivsk region, Lieutenant Shmakov, 1948.

Fedor Tartynskij by deputy department chief, MGB, Stalino/Donetsk region, Colonel Blednykh, 1948 (Iskaradov trial); deputy chief, Investigations Department, MGB, Stalino/Donetsk region, Guards Captain Klejmenov.

Ivan Kondratenko by investigator, MGB, Kiev region, Lieutenant Voloshin; senior investigator, Investigations Department, MGB, Lieutenant Neronov; and deputy military procurator, MVD, Ukraine, Lieutenant Colonel of Justice Kuznetsov, 1948; chief, SBU Archive, Ukraine, A. Pshennikov.

Filip Babenko by case officer, MGB, Kiev region, Lieutenant Krivonos, 1948.

Mikhail Rozgonjajew by deputy chief, Investigations Department, MGB (or Ministry of Defense), Major Nichayev; investigator, Investigations Department, MGB (or Ministry of Defense), Lieutenant Rybalka; and senior investigator, Investigations Department, MGB (or Ministry of Defense), Lieutenant Chernov, Dnepropetrovsk region, 1948; Office of the Attorney General of the USSR, A. Vladimirov; original protocol is located in archive criminal file #5828 against M. Rozgonjajew.

Alexander Yeger by investigator, Investigations Department, MGB, Molotov/Perm region, Lieutenant Popov, 1948; a copy is held with the 1st deputy procurator, Crimean region, Senior Counselor of Justice Kuptsov, February 1978.

Peter Koval by senior operations officer, MGB, Zaporozhe region, Major Bovan, 1948.

Nikolaj Akhtimijchuk by the assistant military procurator of the MVD, western Siberia, Lieutenant Colonel of Justice Ankudimov, and senior investigator, Investigations Department, MGB, Captain Chertishchev, Krasnoyarsk region, 1948.

Dimitri Yarosch by senior investigator, OKR (Counterintelligence Department) of the MGB, Northern Caucasus Military District, Rostov-on-the-Don, Captain Yas, 1949.

Vasili Grigorev by senior investigator, Investigations Department, MGB, Latvia, Lieutenant Andreyanov, 1949.

Ignat Danilchenko by the assistant military procurator, MVD, Ukraine, Major of Justice Pidotov, and senior investigator, Investigations Department, MGB (or Ministry of Defense), Dnepropetrovsk region, Lieutenant Chernov, 1949; attorney general of the USSR; Office of the Attorney General of the USSR, A. Vladimirov; original protocol is located in archive criminal file #15457 against Danilchenko, pp. 47–68. The prosecutor in the case was Natalia Kolesnikova.

Nikolaj Pavli by deputy department chief, Investigations Department, MGB, Stalino/Donetsk region, Major Klajmenov, 1949; attorney general of the USSR; Office of the Attorney General of the USSR, A. Vladimirov; original protocol is located in archive criminal file #56434, vol. 2, pp. 118–121, charging Petro Goncharov, Nikolaj Sherbak, et al.

Ivan Lysij by investigator, Investigations Department, MGB, Sverdlovsk/Yekaterinburg region, Lieutenant Babin, 1949.

Nikolaj Belous by section chief, MGB, Lvov, Major Vasilev, 1949.

Peter Madamov by case officer, MGB, Lieutenant Bayev, 1949.

Andrei Kuchma by case officer, MGB, Kiev region, Lieutenant Krivonos, 1950.

Dimitri Korotkikh by senior investigator, Investigations Department, MGB, Voroshilovgrad/Lugansk region, Lieutenant Yevstigneyev, 1950; a copy is held with the 1st deputy procurator, Crimean region, Senior Counselor of Justice Kuptsov, March 1978.

Anton Streltsov by senior investigator, Investigations Department, MGB, Kharkov region, Lieutenant Novichonok, 1950; a copy is held with the 1st deputy procurator, Crimean region, Senior Counselor of Justice Kuptsov, February 1976.

Vasili Pankov by deputy chief, Investigations Department, MGB (or Ministry of Defense), Stalino/Donetsk region, Captain Klajmanov, 1950.

Ivan Tellman by deputy department chief, Investigations Department, MGB, Novosibirsk region, Major Evstigneyev, 1950.

Vasili Bronov by Investigations Department, MGB, Blagoveshchensk, Amur region, Lieutenant Kuzmin, 1950.

Nikolai Shalayev by investigator, Investigations Department, MGB, Voronezh region, Captain Gorokhov, December 1950; a copy is held by the senior investigator, Investigations Department, KGB, Crimean region, Captain Linnik; original protocol is located in archive criminal file #17214; Procuracy of the USSR, Vladimirov; a copy is held in the criminal file on the accusation against Fedorenko, vol. 15, pp. 158–166.

Ivan Shvidkij by assistant case officer, MGB, Dzerzhinsk District, Stalino/Donetsk region, Lieutenant Evseyev, 1951.

Grigorij Garus/Marusenko by senior investigator, MGB, Lieutenant Pakhomov, 1952.

Fedor Tikhonovskij by senior case officer, KGB, Karaganda region, Lieutenant

Moldashev, January 1955; a copy is held with senior investigator, Investigations Department, KGB, Dnepropetrovsk region, Captain Shkonda; the original is located in the archive criminal file charging V. Podenok, F. Tikhonovskij, et al., KGB Krasnodar region, December 24, 1965.

Fedor Tartynskij by deputy military procurator of the Kiev Military District, Lieutenant Colonel of Justice Vostrikov at the Military Procuracy of the Stalino/Donetsk Garrison, October 31, 1959; original protocol is located in archive investigative file #58228, on Yuri Andreyev; Criminal Archives Directorate, KGB, Kiev region.

Prokofij Rjabtsev by senior investigator, Investigations Department, KGB, Kaliningrad region, Captain Shabanov, Vinnitsa, 1961; original protocol is located in investigative file #11 charging Schults (a.k.a. Vertogradov) et al., which is stored with the KGB in Vinnitsa region; Procurator's Office of the USSR, E. F. Vladimirov.

Alexei Govorov by investigator, Investigations Department, KGB, Lieutenant Loginov, Kiev, 1961.

Sergei Vasilenko by senior investigator, Investigations Department, KGB, Kiev region, Lieutenant Colonel Lysenko, 1961; a copy is held with the 1st deputy procurator, Crimean region, Senior Counselor of Justice Kuptsov, March 1976.

Nikolai Leontev by senior investigator, Investigations Department, KGB, Krasnodar region, Major [name deleted], 1964.

Mikhail Korzhikow by senior investigator, Investigations Department, KGB, Krasnodar region, Major [name deleted], 1964.

Piotr Browzew by senior investigator, Investigations Department, KGB, Krasnoyarsk region, Major Padkin, Moscow, August 1964.

Vasili Shuller by senior investigator, KGB, Krasnodar, Lieutenant Metelkin, December 1964.

Grigorij Kniga by senior investigator, KGB, Krasnodar, Lieutenant Metelkin, December 1964.

Alexander Zakharov/Pruss by senior investigator, KGB, Krasnodar region, Lieutenant Metelkin, January 1965; the original record of the interrogation is located in case #4 against Tikhonovsky, Podenok, et al. and is stored in the KGB archive Krasnodar.

Vasili Podenok by senior investigator, Investigations Department, KGB, Dnepropetrovsk region, Captain Shkonda, March 1965.

Alexander Byschkow by senior investigator, Investigations Department, KGB, Dnepropetrovsk region, Captain Shkonda, 1964 or 1965.

Ivan Tkachuk by senior investigator, KGB, Krasnodar, Captain Pavlyukov, March 1965.

Zaki Tuktarov by senior investigator, KGB, Krasnodar region, Captain Pavlyukov, 1965; original protocol is located in criminal file #4, which charges Nikiforov and others. The file is stored with the KGB in Krasnodar region.

Prokofij Rjabtsev by senior investigator, KGB, Krasnodar region, Captain Pavlyukov, 1965; original protocol is located in criminal file #4, charging Nikolaj Matvienko and others.

Mikhail Laptev/Lapot by senior investigator, KGB, Captain Pavlyukov, Krasnodar region, 1965.

Vasili Orlovskij by Lieutenant Tschirkin, interrogator, Investigations Department, KGB, Dnepropetrovsk region, probably 1965.

Grigorij Nesmejan by Lieutenant Tschirkin, interrogator, Investigations Department, KGB, Dnepropetrovsk region, 1965.

Anastasij Mawrodij by Captain Shkonda, interrogator, Investigations Department, KGB, Dnepropetrovsk region, June 1965.

Petr Browzew by Lieutenant Tschirkin, interrogator, Investigations Department, KGB, Dnepropetrovsk region, August 1965.

Alexander Semigodow by Lieutenant Tschirkin, investigator, Investigations Department, KGB, Dnepropetrovsk region, 1965.

Kiril Prochorenko by Captain Shkonda, interrogator, Investigations Department, KGB, Dnepropetrovsk region, September 1965.

Dmitrij Pundik by Captain Shkonda, interrogator, Investigations Department, KGB, Dnepropetrovsk region, September 1965.

Vladimir Gadsicki by Captain Semikow, investigator, Investigations Department, KGB, Rovno District, September 1965.

Examination of archive file #K-779, July 1966, Lvov, by Lieutenant Boechko, investigator, Investigations Department, KGB, Lvov region: vol. 1, p. 133: a document dated July 13, 1943, giving the number of *Wachmänner* assigned to Janowska as 112. The document further states that on July 27, 1943, Wachmann Nikolaj Grishchenko and Wachmann Nikolai Zhivotov, born in Orlov region, fled. SSPF Lublin ordered the forwarding of the desertion report to the SS & Police Court. Vol. 2, pp. 50–54, Sachsenhausen/Oranienburg Roster, December 1, 1943. Vol. 2, pp. 268–269, Janowska Roster, May 17, 1943 (seventy-five men). Vol. 2, p. 273, Janowska Roster, May 19, 1943 (seventeen men). Vol. 2, p. 195, a report dated July 26, 1943, re: the desertion of nine *Wachmänner*. Vol. 2, pp. 269–273, Sobibor Roster, March 26, 1943. Vol. 2, pp. 276–279, Belzec Roster, March 27, 1943.

Vasili Litvinenko by senior investigator, KGB, Lvov region, Captain Malykhin, 1968.

Yakov Klimenko by senior investigator, Investigations Department, KGB, Lvov region, Captain Kharitonov, Novomoskovsk, Tula region, 1968; original protocol is located in case file #1-16136 on Egor Lobyntsev.

Dimitri Yarosh by senior investigator, KGB, Lvov region, Captain Malykhin, 1968.

Alexander Fedchenko by senior investigator, KGB, Lvov region, Captain Malykhin, 1968.

Ivan Zvezdun by investigator, KGB, Irkutsk region, Lieutenant Tyukavin, 1969; a copy is held with the senior deputy procurator, Irkutsk region. Responsible for monitoring investigations by the KGB: Senior Justice Counselor Malayev.

Alexei Kolgushkin by senior investigator, KGB, Yaroslavl region, Captain Sochnev, as authorized by the Procuracy of the USSR, 1969.

Ivan Zvezdun by Senior Counselor of Justice Zverev, an investigator for especially important cases under the General Procurator of the USSR, along with Procurator Senior Counselor of Justice Kharuto, Court Director K. Oder, and 1st Procurator I. Gnikhvitts. Interrogation took place in the building of the Procuracy of the USSR, Moscow, 1971.

Alexander Moskalenko by senior investigator, KGB, Belgorod region, Lieutenant Bojko, as authorized by the Procuracy of the USSR, 1969; deputy procurator, Belgorod region, Counselor of Justice L. Semenov.

Semen Kharkovskij by senior investigator, Investigations Section, KGB, Kharkov region, Lieutenant Yakovenko, as authorized by the Procuracy of the USSR, 1973.

Prokofij Businnij by senior investigator, KGB, Kiev region, Captain Berestowkij, 1974.

Piotr Browzew by the assistant state attorney of Leningrad, Senior Justice Counselor Ponomarev, on behalf of the attorney general of the USSR, 1975.

Nikolaj Malagon by senior investigator of the Procuracy for Zaporozhe region, Senior Counselor of Justice Litvinenko, *US vs. Fedorenko*, March 1978; a copy is held with the Procuracy of the USSR, G. Shvydak.

Ignat Danilchenko by the department procurator, Procuracy of the Soviet Union, Senior Counselor of Justice Natalia Kolesnikova, Tyumen region,

1979; deputy chief, Office of the Procuracy of the Soviet Union, P. Ryakhovskikh.

Ivan Zvezdun by the senior deputy procurator, Senior Counselor of Justice V. Malyev, on instructions from the Procuracy of the USSR, Irkutsk region, November 1980.

PUNISHMENT OF FORMER TRAWNIKI GUARDS BY SOVIET COURTS

Ivan Shevchenko: convicted by the military tribunal of the 65th Army, 1st Belorussian Front, under the April 19, 1943, executive order (*Ukaz*) 43 and sentenced to death, October 21, 1944.

Pavel Leleko: convicted by the military tribunal of the 2nd Belorussian Front under the April 19, 1943, executive order (*Ukaz*) 43 and sentenced to death, March 19, 1945.

Ivan Terekhov: Convicted by the military tribunal of the 1st Guards Tank Army under Article 58-1b of the Soviet Criminal Code and sentenced to ten years in a labor camp, April 15, 1945. Released in 1953. Reindicted and retried on the basis of newly discovered evidence, 1961 (Schultz trial and others).

Sergej Vasilenko: Convicted under Article 58-1b of the Soviet Criminal Code and sentenced to ten years in a labor camp, April 15, 1945. Released in 1952. Reindicted and retried on the basis of newly discovered evidence, 1961 (Schultz trial and others).

Ivan Zvezdun: arrested by the MGB, Novosibirsk region, sentenced to twenty-five years in ITL (corrective labor camps) by a military tribunal of the MVD, 1947.

Alexander Dukhno: convicted by the military tribunal of the Ural Military District under Article 58-1b of the Soviet-Russian Criminal Code; sentenced to twenty-five years in a labor camp, June 1947.

Mikhail Korzhikow: Convicted by the military tribunal of the Ural Military District under Article 58-1b of the Soviet-Russian Criminal Code; sentenced to twenty-five years' ITL (corrective labor camps), June 1947. Released in an "amnesty" in 1956.

Ivan Voloshin: Convicted by the military tribunal of the Ural Military District under Article 58-1b of the Russian-Soviet Criminal Code; sentenced to twenty-five years in a labor camp, June 1947. Released under amnesty, 1956.

Petr Browzew: Convicted by the military tribunal of the MVD in Leningrad region under Article 58-1b of the Soviet-Russian Criminal Code and sentenced to fifteen years in a labor camp, 1947. Released in 1955 under amnesty.

Alexander Zakharov/Pruss: convicted by the MVD Forces of the Moscow Military District and sentenced to twenty-five years' ITL (corrective labor camp), 1947.

Alexander Moskalenko: Convicted under Article 54-1b of the Soviet-Ukrainian Criminal Code and sentenced to twenty-five years' incarceration, 1947. Released, 1964.

Alexander Byschkow: Convicted under Article 54-1b of the Soviet-Ukrainian Criminal Code and sentenced to twenty-five years in a labor camp, October 1947. Released in October 1955 under amnesty.

Alexei Kolgushkin: convicted under Article 58-1b of the Soviet-Russian Criminal Code, probably in Yaroslavl region.

Vladimir Gadsicki: convicted under Article 54-1b of the Soviet-Ukrainian Criminal Code and sentenced to twenty-five years in a labor camp, 1948.

Ivan Kondratenko: convicted by the military tribunal of the 17th Air Army in Kiev under Article 54-1b of the Soviet-Ukrainian Criminal Code, March 1948.

Nikolaj Gutsulyak: convicted by the military tribunal of the MVD in Stanislavov/ Ivano-Frankivsk region under Article 54-1a of the Soviet-Ukrainian Criminal Code, June 1948.

Vladimir Terletskij: convicted by the military tribunal of the MVD in Stanislavov/ Ivano-Frankivsk region under Article 54-1a of the Soviet-Ukrainian Criminal Code, June 1948.

Zaki Tuktarov: Convicted under Article 58-1b of the Soviet-Russian Criminal Code and sentenced to twenty-five years' ITL (corrective labor camps), 1948. Released, 1955.

Prokofij Rjabtsev: Convicted by the military tribunal of the Voronezh Garrison under Article 58-1b of the Soviet-Russian Criminal Code. Sentenced to twenty-five years' ITL (corrective labor camps), November 16, 1948. He was held in an MVD prison in Vinnitsa region. Released on January 9, 1962.

Filip Babenko: convicted by the military tribunal of the Kiev Military District under Article 54-1b of the Soviet-Ukrainian Criminal Code, December 24, 1948.

Nikolai Leontev: Convicted by a military tribunal, in accordance with Article 58-1b of the Soviet-Russian Criminal Code; sentenced to fifteen years' ITL (corrective labor camps), 1948. Released in June 1956.

Grigorij Nesmejan: Convicted under Article 54-1b of the Soviet-Ukrainian Criminal Code and sentenced to twenty-five years in a labor camp, 1949. Released in 1955 under an amnesty.

Kiril Prochorenko: Convicted in a military district court in Tawritschesk, under Article 58-1b of the Soviet Criminal Code, and sentenced to twenty-five years in a labor camp, 1949. Released in September 1955 on the basis of an amnesty of September 1955.

Alexei Lazorenko: Convicted by a military tribunal under Article 54-1b of the Soviet-Ukrainian Criminal Code and sentenced to twenty-five years' imprisonment, July 1949. Released in October 1955 under amnesty. Reindicted and retried on the basis of newly discovered evidence, 1965 (Zuev trial and others).

Fedor Ryabeka: convicted under Article 54-1b of the Soviet-Ukrainian Criminal Code and sentenced to twenty-five years in a labor camp, 1949. Released in 1955 under amnesty. Reindicted and retried

on the basis of newly discovered evidence, 1961 (Schultz trial and others).

Yakov Karplyuk: Convicted by the military tribunal of Military Installation #77757 under Article 54-1b of the Soviet-Ukrainian Criminal Code and sentenced to twenty-five years in a labor camp, September 1949. Released in 1956. Reindicted and retried on the basis of newly discovered evidence, 1961 (Schultz trial and others).

Nikolaj Pavli: convicted by a military tribunal under Article 54-1b of the Soviet-Ukrainian Criminal Code and sentenced to twenty-five years' ITL (corrective labor camps), December 23, 1949.

Ignat Danilchenko: convicted in a Kiev court under Article 54-1b of the Soviet-Ukrainian Criminal Code and sentenced to twenty-five years' ITL (corrective labor camps), 1949.

Alexander Semenov: convicted and sentenced to twenty-five years' ITL (corrective labor camp), 1949.

Grigorij Kniga: convicted under Article 54-1b of the Ukrainian-Soviet Criminal Code and sentenced to twenty-five years in a labor camp, 1949.

Ananij Kuzminskij: Convicted under Article 54-1b of the Ukrainian-Soviet Criminal Code and sentenced to twenty-five years' imprisonment, 1950. Released in 1955, under amnesty.

Akim Zuev: Convicted under Article 54-1b of the Soviet-Ukrainian Criminal Code and sentenced to twenty-five years' imprisonment, February 1950. Released in October 1955 under amnesty. Reindicted and retried on the basis of newly discovered evidence, 1965 (Zuev trial and others).

Taras Olejnik: Convicted by a military tribunal under Article 54-1b of the Soviet-Ukrainian Criminal Code and sentenced to twenty-five years' imprisonment, February 1950. Released in November 1955 under amnesty. Reindicted and retried on the basis of newly discovered evidence, 1965 (Zuev trial and others).

Georgij Skydan: convicted by the military tribunal of the Belorussian Military District in Baranovichi under Article 63-2 of the Soviet-Belorussian Criminal Code, May 1950.

Alexei Govorov: Convicted under Article 58-1b of the Soviet Criminal Code and sentenced to twenty-five years' imprisonment, 1950. Released in 1955 under amnesty. Reindicted and retried on the basis of newly discovered evidence, 1961 (Schultz trial and others).

Samuel Pritsch: Convicted by the military tribunal of the Kiev Military District under Article 54-1b of the Soviet-Ukrainian Criminal Code and sentenced to twenty-five years in a labor camp, June 1950. Released in 1955 under an amnesty. Reindicted and retried on the basis on newly discovered evidence, 1961 (Schultz trial and others).

Anton Streltsov: convicted by the military tribunal of the Kiev Military District under Article 54-1b of the Soviet-Ukrainian Criminal Code and sentenced to death, June 1950.

Vasili Gajdich: convicted by the military tribunal of the Moscow Military District under Article 58-1b of the Soviet Criminal Code and sentenced to death, December 1950.

Mitrofan Klotz: Convicted under Article 54-1b of the Soviet-Ukrainian Criminal Code and sentenced to twenty-five years' imprisonment, 1951. Released in 1956 under amnesty.

Mikhail Gorbachev: Convicted by the military tribunal of the Ural Military District under Article 58-1b of the Soviet Criminal Code and sentenced to twenty-five years in a labor camp, June 1951. Released in October 1955 under amnesty. Reindicted and retried on the basis of newly discovered evidence, 1961 (Schultz trial and others).

Petro Goncharov: convicted by the military tribunal of the Kiev Military District under Article 54-1b of the Soviet-Ukrainian Criminal Code and sentenced to death, June 1951.

Nikolaj Sherbak: convicted by the military tribunal of the Kiev Military District under Article 54-1b of the Soviet-Ukrainian Criminal Code and sentenced to death, June 1951.

Ivan Machoulin: convicted by the military tribunal of the Kiev Military District under Article 54-1b of the Soviet-Ukrainian Criminal Code and sentenced to death, June 1951.

Dimitri Korotkikh: convicted by the military tribunal of the Kiev Military District under Article 54-1b of the Soviet-Ukrainian Criminal Code and sentenced to death, September 1951.

Nikolai Shalayev: convicted by the military tribunal of the Voronezh Military District under Article 58-1b of the Soviet Criminal Code and sentenced to death, December 1951.

Alexander Semigodow: Convicted under Article 58-1b of the Soviet-Russian Criminal Code and sentenced to twenty-five years in a labor camp, December 1951. Released in 1955 under amnesty.

Dmitrij Pundik: Convicted by the military district court in Prikarpatsky, under Article 54-1b of the Soviet-Ukrainian Criminal Code, and sentenced to twenty years in a labor camp, 1951. Released in October 1955, under the September 1955 amnesty.

Ivan Shvidkij: convicted by the military tribunal of the Kiev Military District in Stalino/Donetsk under Article 54-1b of the Soviet-Ukrainian Criminal Code, January 1952.

Filip Levchishin: Convicted by the military tribunal of the Carpathian Military District under Article 54-1b of the Soviet-Ukrainian Criminal Code and sentenced to twenty-five years in a labor camp, 1952. Released in 1956 under amnesty. Reindicted and retried on the basis of newly discovered evidence, 1961 (Schultz trial and others).

Evdokim Parfinyuk: Convicted by the military tribunal of the Carpathian Military District under Article 54-1b of the

Soviet-Ukrainian Criminal Code and sentenced to twenty-five years in a labor camp, August 1952. Sentence reduced to ten years in prison, February 1955. Released in December 1955 under amnesty. Reindicted and retried on the basis of newly discovered evidence, 1961 (Schultz trial and others).

Alexander Yeger: convicted by the military tribunal of the Kiev Military District under Article 54-1b of the Soviet-Ukrainian Criminal Code and sentenced to death, September 1952.

Anastasij Mawrodij: Convicted by a military tribunal in Odessa region, under Article 54-1b of the Soviet-Ukrainian Criminal Code, and sentenced to twenty-five years in a labor camp, 1952. Released in October 1955 on the basis of the September 1955 amnesty.

Vasili Orlovskij: Convicted under Article 58-1b of the Soviet Criminal Code and sentenced to twenty-five years in a labor camp, May 1953. Released in November 1955 on the basis of the September 1955 amnesty.

Yakov Klimenko: Convicted under Article 58-1b of the Soviet-Russian Criminal Code. Sentenced to twenty-five years' ITL (corrective labor camps), January 19, 1955. Released on May 3, 1966.

Nikolaj Skakodub: convicted by the military tribunal of the Pre-Carpathian Military District under Article 1 of the Soviet Criminal Code and sentenced to fifteen years' ITL (corrective labor camp), February 1961.

Fedor Fedorenko: Deported from the United States back to the Soviet Union by order of the US Department of Justice and the US Supreme Court. Convicted by a court in Simferopol, Crimea, and sentenced to death, 1986. Executed by firing squad, 1987.

APPENDIX D:
REINHARD DEATH CAMP GUARDS
BROUGHT TO JUSTICE

A total of 105 men: thirty-four from Treblinka, twenty-four of whom were sentenced to death, one of which was overturned on appeal and changed to imprisonment; fifty-four from Belzec, thirteen of whom were sentenced to death, one of which was overturned on appeal and changed to imprisonment; and seventeen from Sobibor, one of whom was sentenced to death, which was overturned on appeal (mistaken for a Treblinka guard). The rest of the men generally received fifteen to twenty-five years' imprisonment in labor camps, and they all ended up serving ten years or less of those sentences due to the 1955 amnesty (except for those tried in the 1960s). (Note that this list is not definitive. There may have been more men tried, but further information is currently unavailable.)

Treblinka (34)
Borodin, Dimitri: death sentence
Duschenko, Fedor
Elenchuk, Vlas
Fedorenko, Fedor: death sentence
Gajdich, Vasili: death sentence
Goncharov, Petro: death sentence
Gorbachev, Mikhail: death sentence
Govorov, Alexei: death sentence
Karplyuk, Yakov: death sentence
Korotkikh, Dimitri: death sentence
Kurinnij, Ivan: death sentence
Kuzminskj, Ananij
Leleko, Pavel: death sentence
Levchishin, Filip: death sentence
Lysak, Mikhail: death sentence
Machoulin, Ivan: death sentence
Malagon, Nikolaj
Parfinyuk, Evdokim: death sentence
Pritsch, Samuel: death sentence
Rjabtsev, Prokofij
Ryabeka, Fedor: death sentence
Schultz, Emanuel: death sentence

Senik, Nikolai
Shalayev, Nikolai: death sentence
Sherbak, Nikolai: death sentence
Shevchenko, Ivan: death sentence
Shvidkij, Ivan
Skakodub, Nikolaj
Skydan, Georgij
Streltsov, Anton: death sentence
Terekhov, Ivan: death sentence (overturned
    on appeal; changed to imprisonment)
Tkachuk, Ivan
Vasilenko, Sergej: death sentence
Yeger, Alexander: death sentence

Belzec (54)
Akkermann, Andrej: death sentence
Babenko, Philip
Babin, Boris
Bardachenko, Luka
Baskakov, Ivan
Belyakov, Wasyl: death sentence
Bronov, Vasili
Browzew, Piotr
Byschkow, Alexander
Danilov, Jurko
Didukh, Petro
Diener, Karl: death sentence
Dukhno, Alexander
Emelyanov, Vladimir
Gadsicki, Vladimir
Gorun, Fedor
Greniuk, Mikhail
Gulyj, Wasyl
Gumenyuk, Ivan
Huzuliak, Petro
Klotz, Mitrofan
Kniga, Grigorij
Korzhikow, Mikhail
Kozlowskj, Ivan
Kuchma, Andrei
Lazorenko, Alexei: death sentence
Leontev, Nikolai
Lomov, Vladimir
Lynkin, Grigorij
Mamchur, Nikita: death sentence
Matwijenko, Nikolaj: death sentence
Mawrodij, Anastasij
Nesmejan, Grigorij

Nikiforov, Ivan: death sentence
Niniovskij, Petro
Olejnik, Taras: death sentence (overturned
    on appeal; changed to imprisonment)
Orlovskj, Vasili
Pavli, Nikolaj
Podenok, Vasili: death sentence
Popiliuk, Wasyl
Popov, Wasyl
Prochorenko, Kiril
Prymak, Hryzko
Pundik, Dimitri
Schaefer, Alexander: death sentence
Semigodow, Alexander
Shuller, Vasili
Slowak, Mykola
Tichonowskj, Fedor: death sentence
Voloshin, Ivan
Zagrebajew, Ivan
Zaitsev, Ivan: death sentence
Zakharov, Alexander
Zuev, Akim: death sentence

Sobibor (17)
Businnij, Prokofij
Danilchenko, Ignat
Demjanjuk, Ivan: death sentence (overturned
    on appeal)
Engelhardt, Jakob
Gontcharenko, Nikolaj
Isaenko, Alexei
Ivchenko, Ivan
Kartashev, Wasyl
Marticzuk, Wasyl
Mistyuk, Ivan
Oleksiuk, Wasyl
Pankov, Vasili
Rozgonjajew, Mikhail
Semenow, Alexander
Sendetskij, Milko
Solonina, Anton
Zechmeister, Jakob

**Probably served at Reinhard camps, but
unknown which ones**
Andreyenko, Mikhail
Gordienko, Terentij: died serving his
    imprisonment sentence

APPENDIX E:
AUSCHWITZ-BIRKENAU GUARDS BROUGHT TO JUSTICE

Thirty-five men in total, all of whom had also served at Reinhard death camps, and thirteen of whom received death sentences, one of which was overturned on appeal and changed to imprisonment. The rest received sentences of fifteen to twenty-five years' imprisonment, of which they served less than ten years as a result of the 1955 amnesty (except those tried in the 1960s).

Andreyenko, Mikhail: Treblinka?

Bardachenko, Luka: Belzec, May 1942

Belinskij, Vladimir

Borodin, Dimitri: Treblinka II, July 1942; Sobibor, Feb. 1943; death sentence

Busennij, Prokofij: Belzec, 1942; Sobibor, Feb. 1943

Chernikov, Grigorij: ?

Gajdich, Vasili: Treblinka, death sentence

Gorbachev, Mikhail: Treblinka II, Aug. 1942; Sobibor, Feb. 1943; death sentence

Gordienko, Terentij: ?

Gorun, Fedor: Belzec, May 1942; Sobibor, July 1942

Govorov, Alexei: Treblinka II, July 1942; Sobibor, Feb. 1943; death sentence

Klotz, Mitrofan: Belzec, 1942

Kniga, Grigorij: Belzec, May 1942

Korotnichenko, Fedor: ?

Kozlovskij, Ivan: Belzec

Kuchma, Andrei: Belzec

Kurynnj, Ivan: Treblinka II, Aug. 1942; Sobibor, Feb. 1943; death sentence

Lomov, Vladimir: Belzec, 1942

Lynkin, Grigorij: Belzec

Malagon, Nikolaj: Treblinka II, July 1942; Belzec, Feb. 1943

Mamchur, Nikita: Belzec, 1942; death sentence

Mawrodij, Anastasij: Belzec

Olejnik, Taras: Belzec, 1942; death sentence (overturned on appeal and changed to imprisonment)

Pankov, Wasyl: Sobibor, July 1942

Parfinyuk, Evdokim: Treblinka II, 1942; Sobibor, Feb. 1943; death sentence

Podenok, Wasyl: Belzec, death sentence

Popov, Wasyl: Belzec, 1942

Ryabeka, Fedor: Treblinka II, July 1942; Sobibor, Feb. 1943; death sentence

Safonov, Ivan: Treblinka?

Shuller, Vasili: Belzec

Skakodub, Nikolaj: Treblinka II, June 1942; Sobibor, Feb. 1943

Tikhonovskij, Fedor: Belzec, May 1942; death sentence

Zagrebayev, Ivan: Belzec

Zaitsev, Ivan: Belzec, death sentence

Zuev, Akim: Belzec, 1942; death sentence

AUSHMM: Archive of the United States Holocaust Memorial Museum, Washington, DC

AUSHMM RG 31.018M: Record group (RG) in the Archive of the US Holocaust Memorial Museum containing records of the trials of former Trawniki guards held in the Ukrainian Soviet Socialist Republic, 1940s–1960s

BA Ludwigsburg: Federal Archive Ludwigsburg

BA Ludwigsburg B162/208 AR-Z 251/59: Kurt Bolender trial (Sobibor); stored at the ZStL Archive

BA Ludwigsburg B162/208 AR-Z 252/59: Josef Oberhauser trial (Belzec); stored at the ZStL Archive

BA Ludwigsburg B162/208 AR-Z 673/41: Karl Streibel trial (Trawniki)

delo: File (Russian language)

Dienstausweis: Service identification card. During the war, was used by soldiers and policemen, in German service, as a form of identification.

fond: Collection (Russian language)

FSB: Federal Security Service, Russia (successor to the KGB)

GARF: State Archive of the Russian Federation, Moscow

IPN: Institute of National Remembrance, Poland

Lazarette: Literally, "hospital" (in the German language). In the death camps it was actually an execution pit where people were shot.

MGB: Ministry of State Security (predecessor of the KGB)

MPLW: Museum of the Leczynsko-Wlodawskie Lake District, Wlodawa (Poland)

MVD: Ministry of Internal Affairs (successor to the NKVD)

NCO: Noncommissioned officer

NIOD: Archive of the Dutch Institute of War Documentation, Amsterdam

OKBZ: War Crimes Investigation Commission, Poland

opis: Finding guide (Russian language)

OSI: Office of Special Investigations: A branch of the US Department of Justice's Criminal Division. It specialized in tracking down and prosecuting suspected Nazi war criminals living in the US. Today it has been renamed the Human Rights and Special Prosecutions Section.

Personalbogen: Literally, personal sheet or personnel file. They were stored in an administrative office and contain biographical information and a photograph of the recipient.

procurator: The Soviet equivalent of a prosecutor

RGVA: State Military Archive of the Russian Federation, Moscow

RG 20869 and RG K-779: Wartime documents recovered by the Soviets when they captured the Trawniki camp or the city of Lublin in July 1944. After being sent to Moscow, these documents were consolidated into these two record groups, which are stored in the KGB (now called FSB) Archive. The documents include personnel records, identification documents, reports, and memos and were used after the war to prosecute former Trawniki guards.

SBU: Security Service of Ukraine (successor to the KGB in Ukraine)

SMERSH: Literally "death to spies," it was the Soviet Military Counterintelligence Service during World War II; it was answerable directly to Stalin, in his capacity as head of the Soviet State Defense Committee (GKO).

SS-Sonderkommando: SS-Special Unit

StA Dortmund Js 27/61: Kurt Bolender trial

StA Hamburg 147 Js 43/69: Karl Streibel trial

TPF: Trawniki personnel file

Trawniki guard ranks:
Wachmann: Private
Oberwachmann: Private 1st class
Rottwachmann: Corporal
Gruppenwachmann: Sergeant
Zugwachmann: Sergeant major
Oberzugwachmann: Master sergeant
TsAMO: Archive of the Ministry of Defense of the Russian Federation, Podolsk
UB/SB: Ministry of Public Security / Security Service during the postwar Communist era in Poland
ukaz: Order (Russian language)
U.S.C.: United States Code
Volksdeutsche: Ethnic German; individuals of German ancestry who live outside Germany
ZIH: Jewish Historical Institute, Warsaw
ZStL: Central Office of the State Judicial Administration for the Investigation of Nazi Crimes, Ludwigsburg, Germany. The main office for prosecuting Nazi war criminals in Germany.

Chapter 1

1. David Rich, "Accountability without Limit: Soviet Trials of Aktion Reinhard Soviet Collaborators, 1944–1987," in *Eastern Europe Facing the Shoah: A History of Engagement, 1941–2016*, eds. Raphael Utz and Jochen Böhler (2018).

2. Tanja Penter, "Local Collaborators on Trial: Soviet War Crimes Trials under Stalin (1943–1953)," *Cahiers du Monde Russe* 49, nos. 2–3 (2008): 342.

3. Lev Simkin, "Death Sentence despite the Law: A Secret 1962 Crimes-against-Humanity Trial in Kiev," *Holocaust and Genocide Studies* 27, no. 2 (2013): 312, n. 22. According to a doctoral dissertation by A. Epifanov titled "Otvetstvennost za voennye prestupleniia, sovershennye na territorii SSSR vo vremia Velikoi Otechestvennoi voiny," Akademiia MVD RF, 2001: July 1941–1954, according to data of the Main Military Prosecutor's Office, over 460,000 individuals were convicted of treason in the period of WWII.

4. Penter, "Local Collaborators on Trial," 344n15. See "The Legal Basis for the Organization and Activities of Military Tribunals of the NKVD during WWII," by V. Obuchov, 2002.

5. Sergej Kudryashov, "Ordinary Collaborators: The Case of the Travniki Guards," in *Russia: War, Peace, and Diplomacy*, eds. Ljubica Erickson and Mark Erickson (London: Weidenfeld and Nicolson), 237.

6. Peter Black, "Police Auxiliaries for Operation Reinhard: Shedding Light on the Trawniki Training Camp through Documents from behind the Iron Curtain," in, *Secret Intelligence and the Holocaust*, ed. David Bankier (Jerusalem: Yad Vashem Holocaust Martyrs' and Heroes Remembrance Authority, 2006), 348.

7. Rich, "Accountability without Limit."

8. Ibid.

9. Ibid.

10. Ibid.

11. Black, "Police Auxiliaries for Operation Reinhard," 341.

12. Rich, "Accountability without Limit."

13. Ibid.

14. Ibid. Also see Alexander Statiev, *Soviet Counterinsurgency in the Border Regions*.

15. David Alan Rich, "Reinhard's Foot Soldiers: Soviet Trophy Documents and Investigative Records as Sources," in *Remembering for the Future: The Holocaust in an Age of Genocide*, vol. 1, eds. John Roth and Elisabeth Maxwell (London: Palgrave Macmillan, 2001), 688–701.

16. Simkin, "Death Sentence despite the Law," 302.

17. Rich, "Accountability without Limit."

18. Jonathan Harrison, Roberto Muehlenkamp, Jason Myers, Sergey Romanov, and Nicholas Terry, *Belzec, Sobibor, Treblinka: Holocaust Denial and Operation Reinhard; Critique of the Falsehoods of Mattogno, Graf, and Kues, Holocaust Controversies* (blog), 2011, 85, holocaustcontroversies.blogspot.com.

19. Marek Bem, *Sobibor Extermination Camp, 1942–1943* (Amsterdam: Stichting Sobibor, 2015), 131n46: S. Wileński, B. Gorbowicki, and A. Tieruszkin, eds., *Sobibór*, 79–80.

20. Rich, "Reinhard's Foot Soldiers."

21. Black, "Police Auxiliaries for Operation Reinhard," 349.

22. Ibid., 350.

23. Ibid., 351.

24. Ibid., 352.

25. Rich, "Reinhard's Foot Soldiers": see "Proposal to Rescind Sentence," July 1961, and "Supreme Court Determination regarding Mikhail Petrovich Gorbachev," July 1961, Schults trial, case #14, archive file #66437, vol. 28, pp. 120–125, SBU Kiev. Gorbachev was one of the twelve defendants reinvestigated and tried in the "Schults" case. All of them had served at Treblinka II.

26. Rich, "Accountability without Limit."

27. Ibid.

28. Ibid.

29. Penter, "Local Collaborators on Trial," 342 and 342n7.

30. Ibid., 345.

31. Ibid., 345–346.

32. Ibid., 346.

33. Ibid., 347.

34. Ibid., 347–348.

35. Ibid., 349.

36. Ibid.

37. Ibid.

38. Ibid., 349–350.

39. Ibid., 350.

40. Ibid., 351: see USHMM Archive, RG 31.018M, reel 2, frame #3701.

41. Ibid., 355.

42. Ibid., 356.

43. Kudryashov, "Ordinary Collaborators," 228.

44. Ibid., 229.

45. Rich, "Accountability without Limit."

46. Black, "Police Auxiliaries for Operation Reinhard," 333.

47. Ibid., 334.

48. Testimony of Professor Charles Sydnor Jr., Demjanjuk denaturalization trial, US, 2001.

49. Rich, "Accountability without Limit."

50. Black, "Police Auxiliaries for Operation Reinhard," 334.

51. Ibid., 334–335, n. 19; and USHMM, RG-31.002M, reel 12, folder 331.

52. Black, "Police Auxiliaries for Operation Reinhard," 341.

53. Ibid., 340–341, n. 35: this was the file of Bronislaw Hajda, who had immigrated to the US and was tried by the US Department of Justice. See Note E. B. Makeshov, acting chief of administration, General Procuracy of Ukraine, Consular Section, US embassy in Kiev, May 5, 1995, exhibit 214, *US vs. Hajda*, 94-C-5174, US District Court, Northern District of Illinois.

54. Black, "Police Auxiliaries for Operation Reinhard," 334–335.

55. Ibid., 340.

56. Ibid., 342–343.

57. Ibid., 343.

58. Ibid., 348.

59. Ibid.

60. Ibid., 352.

61. Ibid., 353.

62. Ibid., 353n64.

Chapter 2

1. Igor Nebolsin, *Stalin's Favorite: The Combat History of the 2nd Guards Tank Army from Kursk to Berlin*, vol. 2, *From Lublin to Berlin, July 1944–May 1945* (Solihull, UK: Helion, 2016), 33.

2. Ibid., 36.

3. Ibid., 38.

4. Ibid., 38–39.

5. Ibid., 39.

6. Ibid.

7. Ibid., 39–40.

8. Ibid., 40.

9. Ibid.

10. Ibid.

11. Ibid., 40–41.

12. Ibid., 41.

13. Ibid., 44–45.

14. Ibid., 45.

15. Ibid.

16. Ibid.

17. Ibid., 47.

18. Harrison et al., *Belzec, Sobibor, Treblinka*, 73: *Akt o zverstvakh nemetskikh okkupantov v lagere stantsii Belzhets*, Tomaszow, Lublinskogo, January 25, 1945, TsAMO 236-2675-340, pp. 31–33.

19. Ibid., 355.

20. Ibid., 71: *Prokuratura L'voskoi oblasti, protokol doprosa*, Rudolf Germanovich Reder, September 22, 1944, GARF 7021-149-99, pp. 16–19: Ibid., n. 147; Interrogation of Rudolf Reder, December 29, 1945, Bundesarchiv Ludwigsburg B 162/208 AR-Z 252/59, p. 1177: Ibid., n. 149; Rudolf Reder, Belzec, Krakow, Jewish Historical Commission, 1946.

21. Testimony before Judge Jan Sehn, December 1945, AIPN Lu 1/15/105.

22. Ibid., 318 and n. 190; statement of Rudolf Reder, December 29, 1945, BA Ludwigsburg B 162/208 AR-Z 252/59, p. 1177.

23. Ibid., 319 and n. 196; interrogation of Kazimierz Czerniak, October 18, 1945, BA Ludwigsburg B 162/208 AR-Z 252/59, pp. 1171–1172.

24. Robert Kuwalek, *Das Vernichtungslager Belzec* (Berlin: Metropol Verlag, 2013), 69.

25. Harrison et al., *Belzec, Sobibor, Treblinka*, 323n214: statement of Pfannenstiel, November 1959, BA Ludwigsburg B162/208 AR-Z 252/59, vol. 1, p. 138.

26. Ibid., 324 and n. 218: Heinrich Gley, May 1961, BA Ludwigsburg B162/208 AR-Z 252/59, p. 1291.

27. Ibid., 324 and n. 223: Josef Oberhauser, November 1971, proceedings against Hoffmann et al., 8 Ks 1/70, vol. 3, p. 881, Hessian State Archive, Wiesbaden; exhibit GX-95 in *US vs. Reimer.*

28. Email from Michael Tregenza to the author, via Stephen Tyas, on the Axis History Forum (forum.axishistory.com), May 18, 2020.

29. Email from Michael Tregenza to the author, via Steven Tyas, on the Axis History Forum (forum.axishistory.com), May 20, 2020; Stephen Tyas also added: "Michael [Tregenza] believes there are chinks in this story, but it is the only one available."

30. Interrogation of Maria Warzocha by Sergeant Franciszek Skawinski, Belzec, 1966, AIPN Lu-08/298.

31. Dariusz Libionka, "The Life Story of Chaim Hirszman: Remembrance of the Holocaust and Reflections on Postwar Polish-Jewish Relations," *Yad Vashem Studies* 34 (2006): 238: AIPN Lu 1/15/105, Records regarding the Crimes Committed at Belzec.

32. Ibid., 224: AIPN Lu 028/672, "Hirszmann File."

33. Bem, *Sobibor Extermination Camp, 1942–1943*, 423: Pola Hirszmann, ZIH Archive: Jewish Historical Institute, Warsaw, file #301/1476.

34. Libionka, "The Life Story of Chaim Hirszman," 238.

35. Ibid., 230. For information on the Lublin security apparatus, see *Rok pierwszy. Powstanie i dzialalnosc aparatu bezpieczenstwa publicznego na Lubelszczyznie, Lipiec 1944-czerwiec 1945* (Warsaw: IPN, 2004). In November 1946, Hirszmann's killer, Jerzy Fryze, was tried before the regional military court in Lublin (AIPN Lu 16/458, protocol of the case against Jerzy Fryze, November 1946) and sentenced to life imprisonment. In February 1947, the sentence was reduced to fifteen years' imprisonment, and in 1956 he was released, having served ten years. In 1994, Fryze appealed to the Lublin District Court to repeal his conviction. On the basis that Fryze had intended only to procure a weapon that he thought Hirszmann had, and had not intended to kill him, the court granted the repeal. For the full story, see Libionka, "The Life Story of Chaim Hirszmann."

36. Harrison et al., *Belzec, Sobibor, Treblinka*, 441n6: deposition of Fritz Tauscher, Munich, December 18, 1963, Bundesarchiv Ludwigsburg B 162/208 AR-Z 252/59, vol. 9, p. 1831.

37. Ibid., 441 and n. 4: deposition of Heinrich Gley, Munich, January 7, 1963, BA Ludwigsburg B 162/208 AR-Z 252/59, vol. 9, p. 1697ff.

38. Ibid., 441 and nn. 5–7: deposition of Eustachy Ukrainiski before examining judge Zamosc Godzieszewski, October 11, 1945, BA Ludwigsburg B 162/208 AR-Z 252/59, vol. 6., pp. 1117-1120; deposition of Eugeniusz Goch before examining judge Zamosc Godzieszewski, October 14, 1945, BA Ludwigsburg B 162/208 AR-Z 252/59, vol. 6, pp. 1134–1136; deposition of Stanislaw Kozak before examining judge Zamosc Godzieszewski, October 14, 1945, BA Ludwigsburg B 162/208 AR-Z 252/59, vol. 6, pp. 1134–1136; deposition of Stefan Kirsz before examining judge Zamosc Godzieszewski, October 15, 1945, BA Ludwigsburg B 162/208 AR-Z 252/59, vol. 6, pp. 1134–1136; statement of Alexander Semigodow, Penza, 1973, BA Ludwigsburg B 162/208 AR-Z 643/71, vol. 4, p. 704. Witnesses seem to confirm that cremations ended in March 1943 and that dismantling of the camp lasted until June 1943.

39. Harrison et al., *Belzec, Sobibor, Treblinka*, 442 and n. 10: Report on the Investigation of Belzec, signed by State Attorney Witkowski, BA Ludwigsburg B 162/208 AR-Z 252/59, vol. 6, pp. 1185–1188.

40. Ibid., 442.

41. Ibid., 357 and 442, n. 62: statement of Stanislaw Kozak, BA Ludwigsburg B 162/208 AR-Z 252/59, vol. 1, p. 1227.

42. Harrison et al., *Belzec, Sobibor, Treblinka*, 442.

43. Ibid.: Robin O'Neal, *Belzec: Stepping Stone to Genocide*, chap. 10; BA Ludwigsburg B 162/208 AR-Z 252/59, vol. 2, p. 258 and 286–287; deposition of Rudolf Reder before examining judge Jan Sehn, Krakow, December 29, 1945, BA Ludwigsburg B 162/208 AR-Z 252/59, vol. 1, p. 1175ff, mentioning Szpilke on p. 1180.

44. Harrison et al., *Belzec, Sobibor, Treblinka*, 443.

45. Ibid., 511 and n. 249: report of Rudolf Reder, BA Ludwigsburg B 162/208 AR-Z 252/59, vol. 2, pp. 258 and 286. Reder refers to conversations he had with local residents after the area was occupied by the Red Army.

46. Bem, *Sobibor Extermination Camp, 1942–1943*, 264 and n. 52: Tauscher, hearing report, file # ZStL 252/59-1838/39, Stadelhelm, December 18, 1963, NIOD Archive; Eda Lichtman testimony, ZStL Ludwigsburg Archive, case file #45 Js 27/61, file #208 AR-Z 251/59, Holon, Israel, May 1959, copy in Marek Bem's private collection; Tomasz Blatt account, ZIH Archive, file #4082, Lodz, June 1948.

47. Bem, *Sobibor Extermination Camp, 1942–1943*, 264 and 265, n. 53: Leon Feldhendler account, Lodz, 1946, *Sobibor*, ed. N. Blumental, 202–207.

48. Harrison et al., *Belzec, Sobibor, Treblinka*, 384 and n. 5: excavation protocol of October 12, 1945, and coroner report and opinion of Dr. Mieczyslaw Pietraszkiewicz, October 13, 1945, BA Ludwigsburg, B 162/208 AR-Z 252/59, vol. 6, fol. 1121ff.

49. Harrison et al., *Belzec, Sobibor, Treblinka*, 385n7; Jan Tomasz Gross, *Golden Harvest: Events at the Periphery of the Holocaust* (Oxford: Oxford University Press, 2012), 23–24, n. 30: Commission Report, October 10, 1945, and Report of Investigation by police chief Mieczyslaw Nieduzak, October 17, 1945, Report on the Investigation regarding the Belzec Death Camp, Archive of the State Museum at Majdanek [APMM], sygn. XIX-1284.

50. Gross, *Golden Harvest*, 23 and n. 29: statement of Eugeniusz Goch, October 14, 1945, and Maria Daniel, October 16, 1945, Records of Investigation regarding Crimes Committed at the Belzec Death Camp, APMM, sygn. XIX-1284.

51. Kuwalek, *Das Vernichtungslager Belzec*, 318.

52. Harrison et al., *Belzec, Sobibor, Treblinka*, 518 and n. 1: JuNSV Lfd. #585, vol. 20, pp. 628–647; Munich District Court, January 21, 1965, 110 Ks 3/64; DJuNSV Lfd. #1551, Magdeburg District Court, September 24, 1948, 11 Ks 246/48.

53. Kuwalek, *Das Vernichtungslager Belzec*, 69n24: IPN Archive Lublin, OKBL Ds 20/67, investigative records in the matter of Helmut Kallmeyer, responsible for the construction of the Belzec gas chambers, 1968–1984: official note regarding discovery of gas canisters in the sand quarry, located on the premises of the former death camp. Protocol of site survey, June 9, 1971; report of Tadeusz Wolczyk, February 25, 2004, Chelm.

54. Dieter Pohl, "Die Trawnikimänner im Vernichtungslager Belzec 1941–1943," in *NS-Gewaltherrschaft: Beitrage zur historischen Forschung und juristischen Aufarbeitung*, ed. Alfred Gottwaldt, Norbert Kampe, and Peter Klein (Berlin: Edition Hentrich, 2005), 278–289.

55. Bem, *Sobibor Extermination Camp, 1942–1943*, 319n35: Stanislawa Gogolowska, "The Mass Murderers of Belzec and Sobibor: The Trial in Krasnodar," in *Sztandar Ludu* ["The people's standard"], 1965, #146; and Stanislawa Gogolowska, "After the Trial in Krasnodar: A Letter from the Soviet Union," *Kamena* 13 (1965): 12.

56. Kuwalek, *Das Vernichtungslager Belzec*, 324 and n. 33: Stanislawa Gogolowska, "Ludobojcy z Belzca i Sobiboru: Proces w Krasnodarze," *Sztandar Ludu*, June 6, 1965; and "Po procesie w Krasnodarze: Korespondencja z ZSRR, *Kamena* 13 (1965). Gogolowska was a witness at the trial and also testified against a former *Wachmann* who had served at the Janowska labor camp in Lvov. She made no mention in her journalistic publications concerning Belzec and Sobibor that Jews were killed at these camps. This reflected the politics of postwar Communist Poland, which did not want to emphasize the Jewish tragedy, even when Polish citizens were the victims. Gogolowska was a Jew and a survivor of the Lvov ghetto and Auschwitz-Birkenau, and Ravensbruck concentration camps. In 1945–1946, she was active in the Jewish Historical Commission in Lublin.

57. Harrison et al., *Belzec, Sobibor, Treblinka*, 73 and n. 154: *Zakliuchenie po delu o zverstvakhi zlodeianikah nemetsko- fashistskikh zakhvatchikov v gor.* Lublin, TsAMO 233-2374-25, August 1944, pp. 459–488.

58. Harrison et al., *Belzec, Sobibor, Treblinka*, 73 and n. 155: *Soderzhanie o rezul' tatakh obspedovaniia faktov massovogo istrebleniia naseleniia nemetskimi okkupantami v lagere na stantsii Sabibur*, August 25, 1944, TsAMO 233-2374-58, pp. 225–229.

59. Harrison et al., *Belzec, Sobibor, Treblinka*, 73 and n. 157: *Spravka o zverstvakh nemetsko-fashistskikh zakhvatchikov, vyiavlennykh na territorii Polshi*, July 29, 1944, TsAMO 233-2374-58, pp. 96–98R.

60. Bem, *Sobibor Extermination Camp, 1942–1943*, 74 and n. 158: Akt, July 29, 1944, *stantsia Sabibor*, TsAMO 233-2374-58, p. 131.

61. Bem, *Sobibor Extermination Camp, 1942–1943*, 59n36.

62. IPN Archives, file ref. # Lu/1/9/46/0017.

63. Bem, *Sobibor Extermination Camp, 1942–1943*, 76 and nn. 66 and 68: Jakub Biskupicz, interrogation record, Bolender case, file ref. #13/112, Tel Aviv, May 17, 1961, NIOD Archive; and Jakub Biskupicz, interrogation record, Bolender case, file ref. #13/97, Tel Aviv, June 6, 1962, NIOD Archive: Zachar Poplawski memo to a representative of the Belorussian Communist Party in Brest region, regarding the account of Sobibor death camp by Ivan Karakach, October 7, 1943; copy from Marek Bem private collection.

64. Bem, *Sobibor Extermination Camp, 1942–1943*, 79.

65. Ibid., 86.

66. Ibid., 95.

67. Ibid., 96.

68. Ibid.

69. Ibid., 98. Hodl was Austrian and served in Sobibor from October 1942 to October 1943. He worked the gassing engine.

70. Harrison et al., *Belzec, Sobibor, Treblinka*, 394.

71. Bem, *Sobibor Extermination Camp, 1942–1943*, 101.

72. Ibid.: AIPN Lu 1-9-46-0065.

73. Ibid., 100.

74. Ibid., 99.

75. Richard Raschke, *Useful Enemies: John Demjanjuk and America's Open-Door Policy for Nazi War Criminals* (Harrison, NY: Delphinium Books, 2013), 525.

76. Ibid., 519.

77. Harrison et al., *Belzec, Sobibor, Treblinka*, 90; and Ibid., 24n94: S. Vilenski, F. Gorbovitski, and L. Tyorushkin, eds., *Sobibor: Vosstanie v lagere smerti* (Moscow: Vozvrashchenie, 2010).

78. Bem, *Sobibor Extermination Camp, 1942–1943*, 133n52: report on Sobibor by Ivan Karakach, October 1943.

79. Ibid., 162.

80. Ibid., 163 and n. 62: prosecutor Schnierstein's report on the investigation into Sobibor was published in 1960, in a study called "The extermination of Jews in camps in Poland" (in Polish), by S. Datner, J. Gumkowski, and K. Leszczynski.

81. Bem, *Sobibor Extermination Camp, 1942–1943*, 163.

82. Ibid., 163 and n. 64: report by M. Rozegnal, September 22, 1945, IPN Archive, file ref. # Lu/1/9/46/0004.

83. Ibid., 163 and n. 65: Judge A. Sobieszek, Wlodawa municipal court, November 20, 1945, Sobibor commune, Wlodawa district administrator, Jan Skulski, report. Copy in Marek Bem's private collection.

84. Ibid., 163 and n. 67: IPN Archive, file ref. # Lu/1/9/46/0017.

85. Ibid., 164.

86. Ibid., 166 and n. 73: information of the Jewish Historical Institute for the deputy prosecutor of Lublin Province, T. Kaminski, Warsaw, March 18, 1960, IPN Archive, file ref. # Lu/0/8/298/4/0317.

87. Ibid., 317 and n. 184: Erich Fuchs, April 1963, BA Ludwigsburg B162/208 AR-Z 251/59, vol. 9, p. 1784.

88. Ibid., 317 and n. 185: Erich Bauer, November 1965, StA Dortmund 45 Js 27/6, p. 557.

89. Ibid., 321 and n. 205: interrogation of Ignat Danilchenko, November 1979, Tyumen, Procurator's Office, Procuracy of the USSR, *US vs. Demjanjuk*.

90. Ibid., 322 and n. 206: statement of Hubert Gomerski, November 1965, copy in NIOD Archive 804/48, p. 136.

91. Ibid., 322 and n. 207: statement of Alfred Ittner, BA Ludwigsburg B162/208 AR-Z 251/59, vol. 7, p. 1426.

92. Ibid., 322 and n. 209: statement of Kurt Bolender, 1961, BA Ludwigsburg B162/208 AR-Z 252/59, vol. 11, p. 193.

93. Ibid., 218 and n. 25: Bolender, hearing report, Bavarian State Criminal Investigation Office, Munich, June 5, 1962, MPLW Archive Wlodawa.

94. Ibid., 218 and n. 26: Jakub Biskupicz, witness hearing report, Hagen, November 9, 1965, NIOD Archive.

95. Ibid., 219 and n. 27: Eda Lichtman testimony, ZSt Ludwigsburg Archive, case file #45 Js 27/61, file #208 AR-Z 251/59, Holon, Israel, May 1959.

96. Ibid., 219 and n. 28: Michael Tregenza, "Christian Wirth: Inspektor der SS-Sonderkommandos der Aktion Reinhard," Majdanek Notebooks, 1993, p. 48; and Ibid., 220 and n. 29: Floss also handled the burnings at Treblinka: Tregenza, p. 49.

97. Ibid., 235.

98. Ibid., 430 and n. 150: judgment of Hagen District Court, December 20, 1966, 11 Ks 1/64.

99. Ibid., 444n18: deposition of Bauer, Berlin, December 10, 1962, BA Ludwigsburg B162/208 AR-Z 251/59, vol. 8, pp. 1663–1669.

100. Deposition of Engel before the Information Bureau for Jews, Westerbork, Holland, BA Ludwigsburg B162/208 AR-Z 251/59, vol. 5, pp. 889–892.

101. NIOD Archive 804/20, p. 95

102. Bem, *Sobibor Extermination Camp, 1942–1943*, 501 and n. 223: deposition of Jan Piwonski, Lublin, April 29, 1975.

103. Ibid., 444: deposition of Piwonski, Lublin, May 10, 1984, StA Sob 85 PM III NO 99, pp. 8–9.

104. Ibid., 444 and n. 23: report of Dov Freiburg, Lodz, July 25, 1945, StA Dortmund, Js 2/61, vol. 8, p. 2638; deposition of Jan Krzowski, Lublin, August 1974, BA Ludwigsburg B162/208 AR-Z 643/71, vol. 3, pp. 410–418; and deposition of Bronislaw Lobejko, a railway worker, Olesnica, January 8, 1946, StA Dortmund Sob 85 PM IV NO 178: he witnessed the smell of burning petroleum.

105. Ibid., 394: deposition of Hubert Gomerski, Butzbach prison, February 1964, BA Ludwigsburg B162/208 AR-Z 252/59, vol. 7, pp. 1254–1258, and proceedings against Bolender et al., Hagen, StA Dortmund XI, 1965, pp. 709 and 712.

106. Ibid., 444n24: statement of Ignat Danilchenko, January 25, 1985, Lisakowsk, Kazakhstan, StA Dortmund Sob 85 PM V NO 96; statement of Jan Piwonski, Lublin, April 1975, BA Ludwigsburg B162/208 AR-Z 643/71, vol. 4, pp. 441–452.

107. Ibid., 510 and n. 247: Jakob Biskubisz stated that he had been ordered by SS-Oberscharführer Gustav Wagner to scatter human ashes in the Sobibor vegetable yard: deposition of Biskubisz, Tel Aviv, June 6, 1962, BA Ludwigsburg B162/208 AR-Z 251/59, vol. 7, pp. 1471–1479.

108. Ibid., 510: letter to World Jewish Congress, December 3, 1961, BA Ludwigsburg B162/208 AR-Z 251/59, vol. 5, pp. 1024 and 1044.

109. Ibid., 510: deposition of Lobejko before Judge Zielinski, Olesnica, January 8, 1946.

110. Ibid., 510: deposition of Piwonski, Chelm, November 10, 1945, StA Do Sob 85 PM III NO 109, p. 5.

111. Ibid., 283 and n. 82: Karl Frenzel, hearing report, ZStL file 251/59-6-1113, Gottingen, March 1962, MPLW Archive Wlodawa.

112. Ibid., 413–414, n. 91: deposition of Felix Gorny, Dortmund, September 6, 1962, BA Ludwigsburg B162/208 AR-Z 251/59, vol. 8, pp. 1517–1521.

113. Ibid., 290.

114. Ibid., 291 and n. 97: Franz Suchomel, hearing report, State Criminal Investigation Office, ZStL file 251/59-6-1129f, Altotting, January 1962; Heinrich Matthes, hearing report, State Criminal Investigation Office, ZStL file 251/59-6-1129f, Altotting, Cologne, July 1962.

115. Ibid., 288.

116. Ibid., 291 and n. 98: Robert Juhrs, hearing report, State Criminal Investigation Office, Frankfurt, May 1962, NIOD Archive.

117. Ibid., 292 and n. 100: Antoni Raczynski, letter to the regional commission for the investigation of Nazi crimes in Lublin, Trawniki, December 3, 1966, MPLW Archive.

118. Ibid., 436 and n. 170: deposition of Franciszek Parkola regarding Sobibor, before deputy district attorney Gorgol, Lublin, May 5, 1967, StA Do Sob 85 PM V NO f. 127.

119. Ibid., 331 and n. 65: letter from the Main Commission to the prosecutor of the Lublin District Court, September 28, 1945, Lublin, IPN Archive.

120. Ibid., 331 and n. 66: letter, district judge, Lublin, to the Main Commission, Judge Jozef Skorzynski, Lublin, October 21, 1945, Lublin, IPN Archive.

121. Ibid., 332.

122. Ibid.

123. Ibid., 197n26: Alexander Pechersky, hearing report, IPN Archive Lublin, Kiev, KGB Investigations Department, August 11, 1961.

124. Ibid., 335.

125. Harrison et al., *Belzec, Sobibor, Treblinka*, 73 and n. 156: excerpts of the 65th Army's 1944 investigation file on Treblinka, kept in Podolsk, were published in F. Sverdlov, ed., *Dokumenty obviniaiut: Kholokost; Svidetel'stva Krasnoi Armii* (Moscow, 1996); copies were also passed on to the Extraordinary Commission in Moscow: GARF files 7021-115-8, 9, 10, 11 and GARF 7445-2-136.

126. Ibid., 74

127. Ibid., 394–395.

128. Ibid., 334 and n. 279: *Protokol czynnosci wykomanych w terenie w toku dochodzenia sadowego w sprawie obozu smierci w Treblince*, IPN Archive NTN 69, p. 79R.

129. Ibid., 334.

130. Ibid., 296 and 297n98: statement of Goldfarb, September 21, 1944, GARF 7445-2-134, p. 31.

131. Ibid., 297.

132. Ibid., 320 and n. 199: interrogation of Nikolai Shalayev, December 18, 1950, case against Fedorenko, vol. 15, p. 164; exhibit GX-125 in *US vs. Reimer*.

133. Ibid., 321 and n. 202: interrogation of Ivan Shevchenko, September 8, 1944, GARF 7445-2-134, p. 19.

134. Ibid., 325–326 and nn. 227–230: interrogation of Pavel Leleko, February 1945, SMERSH, 2nd Belorussian Front; interrogation of Nikolaj Malagon, March 1978, Zaporozhe, Procuracy of the Zaporozhe region, Demjanjuk or Fedorenko case; interrogation of Prokofij Rjabtsev, February 1965, Zuev or Matwijenko trial, exhibit GX-121 in *US vs. Reimer*; and testimony of Georgij Skydan, May 1950, Baranovichi, Skydan trial, exhibit GX-141 in *US vs. Reimer*.

135. Raschke, *Useful Enemies*, 474–475.

136. Ibid.

137. Harrison et al., *Belzec, Sobibor, Treblinka*, 446 and n. 34: interrogation of Pavel Leleko, February 20, 1945, SMERSH, 2nd Belorussian Front.

138. Ibid., 448 and n. 42: statement of Pavel Leleko, February 21, 1945, SMERSH, 2nd Belorussian Front.

139. Ibid., 449 and n. 47: file, August 24, 1944, GARF 7021-115-9, p. 109.

140. Ibid., 446 and n. 33: judgment against Franz Stangl, Dusseldorf District Court, December 22, 1970, 8 Ks 1/69, *JuNSV*, vol. 34.

141. Ibid., 493 and n. 201: statement of Henryk Reichman / Chil Rajchman, November 12, 1945, Lodz, IPN Archive NTN 69, p. 29; also published in Z. Lukaszkiewicz, *Oboz stracen w Treblince*.

142. Ibid., 447 and n. 35: judgment against Kurt Franz, Dusseldorf District Court, September 3, 1965, 8 1 Ks 2/64, *JuNSV*, vol. 22.

143. Ibid., 357 and 358n68: Akt, August 24, 1944, GARF 7021-115-9, p. 109.

144. Gross, *Golden Harvest*, 20.

145. Ibid., 22n26: Dr. Jozef Kermisz, *W Treblince po raz drugi*, Jewish Historical Institute (ZIH), Central Jewish Historical Commission [CZKH], 280/XX, pp. 56–72.

146. Ibid., 23n28: Martyna Rusiniak-Karwat, *Neighbors of Treblinka*, ZIH, Warsaw.

147. Ibid., 22 and n. 27: State Archive, Siedlce, Circuit Court of Siedlce, Criminal Division, sygn. 580.

148. Ibid., n36.

149. Harrison et al., *Belzec, Sobibor, Treblinka*, 30.

150. Ibid., 78.

151. Ibid.

Chapter 3

1. Bem, *Sobibor Extermination Camp 1942–1943*, 314n22: letter from Colonel Bryniarski, Ministry of Internal Affairs, to the deputy provincial security chief of the Citizens' Militia (police) in Lublin, January 21, 1965, confidential, no. J-084 T 65, IPN Archive Lublin.

2. Ibid., 315n24: letter from the chief of the Investigation Department of the Citizens' Militia (police) HQ, Lublin, re the depositing of documentation in the archive concerning crimes in Belzec, Sobibor, Trawniki, and Poniatowa, Lublin, March 10, 1965, IPN Archive Lublin.

3. Ibid., 315n25: letter from the Ministry of Internal Affairs to the deputy provincial security chief of the Citizens' Militia (police), Lublin, August 8, 1966, no. J-74/5/66 and no. J-1410/1240/T/67, IPN Archive Lublin.

4. Ibid., 316n27: internal confidential memo, Citizens' Militia (police) HQ, September 23, 1966, IPN Archive Lublin.

5. Ibid., 316n29: letter from the Citizens' Militia (police) chief, Lublin Province, to the deputy district security chief of the Citizens' Militia (police), Wlodawa, September 23, 1966, I, dz. G-1139/66, IPN Archive Lublin.

6. Ibid., 317.

7. See "Criminal Activities of the Wachmänner at Belzec," investigation file, 1965–1968, IPN Archive Lublin, 08/298.

8. Belzec Memorial Museum, wall display.

9. AIPN Lu-08/298.

10. Ibid.

11. Ibid.

12. Ibid.

13. Ibid.

14. "The Case Eugenius Maytchenko," Death Camps, www.deathcamps.org/reinhard/maytchenko.html.

Chapter 4

1. Record of interrogation of Pavel Kozlov, August 24, 1944, Moskalenko trial, case #2871, archival file #11991, SBU Archive Lvov, and *US vs. Hajda*.

2. Record of interrogation of Nikolaj Olejnikov, January 1947, archival criminal case #202, Olejnikov trial, FSB Archive Stalingrad/Volgograd, and *US vs. Zajanckauskas*.

3. Record of interrogation of Vasilij Smetanyuk, July 1947, Smetanyuk trial, archival file #10692, SBU Archive Ivano-Frankivsk, and *US vs. Zajanckauskas*.

4. Record of interrogation of Josef Masyuk, August 1947, Masyuk trial, case #4501, archival file #891, SBU Archive Ivano-Frankivsk, and *US vs. Kwoczak* and *US vs. Reimer*.

5. Record of interrogation of Dimitrij Korzhinskij, August 1947, RG 20869, vol. 22, FSB Archive Moscow, and *US vs. Kwoczak*.

6. Record of interrogation of Vladimir Emelyanov, September 1947, Iskaradov trial, case #5734, archival file #37834, SBU Archive Donetsk, and *US vs. Zajanckauskas* and *US vs. Demjanjuk*.

7. Record of interrogation of Ivan Knysch, January 1948, Iskaradov trial, case #5734, archival file #37834, SBU Archive Donetsk, and *US vs. Reimer*.

8. Record of interrogation of Nikolaj Potyatynik, February 1948, Potyatynik trial, case #4951, archival file #1811, SBU Archive Ivano-Frankivsk, and *US vs. Kwoczak* and *US vs. Reimer*.

9. Record of interrogation of Alexander Yeger, April 1948, *US vs. Fedorenko* or *US vs. Demjanjuk* (or both).

10. Record of interrogation of Fedor Tartynskij, June 1948, Iskaradov trial, case #5734, archival file #37834, SBU Archive Donetsk, and *US vs. Reimer*.

11. Record of interrogation of Nikolaj Tkachuk, September 1948, Tkachuk trial, case #5541, archival file #2609, SBU Archive Ivano-Frankivsk.

12. Record of interrogation of Nikolaj Belous, March 1949, Belous trial, case #2391, archival file #27090, SBU Archive Lvov, and *US vs. Hajda*, *US vs. Kwoczak*, and *US vs. Reimer*.

13. Record of interrogation of Nikolaj Pavli, November 1949, Pavli trial and Goncharov trial, archival file #56434, SBU Archive Donetsk or Kiev.

14. Record of interrogation of Andrej Kuchma, February 1950, Kuchma trial, case #7707, archival file #59446, SBU Archive Kiev, and *US vs. Reimer*.

15. Record of interrogation of Nikolai Shalayev, November 1950, Voronezh, Shalayev trial, archival file #17214, and *Demjanjuk vs. Petrovsky* and *US vs. Reimer*.

16. Record of interrogation of Nikolai Shalayev, December 1950, Voronezh, Shalayev trial, archival file #17214, and *Demjanjuk vs. Petrovsky* and *US vs. Reimer*.

17. Record of interrogation of Nikolai Shalayev, December 1950, Voronezh, Shalayev trial, archival file #17214, and *Demjanjuk vs. Petrovsky* and *US vs. Reimer*; and Fedorenko trial, vol. 15, Simferopol, Crimea.

18. Record of interrogation of Ivan Shvidkij, July 1951, Shvidkij trial, case #7168, archive file #56433, SBU Archive Donetsk, and *US vs. Reimer*.

19. Record of interrogation of Fedor Tikhonovskij, January 1955, Zuev trial, case #44, archival file #31232, vol. 6, SBU Archive Dnepropetrovsk, and *US vs. Reimer*.

20. Record of interrogation of Prokofij Ryabtsev, April 1961, Schultz trial, case #14, archival file #66437, SBU Archive Kiev, and *Demjanjuk vs. Petrovsky* and *US vs. Reimer*.

21. Record of interrogation of Nikolai Leontev, June 1964, Matvienko trial, case #4, archival file #100366, vol. 1, FSB Archive Krasnodar, and *US vs. Reimer*.

22. Record of interrogation of Mikhail Korzhikow, September 1964, Matvienko trial, case #4, archival file #100366, vol. 10, FSB Archive Krasnodar, and *US vs. Reimer*.

23. Record of interrogation of Grigorij Kniga, December 1964, Matvienko trial, case #4, archival file #100366, FSB Archive Krasnodar.

24. Record of interrogation of Alexander Zakharov, January 1965, Matvienko trial, case #4, archival file #100366, FSB Archive Krasnodar.

25. Record of interrogation of Zaki Tuktarov, February 1965, Matvienko trial, case #4, archival file #100366, vol. 13, FSB Archive Krasnodar, and *US vs. Demjanjuk*.

26. Record of interrogation of Prokofij Ryabtsev, February 1965, Matvienko trial, case #4, archival file #100366, vol. 13, FSB Archive Krasnodar, and *Demjanjuk vs. Petrovsky*, and *US vs. Reimer*.

27. Record of interrogation of Mikhail Laptev, February 1965, Matvienko trial, case #4, archival file #100366, vol. 13, FSB Archive Krasnodar, and *US vs. Zajanckauskas*.

28. Record of interrogation of Vasili Podenok, March 1965, Matvienko trial, case #4, archival file #100366, vol. 5, FSB Archive Krasnodar.

29. Record of interrogation of Ivan Tkachuk, March 1965, Matvienko trial, case #4, archival file #100366, FSB Archive Krasnodar, and *Demjanjuk vs. Petrovsky*, and *US vs. Reimer*.

30. Record of interrogation of Vasilij Orlovskij, 1965, Zuev trial, case #44, archival file #31232, SBU Archive Dnepropetrovsk.

31. Record of interrogation of Piotr Browzew, August 1965, Zuev trial, case #44, archival file #31232, SBU Archive Dnepropetrovsk.

32. Record of interrogation of Kiril Prochorenko, September 1965, Zuev trial, case #44, archival file #31232, SBU Archive Dnepropetrovsk.

33. Record of interrogation of Vasili Litvinenko, January 1968, Litvinenko trial, case #158, archival file #57252, vol. 7, SBU Archive Lvov, and *US vs. Demjanjuk*.

34. Record of interrogation of Yakov Klimenko, May 1968, Litvinenko trial, case #158, archival file #57252, SBU Archive Lvov, and *US vs. Zajanckauskas* and *US vs. Reimer*.

35. Record of interrogation of Alexander Fedchenko, November 1968, Litvinenko trial, case #158, archival file #57252, vol. 2, SBU Archive Lvov, and *US vs. Reimer*.

36. Record of interrogation of Roman Pitrow, October 1962, Bad Kissingen, Germany, Hahn trial, file 11 AR-Z 373/59, vol. 30, ZStL Ludwigsburg, and *US vs. Zajanckauskas*.

37. Trial testimony of Karl Streibel, January 1973, Streibel trial, file 147 Js 43/69, vol. 133, State Prosecutor's Office Hamburg, and *US vs. Kwoczak* and *US vs. Reimer*.

38. Record of interrogation of Prokofij Businnij, November 1974, Streibel trial, file 147 Js 43/69, vol. 117, State Prosecutor's Office Hamburg, and *US vs. Reimer*.

Chapter 5

1. Shevchenko trial, case #94, archival file #13199, SBU Archive Cherkassy, and AUSHMM, RG 31.018M, reel 6.

2. Bill of indictment for Sergei Vasilenko, April 14, 1945, case #9; included as an evidence exhibit in Schultz trial, case #14, archival file #66437, SBU Archive Kiev, and AUSHMM RG 31.018M, reel 53-64.

3. Record of court session for Sergei Vasilienko, April 15, 1945; included as an evidence exhibit in Schultz trial, case #14, archival file #66437, SBU Archive Kiev, and AUSHMM RG 31.018M, reel 53-64.

4. Bill of indictment for Ivan Terekhov, April 14, 1945, case #11; included as an evidence exhibit in Schultz trial, case #14, archival file #66437, SBU Archive Kiev, and AUSHMM RG 31.018M, reel 53-64.

5. Record of court session for Ivan Terekhov, April 15, 1945; included as an evidence exhibit in Schultz trial, case #14, archival file #66437, SBU Archive Kiev, and AUSHMM RG 31.018M, reel 53-64.

6. Information sheet on case #6981 against Alexander Dukhno, Mikhail Korzhikow, and Ivan Voloshin, October 1965; included as an evidence exhibit in Zuev trial, case #44, archival file #31232, SBU Archive Dnepropetrovsk, and AUSHMM RG 31.018M, reel 75.

7. Information sheet on the sentencing of Alexander Zakharov, September 1965; included as an evidence exhibit in Zuev trial, case #44, archival file #31232, SBU Archive Dnepropetrovsk, AUSHMM RG 31.018M, reel 75.

8. Record of trial of Ivan Kondratenko, March 22, 1948, case #6056, archival file #57800, SBU Archive Kiev, and *US vs. Hajda, US vs. Kwoczak, US vs. Zajanckauskas,* and *US vs. Reimer.*

9. Record of court appearance of Nikolaj Gutsulyak, June 25, 1948, case #5117, archival file #2180, SBU Archive Ivano-Frankivsk, and *US vs. Kwoczak.*

10. Record of trial of Vladimir Terletskij, June 29, 1948, case #5134, archival file #2345, SBU Archive Ivano-Frankivsk, and *US vs. Kwoczak.*

11. Record of court session of Filip Babenko, December 24, 1948, case #6937, archival file #58240, SBU Archive Kiev, and *US vs. Reimer.*

12. Information sheet on the bill of indictment of Fedor Ryabeka, Mikhail Andreyenko, and Terentij Gordienko, November 2, 1949, case #6491; included as an evidence exhibit in Schultz trial, case #14, archival file #66437, SBU Archive Kiev, and AUSHMM RG 31.018M, reel 53-64.

13. Record of trial of Georgij Skydan, May 26, 1950, Baranovichi, archival file #8309, *Demjanjuk vs. Petrovsky* and *US vs. Reimer.*

14. Record of trial of Nikolai Shalayev, December 20, 1951, Voronezh, archival file #17214, Fedorenko trial, vol. 15, Simferopol, Crimea, and *Demjanjuk vs. Petrovsky* and *US vs. Reimer.*

15. Record of court session of Ivan Shvidkij, January 12, 1952, case #7168, archival file #56433, SBU Archive Donetsk, and *US vs. Reimer.*

16. Background information sheet on the case against Vasili Shuller, 1954, Zaporozhe, case #6636; included as an evidence exhibit in Zuev trial, August 1965, case #44, archival file #31232, SBU Archive Dnepropetrovsk, AUSHMM RG 31.018M, reel 75.

17. Background information sheet on the case against Nikolaj Skakodub, 1960, Vinnitsa, archival file #25190; included as an evidence exhibit in Schultz trial, case #14, archival file #66437, SBU Archive Kiev, AUSHMM RG 31.018M, reel 53-64.

18. Simkin, "Death Sentence despite the Law," 299–312.

19. Ibid., 299.

20. Ibid.

21. Ibid., 300.

22. Ibid., 301.

23. David Rich, email to the author, August 2018.

24. Simkin, "Death Sentence despite the Law," 301, 311n9.

25. Ibid., 301.

26. Ibid., 302.

27. Ibid., 302–303.

28. Ibid., 303.

29. Ibid., 304.

30. Ibid.

31. Ibid., 305.

32. Ibid.

33. Ibid.

34. Ibid., 307.

35. Ibid.

36. Ibid., 307–308.

37. Ibid., 309.

38. Ibid.

39. Schultz trial, case #14, archival file #66437, SBU Archive Kiev, AUSHMM 31.018M, reel 53-64, microfilm #32-41.

40. Zuev trial, case #44, archival file #31232, SBU Archive Dnepropetrovsk, AUSHMM RG 31.018M, reel 75.

Chapter 6

1. Judgment of the State Court Dusseldorf against Franz Swidersky, October 15, 1971, State Prosecutor's Office Dusseldorf, file #8 Ks 4/70, and *US vs. Hajda* and *US vs. Reimer.*

Chapter 7

1. Judy Feigin, *OSI: Striving for Accountability in the Aftermath of the Holocaust* (Washington, DC: US Department of Justice, 2009), iv. For further information on OSI's Trawniki investigations and cases, see Peter Black Papers, Archive of the USHMM, accession #2008.331.1, especially series 3: OSI Reports, 1980–1992, box/folder 12.3: Interim Report on Historical Evidence re: Alleged Activities of Trawniki Camp, 1983 [Restricted access]; subseries 4: index cards, Trawniki Camp Investigations, 2000 [restricted access]; subseries 7: Trawniki Camp Investigations, 1999, boxes/folders 47.12–47.14: Interviews, January and July 1999 [restricted access]; subseries 9: Trawniki Camp Investigations, 1992, boxes/folders 48.15–48.16: Testimony, 1992 [restricted access]; subseries 10: box/folder 51.12: "OSI and the Archives of the Former USSR," by Michael MacQueen, 1995; box/folder 52.28: *US Attorneys' Bulletin* 54, no. 1 (2006), OSI; subseries 14: Trawniki Materials, 1990–2010, box/folder 56.18: Biographical notes on Ivan Shevchenko, Sabit Shirgaliev, and others; box/folder 57.6: catalog records and documents: concentration camp service cards, personnel files, and protocols of interrogation (1940s); boxes/folders 58.1–58.10: FSB Archive Moscow, K-779, index cards, Aktion Reinhard, 1990–2010 (10 folders); boxes/folders 59.3–59.4: FSB Archive Moscow, K-779, index cards: Assignments, 1990-2010; box/folder 60.21: Interrogations, 1940s–1960s (2000–2004); boxes/folders 62.1–62.4: Russian and Ukrainian source materials, 1940s–1960s; boxes/folders 62.5–62.8: Charles Sydnor Jr., Expert Report, Demjanjuk case, 2000; Supplement to Expert Report, Demjanjuk case, 2000–2001; and boxes/folders 62.9–63.7: Trawniki immigration files, 1940s–1950s (14 folders). [*Note that *restricted-access* materials cannot be accessed without the prior permission of Dr. Peter Black, through the year 2032, at which time the restriction terms will be reevaluated.]

2. Feigin, *OSI*, 2–3.
3. Ibid., 4.
4. Ibid., 7.
5. Ibid., ix, n. 4.
6. Ibid., 21.
7. Ibid., 33.
8. Ibid., 40.
9. Ibid., 41.
10. Ibid., 44n15.
11. Ibid.,451n74.
12. Ibid., 46.
13. Ibid., 29.
14. Ibid., 23–24.
15. Ibid., 24.
16. Ibid., 28.
17. Interview with Dr. Elizabeth B. White, p. 18: shfg.org/resources/Documents/FH%208%20(2016)%20White.pdf.
18. Feigin, *OSI*, 22–23.
19. Ibid., 31n16.
20. Ibid., 28–29.
21. Ibid., 11; see 1979 letter from Attorney General Benjamin Civiletti to Lev Smirnov, chairman of the Soviet Supreme Court, p. 535.
22. Ibid., 535.
23. Ibid., 258n45.
24. Ibid., 19n59: 1980 memo from OSI historian David Marwell to OSI director Allan Ryan, re "Soviet Archives"; 1984 memo from David Marwell to OSI director Neal Sher, re "Soviet Archives."
25. Ibid., 19n57.
26. Ibid., 19n58.
27. Ibid., 28.
28. Ibid., 19–20, n. 62.
29. Ibid., 565n1.
30. Lawrence Douglas, *The Right Wrong Man: John Demjanjuk and the Last Great Nazi War Crimes Trial* (Princeton, NJ: Princeton University Press, 2016), 62.
31. Feigin, *OSI*, 566n5.
32. Ibid., 557.
33. Ibid., 558.

34. Ibid., 566n8.

35. Ibid., 559.

36. Ibid., 28.

37. Ibid., 567n20.

38. Ibid., v.

39. Ibid., vi.

40. Dr. White interview, 25.

41. Feigin, *OSI*, 48.

42. Ibid., 49.

43. Ibid., 50.

44. Ibid., 51.

45. Ibid., 53.

46. Ibid., 58.

47. David Rich email to author, August 2018.

48. Feigin, *OSI*, 59.

49. Ibid.

50. Ibid., 63n25; On legal aspects of the Fedorenko case, see Abbe L. Dienstag, "*Fedorenko v. US*: War Crimes, the Defense of Duress, and American Nationality Law," in *Columbia Law Review* 82, no. 1 (January 1982): 120–183.

51. *US vs. Kairys*, leagle.com/decision/19841854600FSupp1254_11667/UNITED%20; "Treblinka Guard Sent Home," the Nizkor Project, nizkor.org/hweb/people/k/kairys-liudas/press/kairys-liudas.html; *INS vs. Liudas Kairys*, US Court of Appeals, projectposner.org/case/1992/981F2d937; and Cordula Meyer, "Alleged Nazi War Criminal John Demjanjuk Trial to Break Legal Ground in Germany," sanfranciscosentinel.com/?p=34414.

52. *US vs. Hajda*, law.justia.com/cases/federal/district-courts/FSupp/963/1452/1644940.html.

53. *US vs. Kwoczak*, civil action #97-5632, June 27, 2002, leagle.com/decision/2002848210FSupp2d638_1785/ US. For additional information on this case, see Peter Black Papers, 1940–2014, Archive of the USHMM, accession #2008.331.1, series 3: OSI Reports, 1980–1992, subseries 6: Kwoczak, 1998–2002, box/folder 21.1-21.10: court transcript of cross-examination of Charles Sydnor Jr., 2000; declaration of Dr. Peter Black, 2000; expert report of Charles Sydnor Jr., 1999; Kwoczak deposition with exhibits, 1998; and opinion, 2002.

54. Mychailo Fostun, "London Man Denies Role in SS Massacres," January 26, 2003, telegraph.co.uk/ education/4792832/London-man-denies-role-in-SS-massacres; Jessica Elgot, "The UK Man Who Tracks Britain's Living War Criminals," January 29, 2015, huffingtonpost.co.uk/2015/01/26/nazi-hunter-stephen-ankie_n_6548; and Peter Black Papers, AUSHMM, Washington, DC: box/folder 20.12-20.15: statement of Dr. Peter Black, 2004 [restricted access], and correspondence, 2003-2004 [restricted access].

55. *US vs. Sawchuk*, nytimes.com/1999/06/11/nyregion/man-accused-in-nazi-case-leaves-country.html.

56. *US vs. Reimer*, fl1.findlaw.com/news.findlaw.com/hdocs/docs/crim/usreimer90502ord.pdf; *US vs. Reimer*, Court of Appeals, openjurist.org/356/f3d/456/united-states-v-reimer; Dan Barry, "About New York: A Face Seen and Unseen on the Subway" *New York Times*, September 17, 2005; Eric Steinhart, "The Chameleon of Trawniki"; and Peter Black Papers, AUSHMM, Washington, DC, accession #2008.331.1, series 5: subject files and source materials, subseries 14: Trawniki materials: FSB Archive Moscow, K-779, index cards, Reimer, 1990–2010.

57. "The Last Nazi Hunters," Warfare History Network, warfarehistorynetwork.com/2018/12/22/the-last-nazi-hunters.

58. Georg Bonisch and Jan Friedman, "The German Demjanjuk: Witness [Samuel Kunz] in War Crimes Trial Could Face Indictment," November 2, 2009, spiegel.de/international/germany/the-german-demjanjuk-witness-in-war-crimes-Trial-Could-Face-Indictment; "German Nazi Suspect Samuel Kunz Dies ahead of Trial," BBC, November 22, 2010; and David Rising, "Samuel Kunz, Nazi Suspect Dead before Germany Trial," *World Post*, January 22, 2011.

59. Raschke, *Useful Enemies*, 518.

60. *US vs. Vladas Zajanckauskas*, March 23, 2006, law.justia.com/cases/federal/appellate-courts/F3/441/32/593478; DOJ press release, August 16, 2007, justice.gov/archive/opa/pr/2007/August/07_crm_619.html; Linda Matchan, "Two Faces of a WWII Case: To US, a Nazi War Criminal; to Family, a Good Man," *Boston Globe*, September 29, 2007; Elizabeth Banicki, "Alleged Nazi Guard Can't Stay in US, Court Rules," July 20, 2010, courthousenews.com/2010/07/20/28981. htm; and "Deportation Orders Can't Dislodge Nazi Suspects from US Homes," Associated Press, July 30, 2013, nydailynews.com/news/national/queens-ex-nazi-nyc-article-1.141279. For further information on this case, see Peter Black Papers, 1940–2014, in the Archive of the USHMM, Washington, DC, accession #2008.331.1, series 4: Expert Witness Cases, subseries 12: Zajankauskas, including, in box/folder 37.10-40.7: correspondence, 2003–2009; affirmation on appeal (Reimer case), 2004; affirmation on appeal, 2006; affirmation on appeal, 2009; answers and counterclaim of Zajankauskas, 2002; decision of immigration judge, 2007; defendant's answers to government's set of interrogatories, 2003; defendant's pretrial memo, 2004; defendant's response to set of requests for production of documents, 2003; deposition of Dr. Peter Black, 2004; deposition of Zajankauskas, 1981 and 2003; deposition exhibits, 2003; expert

report of Dr. Peter Black, 2004; supplement to expert report, 2004; joint statement of undisputed facts and legal conclusions, 2004; memo of decision, 2005; transcript of Dr. Peter Black testimony, 2004; document lists, 2005; excerpts of transcript of Reimer case related to Zajankauskas, 1998; expert report of Charles Sydnor Jr. in Hajda case, 1996, and expert report of Sydnor in Reimer case, 1992; transcript of Reimer testimony, Reimer case; notes, 2003; report, "Roster of men sent to Warsaw," 2003; statements and interrogations (1940s and 1980s), 2003; correspondence re Zajankauskas's POW capture and release (1940s), 2002; Zajankauskas biographical information (1930s–1940s), 2003; Zajankauskas INS file (1950s), 2002; and Zajankauskas questionnaires (1940s), 2003.

Chapter 8

1. Douglas, *The Right Wrong Man*, 30.
2. Michael Hanusiak, "At Different Poles," *News from Ukraine*, March 1976.
3. O. Matviychuk, "Punishment Will Come," *News from Ukraine*, September 1977.
4. Douglas, *The Right Wrong Man*, 37–38.
5. Ibid., 49.
6. Ibid., 122.
7. Feigin, *OSI*, 540.
8. Douglas, *The Right Wrong Man*, 115–116.
9. Jonathan Drimmer interview with author Lawrence Douglas.
10. Feigin, *OSI*, 534. During the Demjanjuk case, there was testimony to the effect that the KGB had a technical department responsible for producing forged documents, and that this department had access to a very large archive of documents compiled during World War II.
11. "OSI and the Archives of the Former Soviet Union," an address by OSI senior historian Michael MacQueen to the Association of Historians in the Federal Government, delivered at the US Holocaust Memorial Museum, April 1994; and Feigin, *OSI*, 549n29.
12. Feigin, *OSI*, 551n42.
13. April 1982 memo to Kairys files, from Neal Sher, re "Testimony of Dr. Ruckerl, OSI #97"; and Feigin, *OSI*, 549n30.
14. Interrogation of Nikolai Shalayev, 1950–1951, FSB Archive Voronezh; also included in evidence at the Schultz trial, 1961–1962, SBU Archive Kiev, and at the Fedorenko trial, 1986, FSB Archive Simferopol.
15. Douglas, *The Right Wrong Man*, 101.
16. Feigin, *OSI*, 105.
17. Ibid., 109.
18. Ibid.
19. Douglas, *The Right Wrong Man*, 91.
20. Ibid., 114.
21. "How Terrible Is Ivan?," *Vanity Fair*, June 1992; "US-Israel Plot Charged in Holocaust Case," *Los Angeles Times*, December 24, 1991; and "Ivan the Terrible: A Case of Mistaken Identity," A&E Television, April 1991. Pat Buchanan was arguably the most influential of OSI's critics. He wrote several articles on OSI's prosecution of Demjanjuk, including "Nazi Hunting—with Guidance from the KGB," *Washington Times*, December 1, 1983; "Nazi Butcher or Mistaken Identity?," *Washington Post*, September 28, 1986; and "Deadly, Dubious ID Card," *Washington Times*, March 19, 1990. Also see Feigin, *OSI*, 174n48.
22. Douglas, *The Right Wrong Man*, 116.
23. Ibid., 117.
24. Feigin, *OSI*, 172n23.
25. Michael Hedges, "Traficant: Heal Thyself and Leave Demjanjuk Alone," *Washington Times*, January 5, 1994.
26. In 2002, Traficant was convicted of corruption, bribery, racketeering, and tax evasion. He was sentenced to eight years' imprisonment and expelled from Congress (Feigin, *OSI*, 553n56).
27. Memo to attorney general from solicitor general re "Demjanjuk vs. Petrovsky, 10 F. 3d 338, 6th Circuit, 1993" (Feigin, *OSI*, 173n30).
28. Feigin, *OSI*, 173n32.
29. "US vs. Demjanjuk, Case: 1:99-cv-01193-DAP"; documents submitted October–November 2011.
30. Affidavits of Storm Watkins, Jonathan Drimmer, Neal Sher, and Eli Rosenbaum.
31. Affidavit of Eli Rosenbaum.
32. Public Law 109-5, Section 1, 803 (d) 119 Stat. 19, 2005.
33. Affidavit of Eli Rosenbaum.
34. Affidavit of Neal Sher.
35. Affidavits of Neal Sher, Eli Rosenbaum, and Jonathan Drimmer.
36. *US vs. Demjanjuk*, 58 F. Supp. 1362, 1367, Ohio, 1981.

37. Feigin, *OSI*, 164.

38. Ibid., 172n28.

39. October 20, 1994, letter to Attorney General Janet Reno re conduct of Allan Ryan in connection with the various cases brought by him to denaturalize, deport, and extradite John Demjanjuk (Feigin, *OSI*, 174n43).

40. Douglas, *The Right Wrong Man*, 135.

41. Ibid., 153.

42. Ibid.

43. Ibid., 157.

44. Ibid., 158.

45. Ibid., 159.

46. Ibid., 190.

47. *Urteil der 1. Strafkammer des Landgerichts Munchen II als Schwurgericht in der Strafsache gegen Demjanjuk, John* ("Proceedings of the 1st Criminal Chamber of the Munich District Court II against John Demjanjuk") and LG Munchen II, February 2, 2010, and May 12, 2011—1 Ks 115 Js 12496/08.

48. Feigin, *OSI*, 550n38.

49. Ibid., 550n39.

50. Residence certificate of displaced-persons camp, Landshut, 1947.

51. Douglas, *The Right Wrong Man*, 21.

52. Ibid., 232.

53. Ibid., 233.

54. Ibid., 235.

55. Ibid.

56. Ibid., 236.

57. Ibid., 238.

58. Ibid., 240–241.

59. Ibid., 218.

60. Ibid., 220.

61. Ibid.

62. Ibid., 221.

63. Ibid.

64. Ibid., 223.

65. Ibid., 224.

66. Ibid., 293n21.

67. Ibid., 226.

68. Ibid., 293n29.

69. Ibid., 217.

70. Ibid., 291n2.

71. *Urteil der 1. Strafkammer des Landgerichts Munchen II als Schwurgericht in der Strafsache gegen Demjanjuk, John.*

72. Ibid.

73. Douglas, *The Right Wrong Man*, 252.

74. Ibid., 253.

75. Ibid., 254.

76. Ibid., 256.

77. Simkin, "Death Sentence despite the Law, 306.

Appendixes

1. Black, "Police Auxiliaries for Operation Reinhard, 51n30.

2. Harrison et al., *Belzec, Sobibor, Treblinka*, 29n120.

SOURCES

Books

Bem, Marek. *Sobibor Extermination Camp, 1942–1943.* Amsterdam: Stichting Sobibor, 2015.

Douglas, Lawrence. *The Right Wrong Man: John Demjanjuk and the Last Great Nazi War Crimes Trial.* Princeton, NJ: Princeton University Press, 2016.

Feigin, Judy. *OSI: Striving for Accountability in the Aftermath of the Holocaust.* Washington, DC: US Department of Justice, 2009.

Gross, Jan Tomasz. *Golden Harvest: Events at the Periphery of the Holocaust.* Oxford: Oxford University Press, 2012.

Harrison, Jonathan, Roberto Muehlenkamp, Jason Myers, Sergey Romanov, and Nicholas Terry. *Belzec, Sobibor, Treblinka: Holocaust Denial and Operation Reinhard; Critique of the Falsehoods of Mattogno, Graf, and Kues.* Holocaust Controversies (blog), 2011. https://holocaustcontroversies.blogspot.com.

Kuwalek, Robert. *Das Vernichtungslager Belzec.* Berlin: Metropol Verlag, 2013.

Nebolsin, Igor. *Stalin's Favorite: The Combat History of the 2nd Guards Tank Army from Kursk to Berlin.* Vol. 2, *From Lublin to Berlin, July 1944–May 1945.* Solihull, UK: Helion, 2016.

Raschke, Richard. *Useful Enemies: John Demjanjuk and America's Open-Door Policy for Nazi War Criminals.* Harrison, NY: Delphinium Books, 2013.

Articles

Black, Peter R. "Police Auxiliaries for Operation Reinhard: Shedding Light on the Trawniki Training Camp through Documents from behind the Iron Curtain." In *Secret Intelligence and the Holocaust.* Edited by David Bankier, 327–366. Jerusalem: Yad Vashem Holocaust Martyrs' and Heroes Remembrance Authority, 2006.

Kudryashov, Sergei. "Ordinary Collaborators: The Case of the Travniki Guards." In *Russia: War, Peace, and Diplomacy.* Edited by Ljubica Erickson and Mark Erickson, 226–239. London: Weidenfeld and Nicolson, 2005.

Libionka, Dariusz. "The Life Story of Chaim Hirszman: Remembrance of the Holocaust and Reflections on Postwar Polish-Jewish Relations." *Yad Vashem Studies* 34 (206): 219–248.

Penter, Tanja. "Local Collaborators on Trial: Soviet War Crimes Trials under Stalin (1943–1953)." *Cahiers du Monde Russe* 49, nos. 2–3 (2008): 341–364.

Pohl, Dieter. "Die Trawnikimänner im Vernichtungslager Belzec 1941–1943." In *NS-Gewaltherrschaft: Beitrage zur historischen Forschung und juristischen Aufarbeitung.* Edited by Alfred Gottwaldt, Norbert Kampe, and Peter Klein, 278–289. Berlin: Edition Hentrich, 2005.

Rich, David Alan. "Accountability without Limit: Soviet Trials of Aktion Reinhard Soviet Collaborators, 1944–1987." In *Eastern Europe Facing the Shoah: A History of Engagement, 1941–2016.* Edited by Raphael Utz and Jochen Böhler, . 2018.

Rich, David Alan. "Reinhard's Foot Soldiers: Soviet Trophy Documents and Investigative Records as Sources." In *Remembering for the Future: The Holocaust in an Age of Genocide.* Vol. 1. Edited by John Roth and Elisabeth Maxwell, 688–701. London: Palgrave Macmillan, 2001.

Simkin, Lev. "Death Sentence despite the Law: A Secret 1962 Crimes-against-Humanity Trial in Kiev." *Holocaust and Genocide Studies* 27, no. 2 (2013): 299–312.

Internet

"The Case of Eugeniusz Maytchenko." www.deathcamps.org/reinhard/maytchenko.html.

Interview with Dr. Elizabeth B. White. shfg.org/resources/Documents/FH%208%20(2016)%20White.pdf.

US vs. Kairys, leagle.com/decision/19841854600FSupp1254_11667/UNITED%20; "Treblinka Guard Sent Home," The Nizkor Project, nizkor.org/hweb/people/k/kairys-liudas/press/kairys-liudas.html; *INS vs. Liudas Kairys*, US Court of Appeals, projectposner.org/case/1992/981F2d937; and "Alleged Nazi War Criminal John Demjanjuk Trial to Break Legal Ground in Germany," by Cordula Meyer, sanfranciscosentinel.com/?p=34414.

US vs. Hajda: law.justia.com/cases/federal/district-courts/FSupp/963/1452/1644940.html.

US vs. Kwoczak, civil action #97-5632, June 27, 2002, leagle.com/decision/2002848210FSupp2d638_1785/U.S.

Mychailo Fostun, "London Man Denies Role in SS Massacres." January 26, 2003, telegraph.co.uk/education/4792832/London-man-denies-role-in-SS-massacres; and "The UK Man Who Tracks Britain's Living War Criminals," by Jessica Elgot, January 29, 2015, huffingtonpost.co.uk/2015/01/26/nazi-hunter-stephen-ankie_n_6548.

US vs. Sawchuk. nytimes.com/1999/06/11/nyregion/man-accused-in-nazi-case-leaves-country.html.

US vs. Reimer, fl1.findlaw.com/news.findlaw.com/hdocs/docs/crim/usreimer90502ord.pdf; *US vs. Reimer*, Court of Appeals, openjurist.org/356/f3d/456/united-states-v-reimer; "About New York: A Face Seen and Unseen on the Subway," by Dan Barry, *New York Times*, September 17, 2005; and "The Chameleon of Trawniki," by Eric Steinhart, warefarehistorynetwork.com/2018/12/22/the-last-nazi-hunters.

Samuel Kunz, "The German Demjanjuk: Witness in War Crimes Trial Could Face Indictment," by Georg Bonisch and Jan Friedman, November 2, 2009, spiegel.de/international/germany/the-german-demjanjuk-witness-in-war-

229

crimes-Trial-Could-Face-Indictment; "German Nazi Suspect Samuel Kunz Dies ahead of Trial," November 22, 2010, BBC; and "Samuel Kunz, Nazi Suspect Dead before Germany Trial," by David Rising, January 22, 2011, *World Post*. *US vs. Vladas Zajanckauskas*, March 23, 2006, law.justia.com/cases/federal/appellate-courts/F3/441/32/593478; DOJ press release, August 16, 2007, justice.gov/archive/opa/pr/2007/August/07_crm_619.html; "Two Faces of a WWII Case: To US, a Nazi War Criminal; to Family, a Good Man," by Linda Matchan, *Boston Globe*, September 29, 2007; "Alleged Nazi Guard Can't Stay in U.S., Court Rules," by Elizabeth Banicki, July 20, 2010, courthousenews. com/2010/07/20/28981.htm; and "Deportation Orders Can't Dislodge Nazi Suspects from U.S. Homes," Associated Press, July 30, 2013, nydailynews.com/news/national/queens-ex-nazi-nyc-article-1.141279.

Archives

Archive of the United States Holocaust Memorial Museum (USHMM), Washington, DC:
Shevchenko trial: RG-31.018M, reel 6
Original held in SBU Archive Cherkassy
Case #94, archive file #13199

Zuev trial: RG-31.018M, reel 75
Original held in SBU Archive Dnepropetrovsk
Criminal case #44, archive file #31232
Vol. 1: Taras Olejnik, pp. 54–58
Alexander Zakharov/Pruss, pp. 82–85
Vasili Shuller, pp. 117–127
Grigorij Kniga, pp. 133–138
Ivan Woloshin, pp. 195–203

Schults trial: RG-31.018M, reel 53–64, microfilm #32–41, image #s 1982–2195
Original held in SBU Archive Kiev
Criminal case #14, archive file #66437
Emanuel Schults, vol. 1, pp. 47–60
Dimitri Borodin, vol. 3, pp. 44–45
Sergei Vasilenko, March 1945, vol. 4, pp.10–16; vol. 5, pp. 4–6; vol. 6, pp. 67–74; vol. 14, pp. 18–20
Ivan Terekhov, vol. 18, pp. 23–31
Filip Levchishin, 1951, vol. 19, pp. 17–33
Evdokim Parfinyuk, vol. 24, pp. 145–151
"Proposal to Rescind Sentence," July 21, 1961, and "Supreme Court Determination Concerning Mikhail Gorbachev," July 25, 1961, vol. 28, pp. 120–125
Ivan Juchnowskij, vol. 31, pp. 1–4
Jakob Engelhardt, vol. 31, pp. 26–30
Petr Goncharov, 1951, vol. 33, pp. 206–215
1962 resolution of the "Presidium of the Supreme Soviet" allowing the military tribunal in Kiev to sentence the defendants to death, if necessary: reel 64, image #00001846.
Investigation of the defendants, conducted by the Ukrainian KGB, in preparation for trial, February–November 1961: reel 64, image #00002003.
1962 resolution of the "Presidium of the Supreme Soviet" reducing Ivan Terekhov's death sentence to fifteen years' imprisonment, with a further reduction for time served in his previous conviction of April 1945: reel 64, image #00002195.
Provisional Disciplinary Regulations for German Police Troops, April 1940: RG-11.001, reel 80 (11 pages); original held in the RGVA (Russian State Military Archive): located by Dr. David Rich, Dr. Jeffrey Richter, and Dr. Todd Huebner, all of whom are DOJ-OSI historians

Archive of the Institute of National Memory (AIPN), Lublin, Poland
FSB (Federal Security Service, Russia) Central Archive, Moscow, Russian Federation
FSB Archive Krasnodar, Russian Federation
SBU (Security Service of Ukraine) Archive; various, but especially Kiev and Dnepropetrovsk
Belzec Memorial Museum, Belzec, Poland

Other

Freedom of Information (FOIA) requests through the US Department of Justice (DOJ), Washington, DC

Chaim Hirszmann, in Polish army uniform. One of only two known survivors of the Belzec death camp. Worked for the Polish Security Service (UB) after the war. Murdered in Lublin, 1946.

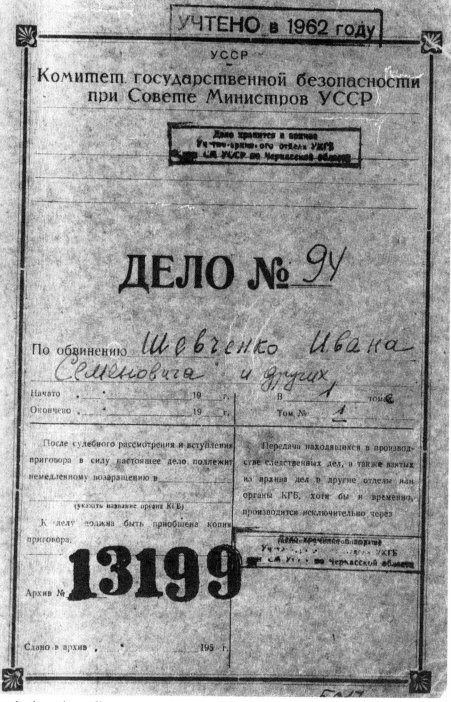

ДЕЛО № 94

По обвинению *Шевченко Ивана Семеновича и других,*

Начато . . . 19 г.   В *1* томах

Окончено . . . 19 г.   Том № *1*

После судебного рассмотрения и вступления приговора в силу настоящее дело подлежит немедленному возвращению в _____

(указать название органа КГБ)

К делу должна быть приобщена копия приговора.

Передача находящихся в производстве следственных дел, а также взятых из архива дел в другие отделы или органы КГБ, хотя бы и временно, производится исключительно через

Дело хранится в архиве
Учетно-архивного отдела УКГБ
при СМ УССР по Черкасской области

Архив № **13199**

Сдано в архив . . . 195 г.

Shevchenko trial, case file cover

UKRAINIAN SOVIET SOCIALIST REPUBLIC

COMMITTEE FOR STATE SECURITY
AT THE COUNCIL OF MINISTERS OF THE
UKRAINIAN SOVIET SOCIALIST REPUBLIC

The case is stored in archives
Illegible... of the Ukrainian KGB
at the Council of Ministers of the
Ukrainian Soviet Socialist Republic
Illegible Cherkassy province

(rubber stamp)

CASE #94

Indictment of   *Shevchenko, Ivan Semenovich*
                  and others

Started in _____ 19___ yr. | In _____1_____ volume
Ended in _____ 19___ yr. | Volume # _____ 1 _____

Upon judicial examination and the sentence coming into force, this case is subject to immediate return to _____
(specify the name of KGB agency)

A copy of the sentence should be attached to the case.

Transfer of active investigation cases, as well as cases extracted from archives onto other departments or KGB agencies, even if only temporarily, is done exclusively through

The case is stored *illegible*
illegible
Illegible of the Cherkassy province

(rubber stamp)

Archive # **13199**

(rubber stamp)

Submitted to archives: _____ 195 yr.

PAGE 1

Shevchenko trial, case file cover translated from Russian to English

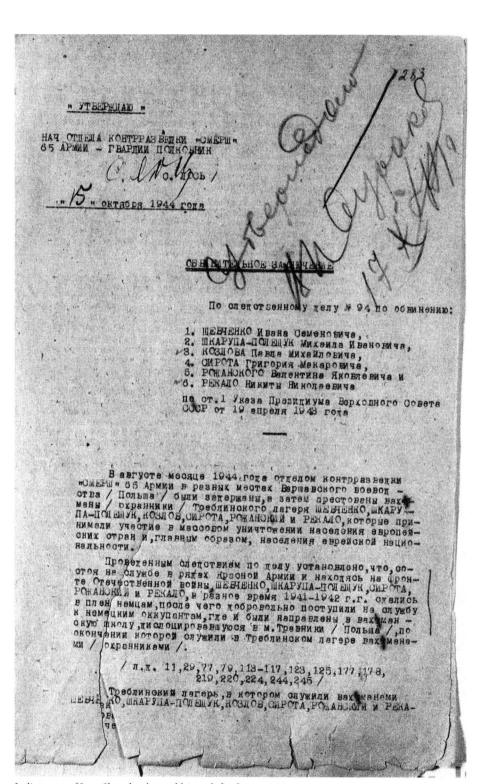

" УТВЕРЖДАЮ "

НАЧ ОТДЕЛА КОНТРРАЗВЕДКИ «СМЕРШ»
65 АРМИИ - ГВАРДИИ ПОЛКОВНИК

/ ... /

" 15 " октября 1944 года

ОБВИНИТЕЛЬНОЕ ЗАКЛЮЧЕНИЕ

По следственному делу № 94 по обвинению:

1. ШЕВЧЕНКО Ивана Семеновича,
2. ШКАРУПА-ПОЛЕЩУК Михаила Ивановича,
3. КОЗЛОВА Павла Михайловича,
4. СИРОТА Григория Макаровича,
5. РОЖАНСКОГО Валентина Яковлевича и
6. РЕКАЛО Никиты Николаевича

по ст.1 Указа Президиума Верховного Совета
СССР от 19 апреля 1943 года

———

В августе месяце 1944 года отделом контрразведки
«СМЕРШ» 65 Армии в разных местах Варшавского воевод -
ства / Польша / были задержаны, а затем арестованы вах-
маны / охранники / Треблинского лагеря ШЕВЧЕНКО, ШКАРУ-
ПА-ПОЛЕЩУК, КОЗЛОВ, СИРОТА, РОЖАНСКИЙ и РЕКАЛО, которые при-
нимали участие в массовом уничтожении населения европей-
ских стран и, главным образом, населения еврейской национальности.

Проведенным следствием по делу установлено, что, со-
стоя на службе в рядах Красной Армии и находясь на фрон-
те Отечественной войны ШЕВЧЕНКО, ШКАРУПА-ПОЛЕЩУК, СИРОТА,
РОЖАНСКИЙ и РЕКАЛО, в разное время 1941-1942 г.г. оказались
в плену немцам, после чего добровольно поступили на службу
к немецким оккупантам, где и были направлены в вахман-
скую школу, дислоцировавшуюся в м. Травники / Польша /, по
окончании которой служили в Треблинском лагере вахманами / охранниками /.

/ л.д. 11, 29, 77, 79, 113-117, 123, 125, 177, 178,
219, 220, 224, 244, 245 /

Треблинский лагерь, в котором служили вахманами
ШЕВЧЕНКО, ШКАРУПА-ПОЛЕЩУК, КОЗЛОВ, СИРОТА, РОЖАНСКИЙ и РЕКА-
ЛО ...

Indictment of Ivan Shevchenko and his codefendants, 1944

234

"УТВЕРЖДАЮ"
НАЧ.ОКР.НКО "СМЕРШ" в/ч 49572
ГВАРДИИ МАЙОР

ВДОВУХИН

" 14 " апреля 1945 года.

ОБВИНИТЕЛЬНОЕ ЗАКЛЮЧЕНИЕ

По следственному делу № 11

По обвинению ТЕРЕХОВА
Ивана Сергеевича по ст.
58-1 "б" УК РСФСР.

Отделом Контрразведки "Смерш" в/ч 49572 25.Ш.45 года арестован и
привлечен к уголовной ответственности за измену родине бывший военно-
служащий Красной армии ТЕРЕХОВ Иван Сергеевич.

В процессе следствия установлено:

ТЕРЕХОВ Иван Сергеевич призван в Красную армию 26.1Х.40 года,
проходил службу в 723 тяжело-артиллерийском полку. В августе 1941г.,
в районе г.Белая Церковь пленен противником, содержался в лагерях
военнопленных в г.г. Хелм, Ораниенбург.

В июле 43г., будучи военнопленным, добровольно вступил в фашист-
ские охранные войска "СС" "Мертвая голова", где проходил специальную
трехмесячную военную подготовку. По окончании подготовки, направлен в
охрану Штуттгофского концентрационного лагеря, в котором служил в
должности охранника. Носил огнестрельное оружие и военное обмундирова-
ние охранных войск "СС" с изображением на головном уборе эмблемы
"мертвая голова".

10 марта 1945 года задержан при исполнении служебных обязаннос-
тей /л.д. 2-21,25,26,28,30

В пред"явленном обвинении ТЕРЕХОВ признал себя виновным. л.л. 11-23

НА ОСНОВАНИИ ИЗЛОЖЕННОГО:

ТЕРЕХОВ Иван Сергеевич, 1922г.р., уроженец с.Афанасьево,
Солнцевского р-на, Курской области, гр-н СССР, русский, из
крестьян, образование 7 классов, холост, бывший военнослужа-
щий Красной армии,-

обвиняется в том, что, будучи военнопленным, добровольно поступил к
противнику на военную охранную службу "СС" "Мертвая Голова", на которой
служил с июля 43г. по 10.Ш.45 года, чем самым изменил Родине, т.е. в
преступлении, предусмотренном ст. 58-1"б" УК РСФСР.

Предварительное следствие по делу считать законченным, а добытые
данные достаточными для предания суду обвиняемого.

Indictment of Ivan Terekhov, April 1945

П Р О Т О К О Л :-

С У Д Е Б Н О Г О   З А С Е Д А Н И Я.-

В расположении ВТ.-   15 апреля 1945 года.

Военный Трибунал 1 Гвардейской танковой армии, в закрытом судебном заседании, в составе:-

Председательствующего- Гвардии майора юстиции
ОВСЯННИКОВА.
Членов- Гвардии майора юстиции КОРОТКИНА и Гвардии майора юстиции КОРОСТЕЛЕВА.
При секретаре- Гвардии капитане юстиции ЯКУШКИНЕ.

В 17 часов 50 минут, председательствующий, открыв судебное заседание об"являет, что рассматривается дело по обвинению -

бывшего красноармейца 723 тяжело-артиллерийского полка ТЕРЕХОВА Ивана Сергеевича, по ст. 58-1 "б" УК
Р С Ф С Р.

Секретарь доложил суду, что подсудимый Терехов, находящийся под стражей, в судебное заседание доставлен под конвоем.

Вызванный в судебное заседание свидетель Нога Василий Яковлевич - явился.

Председательствующий удостоверяется в самоличности подсудимого Терехова, который о себе показал:-

Я- ТЕРЕХОВ Иван Сергеевич, 1922 года рождения, уроженец и житель дер. Тереховка, Солнцевского района, Курской области, по соц.происхождению из крестьян-середняков, по соц.положению из крестьян-колхозник, по национальности русский, гражданин СССР, б/п, член ВЛКСМ с 1938 года по 1941 год т.е. до пленения немцами, холост, мать- Терехова Елизавета Матвеевна проживает по месту моего рождения, образование 7 классов неполно-средней школы, не судим, в Красной армии с 26 сентября 1940 года по призыву Солнцевским РВК и служил до 4 августа 1941 года. Ранений и наград не имею, под стражей содержусь с 25 марта 1945 года.
с обвинительным заключением и определением подготовительного заседания Военного Трибунала - ознакомлен.

Председательствующий предупреждает свидетеля Нога Василия Яковлевича, об ответственности по ст.ст. 92 и 95 УК РСФСР, о чем отбирает подписку и удаляет из зала судебного заседания.

Председательствующий раз"ясняет подсудимому Терехову его права во- время судебного заседания, об"являет состав суда, раз"ясняет порядок отвода составу суда и спрашивает подсудимого не возражает ли он слушать дело с вызванным в судебное заседание свидетелем Нога.

Подсудимый Терехов суду:-

Мои права во-время судебного заседания - мне понятны, ходатайств и отвода составу суда - не имею, слушать дело со свидетелем Нога не возражаю.

Председательствующий оглашает обвинительное заключение и спрашивает подсудимого Терехова понятно ли ему пред"явленное обвинение и признает ли он себя виновным.

Подсудимый Терехов суду:-

Пред"явленное обвинение мне понятно, виновным себя признаю, по существу дела поясняю.

First page of court session of Ivan Terekhov, April 1945

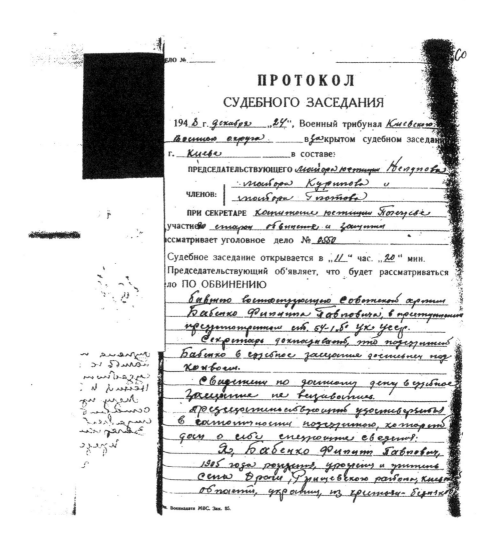

First page of Babenko trial court session, 1948

ВЫПИСКА ИЗ ПРОТОКОЛА СУДЕБНОГО ЗАСЕДАНИЯ

1950г. мая "26" дня, военный трибунал Белорусского Военного округа в закрытом судебном заседании в г.Барановичи в составе

председательствующего   майора юстиции Агафонова

народных   капитана Дементьева
заседателей   лейтенанта Воробьева

при секретаре младшем лейтенанте Грезневе

С участием : Пом.военного Прокурора округа подполковника юстиции Москаленко

и защиты адвоката Барановичской областной коллегии адвокатов Альтшулеры

Судебное заседание открывается в "I4" час 20 мин.

Председательствующий объявляет, что будет рассматриваться дело ПО ОБВИНЕНИЮ Скидан Георгия Александровича в преступлениях, предусмотренных ст.63-2 УК БССР.

Показания подсудимого Скидан.

24 июня I94Iг. Доорянским райвоенкоматом был призван в Советскую Армию и направлен для прохождения службы в 878 артиллерийский полк, где был назначен ездовым 9-ой батареи. В августе I94I года 9 батарея участвовала в бою против немцев недалеко от железнодорожной станции Таганча, в результате которого понесла большие потери личного состава и в том же бою было убито много коней. Командование полка после боя произвело слияние остатков 9 батареи с 8 батареей. В составе 8-ой батареи в середине августа месяца я участвовал в бою, где нам было приказано биться долпоследнего снаряда. Во время боя был ранен командир батареи и его вывезли на машине с поля боя. За командира батареи остался политрук,который,после того как были израсходованы все снаряды,приказал мне и двум другим ездовым подать передки к орудиям и вывезти их с места боя в свой тыл. Я, Тимошенко и другой ездовой,фамилии его не знаю подогнали лошадей к орудиям. На огневой позиции никого кроме нас не было. Втроем мы орудия присоединить никак не смогли и пока мы делали попытки присоединить передки к орудиям,нас окружили немецкие мотоциклисты. Немецкие мотоциклисты продвигались,имея впереди себя танки. При виде немецких мотоциклистов и их танков я испугался и сдался в плен. У меня была винтовка с патронами,но сопротивления я не оказывал. Меня,и бывших со мной ездовых,направили в ближайшую деревушку,где немцы собирали всех военнопленных. В деревне немцы построили всех военнопленных в колонну и в пешем порядке привели в город Белую Церковь,из которого были погружены в вагоны и эшелоном доставлены на территорию Польши в город Хелм и размещены в лагерь для военнопленных.Заключенных в

First page of Skydan trial court session, 1950

238

ПРОТОКОЛ

закрытого судебного заседания Военного трибунала Воронежского военного округа

от 20 декабря 1951 года

В составе: председательствующего - полковника юстиции Кишкурно
ч л е н о в: подполковника адм.службы Михайлова и майора Комолова
при секретаре: ст.лейтенанте юстиции Афанасьеве,с участием,Пом.
Военного Прокурора Воронежского Военного округа-
подполковника юстиции Водопьянова и адвоката Огне-
рубова.

Судебное заседание открывается в 13 час.20 мин.

Председательствующий объявляет,что будет рассматриваться дело по
обвинению Шалаева Николая Егоровича по ст.58-1"б" УК РСФСР.

Подсудимый Шалаев показал:

26 октября 1940 года Ясеновским райвоенкоматом Курской области я был призван на службу в Советскую армию и отправлен в местечко Заболотье,Станиславской области,где был зачислен курсантом
в полковую школу 126 Отдельного саперного батальона. Как только
началась война с Германией я вместе с частью отступал в направле-
нии города Киева. 3-го июля 1941 года в районе деревни Терновка
под городом Белая Церковь в составе подразделения я был пленен не-
мецкими войсками и отправлен в лагерь на территорию Польши в город.
Холм. Из этого лагеря я совершил побег,но был задержан и опять по-
мещен в этот же лагерь. В ноябре 1941 года переводчик лагеря мне
сообщил о том,что немцы набирают из лагеря команду военнопленных
в количестве 40 человек. Я заявил переводчику о своем желании за-
числить меня в эту команду. Куда направлялась эта команда и для
каких целей нам не сказали. В декабре 1941 года всю нашу команду
отвезли в местечко Травники (Польша), по прибытии туда я узнал о
том,что всю нашу команду набрали для зачисления на службу в охранные войска "СС" немецкой армии. Сразу же после прибытия в местечко
Травники,где было уже много русских граждан из числа военнопленных
нас всех разбили по ротам и мы приступили к обучению. На занятиях
мы обучались строевой подготовке,разучивали немецкие песни и изу-
чали винтовку. Обучались мы там около двух месяцев, а в феврале
1942 года,я, в составе 3-й роты вахманов был отправлен в гор.Люб-
лин для несения охраны еврейского гетто.

First page of Shalayev trial court session, 1951

П Р О Т О К О Л

закрытого судебного заседания Военного трибунала Воронежского военного округа

от 20 декабря 1951 года

__В составе:__ председательствующего - полковника юстиции Кишкурно
__ч л е но в:__ подполковника адм.службы Михайлова и майора Комолова
__при секретаре:__   ст.лейтенанте юстиции Афанасьеве, с участием. Пом.
Военного Прокурора Воронежского Военного округа-
подполковника юстиции Водопьянова и адвоката Огне-
рубова.

Судебное заседание открывается в 13 час.20 мин.

Председательствующий объявляет, что будет рассматриваться дело по
обвинению Шалаева Николая Егоровича по ст.58-1"б" УК РСФСР.

Подсудимый Шалаев показал:

26 октября 1940 года Ясеновским райвоенкоматом Курской области я был призван на службу в Советскую армию и отправлен в местечко Заболотье,Станиславской области,где был зачислен курсантом
в полковую школу 126 Отдельного саперного батальона. Как только
началась война с Германией я вместе с частью отступал в направле-
нии города Киева. 3-го июля 1941 года в районе деревни Терновка
под городом Белая Церковь в составе подразделения я был пленен не-
мецкими войсками и отправлен в лагерь на территорию Польши в город
Холм. Из этого лагеря я совершил побег,но был задержан и опять по-
мещен в этот же лагерь. В ноябре 1941 года переводчик лагеря мне
сообщил о том,что немцы набирают из лагеря команду военнопленных
в количестве 40 человек. Я заявил переводчику о своем желании за-
числить меня в эту команду. Куда направлялась эта команда и для
каких целей нам не сказали. В декабре 1941 года всю нашу команду
отвезли в местечко Травники (Польша), по прибытии туда я и узнал о
том,что всю нашу команду набрали для зачисления на службу в охранные войска "СС" немецкой армии. Сразу же после прибытия в местечко
Травники,где было уже много русских граждан из числа военнопленных
нас всех разбили по ротам и мы приступили к обучению. На занятиях
мы обучались строевой подготовке,разучивали немецкие песни и изу-
чали винтовку. Обучались мы там около двух месяцев, а в феврале
1942 года,я, в составе 3-й роты вахманов был отправлен в гор.Люб-
лин для несения охраны еврейского гетто.

First page of Shalayev trial court session, 1951

№ 0858

ПРОТОКОЛ
СУДЕБНОГО ЗАСЕДАНИЯ

12« Января 1952 г., Военный Трибунал Киевского Военного Округа в Закрытом судебном заседании

в г. Сталино в составе:

ПРЕДСЕДАТЕЛЬСТВУЮЩЕГО гв. подполковника юст. Коломийцева,

ЧЛЕНОВ: майора Локтионова и ст. лейтенанта Шлыкова,

ПРИ СЕКРЕТАРЕ ст. лейтенанте юст. Петряева,

с участием пом. военного прокурора КВО полковника юстиции Магудова и адвоката Мизун,

рассматривает уголовное дело № 0858.

Судебное заседание открывается в „12" час. „40" мин.

Председательствующий объявляет, что будет рассматриваться дело ПО ОБВИНЕНИЮ

Швидкого Ивана Даниловича в преступлении, предусмотренном ст.54-1.б" УК УССР.

Секретарь доложил, что подсудимый Швидкий в судебное заседание доставлен под конвоем. Из вызываемых свидетелей в судебное заседание будут доставляться по одному заключенные Еленчук В.И. и Гапенко Г.А.

Вызванные в качестве свидетелей: 1) Лысая М.Ф. осуждена к ВМН и этапирована в тюрьму город Днепропетровск и 2) Погребняк Н.В. осужден к 25 г. ИТЛ и также этапирован в Днепропетровск.

Пред-ющий удостоверяется в самоличности подсудимого, который о себе показал:

TRA   74095

Lieutenant Colonel Kolomjtsev, a military judge of the Kiev Military District, who presided over the case of former Treblinka II guard Ivan Shvidkij in 1952. Photo is dated on the back as January 1953. Author's private collection. This is the only photo the author has ever found of a Soviet judge who was involved in trying the case of a former Trawniki guard.

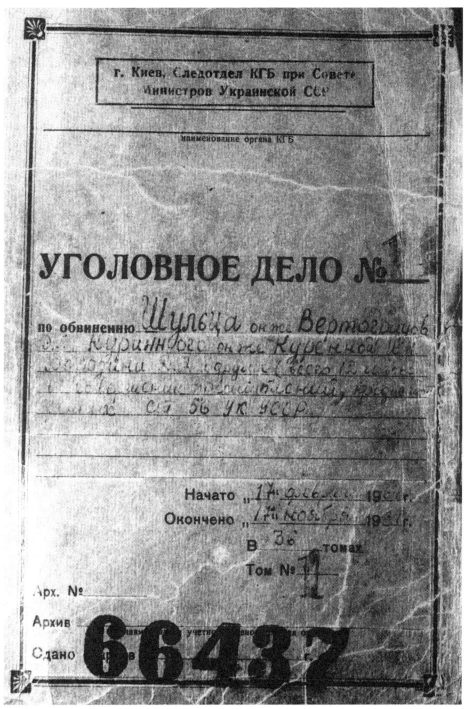

Schultz trial, case file cover

City of Kiev, KGB Investigative Department
at the Council of Ministers of the Ukranian SSR

name of KGB agency

CRIMINAL CASE #14

Indictment of *Shultz, a.k.a. E.G. Vertogradov, Kurinnyi, a.k.a. I.N. Kurennoy, D.A. Borodin, and others (total of 12 individuals) for the crimes under the Article 56 of the Criminal Code of the Ukrainian Soviet Socialist Republic.*

Started: *February "17", 1961*

Completed: *November "17", 1961*

In: *36* **volumes**

Volume # 3

(rubber stamp)

Archive # **66437**

(rubber stamp)

Archive _____

(name of the registering-archiving department/branch)

Submitted to… *(illegible)*

PAGE45

Schultz trial, case file cover translated from Russian to English

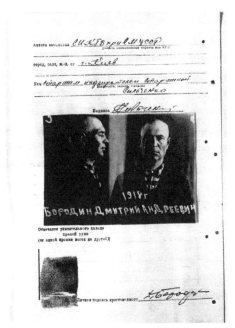

Mug shot of defendant Dmitri Borodin,
Schultz trial

Mug shot of defendant Yakov Karplyuk,
Schultz trial

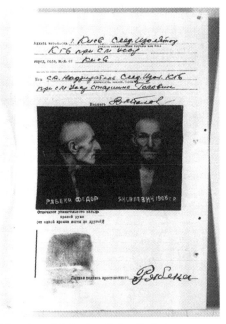

Mug shot of defendant Fedor Ryabeka,
Schultz trial

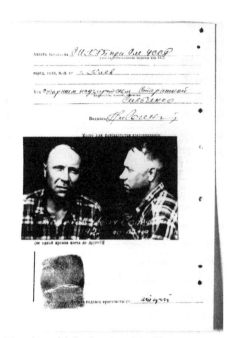

Mug shot of defendant Ivan Terekhov,
Schultz trial

Mug shot of defendant Filipp Levchishin,
Schultz trial

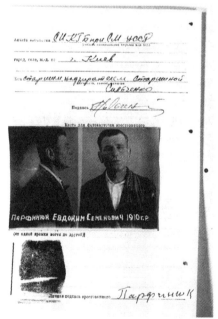

Mug shot of defendant Evdokim Parfinyuk,
Schultz trial

Mug shot of defendant Alexei Govorov,
Schultz trial

"УТВЕРЖДАЮ"

ЗАМ.ГЛАВНОГО ВОЕННОГО ПРОКУРОРА
ГЕНЕРАЛ-МАЙОР ЮСТИЦИИ

/Б. ВИКТОРОВ/

" 13" июля 1961 г.

Секретно
экз.№ 1

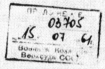

ПР.Л.КЕ.Е
03705
15 07 61
Воен. Колл
Верх суда СС)

В ВОЕННУЮ КОЛЛЕГИЮ ВЕРХОВНОГО СУДА СССР

ЗАКЛЮЧЕНИЕ

/в порядке ст. 387 УПК РСФСР/

По делу ГОРБАЧЕВА М.П.

" 21 " июня 1961 г.   г. Москва

23 июня 1951 г. военным трибуналом Уральского военного округа был осужден по ст. 58-I "б" УК РСФСР к 25 годам лишения свободы, с поражением в правах на 5 лет, без конфискации за отсутствием имущества

ГОРБАЧЕВ Михаил Петрович, 1922 года рождения, уроженец с. Ардабьево, Елатомского района, Рязанской области, русский, беспартийный, с 9-классным образованием, судимый в 1947 г. по ст. I Указа Президиума Верховного Совета СССР от 4 июня 1947 г. "Об уголовной ответственности за хищение государственного и общественного имущества" к 10 годам ИТЛ /срок наказания поглощен приговором по данному делу/.

В приговоре суда указано, что Горбачев, будучи пленен немцами, в мае 1942 г., в сентябре того же года добровольно поступил на службу в немецкие формирования "СС", после чего обучался в Травниковском учебном лагере, получил звание вахмана, а в конце 1942 года был направлен под г. Варшаву, где до мая 1943 г. охранял еврейское гетто. В мае 1943 г. он сопровождал эшелон с еврейскими семьями из г. Варшавы до ст. Малкиния. С мая 1943 г. до апреля 1945 г. Горбачев нес охранную службу в лагерях в г. Аушвиц и в г. Лейпциге. В 1944 г. за усердие по службе Горбачев получил звание обервахмана. /т. I, л.д. 102-103/.

First page of the Soviet Supreme Court determination to set aside the 1951 conviction of Mikhail Gorbachev and retry him in 1961 as one of the defendants in the Schultz trial, in light of new evidence that he had committed crimes as a guard at the Treblinka death camp

н0681   к.0439
№ 163/4.

ПОСТАНОВА ПРЕЗИДІЇ ВЕРХОВНОЇ РАДИ СРСР
ПАСТАНОВА ПРЭЗІДЫУМА ВЯРХОЎНАГА САВЕТА СССР
СССР ОЛИЙ СОВЕТИ ПРЕЗИДИУМИНИНГ КАРОРИ
СССР ЖОГАРГЫ СОВЕТІ ПРЕЗИДИУМЫНЫҢ ҚАУЛЫСЫ
ЬЬА ჯՑᲠᲔᲜᲘᲡ ᲫᲒᲬᲧᲡᲐᲚ ᲮᲐᲡᲘ ᲮᲔᲠᲮᲔᲛᲔᲚᲘᲡ ᲤᲐᲮᲐᲛᲘᲡᲔᲑ
ССРН АЛИ СОВЕТИ РӘJАСӘТ һеJ'этинин ГӘРАРЫ
TSRS AUKŠČIAUSIOSIOS TARYBOS PREZIDIUMO NUTARIMAS

ХОТЭРЫРЯ ПРЕЗИДХУМЛХЭЙ СОВЕТУДЛЙ СУПРЕВ АЛ УНКХНИЙ РСС
PSRS AUGSTĀKĀS PADOMES PREZIDIJA LĒMUMS
СССР ЖОГОРКУ СОВЕТИНИН ПРЕЗИДИУМУЛУН ТОКТОМУ
ҚАРОРИ ПРЕЗИДИУМИ СОВЕТИ ОЛИИ СССР
UHԲI ՉԵᲠᲦᲐᲚᲔᲑ ᲘᲞᲚᲐᲧ ᲮᲘᲛᲮᲩᲔᲚᲘᲐᲠᲘᲮᲐᲚ ᲐᲠᲒᲐᲚᲮᲤᲔ
СССР ЕКАРЫ СОВЕТИНИҢ ПРЕЗИДИУМЫНЫҢ ҚАРАРЫ
NSV LIIDU ÜLEMNÕUKOGU PRESIIDIUMI OTSUS

ПОСТАНОВЛЕНИЕ

ПРЕЗИДИУМА ВЕРХОВНОГО СОВЕТА СССР

О неприменении в виде исключения статей 6 и 41 Основ уголовного законодательства Союза ССР и союзных республик к Шульцу Э.Г., Левчишину Ф.Ф., Василенко С.С., Пришу С.М., Терехову И.С., Карплюку Я.А., Бородину Д.А., Говорову А.Е., Рябеке Ф.Я., Куринному И.Н., Горбачеву М.П. и Парфинюку Е.С.

Разрешить в виде исключения не применять к ШУЛЬЦУ Эммануилу Генриховичу (он же ВЕРТОГРАДОВ Эммануил Григорьевич), ЛЕВЧИШИНУ Филиппу Федоровичу, ВАСИЛЕНКО Сергею Степановичу, ПРИШУ Самуилу Мартыновичу, ТЕРЕХОВУ Ивану Сергеевичу, КАРПЛЮКУ Якову Андреевичу, БОРОДИНУ Дмитрию Андреевичу, ГОВОРОВУ Алексею Евсеевичу, РЯБЕКЕ Федору Яковлевичу, КУРИННОМУ (он же КУРЕННОЙ) Ивану Николаевичу, ГОРБАЧЕВУ Михаилу Петровичу и ПАРФИНЮКУ Евдокиму Семеновичу статью 6 и статью 41 Основ уголовного законодательства Союза ССР и союзных республик в части замены смертной казни лишением свободы, если при рассмотрении дела судом будут установлены активная карательная деятельность Шульца, Левчишина, Василенко, Приша, Терехова, Карплюка, Бородина, Говорова, Рябеки, Куринного, Горбачева и Парфинюка и их личное участие в истязаниях и убийствах советских людей во время Великой Отечественной войны 1941-1945 г.г., поскольку за эти преступления в союзах могла быть назначена смертная казнь.

Председатель Президиума Верховного Совета СССР   Л.БРЕЖНЕВ.

Секретарь Президиума Верховного Совета СССР   (М.Георгадзе)

Москва,
8 февраля 1962 г.

26/736-62н.   21

Resolution of the Presidium of the Supreme Soviet to permit the application of the death penalty as a possible punishment for the defendants in the Schultz trial

To the Chairman of the Committee for
State Security (KGB) at the Council of
Ministers of the USSR
Mr. V.E. Semichastnyi

K 0681   *K 0439*
#163/4.

*This block/paragraph appears to be in
another language (possibly Ukrainian)
which I'm unable to translate*
(*Translator's note)

*This block/paragraph appears to be in
another language,
which I'm unable to translate*
(*Translator's note)

RESOLUTION
OF THE PRESIDIUM OF THE USSR SUPREME SOVIET

On the non-application as an exception of articles 6 and 41 of the Fundamental
Principles of criminal legislation of the USSR and the Union republics in
regards to E.G. Shultz, F.F. Levchishin, S.S. Vasilenko, S.M. Prish, I.S.
Terekhov, Ya.A. Karplyuk, D.A. Borodin, A.E. Govorov, F.Ya. Ryabek, I.N.
Kurinnyi, M.P. Gorbachev, and K.S. Parfinyuk.

To grant, as an exception, to disapply article 6 and article 41 of the Fundamental Principles of
criminal legislation of the USSR and the Union republics – towards SHULTZ, Emmanuel Henrikovich
(a.k.a. VERTOGRADOV, Emmanuel Grigoryevich); LEVCHISHIN, Philipp Fedorovich; VASILENKO,
Sergey Stepanovich; PRISH, Samuel Martynovich; TEREKHOV, Ivan Sergeevich; KARPLYUK, Yakov
Andreyevich; BORODIN, Dmitry Andreyevich; GOVOROV, Aleksey Evseeyvich; RYABEKA, Fedor
Yakovlevich; KURINNYI (a.k.a. KURENNOY), Ivan Nikolayevich; GORBACHEV, Mikhail Petrovich;
and PARFINYUK, Evdokim Semenovich – with regards to replacing the death penalty with incarceration
– if the court finds, during the case investigation, active punitive practices by Shultz, Levchishin,
Vasilenko, Prish, Terekhov, Karplyuk, Borodin, Govorov, Ryabek, Kurinnyi, Gorbachev, and Parfinyuk
– and their direct involvement in torturing and killing of Soviet citizens during the Great Patriotic War of
1941–1945, because those crimes could be punishable by the death penalty during that period.

*(rubber stamp:
Presidium of the USSR
Supreme Soviet)*

Chairman of the Presidium of the
Supreme Soviet of the USSR   L. BREZHNEV

Secretary of the Presidium
of the Supreme Soviet of the USSR
(M. Georgadze)   *Signature*

Moscow, the Kremlin
February 8, 1962

PAGE 10

Resolution of the Presidium of the Supreme Soviet permitting application of the death penalty for
the defendants in the Schultz trial, translated from Russian to English

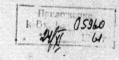

С П Р А В К А

Проходящие по уголовному делу № 14 по обв. ШУЛЬЦА Э.Г.
и других:

1. ГАЙДАК Василий — 13.ХП.50 г. осужден ВТ МВО по ст.
   Степанович   58-1"б" УК РСФСР к ВМН.

2. ГОНЧАРОВ Петр — 27.УI.51 г. осужден ВТ КВО по ст.
   Назарович   54-1"б" УК УССР к ВМН.

3. ЩЕРБАК Николай — 27.УI.51 г. осужден ВТ КВО по ст.
   Кириллович   54-1"б" УК УССР к ВМН.

4. МАЧУЛИН Иван — 27.УI.51 г. осужден ВТ КВО по ст.
   Никифорович   54-1"б" УК УССР к ВМН.

5. КОРОТКИХ Дмитрий — 21.IX.51 г. осужден ВТ КВО по ст.
   Николаевич   54-1"б" УК УССР к ВМН.

6: ШЕВЧЕНКО Иван Се- — 21.Х.44 г. осужден ВТ 65 армии 1 Бе-
   менович   лорусского фронта по ст.1 Указа от
                     19.IУ.43 г. к ВМН.

7. ЛЕЛЕКО Павел — 19.Ш.45 г. осужден ВТ 2 Белорусск.фрон-
   Владимирович   та по ст.1 Указа от 19.IУ.43 г. к ВМН.

8. ШАЛАЕВ Николай — 20.ХП.51 года осужден ВТ Воронежского
   Егорович   ВО по ст.58-1"б" УК РСФСР к ВМН.

9. ЕГЕРЬ Александр — 6-9.IX.52 г. осужден ВТ КВО по ст.
   Иванович   54-1"б" УК УССР к ВМН.

10. СТРЕЛЬЦОВ Антон — 9.УI.50 г. осужден ВТ КВО по ст.
    Иванович   54-1"б" УК УССР к ВМН.

СТ СЛЕДОВАТЕЛЬ ПО ОСОБО ВАЖНЫМ ДЕЛАМ
СЛЕДОТДЕЛА КГБ ПРИ СМ УССР-Подполковник

/ЛЫСЕНКО/

"24" ноября 1961 года

List, in Russian, of ten former Trawniki guards assigned to Treblinka II who were sentenced to death by Soviet courts and executed after the war. This list was included as a document in the Schultz trial.

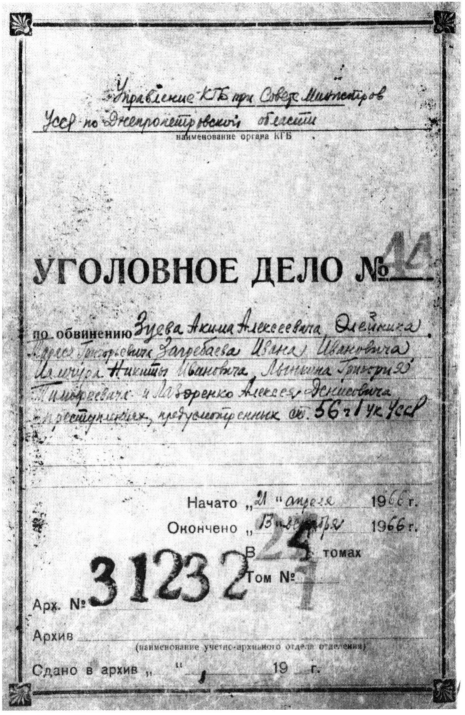

Zuev trial, case file cover

CRIMINAL CASE #44

Indictment of _Zouyev, Akeem Aleskeyevich; Oleynik, Taras Grigoryevich; Zagrebayev, Ivan Ivanovich; Mamchour, Nikita Ivanovich; Lynkin, Gregory Timofeyevich; and Lazorenko, Aleksey Denisovich for the crimes in accordance with the Article 56 of the Criminal Code of the Ukrainian Soviet Socialist Republic._

Started: _April "21", 1966_

Completed: _December "13", 1966_

In: _24_ **volumes**

Volume # 1

Archive # **31232**

Archive _____
(name of the registering-archiving department/branch)

Submitted to archives " " _____ 19 yr.

Zuev trial, case file cover translated from Russian to English

Photo spread included in the Zuev trial file, in which former Trawniki guard Alexander Zakharov identifies photo #1 as the defendant Grigorij Lynkin

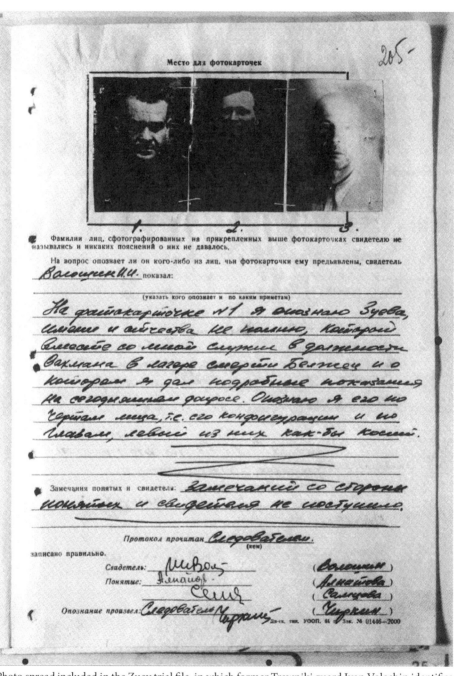

Photo spread included in the Zuev trial file, in which former Trawniki guard Ivan Voloshin identifies photo #1 as the defendant Akim Zuev

Photo spread included in the Zuev trial file, in which former Trawniki guard Ivan Voloshin identifies photo #3 as the defendant Alexei Lazorenko

ВОЕННОЙ КОЛЛЕГИИ ВЕРХОВНОГО СУДА СОЮЗА ССР

Гор.МОСКВА.

адвоката ЛИПАТОВА Бориса Ивановича /юридическая
консультация Октябрьского района гор.Днепропетров-
ска-Гор.Днепропетровск,проспект Карла Маркса
дом № 46 / -защитника осужденного

З У Е В А Акима Алексеевича,содержащегося под
стражей в Днепропетровском следственном изоляторе
УООП,

на
приговор Военного Трибунала Киевского военного
округа от 24-го февраля 1967 года

КАССАЦИОННАЯ ЖАЛОБА.

Приговором Военного Трибунала Киевского военного округа от
24-го февраля 1967 года ЗУЕВ Аким Алексеевич по статье 56 ч.I
УК УССР осужден к смертной казни-расстрелу с конфискацией
имущества.

Указанный приговор в отношении ЗУЕВА А.А. прошу изменить,
так как он без достаточных оснований признан виновным в том,что
он загонял узников по проволочному проходу в "душегубку " и
что в 1942 году он лично расстрелял женщину.

В силу изложенного,на основании ст.ст.369,372,374 УПК УССР
прошу обжалуемый приговор изменить,исключить из приговора
указание о том,что ЗУЕВ А.А. загонял узников по проволочному
проходу в " душегубку " и что он лично расстрелял женщину.

Прошу заменить ЗУЕВУ Акиму Алексеевичу назначенное ему
наказание в виде смертной казни лишением свободы.

ПРИМЕЧАНИЕ: Прошу своевременно известить меня о дне слушания
дела в Военной Коллегии Верховного Суда СССР.

I/Ш 1967г. адвокат 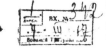 / ЛИПАТОВ Б.И. /

Request made by defense attorneys to the Military Collegium of the Soviet
Supreme Court in Moscow, to pardon the defendant Akim Zuev, who had been
sentenced to death by firing squad

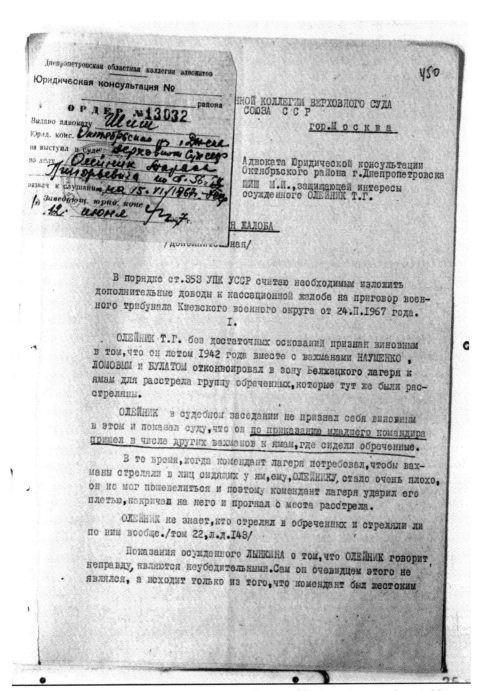

Дніпропетровська областна коллегія адвокатів

Юридическая консультация №

ОРДЕР №13032

района

Выдано адвокату Шиш

Юрид. конс. Октябрьского р-на

на выступ. в суде Верховного Суда

по делу Олейник Тараса

Пригорьевича по ст. 56 УК

назнач. к слушанию на 15.VI.1967 года

Заведующ. юрид. конс.

12 июня

450

НОЙ КОЛЛЕГИИ ВЕРХОВНОГО СУДА
СОЮЗА ССР

гор. Москва

Адвоката Юридической консультации
Октябрьского района г. Днепропетровска
ШИШ М.И., защищающей интересы
осужденного ОЛЕЙНИК Т.Г.

Я ЖАЛОБА

/дополнительная/

В порядке ст. 353 УПК УССР считаю необходимым изложить
дополнительные доводы к кассационной жалобе на приговор военного трибунала Киевского военного округа от 24.II.1967 года.

I.

ОЛЕЙНИК Т.Г. без достаточных оснований признан виновным
в том, что он летом 1942 года вместе с вахманами НАУМЕНКО,
ЛОМОВЫМ и БУЛАТОМ отконвоировал в зону Белзецкого лагеря к
ямам для расстрела группу обреченных, которые тут же были рас-
стреляны.

ОЛЕЙНИК в судебном заседании не признал себя виновным
в этом и показал суду, что он по приказанию младшего командира
пришел в числе других вахманов к ямам, где сидели обреченные.

В то время, когда комендант лагеря потребовал, чтобы вах-
маны стреляли в лиц сидящих у ям, ему, ОЛЕЙНИКУ, стало очень плохо,
он не мог пошевелиться и поэтому комендант лагеря ударил его
плетью, накричал на него и прогнал с места расстрела.

ОЛЕЙНИК не знает, кто стрелял в обреченных и стреляли ли
по ним вообще. /том 22, л.д. 143/

Показания осужденного ЛЫНКИНА о том, что ОЛЕЙНИК говорит
неправду, являются неубедительными. Сам он очевидцем этого не
являлся, а исходит только из того, что комендант был жестоким

Request made by defense attorneys to the Military Collegium of the Soviet Supreme Court in Moscow, to pardon the defendant Taras Olejnik, who had been sentenced to death by firing squad

Председателю Верховного Суда СССР
тов.Горкину А.Ф.

480

ПОСТАНОВА ПРЕЗИДІЇ ВЕРХОВНОЇ РАДИ СРСР
ПАСТАНОВА ПРЭЗІДЫУМА ВЯРХОЎНАГА САВЕТА СССР
СССР ОЛИЙ СОВЕТІ ПРЕЗИДИУМИНИНГ ҚАРОРИ
СССР ЖОГАРГЫ СОВЕТІ ПРЕЗИДИУМЫНЫҢ ҚАУЛЫСЫ
ЫА АЗГЫЛЬ ВЮСҚЫ ЫЫАЗ ХАЗЫҒЫЫЫ Һ
СССРИ АЛИ СОВЕТИ РЭЈАСЭТ НЕЈ'ОТНИНИ ГОРАРЫ
TSRS AUKŠČIAUSIOSIOS TARYBOS PREZIDIUMO NUTARIMAS

ХОТ3РЫРЕ ПРЕЗИДИУМУЛУЙ СОВЕТУЛУЙ СУПРЕМ АЛ УНИУНИЙ РСС
PSRS AUGSTĀKĀS PADOMES PREZIDIJA LĒMUMS
СССР ЖОГОРКУ СОВЕТИНИН ПРЕЗИДИУМУНУН ТОКТОМУ
ҚАРОРИ ПРЕЗИДИУМИ СОВЕТИ ОЛИИ СССР
ООИУ ЧЫРОЧОЬ5Ы ПУЬ5Ъ ЧЕМЧОЗОЬРОЫЪ ЯРООЛ'ҒЕ
СССР ЁКАРЫ СОВЕТИНИҢ ПРЕЗИДИУМЫНЫҢ ҚАРАРЫ
NSV LIIDU ÜLEMNÕUKOGU PRESIIDIUMI OTSUS

ПОСТАНОВЛЕНИЕ
ПРЕЗИДИУМА ВЕРХОВНОГО СОВЕТА СССР

Об отклонении ходатайств о помиловании
Зуева А.А., Мамчура Н.И. и Лазоренко А.Д.,
осужденных к смертной казни

Рассмотрев ходатайства о помиловании Зуева А.А., Мамчура Н.И. и Лазоренко А.Д., осужденных к смертной казни, предложения в связи с этим Прокуратуры СССР и Верховного Суда СССР,
ввиду исключительной тяжести совершенных ими преступлений,
Президиум Верховного Совета СССР п о с т а н о в л я е т
отклонить ходатайства о помиловании:

ЗУЕВА Акима Алексеевича, рожд.1912 года, уроженца с.Паш-
ковки Фастовского района Киевской области;

МАМЧУРА Никиты Ивановича, рожд.1906 года, уроженца с.Коло-
денки Тульчинского района Винницкой области;

ЛАЗОРЕНКО Алексея Денисовича, рожд.1909 года, уроженца
с.Волошновки Роменского района Сумской области.

Председатель Президиума
Верховного Совета СССР   Н.ПОДГОРНЫЙ.

Секретарь Президиума
Верховного Совета СССР

Москва, Кремль.
13 октября 1967 г.
№ 1966-УП.

Denial of the appeal to pardon the defendants Akim Zuev, Nikita Mamchur, and Alexei Lazorenko,
all of whom had been sentenced to death by firing squad

To the Chief Justice of the
USSR Supreme Court
Mr. A.F. Gorkin

This block/paragraph appears to be in
another language (possibly Ukrainian)
which I'm unable to translate
(*Translator's note)

This block/paragraph appears to be in
another language,
which I'm unable to translate
(*Translator's note)

RESOLUTION
OF THE PRESIDIUM OF THE USSR SUPREME SOVIET

On denying the appeals to pardon
A.A. Zouyev, N.I. Mamchour, and A.D. Lazorenko,
who were sentenced to the death penalty

Having examined the motion to pardon A.A. Zouyev, N.I. Mamchour, and A.D. Lazorenko, sentenced to the death penalty, and the suggestions associated with this case by the USSR Prosecutors Office and by the USSR Supreme Court, considering the extreme severity of the committed crimes, the Presidium of the Supreme Soviet of the USSR I S H E R E B Y R U L I N G to dismiss the motion to pardon:

ZOUYEV, Akeem Alekseyevich, born in 1912 in the town of Pashkovka, Fastovskiy region, of the Kiev province;

MAMCHOUR, Nikita Ivanovich, born in 1906 in the town of Kolodenka, Tulchinsk region, Vinnitsa province;

LAZORENKO, Aleksey Denisovich, born in 1909 in the town of Voloshkovka, Romensk region, of the Sumskaya province.

(rubber stamp:
Presidium of the USSR
Supreme Soviet)

Chairman of the Presidium of the
Supreme Soviet of the USSR   N. PODGORNYI

Secretary of the Presidium
of the Supreme Soviet of the USSR

Signature

Moscow, the Kremlin
October 13, 1967
#1966-UP (Criminal Procedures)

PAGE 22

Denial of the appeal to pardon defendants Zuev, Mamchur, and Lazorenko, translated from Russian to English

Председателю Верховного Суда СССР
тов. Горкину А.Ф.

479

УКАЗ
ПРЕЗИДИУМА ВЕРХОВНОГО СОВЕТА СССР

О помиловании Олейника Т.Г., осужденного
к смертной казни

Рассмотрев ходатайство о помиловании Олейника Т.Г.,
осужденного к смертной казни, предложения в связи с этим Прокуратуры СССР и Верховного Суда СССР и принимая во внимание его
возраст, данные, положительно характеризующие его по работе до
осуждения, конкретные обстоятельства дела и то, что со времени
совершения им преступлений прошло более 20 лет, Президиум
Верховного Совета СССР п о с т а н о в л я е т:

Помиловать ОЛЕЙНИКА Тараса Григорьевича, рожд. 1910 года,
уроженца с. Сурско-Покровского Днепропетровского района Днепро-
петровской области, и заменить ему смертную казнь пятнадцатью
годами лишения свободы.

Председатель Президиума
Верховного Совета СССР   Н. ПОДГОРНЫЙ.

Секретарь Президиума
Верховного Совета СССР

Москва, Кремль.
13 октября 1967 г.
№ 1965-УП.

Approval of the appeal to pardon the defendant Taras Olejnik, who had been sentenced to death by firing squad

260

To the Chief Justice of the
USSR Supreme Court
Mr. A.F. Gorkin

This block/paragraph appears to be in another language (possibly Ukrainian) which I'm unable to translate (*Translator's note)

This block/paragraph appears to be in another language, which I'm unable to translate (*Translator's note)

DECREE
OF THE PRESIDIUM OF THE USSR SUPREME SOVIET
On the pardon of T.G. Oleynik,
sentenced to the death penalty

Having examined the motion to pardon T.G. Oleynik, who has been sentenced to the death penalty, and the suggestions associated with this case by the USSR Prosecutor Office and by the USSR Supreme Court and taking into account his age, statistics, which characterized him positively in his work prior to indictment, specific circumstances of the case, and the fact that more than 20 years have passed since him committing those crimes, the Presidium of the Supreme Soviet of the USSR IS HEREBY RULING:

To grant pardon to OLEYNIK, Taras Grigoryevich, born in 1910 in the town of Sursko-Pokrovskoe, Dnepropetrovsk region, of the Dnepropetrovsk province, and to replace the death sentence with fifteen years of imprisonment.

(rubber stamp:
Presidium of the USSR
Supreme Soviet)

Chairman of the Presidium of the
Supreme Soviet of the USSR   N. PODGORNYI

Secretary of the Presidium
of the Supreme Soviet of the USSR

Signature

Moscow, the Kremlin
October 13, 1967
#1965-UP (Criminal Procedures)

PAGE 21

Approval of the appeal to pardon defendant Taras Olejnik, translated from Russian to English

г. Киев, Следотдел КГБ при Совете
Министров Украинской ССР

наименование органа КГБ

УГОЛОВНОЕ ДЕЛО №14

по обвинению *Шульца он же Вертоградов*
Э. Г. Куринного он же Куренной И.и.
Володина Д. А и другие (всего 13 человек)
в совершении преступлений
предусмотренных ст 56 УК УССР

Начато „17" февраля 1961 г.
Окончено „17" ноября 1961 г.
В 36 томах
Том №9

Арх. №

Архив

наименование учетно-архивного подраздела органа КГБ

Сдано архив

66437

Schultz case, file cover, volume 9

г. Киев, Следотдел КГБ при Совете
Министров Украинской ССР

ДЕЛО №16469 14

Терехов

Иван Сергеевич

(материалы проверки)

Начато_____19__г.

Окончено_____19__г.

На 87 листах *N 16469*

ТОМ №2.

66437 т.**17**

Schultz case, file cover, volume 17 (this volume covered the defendant Ivan
Terekhov)

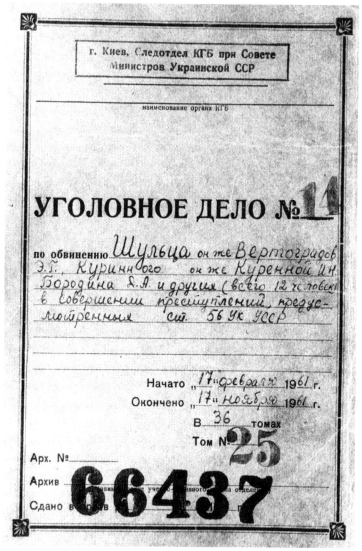

УГОЛОВНОЕ ДЕЛО №14

по обвинению *Шульца он же Вертоградов
Э.Г. Куринн ого он же Куренной и н.
Бородина Д.Я. и других (всего 12 человек)
в совершении преступлений, предусмотренных ст. 56 Ук УССР*

Начато „17" февраля 1961 г.
Окончено „17" ноября 1961 г.
в 36 томах
Том № **25**

Арх. №

Архив **66437**

Сдано в

Schultz case, file cover, volume 25

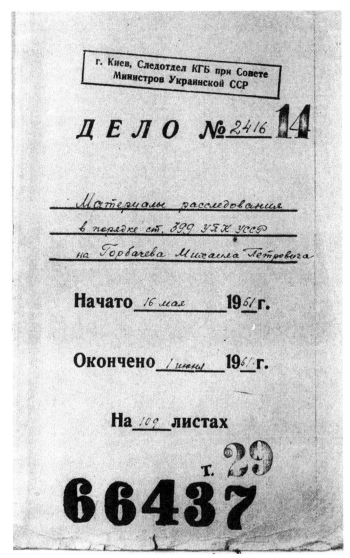

г. Киев, Следотдел КГБ при Совете
Министров Украинской ССР

ДЕЛО №2416 14

Материалы расследования

в порядке ст. 399 УПК УССР

на Горбачева Михаила Петровича

Начато 16 мая 19 61 г.

Окончено 1 июня 19 61 г.

На 109 **листах**

т. **29**

66437

Schultz case, file cover, volume 29 (this volume covered the defendant
Mikhail Gorbachev)

‚ министер тво бор ны СССР

Военный трибунал

КВО

Приговор

ДЕЛО № 9

по обвинению Шульца, он же Вертоградов Э.Г., Куринного, он же Куренной
Бородина Д.А. и других (всего 12 чел.)
по сш 56 УК УССР   Том 37

Начато „___" _____ 19__ г.

Окончено „___" _____

На „___" _____

рои ср: внут   Форма 1
‚ ЧНАЯ КОЛЛЕ ИЯ ВЕРХСУДА СССР

Докладчик _____

Прокурор _____

Schultz case, file cover, volume 37

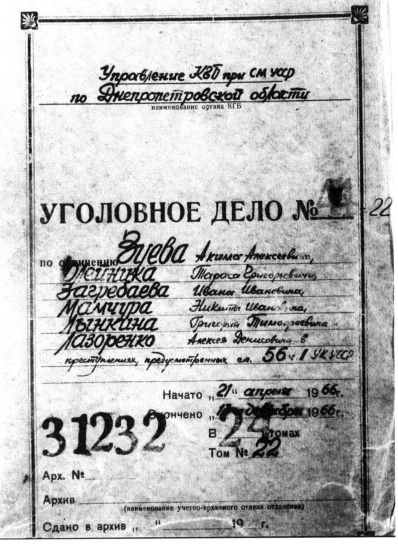

Zuev case, file cover, volume 22

Zuev case, file cover, volume 23

268

ТВ-2

Экз. № 1

ФЕДЕРАЛЬНАЯ
СЛУЖБА БЕЗОПАСНОСТИ
РОССИЙСКОЙ ФЕДЕРАЦИИ
(ФСБ России)

Mr. Joshua Baldwin

УПРАВЛЕНИЕ РЕГИСТРАЦИИ
И АРХИВНЫХ ФОНДОВ

27.07.2010   № 10/А-Б-1999
г. Москва, 101000

Ваше обращение от 3 июня 2010 рассмотрено в Центральном архиве ФСБ России.

Сообщаем, что копии архивных материалов немецкого лагеря СС «Травники» предоставляются Центральным архивом ФСБ России по официальным запросам судебных органов, органов юстиции и прокуратуры Российской Федерации и иностранных государств. Исследователям копии указанных материалов предоставляются в читальном зале Центрального архива ФСБ России после направления в наш адрес плана исследования.

Первый заместитель начальника Управления   А.В. Васильев

Response letter to the author, in Russian, from the FSB Archive Moscow, dated July 27, 2010, stating that access to Record Group 20869 (containing the Trawniki personnel files that the Soviets had captured) would require the permission of the Russian Procurator's Office, signed A. Vasilyev

Immigration photo of Feodor Fedorenko, a Ukrainian and former Treblinka II guard. Deported from the US in 1984, on the basis of a decision by the US Supreme Court. Tried in the Soviet Union, sentenced to death, and executed by firing squad in 1987.

Photo of Jakob Reimer, a Volksdeutscher, from his Trawniki *Personalbogen* (personnel file)

Photo of Vladas Zajanckauskas, a Lithuanian, from his Trawniki *Personalbogen* (personnel file)

Immigration photo of Vladas Zajanckauskas

U.S. Department of Justice

Criminal Division

Washington, D.C. 20530

CRM-200900706F

DEC **2 3** 2009

Mr. Joshua Baldwin

Dear Mr. Baldwin:

This is in response to your undated request for access to the Trawniki Personalbogens (personnel files) of the 10 individuals listed in your letter.

We located (items 1-10) in the Criminal Division within the scope of your request. We have processed your request under the Freedom of Information Act (FOIA) and will make all records available to you whose release is either required by that statute, or considered appropriate as a matter of discretion.

In light of our review, we have determined to release items 1-7 in full and to withhold items 8-10 (as described on the enclosed schedule) in full. We are withholding the records pursuant to the following FOIA exemptions set forth in 5 U.S.C. 552(b), which permit the withholding of:

(6) personnel and medical files and similar files the disclosure of which would constitute a clearly unwarranted invasion of personal privacy; and,

(7) records or information compiled for law enforcement purposes, but only to the extent that the production of such law enforcement records or information . . .

(C) could reasonably be expected to constitute an unwarranted invasion of personal privacy; and,

Author's FOIA request response from the US Department of Justice after asking for access to Trawniki *Personalbögen* (personnel files), dated December 2009. Note the interesting reasons given for the withholding of certain information.

274

(D)   could reasonably be expected to
disclose the identity of a
confidential source, including a
State, local, or foreign agency or
authority or any private
institution which furnished
information on a confidential
basis, and, in the case of a record
or information compiled by criminal
law enforcement authority in the
course of a criminal investigation
or by an agency conducting a lawful
national security intelligence
investigation, information
furnished by a confidential source.

You have a right to an administrative appeal of this partial
denial of your request. Your appeal should be addressed to: The
Office of Information Policy, United States Department of
Justice, 1425 New York Ave., NW, Suite 11050, Washington, DC
20530-0001. Both the envelope and the letter should be clearly
marked with the legend "FOIA Appeal." Department regulations
provide that such appeals must be received by the Office of
Information Policy within sixty days of the date of this letter.
28 C.F.R. 16.9. If you exercise this right and your appeal is
denied, you also have the right to seek judicial review of this
action in the federal judicial district (1) in which you reside,
(2) in which you have your principal place of business, (3) in
which the records denied are located, or (4) for the District of
Columbia. If you elect to file an appeal, please include, in
your letter to the Office of Information Policy, the Criminal
Division file number that appears above your name in this letter.

Sincerely,

Rena Y. Kim
by ﬀ

Rena Y. Kim, Chief
Freedom of Information/Privacy Act Unit
Office of Enforcement Operations
Criminal Division

2

Page 2 of the previous document

U.S. Department of Justice

Criminal Division

Washington, D.C. 20530

CRM-200900706F

APR **6** 2010

Mr. Joshua Baldwin

Dear Mr. Baldwin:

This is in reference to your appeal (No. 2010-0810) of the Criminal Division's response to your Freedom of Information Act request for the Trawniki Personalbogen of ten individuals.

Since you have provided proof of death for Eugen Binder we are now releasing his Personalbogen (item 8, previously withheld in full) to you in its entirety. A copy of that document is enclosed.

Sincerely,

Rena Y. Kim

Rena Y. Kim, Chief
Freedom of Information/Privacy Act Unit
Office of Enforcement Operations
Criminal Division

Author's FOIA request response from the US Department of Justice, dated April 2010, after asking for access to the Trawniki _Personalbogen_ (personnel file) of Eugen Binder. Access was granted after the author had shown documentation that Binder was deceased.

Am 10.4.43 wegen Meuterei in Belcek von H. Sonder-
kommando Belcek erschossen worden.

Trawniki, den 24.10. 1941.

Meister der Schutzpolizei

Vorgang.

Personalbogen Nr. 81

Name:	B i n d e r
Vorname:	Eugen
Vatersname:	Valerie
geb. am:	20.1.1921
in:	Schjolkowa, Krs.Woskan
Nationalität:	Volksdeutsch
Staatszugehörigkeit:	UdSSR
Beruf:	Schlosser
Stand:	ledig
Kinderzahl:	

rechter Daumen

Mädchenname der Frau: _____

Mädchenname der Mutter: Okuline,geb.Rusakowa

Militärdienst — Waffengattung: Panzer

Letzter Dienstgrad: Soldat   Dienstzeit: seit 7.4.40

Bemerkungen: _____

Sprachkenntnisse: Russisch

Besondere Fähigkeiten: _____

Grösse: 170 cm

Gesichtsform: oval

Haarfarbe: blond

Augenfarbe: blaugrau

Besondere Merkmale: Schramme auf der rechten Hand

Obige Angaben wurden – belegt mit:

1.) _____

2.) _____

3.) _____

— auf Grund eigener Angaben aufgenommen

Aufgenommen durch:

Unterschrift: _____
Dienstgrad: Hptw.d.Schupo

359

TRA048100

First page of the Trawniki *Personalbogen* (personnel file) of Eugen Binder. Binder was a Volksdeutsche (ethnic German). Note the line crossing out the file, and the notation at the top of the file: it states that Binder was shot by the SS on April 10, 1943, after he had attempted to instigate a mutiny with other Trawniki guards against the SS staff at Belzec death camp.

U.S. Department of Justice

Criminal Division

CRM-201100285F

Washington, D.C. 20530

MAY 2 7 2011

Mr. Josh Baldwin

Dear Mr. Baldwin:

This is in response to your Freedom of Information Act request dated April 4, 2011 for access to records concerning 1) Modrega, Nikolaj; 2) Modschuk, Dimitrij; 3) Pochwala, W; 4) Skorokhod, Nikolaj; 5) Terletskij, Wladimir; and 6) Zechmeister, J. Your request has been assigned file number CRM-201100285F. Please refer to this number in any future correspondence with this Unit.

Our search of Criminal Division files located six (6) records within the scope of your request. We have processed your request under the Freedom of Information Act and will make all records available to you whose release is either required by that statute, or considered appropriate as a matter of discretion.

In light of our review we have determined to release three (3) records in full and to withhold three (3) records in full. We have been advised by the Human Rights and Special Prosecutions Section (HRSPS) (DOJ), that the three (3) records located concerning 1) Modrega, Nikolaj, 4) Skorokhod, Nikolaj, and 6) Zechmeister, J., are not Department of Justice records, but foreign government records that were provided to DOJ, pursuant to a bi-lateral agreement, for **law enforcement purposes only**. As they have never been used in a prosecution in the United States, they have not become public documents.

Therefore, pursuant to the recommendations of the Human Rights and Special Prosecutions Section, we will withhold these three (3) records in full. We are withholding the information indicated pursuant to the following FOIA exemption set forth in 5 U.S. C. §552(b):

> (7) which permits the withholding of records or information compiled for law enforcement purposes, but only to the extent that the production of such law enforcement records or information...
>
> (D) could reasonably be expected to disclose the identity of a confidential source, including a State, local, or foreign agency or authority or any private institution which furnished information on a confidential basis, and, in the case of a record or information compiled by criminal law enforcement

Author's FOIA request response from the US Department of Justice, dated May 2011, after asking for access to Trawniki *Personalbögen* (personnel files). Note the interesting reasons given for the withholding of information.

278

U.S. Department of Justice

Criminal Division

Office of Enforcement Operations   *Washington, D.C. 20530*
CRM- 201200013F

Joshua Baldwin

FEB   2 2012

Dear Mr. Baldwin:

   The U.S. Department of Justice, Criminal Division acknowledges receipt of your Freedom of Information Act (FOIA) request dated December 20, 2011. In your request, you asked for copies of the Trawniki Personalbogens (Personnel Files) for:

1. Viktor Bogomolow
2. N. Bukowjan
3. Yurji Danilow
4. T. Denkewicz
5. Mykola Huculak
6. Nikolai Kototschilow
7. Josef Loch
8. G. Pankratov
9. Alexander Potschinok
10. Wladimir Pronin
11. I. Saplawny
12. Nikolaj Skorokhod
13. Johann Tellmann
14. J. Zechmeister.

   Your request has been assigned file number 201200013F. Please refer to this number in any future correspondence with us.

   You have requested records concerning third parties. We cannot confirm or deny the existence of any such records without causing an unwarranted invasion of personal privacy. Specifically, records about a third party generally cannot be released absent (1) express written authorization and consent by the third party; (2) proof that he is deceased; or (3) a clear demonstration that the public interest in disclosure outweighs the personal privacy interests of the third party and that significant public benefit would result from the disclosure of the requested records. Because you have not furnished a release, proof of death, or public justification for release, the release of records concerning the third parties would result in an unwarranted invasion of personal privacy and thus these records are exempt from disclosure under the FOIA under Exemption 6, which permits withholding personnel, medical and similar files when disclosure would constitute a clearly unwarranted invasion of personal privacy, and Exemption 7(C), which permits withholding records or information compiled for law enforcement purposes when disclosure could reasonably be expected to constitute an unwarranted invasion of personal privacy. 5 U.S.C. § 552(b)(6), (7)(C).

Author's FOIA request response from the US Department of Justice, dated February 2, 2012, after asking for access to Trawniki *Personalbögen* (personnel files). Note the interesting reasons given for the withholding of information.

For purposes of FOIA Exemptions 6 and 7 (C), a "public interest" exists only when information will contribute significantly to the public understanding of the operations or activities of the government. We have concluded that this standard is not satisfied regarding personal information – in the form of personnel files – about third parties.

Furthermore, the public domain doctrine applies only when the specific information requested is duplicated by information in the public realm. As the information you provided does not indicate that the Trawniki Personalbogens of the fourteen individuals you identified are in the public domain, we have concluded that this doctrine does not apply here.

We have not performed a search for records and you should not assume that records concerning the third party exist. If you obtain proof of death or the written authorization and consent of the third party for release of the requested records, you should submit a new request for the documents accompanied by the written authorization or proof of death. A form is enclosed to assist you in providing us the authorization and consent of the subject(s) of your request. The authorization must be notarized or signed under penalty of perjury pursuant to 18 U.S.C. § 1001.

If you treat this response as a denial of your request, you have a right to an administrative appeal of this determination. Your appeal must be in writing and addressed to:

Office of Information Policy
United States Department of Justice
1425 New York Ave., N.W., Suite 11050
Washington, D.C. 20530-0001.

Both the envelope and appeal letter should be clearly marked "FOIA/PA Appeal." Department regulations provide that such appeals must be received by the Office of Information Policy no later than sixty days (60) from the date of this letter. 28 C.F.R. § 16.9. If you exercise this right and your appeal is denied, you also have the right to seek judicial review of this decision in the U.S. District Court for the District of Columbia or the federal judicial district in which (1) you reside, (2) you have your principal place of business, or (3) the records denied are located. If you elect to file an appeal, please include the Criminal Division file number above in your letter to the Office of Information Policy.

If you have any questions regarding your request, please contact us at (202) 616-0307. Thank you for your interest in the Criminal Division.

Sincerely,

Rena Y. Kim, Chief
FOIA/PA Unit

Enclosure

Page 2 of the previous document

U.S. Department of Justice

Criminal Division

Office of Enforcement Operations   *Washington, D.C. 20530*

CRM-201100881F

FEB 1 0 2012

Mr. Joshua Baldwin

Dear Mr. Baldwin:

    This letter is in response to your Freedom of Information Act (FOIA) request to the U.S. Department of Justice (DOJ), Criminal Division dated December 10. 2011. In that request, you asked for copies of World War Two, German documents concerning the Trawniki Training Camp, specifically-

    1) List of guards on the run, drawn up by Trawniki Training Camp on August 10, 1943
    2) Circular letter dated December 15, 1943, concerning fugitive Ukrainian auxiliaries
    3) List of fugitives up to April 30, 1943, contains the names of 42 Ukrainian guards and their service numbers
    4) Report on the escape of Ukrainian guards from Auschwitz concentration camp, dated July 5, 1943
    5) Report on the escape of Ukrainian guards from Treblinka, dated March 17, 1943

    In responding to a FOIA request, the Criminal Division's search will include responsive records in its control on the date the search began. Our search began on January 19, 2012.

    We have been advised by the DOJ, Human Rights and Special Prosecutions Section (HRSPS), that the records were located at the archive of the Russian Federal Security Services (FSB), which is not accessible to the public. These records were provided to the DOJ for **law enforcement purposes** and have not entered the public domain in the United States.

    Therefore, we are denying your request in full. We are withholding twenty-four (24) pages based on the following FOIA exemptions:

    Exemption 7(C), which permits withholding records or information compiled for law enforcement purposes when disclosure could reasonably be expected to constitute an unwarranted invasion of personal privacy. 5 U.S.C. § 552(b)(7)(C).

Author's FOIA request response from the US Department of Justice, dated February 10, 2012, after asking for access to five German reports concerning the desertion of Trawniki guards from their assigned posts. Note the interesting reason given for denying access to the information.

INDEX